A STUDENT'S GUIDE TO
COGNITIVE NEUROPSYCHOLOGY

Sara Miller McCune founded SAGE Publishing in 1965 to support the dissemination of usable knowledge and educate a global community. SAGE publishes more than 1000 journals and over 800 new books each year, spanning a wide range of subject areas. Our growing selection of library products includes archives, data, case studies and video. SAGE remains majority owned by our founder and after her lifetime will become owned by a charitable trust that secures the company's continued independence.

Los Angeles | London | New Delhi | Singapore | Washington DC | Melbourne

A STUDENT'S GUIDE TO COGNITIVE NEUROPSYCHOLOGY

ASHOK JANSARI

Los Angeles | London | New Delhi
Singapore | Washington DC | Melbourne

Los Angeles | London | New Delhi
Singapore | Washington DC | Melbourne

SAGE Publications Ltd
1 Oliver's Yard
55 City Road
London EC1Y 1SP

SAGE Publications Inc.
2455 Teller Road
Thousand Oaks, California 91320

SAGE Publications India Pvt Ltd
B 1/I 1 Mohan Cooperative Industrial Area
Mathura Road
New Delhi 110 044

SAGE Publications Asia-Pacific Pte Ltd
3 Church Street
#10-04 Samsung Hub
Singapore 049483

Editor: Donna Goddard
Editorial assistant: Emma Yuan
Production editor: Martin Fox
Copyeditor: Tom Bedford
Proofreader: Derek Markham
Indexer: Adam Pozner
Marketing manager: Fauzia Eastwood
Cover design: Wendy Scott
Typeset by: C&M Digitals (P) Ltd, Chennai, India
Printed in the UK

Library of Congress Control Number: 2022930788

British Library Cataloguing in Publication data

A catalogue record for this book is available from the British Library

ISBN 978-1-4129-4744-2
ISBN 978-1-4129-4745-9 (pbk)

At SAGE we take sustainability seriously. Most of our products are printed in the UK using responsibly sourced papers and boards. When we print overseas we ensure sustainable papers are used as measured by the PREPS grading system. We undertake an annual audit to monitor our sustainability.

CONTENTS

ABOUT THE AUTHOR AND CONTRIBUTORS

Dr Ashok Jansari is a cognitive neuropsychologist at Goldsmiths, University of London, and has been working in the field for over 30 years. Ashok has trained with important neuropsychologists in the UK (Rosaleen McCarthy & Alan Parkin) and in the US (Antonio Damasio, Dan Tranel & Ralph Adolphs), and his research spans three areas (memory, face-recognition and assessment of executive functions). In 2004, he was awarded the International Neuropsychological Society's Cermak Award for best research in memory disorders. Ashok is passionate about teaching, mentoring and public engagement with science; he has contributed to TV documentaries around the world and during the Covid-19 global lockdown, he gave a series of free online talks to open the field of neuropsychology to the general public.

Dr Mary Jane Spiller is a cognitive psychologist at the University of East London who specialises in perceptual phenomena including the cross-sensory experience known as synaesthesia.

Jwala Narayanan is a clinician and researcher in Bangalore, India, and authored one of the first ever papers on the impact of Covid-19 on the brain.

Anisha Desai is a Highly Specialist Speech & Language Therapist in Neurorehabilitation who has worked clinically as well as in research; she is currently a lecturer at the University of Essex.

PREFACE

The aim of this book is to introduce the student to the fascinating field of Cognitive Neuropsychology, which is the understanding of normal mental processes by the study of individuals who have lost some aspects of this behaviour largely through brain damage. The field has had a rocky road, starting with the descriptions of patients with very specific problems in the middle of the Nineteenth Century, then a period in the doldrums for the first two-thirds of the Twentieth Century, then a renaissance since the 1970s followed by a slightly tricky position during the beginning of the Twenty-first Century. The latter has been due to the rise of the related field of Cognitive Neuroscience and at least in part, the use of neuroimaging which has made this more 'sexy' than the precise study of patients with selective brain damage. This is reflected in the types of research that attract funding and get published (see Chapter 1); further, many neuropsychology conferences have ended up becoming dominated by studies using an ever-increasing number of new neuroimaging techniques. However, I believe that newer is not necessarily better and this book is my attempt to show the very special ability of neuropsychology to reveal secrets of the brain that other methodologies simply cannot. My aim is not to provide an exhaustive account of all of cognitive neuropsychology but to guide students new to the field through the various issues and principles involved and then a survey of the main areas of research.

STRUCTURE OF THE BOOK

The book consists of three introductory chapters followed by nine chapters on specific areas of research. Chapter 1 (Why Study Damaged Brains) provides a general background to the field including its historical development. Chapter 2 (Methods in Cognitive Neuropsychology: A Tool Kit) provides the student with the building blocks for understanding terminology including basic neuroanatomy, a review of the main causes of brain damage, the basics of neuroimaging and how patients with brain damage are studied. Chapter 3 (Principles and Issues in Cognitive Neuropsychology) goes through conceptual issues that are crucial for studying and interpreting the cognitive behaviour of patients with brain damage.

Chapters 4 to 10 then address the principal areas studied by neuropsychologists. Each chapter takes a particular aspect of cognition and describes how brain damage affects that particular function resulting in a neuropsychological disorder. For example, the first thing that we need to do when interacting with the world is to pay attention to it; when this is damaged, it can result in attentional Neglect, whereby the sufferer may only pay attention to one side (usually the right side) of the world (Chapter 4). To interact with the world, we need to understand what we see and coordinate movements towards the objects that we see; this system can be damaged impacting the way that a person manually tries to use objects, a condition known as Apraxia (Chapter 5). Even if we don't interact with objects, we still need to recognise them and when this system breaks down, the result is Agnosia (Chapter 6). For social interaction, recognition of others is vital; the complexity of this skill that we all take for granted is revealed in the rare disorder Prosopagnosia (Chapter 7). One of our most important skills is being able to store information, conversations and our experiences so that we can recall them later when necessary; this process of memory is one of the most easily affected abilities because of its complexity and results in different forms of Amnesia (Chapter 8). To allow us to make decisions, juggle a number of things at the same time (multi-tasking) and plan for the future, we need a central coordinator; this system develops through childhood and adolescence with damage to it affecting a myriad of 'higher level' abilities known as Executive Functions (Chapter 9). One of the cognitive skills that seems more evolved in humans than in other animals is our ability to communicate both through speech and writing; disruption of this complex skill can result in a plethora of different verbal and reading disorders such as Aphasia and Dyslexia (Chapter 10).

The book ends with two chapters that are rarely covered in undergraduate neuropsychology books but which I feel are both extremely important. While studying people who have unfortunately suffered brain damage gives us a window into how the healthy brain functions, an important emerging field is Cognitive Rehabilitation (Chapter 10). This is a recent development within the field starting in the 1990s which at some levels is the coming together of cognitive neuropsychology and clinical neuropsychology. Slowly, it is becoming possible to use the insights gained from studying individuals with brain damage to develop new methods of rehabilitation for future patients and the advances made in this field will be an optimistic view towards what may be possible in the future. The final chapter is an exception to the classical field of cognitive neuropsychology because it deals with a fascinating new area of research known as Synaesthesia (Chapter 11). Whilst the majority of the book will draw on evidence from individuals with brain damage who have a particular impaired function (e.g. severe memory problems) to try to understand normal function, synaesthesia at some level is the understanding of individuals who possess an 'extra ability' in that they experience 'multi-sensory perception'. Studying individuals who have *two* experiences from one sensory input (for example, hearing the word 'Monday' and thinking of the first day of the week but *also* 'seeing' a colour at the same time) is providing researchers with an insight into how we 'bind' sensory information from the outside world together to allow us to perceive and interact with our environment.

The general structure of each chapter is to give a historical background to the field which has often been the insights from neurologists working with patients who have experienced some sort of trauma that has needed medical attention; some of these medical doctors began to explore what the unfortunate experience of the patient revealed about how their brain may have been functioning before the damage, and these early thoughts have led to what the field has eventually become. I believe that a historical background of the initial work in the field is important since most current research is simply expanding on this seminal work; therefore, I have tried to lay the solid foundations for understanding each area such that students who are particularly interested can explore the more recent developments. Since it is impossible to cover everything in an area, the chapter gives suggestions for further reading for those who want to dig a bit deeper.

Each chapter closes with a summary of main points followed by Questions for Reflection which can be used by a lecturer to suggest ways to explore understanding of the material that is covered. This is followed by a Go Further section which outlines some of the issues that have *not* been addressed in the chapter and point a keen student to what researchers are trying to currently address in their investigations. Since video material can be extremely helpful for consolidating information, there is a second Go Further section which gives QR codes for videos on my YouTube channel which are either from the talks that I gave during the Covid-19 global lockdown or TV documentaries that I have been involved in. I would encourage the reader to subscribe to this channel (it's free) so that you can get notifications every time we add another video to the channel. The final section is a Further Reading list with suggestions of papers or books that are not already cited in the main text.

An extra feature of each chapter is an attempt to personalise the book by showing who the greats of the field are. This is because in a number of the different fields, one or two individuals have been instrumental for kickstarting the interest in an area and their novel insights have effectively allowed a whole field of enquiry to flourish. Therefore, where possible, each chapter has an Important Researcher box introducing the student to these giants of the field. In a similar vein, some of the areas have been hugely impacted by the intense study of one patient or by a particular research study that set the scene for future work. Therefore, where possible, each chapter has an Important Research Study box which explains in more depth than is possible in the main text, who the patient was or what the study was about and why it was so formative for the field.

I hope that my passion for this field comes across in the way that I have written the book and provided the reader with information that will allow them to explore this fascinating field further. And if some of those readers decide to pursue the field, I will consider all the effort that I have put into this book over the last 15 years well worth it 😊

ACKNOWLEDGEMENTS

First and foremost, I would like to dedicate this book to my darling parents Damyanti (Oggi) and Surendra and offer them my endless thanks; this book has been a labour of love but the unbounding and unconditional love that I have received from them has made me carry on even when it was tough, and finishing seemed like an unsurmountable task. As immigrants to London from Kenya, and with no-one having been to university in the family, there was little knowledge about degrees, careers etc., so the obvious choice for an Indian boy would have been to study medicine! Therefore, for me to apply for this odd thing called 'Natural Sciences' at Cambridge and then to specialise in the equally unfamiliar 'Experimental Psychology' was not written on my cards and yet my parents were happy for me to find my way without any pressure. Whatever I have achieved is a testament to their love, devotion and free spirit. In addition, I would like to thank my siblings Chandrashekhar, Anjana, Bhavna, Ajit and Ajay for the love, encouragement and help that they've provided me at different points in my life, studies and career. Anyone who knows me will know that my darling cat Rover is also central to anything I do well ☺

The person who was effectively instrumental in getting me even close to making a career in this field is Rosaleen McCarthy. I had only chosen to study this strange Experimental Psychology for one of my courses in the second year of my degree because the other options were not of any interest to me. I had never heard of 'neuropsychology' and yet in October 1987, the second lecture of the year, given by Ros, changed my life as it opened my eyes to the wonders of studying individuals with brain damage. Doing my research dissertation for my final year with her got me hooked on this beguiling field; but while the field itself is amazing, it was Ros's enthusiasm that infected me and started my love affair with cognitive neuropsychology! Other leading researchers who have provided me mentorship and encouragement (especially in the dark days of lacking self-belief) are Barbara Wilson, Narinder Kapur, Alan Baddeley, Graham Hitch and my 'academic big brother' Jonathan Evans – they have been shining examples of how it is possible to work in this field, be generous, collegiate and inspiring. My mentors from my postdoctoral fellowship at the University of Iowa Hospitals & Clinics (Ralph Adolphs, Dan Tranel, Hannah Damasio and Antonio Damasio) opened my eyes to a whole new world of possibilities. Two gods of the field, Andy Ellis and Andy Young, wrote the 'bible' that I used as an undergraduate more than 30 years ago, so you can imagine then how honoured I felt when approached to write a book that could be a successor to their book. All the more wonderful was when they offered to give me some advice – one piece of advice was to include the brain in my book since their book had not dealt with the physical brain itself! I would also like to thank Kathy Haaland for encouraging me to include a chapter on Apraxia in this book, an area that I didn't know well; she kindly leant me some of her materials which helped me start my journey to understanding and therefore being able to include it in the book. Finally, two other mentors are Bill Hirst from the New School in New York and Ernie Govier from the University of East London. Both have been extremely wise mentors who I have been able to turn to for advice when navigating through the sometimes complex world of academia.

While my mentors have given me support and guidance, it is the next generation that has made this book possible, especially members of ART (Ashok's Research Team). First and foremost are people who have authored or co-authored chapters for the book, namely Anisha Desai, Mary Spiller and Jwala Narayanan; their specialist knowledge in each of their respective chapters has given the book a level that I myself could not have achieved. In particular, Anisha was instrumental in helping me build up the momentum during 2021 to make finishing the book a possibility. In addition, a wonderful small army of students and research assistants have beavered away in the background; their contributions included finding literature, chasing copyright permissions for the figures in the book, formatting the all-important bibliography, reading draft versions of chapters and just general cheerleading from the side when I was flagging in energy. In particular, I feel that Oromia Eshete, Lewis Philippe and Alana Wickham went beyond the call of duty in the incredible amount of work they did at times when it almost felt too much! In addition, I would like to thank Francesco Innocenti, Oscar Knockton, Kruti Rathi, Lubna Kumar, James Hunt, Kim Clark, Terry McGibbon, Claudia Pulcini, Maddie Taylor, Will Mayes, Andrea Chebat, Vytautė Gavelytė, Tristan Hornak, Max Bowman and Oli Iggstrand Darvill. Finally, I would like to thank Anna Sedda and Nanda Rathi for their very generous feedback on early versions of one of the chapters; it felt like showing another parent your baby praying that they would like it; the comments that both made were extremely helpful at a tricky stage in the book.

In a rather macabre way, I need to 'thank' Covid-19 for this book. The strange global lockdown resulted in me taking a public talk I was going to give, onto a live online format; much to my surprise, there was a wonderful response to the first talk which then grew into a series of ten talks! This then grew further into four series, totalling 22 talks, which then turned into a YouTube channel. The feedback that I received encouraged me to go back to the book manuscript that had constantly been put on the back burner for 13 years! Whilst lockdown allowed some people to finally learn to play a musical instrument, learn a new language or get into baking sourdough bread, my main thing was this book that you are reading, so in a way, I owe a 'thank you' to Covid-19. For the record, I aced the sourdough baking and am enjoying learning Spanish after being encouraged by my friend Enrique a few months into lockdown…

Last but definitely not least are some people who have encouraged me from the outset. My friend Ewan Clayton, an author himself on the art of writing, has always provided wise advice and encouragement through a process that I think most writers face – the enormity of the task, juggling the project with everything else and battling periods of lack of self-belief. I would like to thank my publishers Sage for their belief in me despite it taking so long from signing the contract to delivering the manuscript! Donna Goddard has been fantastic in guiding me through the latter stages of this process, so huge thanks to her as well as Esmé Carter and Emma Yuan for all their help in the tricky world of obtaining copyright permissions. The biggest thanks go to Michael Carmichael who recruited and signed me up. Despite my concerns (that I was not good enough to deliver the manuscript) at a number of points on this long journey, Michael was always incredibly consistent in his support and his belief that my 'voice' was one that he knew would make this book happen. Thanks Michael – I will always associate this book with you!

1
WHY STUDY DAMAGED BRAINS?

Chapter Overview

Why do psychologists who are ultimately interested in understanding how the healthy brain functions study individuals who have brain damage? This chapter will provide a background to how this field developed. Given that there are a number of related but different fields, the connections and differences will also be addressed.

Chapter Outline

- Introduction
- Historical Background
- Modern Cognitive Neuropsychology
- Connectionist Modelling
- The Many Faces of 'Neuro'
- Chapter Summary

INTRODUCTION

If, as stated above, one of the main goals of cognitive psychology is to understand normal (intact-brain) human behaviour, in particular mental abilities, it may initially seem strange that cognitive neuropsychologists accomplish this by studying damaged brains. To answer why they are effectively working 'backwards' from an incomplete system, a succinct quote from an important Scottish philosopher and psychologist, Kenneth Craik – who was the first director of one of the most important psychology research centres in the world, the Applied Psychology Unit – is very useful. Craik said, 'In any well-made machine one is ignorant of the working of most of the parts – the better they work, the less we are conscious of them… it is only a fault which draws attention to the existence of a mechanism at all' (1943, p. 84). The human cognitive system is a finely tuned 'machine', having evolved over millions of years, and while we may have access to *some* aspects of how and why we do things (for example, how we might plan a weekend away), for many abilities (for example, how you manage to convert the black ink on this page into an understanding of what I am trying to say) such an understanding is quite difficult. In fact, some skills that we think are effortless such as seeing or walking are the most complex, such that the best artificial intelligence systems cannot mimic them (Moravec, 1988). Although cognitive psychologists attempt to address this difficulty through research, in some aspects of behaviour, it is only when the intact system malfunctions, through for example brain damage, that it is possible to get a real sense of the complexity. It is in this sense of looking at a damaged system that cognitive neuropsychologists study the complex processes of memory, object recognition, face recognition, reading, problem solving, etc.

HISTORICAL BACKGROUND
The Ancients

Given that in the modern world the importance of the brain is taken for granted, it is interesting that much of the insights that have been gained into its functioning have happened since the middle of the nineteenth century; in fact, the vast bulk of knowledge gained has been only in the second half of the twentieth century. Compared to some other disciplines such as biology, physics and astronomy, psychology and particularly knowledge of the role of the brain in human behaviour is a very new discipline. A brief review of the history of the study of the brain will help in understanding why this has come about.

Figure 1.1 Portion of the Edwin Smith Surgical Papyrus with the ancient Egyptian hieroglyphics for the word 'brain' (Reprinted with permission from Wikipedia Commons)

It is known that at different times in ancient history and in civilisations that were quite far from one another, some knowledge of the brain existed. In an ancient Egyptian document known as the Edwin Smith Surgical Papyrus, the first written documentation of the word 'brain' appears; the papyrus gives physical descriptions of the brain, the consequences of damage to it and also proposed treatments (see Figure 1.1). While the physical document is from around 1700 BCE it is thought to be a copy of an earlier manuscript dating from between 3000 and 2500 BCE! In the Hindu culture in ancient India thousands of miles away, the *Atharava Veda* – one of the holy Hindu scriptures known as the *Vedas* (which were composed around 1000 BCE) – speaks of nine areas in the brain which map to different points along the spinal cord. These areas known as *chakras* are still much-used in contemporary alternative medicine. Within the same culture, the father of medicine was a physician called Jivaka who was known to have treated Lord Buddha (c. 563 BCE to 483 BCE). Ancient texts state that Jivaka learnt how to open the skull and is said to have removed two tumours from the brain of a merchant.

Moving to ancient Greece, there was great debate as to which organ controlled the body, the heart or the brain. While the prevailing view was that it was the heart, the father of Western medicine Hippocrates (c. 460 BCE to 375 BCE) wrote 'Men ought to know that from the human brain and from the brain only arise our pleasures, joys, laughter, and jests as well as our sorrows, pains, griefs and tears… It is the same thing which makes us mad or delirious, inspires us with dread and fear… brings us sleeplessness, inopportune mistakes, aimless anxieties, absent-mindedness and acts that are contrary to habit…' (pp. 174–175).

Phrenology and Diagram-Makers

Despite Hippocrates and later thinkers, the heart-centric view prevailed; this is seen all the way into the sixteenth century in the works of possibly the greatest playwright ever, William Shakespeare. For example, in *The Merchant of Venice* he wrote: 'Tell me where is the fancy bred, Or in the heart or in the head?' It wasn't until the seventeenth century, in the middle of the scientific revolution, that the Aristotelian, heart-centric view was rejected and the primacy of the brain recognised. However, although an understanding of the *physical* aspects of the brain was developed in the next two centuries, it wasn't until the end of the eighteenth century, largely thanks to pioneers like the Italian scientists Galvani and Volta, that thoughts that correlate in any way to modern knowledge of the brain were proposed.

The very earliest roots of neuropsychology lie in the field of phrenology developed primarily by a German doctor, Franz Joseph Gall, in 1796. The phrenologists believed that certain mental 'faculties' (or abilities) were located in different parts of the head and that the strength of this faculty determined the size of bumps on the skull. The American Lorenzo Niles Fowler believed, for instance, that the 'literary, observing and knowing faculties' were situated above the right eye, that selfish properties resided under the skull above the right ear whilst 'marriage, conjugality, constancy' was found near the base of the skull at the back of the head slightly to the left of centre. Given this correspondence between a mental ability and contours on the skull, this approach suggested that measuring the size of the bumps would reveal how much of a particular faculty an individual had (see Figure 1.2). Given its novelty, phrenology seemed exciting at the time and was even used as the basis for therapy in psychiatry for a while, but in the end it did not gain any support within the scientific community and therefore, as a basis for a theory, was discredited and forgotten. However, its importance was that it started to build momentum behind the concept of functional specialisation – the idea that our mental abilities were separable into modules (such as memory and language) and that these modules may be localised in specific parts of the human brain.

The true roots of contemporary neuropsychology can be found in the work of the French neurologist Paul Broca. In 1861, he reported the case of a man who had suffered a stroke, which is the bursting of a blood vessel in the brain (see Chapter 2 for more on causes of brain damage). Broca reported that his patient had great difficulty making intelligible utterances. At most, only a few syllables were ever produced at any one time, i.e. nothing that sounded like real connected language, and due to the sound of one of the syllables that the patient could make, he became known as 'Tan'. Despite this profound inability to produce intelligible language (which later became known as aphasia), the interesting thing was that Tan was able to fully understand what was said to him. He could follow verbal commands, could show that he could remember something said to him earlier that day, point to objects if asked to do so, etc. as long as no verbal response was required. As a result of his work with Tan, Broca proposed that the part of the brain

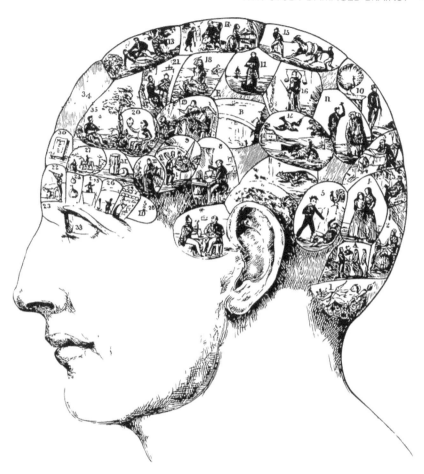

Figure 1.2 Diagram of a phrenology head map or of a classic phrenology bust (Reprinted with permission from Upsplash.com)

that was damaged was responsible for co-ordinating the patterns of muscle movements required for saying individual words. He suggested that damage to this area would mean that, although the vocal apparatus in the throat and mouth probably worked, they were not sent the appropriate signals by the brain to make the correct movements for speech, resulting in the pattern of behaviour found in Tan. After Tan's death, analysis of his brain revealed what Broca had suspected – that a particular area of his brain had been damaged with the rest of the brain being relatively intact; Figure 1.3 shows Tan's brain which has been preserved at a museum in Paris, with the blackened area towards the front of the brain being that which once occupied brain tissue but was destroyed following Tan's stroke. This area of the brain is now known as Broca's area, in recognition of his pioneering work in the field of language production.

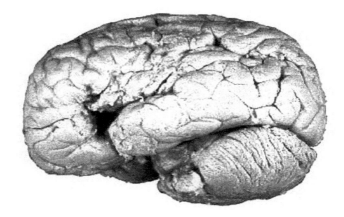

Figure 1.3   Tan's Brain (Copyright © 1997, rights managed by Georg Thieme Verlag KG, Stuttgart & New York)

Just a decade after Broca's seminal work, in 1874, Karl Wernicke, another neurologist was working with a number of patients who demonstrated a pattern of problems that seemed to be the reverse of those shown by Tan. These patients appeared to be able to speak fluently (in that whole words were produced in continuous speech that, superficially at least, *sounded* like full sentences), but they had difficulties in understanding what was said to them. However, although the speech sounded fluent, it had many errors (known as 'neologisms') and was almost incomprehensible. In an attempt to explain this pattern of impaired speech, Wernicke proposed that the area affected in his patients was responsible for storing the sound patterns of words and that damage to this area resulted in difficulties in comprehending speech. Although Wernicke's suggestion explained poor comprehension, it didn't account for the patients' problem in *producing* fluent speech; this issue is still not fully understood. Following the death of one of the patients, a post-mortem revealed a clear specific area of damage. The damage was slightly further back in the brain than Broca's area, this time in an area known as the left temporal lobe; this area is now known as Wernicke's area (see Figure 1.4).

Although both Broca and Wernicke were neurologists (medical doctors who treated patients with brain damage), they can be regarded as the forefathers of modern neuropsychology; the reasons are twofold. The first was a demonstration of the separation of mental abilities, since the patients documented by these neurologists had deficits that were largely restricted to their language, leaving other abilities (e.g. memory) intact. This dissociation of abilities has been instrumental in the development of modern neuropsychology (see Chapter 3). The second important contribution was that by examining the patients' brains at post-mortem and showing that their damage was restricted to very specific areas, there was some vindication of the idea of functional specialisation within the brain that the phrenologists had promoted. Whilst the actual faculties proposed by

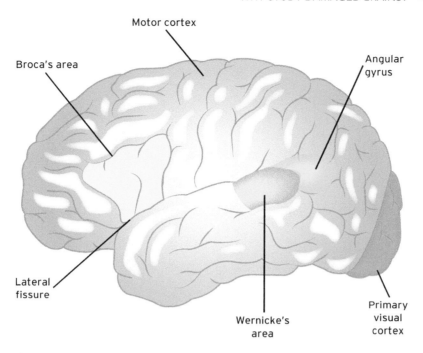

Motor cortex

Broca's area

Angular
gyrus

Lateral
fissure

Primary
visual
cortex

Wernicke's
area

Figure 1.4   Broca's and Wernicke's areas on one brain image (Garrett & Hough, 2017)

the phrenologists were largely wrong, at a basic level, their idea of discrete functions in specific areas of the brain was supported.

As a result of their approach, Broca and Wernicke became known as 'localisationalists' because they believed that certain functions were firmly localised in particular areas of the brain, i.e. speech production in Broca's area and comprehension in Wernicke's area. The result of this trend towards localising functions anatomically was that, eventually, other neurologists like Lichtheim (1885) started attempting to create models of the production of spoken language. Due to the box-and-arrow visual models that were created, they became known as the 'diagram-makers' (see Figure 1.5).

Initially, this approach received considerable support. In fact, Wernicke even made predictions based on such models about the possible existence of another form of language problem which *as yet* had not been documented by any clinician. Lichtheim (1885) went on to discover a patient with such a problem, thus demonstrating the scientific validity of the methodology; from clinical observations, claims were made about certain aspects of language and their physical location in the brain, a model was proposed to incorporate these suggestions, a new prediction came out of the model and this prediction was upheld with a new discovery. Such was the impact of the early diagram-makers and localisationalists that Shallice refers to the period between 1860 and 1905 as the 'golden age of the flowering of neuropsychology' (p. 3, 1988).

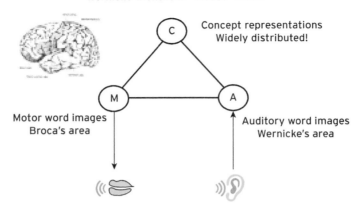

Figure 1.5 Lichtheim's model of language (Speak by Gregor Cresnar from NounProject. com, Listen by Rémy Médard from NounProject.com)

Disfavour with 'Black Boxology'

Although the diagram-makers had created a very energetic momentum, unfortunately, during the early part of the twentieth century, their approach weakened. This happened for a number of reasons, both from within the field of neurology and from outside the field. Many neurologists criticised the earlier work saying that while the localisation of suggested functions was very precise, the descriptions of both the patients' problems and the concepts that were used to explain the problems were rather vague. For example, Broca interpreted Tan's problems as being caused by a loss of 'motor images' required for making intelligible sound. However, patients who suffer the same fate as Tan (known as Broca's aphasia: see Chapter 10) tend to be able to make individual sounds and therefore seem to have the 'motor images' to make these utterances, but they cannot create connected meaningful sentences to communicate effectively. Therefore, there was a lack of clarity concerning how each of the centres in the elaborate models functioned. A particularly damning definition of this 'black boxology' (since the centres were likened to boxes that couldn't be looked into) comes from Sutherland who defined it as 'the construction and ostentatious display of meaningless flow charts by psychologists as a substitute for thought' (1989, p. 58).

In addition to the criticism of the level of clarity, another challenge came in the form of Lashley's (1929) theory of 'mass action'. This was the suggestion that many parts of the brain can serve the same functions as one another and so loss of a particular part of the brain does not result in any specific loss of behaviour but a general decrease in efficiency proportional to the amount the brain that was damaged. If it didn't matter which part of the brain was damaged, just the extent of the damage, that challenged one of the bedrocks of the nineteenth-century diagram-makers, i.e. functional specialisation. Although Lashley's views have largely been disproved, at the time that he proposed his theory, it added a further nail in the (temporary) coffin of the diagram-makers.

A final major reason for the demise of the diagram-makers' approach was a shift in the focus of the general field of psychology. While the neurologists had been studying patients with brain damage to understand some aspects of behaviour, parallel to that, in Germany Wilhelm Wundt founded what many people see as the first systematic methodology in psychology known as introspection. This approach flourished between 1860 and its eventual demise in 1927 and, in brief, involved the observation of one's own thoughts, feelings and mental states to try to derive theories of general human behaviour. They trained participants on how to report their experiences and, after this training, they might have asked the person how they solved a mathematical problem and the way that they described it would be seen as indicative of mental processes common to everyone when carrying out the same task. Whilst this approach flourished for over half a century in Europe, its demise came when there was a huge shift in psychology. There was criticism of the unreliable and subjective nature of much of the findings that came from individuals' observations of their own thought processes.

Instead, in 1913, John Watson in America suggested that the proper scientific study of human behaviour should be based on what was observable, measurable and replicable. A classic example from the school of behaviourism was the work of the Russian physiologist Ivan Pavlov who was studying the digestive system in dogs. He noticed that dogs would start salivating when they heard the footsteps of the researchers bringing them food. This anticipatory behaviour at the sound of the footsteps then became formalised in experiments where he began to play sounds from different objects (buzzer, harmonium, etc.) just before the dogs were meant to be fed; what he found was that eventually the dogs had become 'conditioned' to the sounds and would salivate simply when they heard them being played. This work, which won Pavlov a Nobel Prize for Medicine/Physiology in 1904, was seen as a perfect example of solid observable, measurable and replicable work that could be applied to the understanding of both animal and human behaviour. Given the criticisms that were coming from within neurology concerning the unscientific observations and explanations offered by the diagram-makers, it was no surprise that, for psychologists investigating normal human behaviour, the subjective research on rare individuals with brain damage didn't take off.

Consequently, for a number of different reasons, the approach of the nineteenth century neurologists faded into the background for those attempting to study the human mind. During the middle of the twentieth century, therefore, while some neurologists continued studying individuals with brain damage, their approach was a different one, that involving studying large groups of patients who all had similar areas of brain damage.

The Emergence of Cognitive Psychology

The next milestone in research on mental functions happened with what has become known as the 'cognitive revolution'. There are a number of different factors that resulted in what was to be a huge shift in focus. In 1959, two quite pivotal events occurred.

Noam Chomsky presented a paper at the Massachusetts Institute of Technology which criticised the dominance of the behaviourist approach, particularly with respect to a theory by one of its prominent leaders, B. F. Skinner who had claimed that human language could be explained using principles derived from an offshoot of Pavlov's conditioning work. Chomsky outlined a number of areas where this was not possible and argued strongly that there was at least some biologically inherited aspect to the learning of language. This weakening of the behaviourist stranglehold on psychology was mirrored by the events in Cambridge in the UK where Donald Broadbent in 1958 proposed that human mental abilities could be seen as a sequence of processing stages. This view has become known as the information processing approach and was partly driven by the very early stages of the development of computers. At the time, these devices were only known within the scientific research arena and were being used for processing of information through a series of defined stages.

This comparison between a computer and the human brain can be seen at a number of levels (see Figure 1.6). Both systems have got input devices, physical hardware that does the processing of information and some form of output. In the case of a simple computer its input device is the keyboard, the physical hardware is the range of internal circuit boards and the output device is the screen or a printer. To allow someone to use the computer, it needs software such as a word-processing programme; the result is that a series of ordered key presses on the input device (keyboard) is transformed by the circuit boards (hardware) using the word-processing programme (software) into a written piece on the computer screen or printed onto paper (output). In an analogous

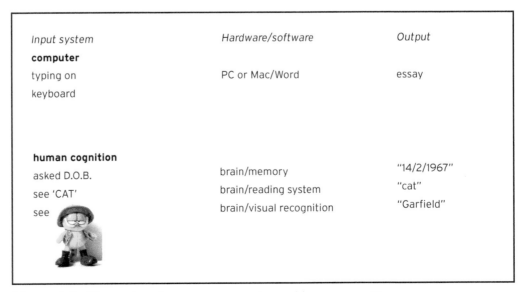

Figure 1.6 The analogy between a computer and human cognition

way, human cognition has five input devices which are the five senses which transform different external stimuli (light, sound, tastes, odours and skin pressure) into nerve signals that are sent to the brain. These signals are processed here and depending on the particular cognitive function and the action you are aiming to perform, there is usually some sort of behaviour towards this input. Sometimes it may simply be to pay attention to it to decide what you are going to do later, or it may be to visually recognise what you are seeing, or it may involve acting towards the input; this action can either be a physical movement such as reaching out to pick up an object or it may be a verbal response. The functioning of the input and output devices (the five senses and motor control) is studied by physiologists and is relatively well understood. Therefore, for example, a substantial amount is known regarding the effect of light on the various components of the eye, on the physical rods and cones found on the retina and then the conduction of nerve signals from there via a major bundle of fibres known as the optic nerve. Similarly, the physical structure of the brain is fairly well understood and had been mapped out to some degree of accuracy by the end of the nineteenth century. What is not well understood about the human system, however, is the equivalent of the word-processing programme, i.e. the 'software' that processes information in the brain. The software that is involved in mental abilities is known as cognition. For example, looking at a cartoon of a cat activates the 'visual recognition' software (see Figure 1.6). This software processes the series of shapes, colours and possibly even context to finally derive the 'output' which is the name of this object, i.e. Garfield the cat. Similarly, if I was asked my date of birth, this would activate my memory software which would access that bit of information about myself to give you the answer. Finally, seeing a series of letters on a page will activate the reading system to name the word as /cat/. In each of these examples a different aspect of cognition is accessed to enable the brain to process the external information to produce the desired behaviour. The work of the cognitive psychologist is to unravel the extremely complex programmes that have effectively been written through the very long process of human evolution.

This analogy between a computer and the way that the brain processes information has proven very fruitful. In the same way that the computer has a series of subroutines (that are usually chugging away in the background without you realising it), so does human cognition. For example, a very important part of visual recognition involves edge-detection and working out which lines belong to which object. It is only once this subroutine has been completed that the next stage of visual recognition can proceed. Similarly, the computer performs many tasks in parallel, i.e. a number of processes can occur at the same time. For example, my laptop is playing me soothing music at the same time as converting my finger-strokes into words on the screen. In the same way, my hearing apparatus can listen to and enjoy the music whilst simultaneously letting my language system produce the text you see before you. Similarly, the computer can take information stored in one format, for example on a numerical spreadsheet, and use it in a word-processing format. This interaction between different aspects of the computer can be seen in the interaction between the modules of human cognition. For example, when watching a film, while it is the visual recognition system that is making sense of what you are seeing, the memory system will be activated if trying to remember where you have seen a particular actor before.

The importance of the cognitive revolution is that a number of the criticisms made against the diagram-makers at the end of the nineteenth and beginning of the twentieth centuries were no longer valid. Cognitive psychology resulted in more box and arrow diagrams but armed with the ideas about information processing, computation and representation, researchers are now able to put something inside the black boxes that had been the downfall of the early diagram-makers. For example, whereas Lichteim may have said that there was a centre for word recognition which, if damaged, would result in difficulties in understanding language, cognitive psychologists could now attempt to describe what might happen in such centres. So for example, there now exist very complex models of reading (e.g. Patterson et al., 2017: see Chapter 10).

MODERN COGNITIVE NEUROPSYCHOLOGY

With the advent of cognitive psychology, it was possible for clinical neuropsychologists to work with those who were building cognitive models to try to better understand the disorders suffered by neurological patients. Two vital papers that seemed to really signal the birth of modern cognitive neuropsychology were those by British researchers Marshall & Newcombe (1966) on a patient with a very specific reading disorder (see Chapter 10), and Warrington & Shallice (1969) on a patient with a very selective short-term memory deficit (see Chapter 8). Within a decade of this, in 1980, Max Coltheart wrote the first ever book to discuss the use of neuropsychology as a cognitive approach, *Deep Dyslexia*. The arrival of this approach as a field was signalled by the founding of the journal *Cognitive Neuropsychology* in 1984.

A final important factor in the history of cognitive neuropsychology was the development of more and more sophisticated techniques for looking at the brain (e.g. PET, MRI and fMRI: see Chapter 2). Whereas Broca and others had to wait until their patients' deaths to be able to look at their brains, now it is possible to look at the patients' brain while they are alive. This has a huge impact for a number of reasons. Firstly, before the development of these techniques, researchers had to rely on simple paper and pencil tests which were developed with the rationale that bad performance on them indicated damage to specific parts of the brain (e.g. bad performance on certain subtests in an aphasia battery would imply damage in Broca's area). Now, however, it is possible to 'see' the damage in the living brain. This has a significant impact on being able to treat patients – if surgery is involved, surgeons have a much more accurate picture of what they need to work on. Secondly, the information on which parts of a brain are damaged in particular patients allows psychologists to develop more accurate models of the behaviour that they are trying to explain. Techniques such as fMRI make it possible to look at what parts of the brain are particularly active when normal healthy participants carry out tasks (e.g. reading). This allows cognitive neuropsychologists to bring together data from both the healthy and the damaged brain.

Overall, the aims of cognitive neuropsychology are:

1   The attempt to understand healthy function by studying dysfunction.
2   The use of the new understanding of healthy functions to help diagnose and understand difficulties of new patients.
3   The application of knowledge about both impaired and intact functions to develop methods of rehabilitation for patients.
4   The localisation of cognitive functions to specific parts of the brain.

Very few neuropsychologists work at all the levels above. For example, some might exclusively work with patients as a mirror onto healthy functions while others might do this but also use their understanding to develop new assessments of the dysfunctions they have studied. In general, those working in clinical settings are the only ones likely to attempt to develop rehabilitation techniques. Finally, only some neuropsychologists will be interested in trying to localise functions; they may be particularly interested in trying to develop functional architectures of brain systems to show how different parts work together in networks to perform the intricate cognitive functions that most humans can perform effortlessly. As an example, however, Figure 1.7 is a 'map' with landmarks of the specialisations of different parts of my brain (the image has been created using the Brainvox system described in Chapter 2). However, many neuropsychologists will seldom do this since they feel that working on the 'programme' of how we perform a cognitive function is much more important than where the hardware for that programme is situated.

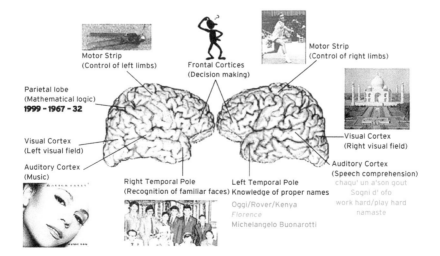

Figure 1.7   Three-dimensional images of AJ's brain showing the localisation of some of the main cognitive functions

It is important to note that the brain works in networks so although the areas that are marked specialise in the named specific functions, they will be receiving input from and sending output to other brain areas as well.

CONNECTIONIST MODELLING

In the 1980s a new piece of the arsenal for some neuropsychologists was the birth of connectionist modelling, which came from the broader field of cognitive science. The principle behind this approach is that it is possible to describe mental processes (such as how you translate the visual input CAT into the sound /*cat*/ by very simple units in an interconnected network. The network would have a layer of input units, a layer of output units and either one or more 'hidden' layers (see Figure 1.8). The individual units between two adjacent units would be connected to one another and have the possibility of activating or inhibiting each other; the strengths of these connections varied and could *change* depending on how the model was programmed; this change was to mimic learning that can occur after we experience something a number of times. It should be noted that these networks were *not* developed to be a *direct* representation for the three layers in Figure 1.6 (on p. 10); however, at some levels, the attempt is to *eventually* try to scale up to that level of explanation. So although units are not supposed to represent individual neurons and their connections, the synapses between neurons (see Chapter 2), the analogy would be appropriate.

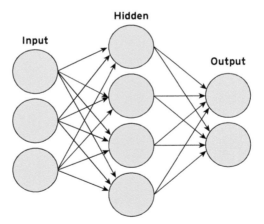

Figure 1.8   An example of a simple connectionist network model (CC BY-SA 3.0)

The process would involve programming the model to define what the input layers could process, what the form of the output would be and importantly how the individual units connect to one another. Do some units in the input layer have very strong connections with some of the hidden units but virtually no connection with the remainder? Do units in the hidden layer only activate the ones in the output layer if they receive a *minimum* level of input from the input layer? The actual process of how the model is programmed and how it 'learns' is beyond the scope of this chapter but the overall aim is that if the programme and its 'output' mirrored that of healthy or brain-damaged individuals then the programme could represent those cognitive processes in the brain.

In this approach, mental representations (such as reading) were programmed as information units and the models were then given inputs (such as the letter string CAT and the output was evaluated to see if it was the *same* as human performance. Importantly, in connectionist models, it was important that the output was the *same* as the output of human cognition *including* the errors that are made. If there was a difference between the two, then this meant that the processes programmed into the model did not *yet* represent human cognition. By a process of trial and error, the *strengths* of the connections or the representations themselves were adjusted and then the model was tested again with inputs and the output evaluated. This process of testing with inputs, evaluating the output, adjusting the strengths, and then repeating the process was run many times until the model produced an output that resembled human performance. Within cognitive neuropsychology, connectionist modelling was used to try to explain the difficulties shown by patients. To do this, a model was 'lesioned' by either 'damaging' the representations or the connections between them; the damaged model was then tested again to see whether it produced the same errors as the patients. If the model mimicked either intact or brain-damaged performance, it was plausible to suggest that the representations and the processes within the model were simulating human cognitive processes.

As an example, in the field of object recognition, Farah and McClelland (1991) attempted to create a model to explain an intriguing finding whereby some patients had difficulties recognising only certain categories of visually presented objects (see Chapter 6: Visual Agnosia & Object Recognition). They took the prevailing understanding within the field and created a model which involved the input units representing either visual or functional information about objects; so for example with a bicycle, visual information is useful but the functional information is much more important, whereas deciding whether a banana is ready to eat relies very heavily on the visual information. Their model was able to mimic a number of findings in general 'healthy' object recognition, but importantly they were able to 'lesion' their model by damaging some of the units in the hidden layer. Depending on whether they damaged visually-based information or function-based information, the Farah and McClelland (1991) model had difficulties 'recognising' visually presented living things or non-living things respectively. This perfectly mirrored the pattern of object recognition difficulties of the patients being documented in the 1980s; this finding therefore helped to inform the cognitive theories that were being developed at the time to explain the patterns of problems that patients were exhibiting (see Chapter 6 for more on this specific disorder).

Renewed Connectionism in the Age of Deep Learning

In the early 90s the parallel distributed processing (PDP) or connectionist movement went out of fashion, in what was then recognised as 'the second artificial intelligence (AI) winter'. More than two decades later, there has been a true renaissance of PDP under the name of 'deep learning' thanks in part to technological advances in both hardware (increasing computing power) and software (open-source software, and better machine learning algorithms). The new generation of models, called deep neural networks (DNNs), are 'deep' in the sense that they have many layers of units or 'neurons' (sometimes hundreds). Such DNNs are starting to pervade almost every aspect of our society, and can rival human object recognition ability, master natural language, beat humans at games such as chess, predict the weather and, most recently, assist mathematicians in proving new theorems.

DNNs have also proven to be the best (i.e. most predictive) computational models of brain function, leading to a renewed convergence between AI and neuroscience. As an example, Higgins et al. (2021) recently found that a DNN trained to process certain aspects of face recognition best accounted for how the inferotemporal cortex of macaque monkeys responded to faces. This is a quickly advancing area of research and is likely to mushroom further in the next decade.

Given the success in mimicking some aspects of human cognition, the next big step is that the lesion method used in neuroscience and cognitive neuropsychology is now being applied to gain insights into how DNNs work. The basic idea in these so-called 'ablation' experiments is similar to the experimental surgeries conducted on animals whereby part of a DNN is 'damaged' and the impact on the behavioural output of the network is observed. For example, Zhou et al. (2018) ablated individual units within a DNN that had already been trained to classify objects finding that specific units were selective to specific object categories. This is clearly analogous to cognitive neuropsychologists assigning a function (or functions) to a brain area based on the deficits following lesion to that area. Therefore, more than 160 years after the seminal work by Paul Broca, this emerging work on brain-damaged DNNs or *in silico* neuropsychology (Innocenti, 2022, personal communication) may well be the next stage in our understanding of cognitive functions.

This research also reveals that the lesion method, though closest to cognitive neuropsychology, does not belong to any particular field. It can instead be viewed as a general principle to gain insights about the workings of a system, although it might need further development to provide more informative insights into complex systems such as the brain.

Cognitive neuropsychology has therefore had a rocky ride since its 'golden flowering' in the nineteenth century and has entered the twenty-first century with a growing momentum, which makes it an extremely fascinating field. However, there are various challenges that the field needs to address. The first is societal pressures on the ethics of working with individuals with brain damage. The need for appropriate ethics is obvious since the individuals being studied have sometimes suffered extremely distressing illnesses or accidents and so great care needs to be taken when working with them. However, unless there is a deeper understanding of the vital clues that can emerge from this type of work, the field could be under serious threat. A second related challenge is the rise of other methods of research that entered the arena towards the end of the twentieth century. The emergence of cognitive neuroscience has led some to see cognitive neuropsychology as redundant. Chapter 2 will address the importance of this issue but the main point is that it is important for the field to be seen as a vital contribution to the understanding of the incredible complexity of the human mind.

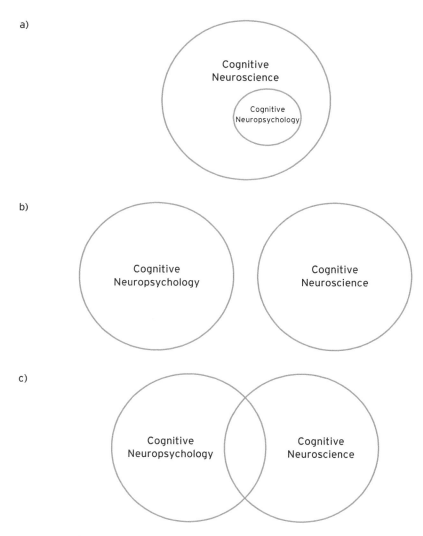

Figure 1.9 The relationship between neuroscience and neuropsychology: a) Neuropsychology is simply a part of neuroscience; b) The two fields are not related at all; c) The two fields have commonality and can borrow from one another but are also independent of one another

THE MANY FACES OF 'NEURO'

Given that there are a number of different aspects of studying with or working with the brain, along with the fact that compared to some of the other sciences, it is a relatively new area, there can be some confusion, *even among scientists*, as to what the many faces of 'neuro' are. For students, therefore, it is unsurprising that cognitive neuropsychology, clinical neuropsychology, cognitive neuroscience, clinical neuroscience, clinical neuropsychiatry, etc. all sound more or less the same. Sometimes even people within the field can get confused, or rather misunderstand the relationship of their field to the other related fields. For example, just taking two of the big ones, cognitive neuropsychology and cognitive neuroscience, some people (mainly within the neurosciences) feel that the situation is what is seen in Figure 1.9a, with neuropsychology being entirely within neuroscience. It is unsurprising that many think like this because of the rapid rise of the field which has effectively swamped the other areas. Figure 1.10 shows the number of scientific publications which had the words/phrases 'neuroscience', 'neuropsychiatry', 'cognitive neuropsychology' and 'clinical neuropsychology' in them for each year from 1960 to 2020; there will have been some overlap between the publications but the picture is pretty clear; since the early 1990s, there has been an enormous increase in the neuroscience field which has often led some to feel that it's the only 'neuro' left on the block… This issue is picked up again in Chapter 2.

Returning to the relationship between neuropsychology and neuroscience, some could be extreme and say that there is no relationship whatsoever; perhaps to be controversial, Max Coltheart might say that it is more like Figure 1.9b, with neuroscience not informing

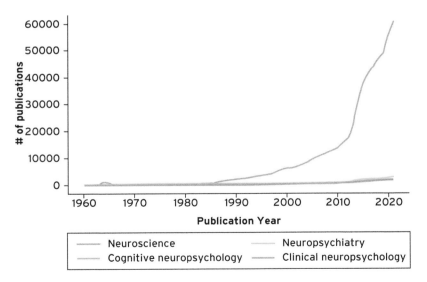

Figure 1.10   The number of papers published each year that included the terms neuroscience, neuropsychiatry, cognitive neuropsychology and clinical neuropsychology from 1960 to 2020

neuropsychology at all. This extreme position effectively would be suggesting that nothing that we learn from the neurosciences can help us in the endeavour to use individuals with brain damage to try to understand healthy cognitive functions. The most likely position, and one that most cognitive neuropsychologists would agree with, is that in Figure 1.9c, which admits that neuroscience can help us understand aspects of cognition but that there are many aspects of the field that do *not* require knowledge of neurons, pathways in the brain, etc.

Turning to the relationship between cognitive and clinical neuropsychology, this grew with the birth of cognitive psychology with there being clear links between the two. At an informal level, *depending on the country*, cognitive neuropsychologists are not trained clinicians but simply scientists who happen to work with patients with brain damage for their research. On the other hand, many clinical neuropsychologists do not conduct research since all their time is taken up with the assessment and care of their patients. However, some will work with scientists to conduct research. In terms of training, clinical neuropsychology is a specialist training that occurs within a health setting and is often done after formal studies (at Bachelors or Masters levels) have been completed. The pathways and the amount of time varies considerably in different countries. So for example, in the United States and Australia, it is possible to enter a doctoral clinical neuropsychology programme after completing the relevant undergraduate or postgraduate studies. In the UK, however, it is necessary first of all to complete a doctoral training in clinical psychology to get an overall grounding as a clinician and then, after that, to specialise in clinical neuropsychology.

Chapter Summary

- Early thinkers in the field were known as localisationalists because they believed that particular mental functions were situated in specific locations in the brain.
- The diagram-makers formulated the earliest models of mental processing by synthesising the ideas of the localisationalists in 'box and arrow' models.
- The field decreased in popularity at the beginning of the twentieth century but this was rekindled by the birth of the information processing approach and cognitive psychology.
- The development of more advanced techniques such as standardised research methodologies and brain-imaging technology further developed the field towards the end of the twentieth century.

Important Researcher

Paul Broca

Paul Broca (1824–1880) was a French polymath who was a physician, anatomist, and anthropologist, publishing research across all these areas. The event that has secured his place in history is the revolutionary thinking he proposed when he studied patient Tan.

While similar thoughts may have been around at the time, it was Broca who meticulously documented his observations and spoke about it through the various intellectual groups and salons that he was very involved in. If Broca's suggestions about Tan had not been heard by others and promoted similar lines of enquiry in other doctors working with patients with brain damage, then we may never have heard of Broca or Tan, or at the very least the pace of understanding would have been extremely slow. This demonstrates that science requires excellent quality work but it also requires communication to other audiences; this can be through written papers and scientific conferences. In the modern world public engagement with science is particularly valued, bringing science to the general population so that they can think about it and maybe even contribute to the debate. So Broca was important not only for his scientific work but also for his prolific communication of his ideas that spread quickly to other neurologists such as Carl Wernicke and Ludwig Lichtheim. Interestingly, as well as his medical career, Broca, founded a society of free thinkers who were very impressed with Charles Darwin's theories on evolution which had just been published in 1859. Broca, who was an atheist, is quoted as saying, 'I would rather be a transformed ape than a degenerate son of Adam'.

Important Research Study

Patient Tan

Tan was the name given to Louis Victor Leborgne when he was admitted to a hospital in Paris having lost the ability to speak at the age of 30; the name was simply because that was the only guttural sound he could make. He had suffered from **epilepsy** for much of his life and spent the next 21 years at the hospital. Although some of the details about the specific brain area that Paul Broca suggested was the centre of spoken language have been disputed (see Chapter 10), Tan will go down in history because of the incredible contribution to science that his condition gave through the observations that Broca made.

Questions for Reflection

- Why was it necessary for the cognitive revolution to happen before the amazing observations by the nineteenth century diagram-makers were rediscovered in the creation of the field of cognitive neuropsychology?
- In what ways is cognitive neuropsychology different from cognitive neuroscience?

Go Further

Dr Jansari's YouTube Videos

Why do we know less about the human brain than the dark side of the moon? (Parts 1 and 2)

Go on a guided tour of the functioning of the human brain, dispelling some of the many myths about the grey stuff while also revealing some true wonders. The fascinating field of cognitive neuropsychology is explored through examples of patients with very selective disorders. How these findings can help others with brain damage is shown and the exciting techniques for improving functioning in healthy adults are described. Finally, in a coming-together of Eastern philosophy and neuroscience, the incredible impacts of mindfulness meditation both on the physical body and the brain are introduced.

Further Reading

- Sacks, O. (1985). *The Man Who Mistook His Wife for a Hat*. Summit Books.
- Ramachandran, V. S., Blakeslee, S., & Dolan, R. J. (1998). Phantoms in the brain: Probing the mysteries of the human mind. *Nature, 396*(6712), 639–640.
- Graves, R. E. (1997) The legacy of the Wernicke-Lichtheim model. *Journal of the History of the Neurosciences, 6*(1), 3–20.

2
METHODS IN COGNITIVE NEUROPSYCHOLOGY: A TOOL KIT

Chapter Overview

This chapter will provide a 'tool kit' for students that can allow them to understand the methodologies and terminology that are used in many research articles. Some of these are not strictly part of cognitive neuropsychology but knowing some basic neuroanatomy and what the main causes of brain injury are helps to understand the types of damage that a patient has suffered and also why two patients may differ enormously. Similarly, neuroimaging is not a part of classical cognitive neuropsychology but it has become so omnipresent in research that it is useful to have a basic understanding of what is and isn't important to know. Finally, knowing how research is conducted on single cases and how the data is analysed will be of use for understanding the language used in research papers.

Chapter Outline

INTRODUCTION

As seen in Chapter 1, cognitive neuropsychology is a methodology within cognitive psychology, and depending on the aims of a particular neuropsychologist, they may or may not be interested in what is happening within the physical brain (see 'The Many Faces of Neuro' section in Chapter 1). Nonetheless, research papers are usually peppered with information about areas of the brain, their brain damage and possibly images of the brain. The methodological section usually has information about the testing that was conducted before the experimental work was started. All of this tends to contain a lot of dense information that is almost another language which is rarely taught to students. Therefore, the aim of this chapter is to provide a tool kit that will allow students to understand a number of important concepts that are useful in the field.

BASIC NEUROANATOMY

The brain is made up of approximately 86 billion nerve cells and while there are a number of different types of nerve cells, each one has a central cell body (also referred to as the soma), a major fibre that transmits information from this to other cells known as the axon and many smaller fibres known as dendrites which allow the nerve cell to communicate with other nerve cells at a junction known as a synapse (see Figure 2.1). Neurons are clustered within the brain in larger units called nuclei with the neurons in an individual nucleus having similar functions. Nuclei are connected to each other via their axons which together form tracts.

A nucleus is one of the two most common forms of nerve cell organisation, the other being layered structures such as the cerebral cortex or cerebellar cortex. In anatomical sections, a nucleus shows up as a region of grey matter, often bordered by white matter. The two cerebral hemispheres are divided into four major areas known as lobes, namely the frontal, parietal, occipital and temporal lobes (see Figure 2.2). The brain has a grooved walnut-like appearance which is caused by the gyri (singular gyrus) which are the visible ridges or bumps and the shallow grooves being the sulci (singular sulcus)

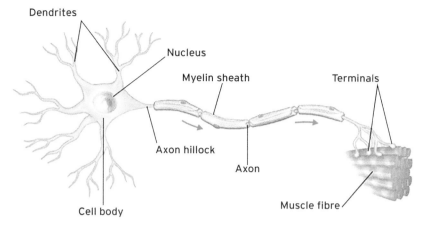

Figure 2.1   A simple nerve cell (Garrett & Hough, 2017)

between the gyri; the larger sulci are also called fissures – for example, the one between the frontal and temporal lobes is known as the lateral fissure or also the Sylvian fissure. Gyri and sulci are only found on the surface of the cortex and are made up of grey matter (the nerve cell bodies and dendrites). Therefore, using this system, it is possible to work out the area of brain that is referred to in some descriptions. For example, the 'middle frontal gyrus' is one of the main ridges found in the frontal lobes and is differentiated from the superior and inferior frontal gryi which are the upper and lower ridges respectively; similarly, the intraparietal sulcus is the main groove found within the parietal lobe (intra meaning 'within'). Confusingly, some articles and textbooks may refer to the same areas using a numbering system which refers to Brodmann areas, which is a terminology based on the physical structure of the cells within a particular area. This is a complex system but can sometimes give more precise localisation. Therefore Brodmann area 46 (also known as BA46), for example, is the middle part of the middle frontal gyrus and the end part of the inferior frontal gyrus.

All the brain's gyri are linked very intricately and extensively by tracts of fibres with the result that there is a staggering amount of communication going on within the brain. The result is that although each lobe may be *primarily* involved in a particular cognitive function, interaction between different lobes is required to allow the system to function efficiently. As a simple example when making a choice between three different types of fruit, the visual system (see Chapter 6: Visual Agnosia & Object Recognition) needs to recognise what the three options are, a decision needs to be made on which one to select (see Chapter 9: Executive Functions) and then the motor planning system (see Chapter 5: Apraxia & Motor-Planning) needs to send instructions to the motor cortex to activate the sequence of skeletal and muscular changes for picking up the banana.

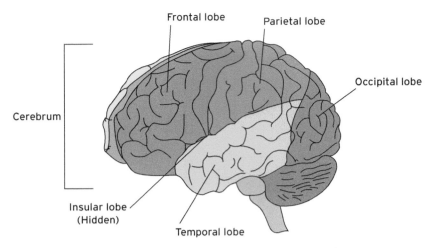

Figure 2.2   The four lobes of the human brain (Boore et al., 2016)

CAUSES OF BRAIN DAMAGE

Brain function can be disrupted either temporarily or permanently in a number of different ways. Each cause or aetiology (sometimes also written as etiology) may result in a different extent of brain damage which may then determine the range and severity of the difficulties experienced. An acquired brain injury (ABI) is any injury to the brain that is *not* inherited, degenerative or caused by trauma during the process of birth. There are developmental disorders that can impact cognitive abilities but as will be seen later in this chapter, the types of inferences we can make from the study of acquired and developmental disorders are quite different. Similarly, there are degenerative brain disorders which cause either abnormal or accelerated death of nerve cells which impact behaviour, the two most common ones being Alzheimer's disease and Parkinson's disease. However, given that one of the cornerstones of cognitive neuropsychology is the attempt to infer the workings of the intact healthy brain by studying those with brain disorders, since the disease processes in these conditions are ongoing, they tend to be studied less within the field.

Within the umbrella term of ABI there are two major sub-divisions, traumatic brain injury (TBI) and non-traumatic brain injury (NTBI), with the difference effectively being whether the cause is external or internal respectively. A TBI is any sudden external impact on the brain which can either penetrate the skull or leave it intact. The former, which breaks the skull, can happen because of objects such as bullets or freak accidents (see the example of Phineas Gage in Chapter 9: Executive Functions). In a grizzly way, the impact of the types of bullets that were used during World War II has ended up contributing to the field of cognitive neuropsychology. This is because bullets at this time in history had become smaller and could penetrate the skull but sometimes without leading to death. Depending on the trajectory of the bullet and how far it went into the brain, there were instances where the soldier was left with damage in a quite specific area which did not affect the functioning of the rest of the brain. The British neuropsychologist Freda Newcombe (1969) studied ex-servicemen to derive amazing insights into areas of the brain that until then had not been studied extensively; for instance, helmets that left the lower portions of the back of the head exposed meant that bullets could penetrate the occipital lobes creating visual disorders that had not been documented before.

However, given that the brain is effectively a soft spongy object inside a very hard bony casing, an object does not need to penetrate the skull to result in brain damage. Rapid forward or backward movement of the head can result in the softer brain hitting the harder bony skull. This can result in bruising or damage of brain cells, tearing of the fibre tracts that communicate between the cells or tearing of the blood vessels feeding oxygen to the cells. This sort of damage can occur when the skull hits a hard object such as the windshield of a car (see Figure 2.3), or against another individual (as is being documented more increasingly through contact sports such as football and rugby) or sadly when a baby is shaken repeatedly (known as shaken baby syndrome).

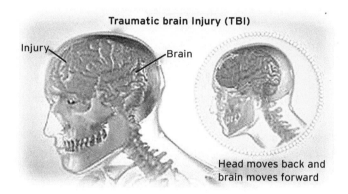

Figure 2.3   A traumatic brain injury in which the front of the head hits a solid object such as the windshield of a car and although the skull does not break, the front of the brain gets damaged because of it hitting the inside of the skull (Reproduced with permission of hopkinsmedicine.org)

Non-traumatic brain injury comes about because of internal factors, the primary reasons being interruption or lack of oxygen, pressure from a tumour and the consequences of infections within the brain. Since all living tissues require oxygen to survive, any sustained interruption of blood to the brain can result in a stroke of which there are two types. An ischemic stroke occurs when there is a clot in a blood vessel which blocks the flow of the blood with the result that brain areas further downstream can be starved of oxygen while the clot remains in place. A haemorrhagic stroke (or haemorrhage) is the bursting of a blood vessel either because of weakened walls or because of the build-up of pressure because of a clot that has not been dealt with. Again, there is damage to areas of the brain that are starved of oxygen and usually the impact can be much more severe than that due to an ischemic stroke. A related problem is an aneurysm which is a swelling in the wall of a weak blood vessel and looks like a blister protruding from the vessel. While in itself it may not cause significant problems, the danger is that if the pressure within the aneurysm gets to a certain point, the blood vessel will burst, again causing cell death to adjoining areas.

Issues outside the brain can also cause damage if they interrupt the steady flow of oxygen, known interchangeably as cerebral anoxia or hypoxia. If it is interrupted for as little as 15 seconds then the person could become unconscious, while if the interruption extends to more than four minutes, brain damage can occur. Just as with the rest of the body, infections can cause swelling/inflammation of cells in and around the brain; encephalitis is when the brain tissue becomes inflamed while meningitis is inflammation of the lining of cells (known as the meninges) around the brain and the spinal cord. Finally, a tumour anywhere in the body is when there is an abnormal growth of a particular type of tissue; within the brain, in addition to affecting the functioning of the abnormal cells, as the tumour grows, it will start exerting pressure on the surrounding areas. This pressure can then interrupt the functioning of brain tissue or squeeze blood vessels, thereby reducing oxygen flow to other areas of the brain.

Finally, an abnormality which does not involve specific brain damage is epilepsy, in which rather than the smooth coordinated electrical signals that are sent through nerves as different parts of the brain communicate with one another, there is an uncontrollable pulse or pulses that can shoot around the brain. These interrupt the smooth functioning of the brain resulting in seizures (or fits). The condition is complex and not well understood such that in half of those who suffer it, there is no identifiable cause. In the other half, the cause could be genetic or brought about by abnormalities resulting from some sort of damage to the brain such as a head injury or the viruses mentioned above. Finally, some developmental disorders such as autism can also carry a risk of epilepsy. Due to the large variety within and severity of epilepsy, there is no one set treatment. For many patients their treatment can be controlled by medication, but in severe cases where this is not sufficient (for example, see the case of HM in Chapter 8: Amnesia & Memory), surgery is required to remove the area of the brain that is generating the epileptic seizures.

BASIC NEUROIMAGING

As described in Chapter 1, an important contribution to the revival of the study of individuals with brain damage that started with the work of Broca in the nineteenth century was the development of methods and technologies that made it possible to 'look' at the brain while someone was alive rather than only at post-mortem. Thanks to advances in technology, nowadays researchers have an expanding and diverse arsenal of techniques to probe the structure and function of the brain, at different levels of spatial and temporal resolution. These methods fall into two broad categories: structural and functional imaging. Structural brain imaging, as its name suggests, refers to techniques that resolve the structure of the brain, taking static 'pictures' or 'snapshots' of the brain at a given point in time. The most popular structural techniques are computerised axial tomography (CAT or simply CT) and magnetic resonance imaging (MRI). Functional imaging techniques allow us to go beyond structure and examine certain functional properties of the brain over time allowing us to see the brain 'in action'. These techniques include (but are not limited to) functional MRI (fMRI), electroencephalography (EEG) and magnetoencephalography (MEG).

CAT is a technique that uses X-rays to create a 3D image of the brain. It basically works by taking multiple X-ray scans from different angles and then combining them to construct a representation of the patient's brain. Due to improvements made since their development in the 1970s, modern CAT scanners can show detail (known as spatial resolution) of brain structure down to a millimetre.

MRI is nowadays the method of choice when it comes to imaging brain structure, both for clinical and research purposes. There are a number of different types of MRI scans, but in the most typical known as 'T1-weighted', grey brain matter will look grey, white matter, white, and cerebrospinal fluid, black. MRI has a much higher spatial resolution than CAT scans, with modern scanners reaching 100 micrometre resolution.

While CAT and MRI allow researchers and clinicians to see physical structures and areas of damage accurately, they don't provide information on how those areas are functioning. In the 1990s a Japanese bioscientist called Seiji Ogawa developed a technique that relies on the fact that, just as your legs require more energy if you are running, a part of the brain that needs to process information needs energy to function. To do this, it needs oxygen and therefore, just as the blood flow to your legs increases to provide the necessary oxygen, active parts of the brain pull more blood to allow them to function. fMRI capitalises on this principle and works on the same principles of MRI by tracking the level of oxygen in the blood throughout the brain. While the spatial resolution of fMRI is extremely good, the temporal resolution (accuracy of the timing of activity) is relatively low. Therefore, fMRI is good for letting researchers see *where* activity is happening with a great level of detail but the accuracy of saying *when* it happened is quite limited. Over the last two decades, there has been a huge explosion in neuroimaging techniques that are advancing our understanding of brain functions *in vivo* – this has created a veritable alphabet soup of techniques including EEG, ERP, MEG, TMS, SPECT, DTI, DOT, tDCS, etc.

Lesion Overlap Analysis

As you will see in Chapter 3, one of the issues when comparing the brains of two people is that even with identical twins, there are slight differences between two brains.

Therefore, how can we compare the brains of two patients which even before the neurological incident were different to one another? If two patients have both suffered from strokes, how do we know whether the areas damaged in them are similar or not? To address this conundrum, a remarkable scientist, Hanna Damasio, developed a method that has formed the basis of many subsequent forms of analysis. Damasio & Damasio (1990) created a detailed 'atlas' of the brain, meticulously going through the brain layer by layer; this brain and its atlas then could be used as a 'reference brain' for analysing all other brains. The atlas came with instructions of how to locate the equivalent levels of a brain scan for a particular patient and then using 'landmarks' of specific brain structures to manually copy over areas of damage onto the reference brain. By doing this, different types and extent of brain damage could be 'normalised' to a single brain. As a result, by doing this for two, three or more brains, the above difficulty of the heterogeneity of everyone's brains being different is no longer an issue since they have all been normalised to the reference brain.

This lesion overlap analysis proved invaluable to researchers around the world. For years, this method made it possible to look at patients who had a particular cognitive disorder and to locate the common area of damage; this then allowed for the potential localisation of specific functions. This manual method was then automated to create Brainvox, which is a system that allows the normalisation of an individual's brain to the reference brain without the use of the earlier paper and pencil method (Frank et al., 1997). An added benefit of this system is that if this normalisation is conducted for a number of layers through the brain, Brainvox can turn these 2D images into 3D 'volumes' of the brain. This allows the researcher to 'see' the living patient's brain in a way that had not previously been possible until the patient's death; for example, the images of my brain shown in Figure 1.7 were created by Hanna Damasio using Brainvox. Further, looking across a group of patients, it is possible to start inferring what the 'maximum area of overlap' is that affects specific cognitive functions. For example, Figure 2.4 shows the lesion overlap analysis conducted by Tranel et al. (2003) to look at the brain areas involved in our ability to use manipulable tools correctly (see Chapter 5: Apraxia & Motor-Planning). By overlapping the normalised brains of a number of patients who all had difficulties in tool use, they were able to see which areas were the most commonly affected across the patients. As seen in Figure 2.4, Brainvox provided a three-dimensional image of the brain in which the 'hotter' colours show that more patients had damage in that particular area. Then the letters show the points at which this lesion overlap brain has been 'sliced' to show how the maximum areas of overlap change going further back in the brain. It is obvious how systems like Brainvox and those that have been developed subsequently can contribute enormously to our understanding of the neural basis for specific cognitive functions, which up until relatively recently could only be inferred after the analysis of a deceased patient's brain.

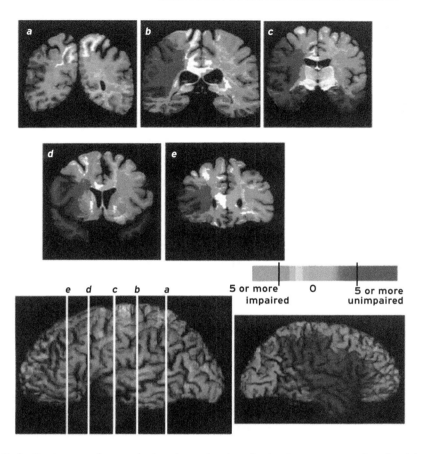

Figure 2.4 Lesion overlap analysis – investigating the brain areas most involved in the conceptual understanding of tool use (Tranel et al., 2003. Reprinted with permission from Taylor and Francis Ltd)

Caveats Regarding Neuroimaging

This increase in neuroimaging techniques has been extremely useful for researchers studying cognitive functions in healthy individuals. However, it is important to note that at the moment, many of them are not suitable for use with patients with brain damage; this will probably change over the coming decades. Also, as described in Chapter 1, there are differences between cognitive neuropsychology and cognitive neuroscience, so the recent techniques are not necessarily applicable to the types of questions regarding cognitive abilities being studied with patients.

Another important point is that all of the neuroimaging techniques are based on complex physics and increasingly an immense amount of mathematics. Unless one understands these issues, it is very easy to over-interpret the compelling images that are produced. A hilarious and shocking example of how extreme this can be is a study that won its authors the IgNobel Prize for science that first of all makes us laugh and then makes us think. Bennett et al. (2009) demonstrated that unless the mathematics is applied carefully, it is possible to get some very 'interesting' findings. They were about to conduct a study on social perspective taking (in humans) and were setting up the experimental and fMRI scanning procedures. Their procedure involved displaying photographs to the participant within the scanner of people showing a variety of emotions; the participant's task was to judge what emotion was being experienced in the photo. To trial this experimental protocol, since they needed organic material within the scanner, and one of them had been shopping for dinner, 'one mature Atlantic Salmon (Salmo salar) participated in the fMRI study. The salmon was approximately 18 inches long, weighed 3.8 lbs, and was not alive at the time of scanning' (Bennett et al., 2009, p. 47). What they found was that, using the mathematical procedures that were common at the time for analysing the results from such fMRI protocols, parts of the salmon's brain looked as if they had been activated (see Figure 2.5). So not only was this a salmon who could understand English, and not only was it a salmon that could understand English and work out what emotions humans were displaying in a photograph, but it was a dead salmon who could do all of this!!!! This study was not a spoof but a real study and was presented at a conference as a warning against how, unless appropriate mathematical procedures are applied, it is very easy to make a dead salmon understand human emotions.

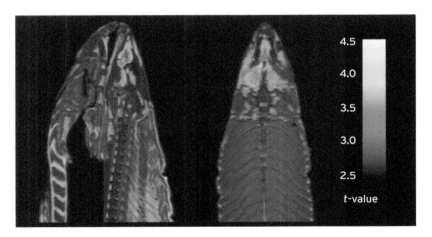

Figure 2.5 The dead salmon 'recognising' human emotions (Bennett et al., 2009. Reprinted with permission from Elsevier Science & Technology Journals)

Research has demonstrated that even if researchers conduct the correct mathematical procedures, it can still result in levels of 'belief' in the images that are produced that might be unwarranted. McCabe & Castle (2008) demonstrated this rather starkly in a study in which groups of participants were given fictitious scientific articles to read which contained dubious claims such as the suggestion that watching TV activated the same part of the brain as solving maths problems and therefore watching TV was good for one's overall mathematical abilities! One group of participants was presented a version of the paper with a bar graph showing the apparently similar levels of activation in the temporal lobes while the other group was presented with a classic fMRI type of image showing activation in similar areas of the brain for the two activities (see Figure 2.6a). After reading the articles, participants had to give a rating for how much sense was made by its scientific reasoning. What McCabe & Castle found was that even though the text for the two conditions was identical, the ratings given for the version with the brain image were significantly higher; indeed, the ratings for the version including the bar graph were no greater than for a control condition in which only text was presented (see Figure 2.6b).

D.P. McCabe, A. D. Castel / Cognition 107 (2008) 343-352

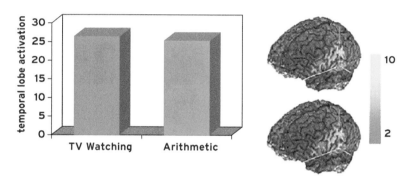

Figure 2.6a   The two versions of the images shown by McCabe & Castle (2008) to explore whether brain images make an article more compelling

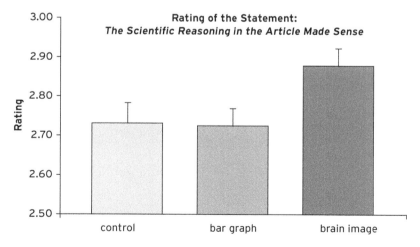

Figure 2.6b   The ratings given for the scientific sense made by the articles for the two experimental conditions compared to the control one in which no text was shown (McCabe & Castle, 2008)

Ali et al. (2014) took things one step further and created a mock neuroimaging laboratory 'assembled from discarded odds and ends including a scrap salon hair dryer' (p. 2). They seated participants underneath the supposed brain scanning device and displayed a pre-recorded video of 3D brain slices along with audio that made it sound like they were in a real brain scanner (see Figure 2.7). Participants were told that the scanner was able to decipher their internal thoughts and that these were being presented on the computer screen; their task was to give subjective ratings of their beliefs in the ability of the neuroimaging equipment to understand what they were thinking. Based on their findings, the authors stated that participants believed in the

> …over-promise-&-under-deliver mentality, which portrays brain imaging as an omniscient strategy for unscrambling the neural correlates of thought. Fuelled by popular media and lay accounts, neuroenchantment further blurs fact from fad and leads to accepting tentative suppositions as indisputable fact… even participants explicitly educated about the limits of neuroimaging succumbed to our simple trick, albeit less so than their naïve peers. (Ali et al., 2014, p. 3)

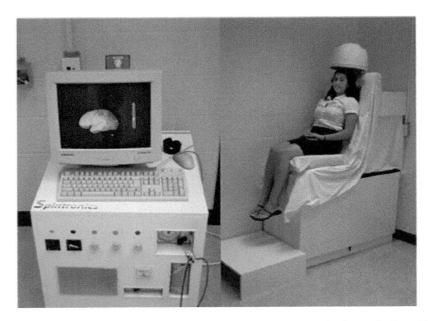

Figure 2.7　'Neuroenchantment' set up (Ali et al., 2014; Copyright © 2014 Ali, Lifshitz and Raz, CC BY 3.0)

The above issues are relevant for two important reasons. One of these is the volume of research papers published. For example, Eklund et al. (2016) estimated that already by 2016 there were 40,000 papers published using fMRI. Given the pace at which neuroimaging has been developing, by the time you are reading this, the number will be quite a bit larger. This is important because for a number of years, there has been a concern within psychology about the fact that if a result is statistically significant someone repeating the same study should get similar results, but in cognitive neuroscience in particular there is a replication crisis. This difficulty for scientists to replicate the findings that have already been published is of concern, leaving them to wonder whether they did something incorrect in their study or the original study itself was at fault. As an example, although not directly to do with brain damage, Horster et al. (2020) found that fMRI results on the brain dysfunction driving anorexia nervosa published previously were not replicable. Since in general science proceeds by attempting to replicate and then extend established findings, this can result in wasted resources or research theorising going in a direction that actually could be a blind alley.

Attempts are being made to address these issues with researchers being asked to be more transparent and to share their methods and data with one another. There is a move towards 'big data' whereby scientists can share their results so that there is an accumulation from many different studies which allows anyone to analyse the data to look at patterns that any single study would not be able to (see Further Reading below). This is a very positive move forward; however, some scientists suggest that we should still be cautious since 'there is a concern that claims regarding "big data" approaches for the cognitive sciences may overpromise and underdeliver' (Medina & Fischer-Baum, 2017, p. 443).

TESTING A NEUROPSYCHOLOGICAL PATIENT

As outlined in Chapter 1, a clinical neuropsychologist and an experimental cognitive neuropsychologist work with a patient with brain damage for different reasons. However, when looking at their cognitive abilities, initially at least, there will be commonality in the work that they conduct.

Generally speaking, the clinician will tend to use standardised tests which have been developed rigorously to evaluate performance on different abilities in a clear and objective manner. The point of this is that anyone with sufficient understanding or training on the particular test materials can conduct an assessment on an individual without there being a danger of their own thoughts about the test participant affecting the way that their performance is scored. This latter point is extremely important since if the assessor's *subjective* thoughts about what the patient is trying to say or do on a test makes them alter their scoring, they may overestimate or underestimate the patient's abilities resulting in an inaccurate overall evaluation of the impact of the brain damage. A standardised test therefore comes with very clear instructions on how to set up the testing material, what to say to the patient, whether or not any feedback can be given during the assessment and how to interpret the results. Usually, rather than taking the raw score of the patient on the test (for example the number of correct words remembered in a memory test), the patient's score is evaluated relative to a set of norms which is effectively the performance of a control group of healthy participants. Such norms could be stratified by the different factors that could affect performance on that particular task – examples of factors are age, education level, gender or even ethnicity. This is important because a raw score of 20 out of 30 on a face recognition test in itself is not informative until we know something about the individual participant and what the typical performance is of healthy individuals who are of a similar demographic. For example, if the individual is relatively young and the average person of their age scores 18 out of 30, then this score is actually quite good; however, if the individual is older and the average score for their age group is 25, then the score of 20 implies that there is possibly an impairment. This is just an abstract example but a test that provides norms will have clear cut-off scores for different demographic factors and clear categorical interpretations such as 'highly impaired', 'impaired, 'below average', 'average', 'above average', etc.

Another way to present an individual's score is to provide a numerical score for their performance. The most widely used statistical method is based on a 'bell-shaped' normal distribution of natural observations – therefore, whether you are measuring people's heights, their IQs or their ability to remember a series of unrelated words, generally it is found that the spread of performance across a large group of individuals will have most scores clumping around a central average and then fewer and fewer scores as you move to either higher or lower scores (see Figure 2.8). There are various properties of this type of distribution, the most important being the standard deviation which is a measure of how 'spread out' or varied the distribution is across all the scores. A small standard deviation implies that most scores in a population are very close to the average (and so scores across the whole population show little variation), while a big standard deviation implies a big spread of scores. Due to the mathematical properties of such a 'distribution' it is possible to define 'outliers' as scores that are more than two standard deviations from the average score. Therefore, a method adopted by many neuropsychologists is to convert an individual's performance into a z-score which is the number of standard deviations from the mean. As a convention, any z-score that was more than 2 would be considered outside the normal range and therefore it could be stated that the patient's performance was significantly different to the control mean. For classical IQ tests, the average score is 100 and one standard deviation is 15. Therefore, any scores that are below 70 or above 130 would be considered 'outside' normal limits.

The properties of the bell-shaped curve also allow the same score to be stated in a different way which is used more for clinical purposes than research. With the z-score method, a statement is made relative to the *average for the population*, but sometimes it is more useful to know how the score *compares to the whole population* rather than the average. In such situations, a percentile score is computed which effectively involves drawing a line in the distribution where the patient's score falls and computing the proportion of people who have *lower* scores – this number then tells the researcher what proportion of population the patient scores *better* than. This method is used a lot in clinical psychology where a low percentile score for one ability (e.g. face memory) compared to an average or higher than average one for another ability (e.g. verbal memory) would suggest that the brain injury has significantly affected one ability but not the other. Taking the IQ example, a score of 130

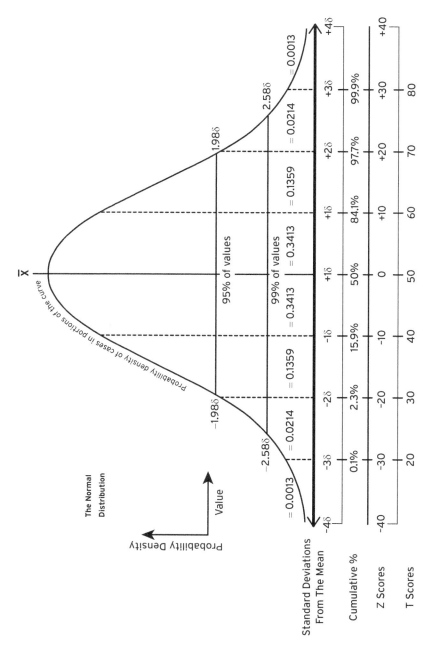

Figure 2.8 The normal 'bell-shaped' curve, the percentage of the curve that is in successive standard deviation blocks from the mean, and the percentile score for an individual score that falls at each of these points (Reproduced with permission from investopedia.com and Julie Bang)

would be two standard deviations above the mean and that would be equivalent to the 97.7th percentile. See Table 2.1 for standard neuropsychological testing on a patient with a specific memory problem tested by Jansari et al. (2010). It is obvious from seeing the right-hand column that on some measures he scored well above average (percentile scores above 50), but on others such as the AMI sub-tests he scored in the abnormal range.

Table 2.1 The performance of patient RY tested by Jansari et al. (2010) on a series of cognitive tests. The right-hand column gives the patient's raw score, or the raw score and the interpretation against set norms, or the raw score and its percentile, or simply its percentile

Neuropsychological assessment of RY.

Test	Sub-test	RY's performance
NART (errors = 10)		Pre-morbid IQ 118
WAIS-R	Performance IQ	124
	Verbal IQ	123
WMS-R	Stories immediate recall	28 (80th percentile)
	Stories delayed recall	25 (82nd percentile)
	Designs immediate recall	36 (95th percentile)
	Designs delayed recall	34 (94th percentile)
WMS-III	Faces immediate retention	41 (scaled score 14)
	Faces delayed retention	44 (scaled score 18)
Rey-Osterieth Figure	Delayed visual recall	70th percentile
WRMT	Faces	67.5th percentile
	Words	86.7th percentile
AMI	Childhood semantics	10.5/21 (definitely abnormal)
	Childhood autobiographical	4/9 (probably abnormal)
	Early adulthood semantics	11.5/21 (definitely abnormal)
	Early adulthood autobiographical	4/9 (probably abnormal)
	Recent semantics	15/21 (definitely abnormal)
	Recent autobiographical	4/9 (definitely abnormal)
WSCT		6 categories (normal)
Graded naming test		24/30 (normal)

WAIS-R = Wechsler Adult Intelligence Scale Revised; WMS-R = Wechsler Memory Scale Revised; WMS-III = Wechsler Memory Scale III; WRMT = Warrington Recognition Memory Test; AMI = Autobiographical Memory Interview; WSCT = Wisconsin Card Sorting Test.

While a clinical neuropsychologist will tend to use largely standardised tests, the cognitive neuropsychologist usually uses these simply to get an overall view of the patient's main cognitive abilities. Then, having isolated the problem to a particular domain, for example to visual recognition, they would then start focusing on that particular ability. Initially, they would generally try to look at the pattern of both intact and impaired abilities; this is similar to Broca's observations with patient Tan in that he was able to isolate the problem to the production of language, having seen that all the other cognitive abilities were intact. Similarly, in their work with a patient with a face-recognition problem (see Chapter 7: Prosopagnosia & Face Processing), Jansari et al. (2015) used standardised testing to get a 'general picture' of the patient's abilities to establish objectively that he had prosopagnosia. Following this, however, they developed bespoke experiments to investigate the patient's face-recognition difficulties in more detail. Whereas for the standardised tests, it is possible to evaluate the patient's performance against a set of established control scores (the norms), when a new test is developed, this is not possible. Instead, the patient's score is usually compared against those of other individuals who are of similar demographic characteristics, typically similar age, educational level and possibly gender.

Historically, a number of different methods have been used to evaluate the patient's score against the control group and therefore, depending on how long ago a study was conducted, you may well find different methods in different papers. In the very early days of the field, simple histograms or tables were used to demonstrate that a patient had scored substantially worse than the control participants. However, as will be seen in Chapter 3, there are many pitfalls to judging whether or not an individual has a deficit by direct comparison. Following this 'visual analysis' method, neuropsychologists began to use statistical techniques to make decisions about whether or not a patient's performance on a task was significantly different from 'the norm'.

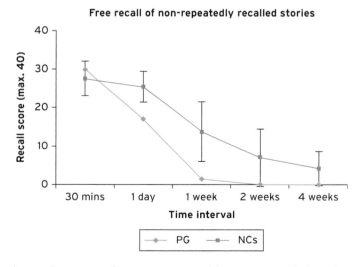

Figure 2.9   The performance of patient RY tested by Jansari et al. (2010) compared to healthy controls on a specially developed memory test. Using Crawford & Garthwaite's (2002) method, it was possible to compute specific probability values for RY's performance relative to the controls (adapted from original)

The most recent step in analysing data from single cases has come about with procedures to compute exact probabilities for a patient's score compared to a group of matched controls. For example, Crawford & Garthwaite (2002) have developed a free suite of web-based programmes that allow a researcher to enter a patient's individual score, the average of the matched controls, the standard deviation for the controls' scores and the size of the control sample – the output is an exact probability (p) value for the patient's score and, following standard convention, if the score is less than 0.05 it can be stated that the patient's score is significantly different. As seen in Figure 2.9, Jansari et al. (2010) were able to show that on a specially developed memory task, their patient RY began to perform very poorly compared to health controls; this showed that although the patient scored within normal limits on standardised tests of memory (see Table 2.1), he was actually showing catastrophic forgetting of information within one day of learning.

Chapter Summary

- The brain has a clear anatomy with different areas specialising in specific abilities.
- There are multiple causes of brain dysfunction and therefore knowing the history that brought a patient to a clinician or a researcher is an important part of helping them or for experimentation and theorising.
- Neuroimaging can be extremely useful for visualising the brain, areas of damage and functioning in a healthy brain; however, there are a number of issues that need to be borne in mind when looking at and interpreting brain scans.
- Testing a patient involves a number of standard procedures which allows the clinician or researcher to understand the deficits that are being exhibited and also to compare them with other patients.

Important Researcher

John Crawford

John Crawford is a clinical psychologist and neuropsychologist currently at the University of Aberdeen in Scotland. His special interests are in the development, evaluation and application of quantitative methods in neuropsychology. This has had a very significant impact in the field because one of the criticisms of some of the work in the field was that it was relatively descriptive with some theorising involving researchers saying that a patient performed better on condition X than on condition Y and therefore this showed that condition Y was impaired. Since the rest of psychology was using statistical techniques for demonstrating the differences between conditions X and Y, this seemed somewhat simplistic. However, since most statistical techniques in psychology are based on needing two *groups* of participants, John's very influential contribution to cognitive neuropsychology has been the development of techniques that allow researchers to perform formal statistical analysis even on single case studies. He has developed a set of programmes that are free to download and have become invaluable resources for researchers around the world. John is one of the most highly cited neuropsychologists in the UK, having published over 150 scientific papers in neuropsychology and in clinical psychology.

Questions for Reflection

- Does the etiology (or cause) of brain dysfunction impact the amount of damage that can be caused? Why would this be important to know?
- Why is it important to avoid neuroenchantment?
- When testing a patient, what does a research neuropsychologist need to do to ensure that they are scientifically rigorous?

Go Further

Dr Jansari's YouTube Videos
Never mind the neuro-bollocks! A beginner's guide to separating neuro-fact from neuro-trash

While great strides are being made in our understanding of the brain, there has also been an expansion of work which has hijacked the term 'neuro'. Sometimes this is to add a level of legitimacy to otherwise questionable work, sometimes it is to drive sales of products or services, and sometimes it is simply to make something sound, for want of a better word, more 'fancy'! This talk provides a guide through some fundamental aspects of this area to demonstrate some of the issues that we need to be careful about, and therefore when to mind the neuro-bollocks.

Further Reading

- Gilmore, R. O., Diaz, M. T., Wyble, B. A., & Yarkoni, T. (2017). Progress toward openness, transparency, and reproducibility in cognitive neuroscience. *Annals of the New York Academy of Sciences, 1396*(1), 5-18.
- Medina, J., & Fischer-Baum, S. (2017). Single-case cognitive neuropsychology in the age of big data. *Cognitive Neuropsychology, 34*(7-8), 440-448.

3
PRINCIPLES AND ISSUES IN COGNITIVE NEUROPSYCHOLOGY

Chapter Overview

This chapter will provide an overview of some of the most important principles that allow researchers to study individuals with brain damage and make inferences about how healthy cognitive abilities function. In addition, it is important to consider some of the 'danger zones' when conducting such research so that theories are not based on highly specific individuals who are not representative of the general population. Finally, given that the studies are conducted on either specific individuals or groups, rather than a random sample of the general population as happens with most studies, there will be an overview of the research issues that need to be considered.

Chapter Outline

- Introduction
- Recreating the 'Cognitive Jigsaw'
- Comparing Two Individual Brains
- Research Decisions
- Chapter Summary

INTRODUCTION

A neuropsychologist has a number of approaches that are available when either assessing a patient clinically or conducting empirical research. Whichever of these two is the major aim, he or she needs to pay careful attention to principles and decisions about participants that are relevant when working with patients with brain damage. If the patient is being used for research purposes, how representative they are of the normal population is a very important consideration since the whole point of research is to generalise to intact cognitive processes. Similarly, in trying to compare two patients, the extent to which it is possible to compare any two individuals who have physically different brains and whose brain damage could differ either only subtly or greatly needs to be given careful thought. One of the major assumptions behind the use of damaged cognitive systems to infer normal intact processing, known as subtractivity, is an issue that a neuropsychologist needs to consider very carefully. Similarly, the appreciation that the brain may show some changes as part of its recovery after being damaged needs to be cautiously considered. A big question when conducting empirical research will be the choice and number of patients in a study – is it better to do a very fine-grained analysis of one patient or is it better to study a group of patients with a common deficit? Finally, when the patient suffered brain damage will have a large impact on both the profile that emerges and also on how the findings can be interpreted. This is because damage early in life, when the brain is still forming, can have different consequences to damage that happens to a fully formed brain.

RECREATING THE 'COGNITIVE JIGSAW'
Subtractivity

If one of the aims of psychology is to understand human behaviour functions – and within cognitive psychology, to understand mental functions such as memory or face recognition – it is reasonable to pose the question 'Then why are you studying people who have *problems* with those very abilities?' given that the majority of us can remember or recognise faces without even thinking about it. This brings up one of the fundamental principles of neuropsychology, but to introduce it, it is useful to think of an important quote by Craik who said, 'in any well-made machine one is ignorant of the working of most of the parts – the better they work, the less we are conscious of them… it is only a fault which draws attention to the existence of a mechanism at all' (1943, p. 84). To understand why this quote is so vital, think about how a car works. It is a highly complex system whose design is known to engineers and mechanics but unknown to me and in all likelihood to yourself too. If my car broke down, it could be for a number of reasons and since I don't understand the internal workings, I would need to go to a mechanic to have it fixed. While there, I could ask them what is wrong and they might say that the fan belt was broken. Since I don't know what a fan belt is, I could then ask for a description of what it is and how it works within my car. Now if I was unfortunate enough, my car might break down again a few months later but this time it might not be the fan belt so I would have to go back to the mechanic who would work out that it is something called the gear box; again, I could ask them to explain to me how that works. Continuing on the theme of my bad luck, I could go round the entire car with different parts malfunctioning and eventually know how all the different parts work; however, initially looking at the smoothly running piece of transport gave me very few clues about its internal intricacy.

In this analogy, it should be noted that the design of the car is something that is *already known*, and therefore for someone to understand how or why it is malfunctioning isn't a difficult process. Also, whereas the mechanic might be able to repair the problem with the car, the same is not true in neuropsychology, since brain damage is, on the whole, irreversible. Further, the human brain and cognitive system are *much* more complex than a car and we do not know the design or internal processes until we conduct rigorous experimental research; however, the analogy of the complexity of a well-made machine and studying it when it is broken applies very well to the study of the human brain.

One way of conceptualising cognitive neuropsychology is to see it as a recreation of an originally intact jigsaw that has been broken up by some form of brain damage, and with some pieces now missing. Importantly, the rest of the brain is assumed to function in exactly the same way as that of a healthy brain-intact individual. This has been termed the transparency or universality assumption by Alfonso Caramazza (1986). In the healthy adult state, all elements of the complex aspects of a particular cognitive ability (such as memory for example) function normally. This system could be seen as an intricate jigsaw. Figure 3.1a is a conceptual representation of a rather simple nine piece jigsaw that would represent memory. However, due to the very efficient functioning of this system, despite the underlying intricacy, we are unaware of all the complex mechanisms and in reality (referring to the jigsaw) we only know the general outer shape, as seen in Figure 3.1b.

Now consider for example Patient A, who is seen by a neuropsychologist (Figure 3.2a). By carefully studying this patient, the neuropsychologist maps out what he or she can and cannot do. If done properly, this process will allow a general understanding of the outer 'shape' of A's memory functioning. From this, it is possible to infer the shape of the missing piece in Patient A (Figure 3.2b). Using this knowledge, the neuropsychologist can make a hypothesis about the shape of one of the pieces of the normal memory system found in all healthy adults; this is the principle of subtractivity. Using the same rationale, Patient B with a *different* memory problem might also be seen by the neuropsychologist (Figure 3.3a). From studying B, it is found that the 'shape' of his memory is quite different to that of A. Again, by carefully studying this new patient, it is possible to infer his 'missing piece' (Figure 3.3b). Using this rationale, depending on first of all the existence, and second the extremely careful study of different patients, cognitive neuropsychologists aim to infer the workings of the entire system and its many sub-processes (Figure 3.1a).

Figure 3.1a   Cognitive neuropsychology: Recreating the jigsaw

Figure 3.1b   Due to the complexity of cognitive abilities, sometimes all that is known is the 'outer shape'

Figure 3.2a   Patient A

Figure 3.2b   Inferring what is missing in patient A

Figure 3.3a   Patient B

Figure 3.3b   Inferring what is missing in patient B

Associations, Dissociations and Double Dissociations

Associations

Once the neuropsychologist has used the various available standardised assessments and specially designed experimental techniques to study the deficits and intact abilities of a patient, the task now turns to making inferences from the evidence gained. How do neuropsychologists infer the existence of separate cognitive functions within the brain, and how do they then decide whether or not each of these contains separate processes? For example, is language a separate function from memory? Or within face processing are there different pathways for recognition of faces and recognition of the emotion in the face? Neuropsychologists look to see which cognitive problems tend to occur together and these are known as associations.

Sometimes, if a number of problems co-occur consistently, they can be grouped together as a syndrome. An example is Wernicke-Korsakoff syndrome which is a constellation of deficits that can occur following very chronic alcohol abuse. The most striking sign is a dense inability to lay down new memories. Coupled with this is a difficulty in retrieving memories laid down during earlier points in life before brain damage as well as a difficult walking gait. Between patients there can be variance in the extent of each of these individual deficits but by and large the association between them is strong, hence the syndrome label. It would be tempting to think that if the deficits in memory and walking gait occur together with such consistency following brain damage that they are all caused by one specific functional problem at the cognitive level, and this could result in localising each of these functions to the area of the lesions.

However, such a conclusion could be inaccurate and premature. For instance, the brain damage that causes the Wernicke-Korsakoff syndrome may be quite widespread affecting a number of different areas, and each of these is responsible for a different aspect of the syndrome. It may be that the initial disorder that initiates the brain damage (for example, a thiamine deficiency that is caused by the poor diet of chronic alcoholics) triggers cell death in a number of different areas which in themselves are not related to one another. For this reason, association of symptoms needs to be interpreted with great care. McCarthy & Warrington (1990) state that some syndromes could occur simply due to the fact that separate functions may be controlled by brain areas that are very close to one another. A brain lesion that is large may therefore cover an area that controls a number of unrelated abilities. For example, in Gerstmann's syndrome there are four main symptoms: agraphia (deficiency in the ability to write), acalculia (difficulty in learning or comprehending mathematics), finger agnosia (inability to distinguish the fingers on the hand) and left-right disorientation. This does not, however, mean that these functions are all related to one another or even controlled by the same brain area, but probably that a lesion has affected a number of different areas that are very close to one another and which control different functions.

Dissociations

A stronger inference about functions can be made when certain symptoms consistently occur in the *absence* of other problems. For example, it has been repeatedly observed that certain patients retain an ability to remember items for a few minutes, but lose their ability to remember the same information for longer periods (e.g. patient HM reported by Scoville & Milner, 1957). One initial conclusion could be that two types of memory are involved and that in these patients, they dissociate from one another – it is possible to lose one whilst retaining the other intact. This sort of dissociation has been used to support very influential early models of memory such as the Modal Model proposed by Atkinson & Shiffrin (1968) which has separate components for holding information for a brief amount of time, known as short-term memory (STM), or for much longer periods, known as long-term memory (LTM) (see Chapter 8).

Double Dissociations

However, even if this pattern of good STM and bad LTM is found very consistently, it could be argued that we don't actually have enough evidence to propose such a complicated system of two different forms of memory. If an easier explanation can be found it should be adopted instead – this is known as the 'law of parsimony', which means that we should look for the simplest explanation for an observation that we are trying to understand. For example, 'unidentified flying object' in the sky could well be an alien spaceship but it is more likely to be a simple silver weather balloon! Teuber (1955) argued that the neuropsychologist should consider the question: What if one of these two abilities was simply *easier* than the other? The pattern of observed behaviour could then be explained without suggesting a complicated multi-component system.

For instance, just hypothetically, suppose that there was just *one* memory system, and in that system the more 'effort' (conscious or unconscious) you put into retaining information, the more likely it was that you would retain it for longer periods. So for example, more 'effort' (such as more concentration or more efficient neural processing) is required to retain information for a few hours than it is to do so for just a few seconds or a few minutes (see Figure 3.4a). Now if this system was damaged by brain injury, perhaps rather than losing the entire memory system, only the ability to hold onto information for a long time, i.e. the 'difficult-to-hold-onto' memory could be affected. This does not affect 'easy-to-hold-onto' memory since that only requires a bit of effort/processing and therefore it could be possible to see the pattern described in patients such as Henry Molaison, who during his life for the sake of anonymity was known in the literature as HM (see Figure 3.4b). This situation would be similar to having a heavy illness for a few weeks which would generally reduce energy levels; following recovery, easy exercise such as walking would be possible but more strenuous activities such as running or swimming would prove more challenging.

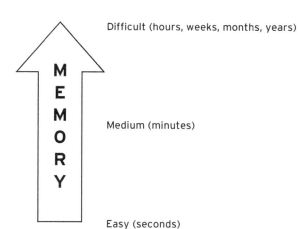

Difficult (hours, weeks, months, years)

Medium (minutes)

Easy (seconds)

Figure 3.4a A hypothetical unitary memory system with different degrees of difficulty as the hierarchy is ascended

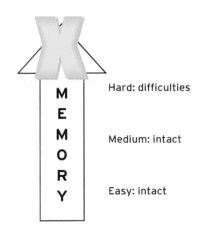

Figure 3.4b Damage to the hypothetical unitary system is most likely to affect the most difficult aspects of memory. This *could* explain cases such as HM who have an inability to remember information that happened more than a few minutes ago

The scientific rationale is that if a simpler explanation can suffice for all available data, it is not *yet* possible to suggest a more complex system – basically, nature and evolution prefers simplicity! Therefore, the evidence from amnesics such as HM does not *yet* allow us to suggest multiple forms of memory.

What would the prediction be if this unitary hierarchical system was damaged at its midpoint? An impairment at the midpoint would allow easy levels of processing but would affect medium levels of difficulty (see Figure 3.4c). In our memory example, this would mean that a patient should be able to hold onto information for a few seconds but beyond that should have problems. Additionally, in such a hierarchical system, the patient should have problems in retaining anything at the 'hard' end of the spectrum, so the prediction would be that a patient who has a problem with holding onto information for anything more than a few seconds should *also* have problems holding onto information for any long periods of time such as days, weeks and years.

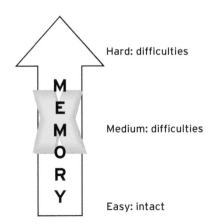

Figure 3.4c If the hypothetical unitary system is damaged in its middle portion the prediction would be that both 'medium' and 'hard' levels of memory would prove difficult

However, what if a patient was found who cannot repeat back a list of six single digit numbers after ten seconds and yet has no problems with remembering information from a few weeks ago? This is the pattern depicted in Figure 3.4d and has been found in some patients. Shallice & Warrington (1970) documented the case of patient KF who, following a motorcycle accident that caused brain damage, had problems with certain aspects of STM but no problems with his LTM. Can such a pattern be explained by our simple 'one-memory' model? The answer is 'no', and the result of such a finding would be that we would have to abandon the concept of a single unitary hierarchical model in favour of at least two separate memory systems, one which primarily caters for the medium-difficulty level whilst the other caters for the harder level of difficulty.

The reverse pattern between two patients, where HM had intact STM but impaired LTM, and KF had impaired STM but intact LTM, is known as a double dissociation. This type of finding is extremely useful for neuropsychologists because, as it cannot be explained in the one-system model that varies along 'ease' (Figure 3.4d), it seems to imply the existence of two separate systems (thus allowing both patterns of impairment to occur). Such a double dissociation allows researchers to then conclude that (at least to some degree) STM and LTM are separate processes. The existence of further double dissociations then allows for further fractionation of memory (see Chapter 8: Amnesia & Memory).

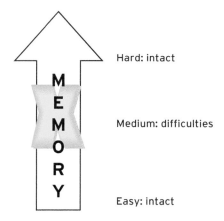

Hard: intact

Medium: difficulties

Easy: intact

Figure 3.4d If the hypothetical unitary system is damaged in its middle portion resulting in problems with memory for information heard a few minutes ago, it is impossible to explain how a patient such as KF can still be able to remember what happened an hour, a week or many months ago

Other very clear examples of double dissociations in cognitive neuropsychology occur in face processing, between recognition of someone's identity and the emotion they are expressing (e.g. Adolphs et al., 1994; Jansari et al., 2015; see Chapter 7), and in reading, between phonological and surface dyslexia (e.g. Coltheart et al., 2001; see Chapter 10).

Generally speaking, if applied appropriately, double dissociations can be extremely useful in the development of cognitive models of normal functions. Researchers do not go looking for double dissociations since they are not common, but noticing patterns that may dissociate like this is useful as part of the 'tool kit'. For example, we (Jansari et al., 2015; see Chapter 7) noticed that our patient's face-recognition problem was almost exactly the reverse of that of a patient with object recognition difficulties studied by Moscovitch et al. (1997). Therefore, we developed a study using their paradigm to demonstrate a double dissociation between the two patients. Following the discovery of a double dissociation, if specific anatomical differences exist between the two patients who demonstrate a double dissociation, it is possible to make claims about the localisation of particular functions. However, even in the absence of anatomical information, the functional significance is still very important.

Caution Regarding Double Dissociations

Double dissociations are a very powerful tool in cognitive neuropsychology but a number of authors suggest caution when interpreting such findings to conclude either functional or physical separation of processes (e.g. Law & Or, 2001; Shallice, 1986; Young et al., 1993). The issues revolve around how data from different studies is compared, how to judge a deficit and how to evaluate normality.

Comparison of Data from Different Studies

Patients who demonstrate double dissociations from one another are often studied in different laboratories by different researchers using methods that are not standardised. As a result, different stimuli may have been used to demonstrate the pattern of problems exhibited in the two patients. A classic example is in the field of object recognition where some researchers (e.g. Warrington & Shallice, 1984) have reported patients who have much greater problems visually recognising living things than non-living things whilst others (e.g. Sacchett & Humphreys, 1992) have reported the reverse case (see Chapter 6). This has led many (e.g. McCarthy & Warrington, 1990) to argue that the system responsible for storing conceptual knowledge (known as the semantic system) consists of at least two separate systems, split along categorical lines with a major sub-division between living and non-living objects.

However, many critics (e.g. Gaffan & Heywood, 1993) have argued that the double dissociation may be an artefact of the different studies using different materials for testing that were not matched appropriately. Since Warrington & Shallice will have used one set of stimuli to demonstrate that their patients had difficulties in recognising living things but not in recognising non-living things, while Sacchett & Humphreys used different stimuli to demonstrate the reverse pattern in their patient, a direct comparison is difficult. For some scientists, this brings into question the inference of a double dissociation.

However, there have also been studies reported that counter this concern. Hillis & Caramazza (1991) have shown a clear double dissociation between two patients, tested at similar times, in the same laboratory and on the same material.

Judgement of Deficits and Normality

How a deficit, dissociation or even 'normal performance' in a patient is judged can sometimes be a subjective matter. Law & Or (2001), for example, have shown that depending on whether or not appropriate data from healthy normal controls is used, it is possible to seriously misinterpret data. For example, imagine a patient who performs sub-normally on two tasks, where the average score for health individuals is 9 and the normal limits are between 7.5 and 10; however, the patient is better on task A than task B (see Figures 3.5a and 3.5b). If a second patient is found who also performs sub-normally on both tasks but shows the reverse pattern (i.e. better performance on task B than A), can these two patterns be interpreted as a double dissociation?

Some argue that it is necessary for *each patient* to be relatively intact, and to perform within the normal limits on one of the two functions to justify the use of the data from the two patients to claim a double dissociation. Shallice (1986) refers to a situation where at least one of the abilities is performed within normal limits as a 'classic dissociation'. In the hypothetical example above, since neither patient shows intact performance on at least one of the two tasks, some would suggest that the evidence is not strong enough for a double dissociation. However, if one patient scores 9 on task A and the other scores 8 on task B, then both meet Shallice's criterion for their performance on the two tasks to show a double dissociation (see Figure 3.5b). As an example, HM performed fully within the normal range for short-term memory tasks but extremely poorly on long-term memory tasks while KF was the exact opposite.

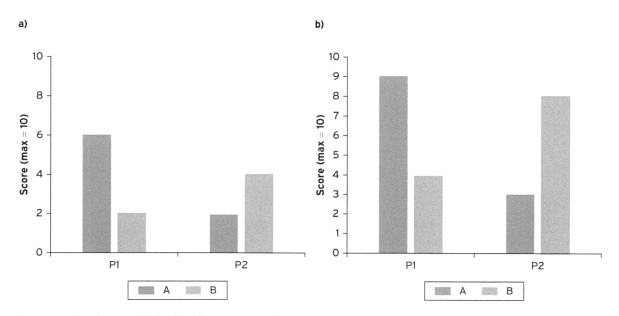

Figure 3.5   a) A 'weak double dissociation' with patients 1 and 2 both performing sub-normally on tasks A and B; b) A 'classic double dissociation' whereby both patients perform within normal limits on at least one of the two tasks and poorly on the second task

What Does 'Normal' Mean?

When we say 'normal' in neuropsychology, what do we mean? 'Normal' performance on a task does not necessarily mean normal cognitive functioning, since a patient may be using a compensatory strategy not found in the intact cognitive system (see below). For example, Humphreys & Riddoch's (2013 patient HJA seemed to be able to copy line drawings well, implying an intact ability to perceive the drawings properly. However, detailed analysis of his *strategy* when drawing showed a very laborious piecemeal line-by-line drawing, concentrating on different parts of the object selectively, rather than what one might expect if HJA perceived the object as a complete whole. Similarly, Jansari et al. (2015) examined a patient with face-recognition difficulties (see Chapter 7) but who was still able to recognise some famous faces. However, by not relying simply on his accuracy at recognising a famous face, but looking at how long it took him to name the face, they were able to show that the patient's 'recognition' was far from normal. It is therefore important to ensure that a patient is tested in a variety of ways to make sure that what seems 'within normal limits' is in fact 'normal'.

The above discussion shows that it is necessary to observe caution when interpreting dissociations and double dissociations. Since these interpretations can have a large impact on theories, it is important that patients are tested as rigorously as possible. Finally, as a cautionary note, Ellis and Young say that it 'would be unwise to regard the search for double dissociations as some sort of royal road to understanding the structure of the mind' (1988, p. 5). In other words, double dissociations are *one* of a set of tools but not the *only* tool that can be used.

Overall, it is clear that it is necessary to carefully scrutinise the evidence regarding the types of patients, the stimuli that are used and the judgements of the level to which an ability is intact or impaired to argue for double dissociations between functions. Therefore, anyone entering the field needs to ask themselves questions such as 'Although on the surface, two patients seem to be performing in quite opposite directions, were their abilities tested in sufficiently similar ways for the double dissociation to be convincing?'

General Caveats When Intrepreting from Damaged Brains

The Alien Within Us

One of the major assumptions made in neuropsychology to allow the principle of subtractivity to be valid is that before brain damage, the patient's cognitive system worked in exactly the same way as any other person's. If this is the case, then it may be possible to extrapolate from this one person's damaged system as to how the normal intact system functions. However, what if the assumption is invalid and, in fact, even before brain damage the patient had an unusual cognitive system, quite unlike the rest of the population; their system would be somewhat 'alien' to the normal one. The consequence of this would be that any inferences that are made from their damaged system for the intact system would not satisfy one of the goals of neuropsychology which is to investigate the functioning of the normal intact system.

This of course, is a serious issue, especially since it is impossible to go back in time and check that the patient's intact system was indeed 'normal' before brain damage. This potential problem is particularly the case when there is an underlying abnormality. For example, if a patient complains of memory problems but it is discovered that they have suffered from epilepsy for 20 years, then it is important to consider that as a result of the physical abnormality that is the cause of the epilepsy, the patient's cognitive system has not developed normally over the last two decades, or they have developed 'compensatory strategies' that are not found in the normal state.

A famous example is that of Kim Peek, who was the inspiration for the Hollywood film *Rain Man*, which was about an autistic savant with an exceptional memory for numbers. Although Kim was seen as autistic and some of his cognitive abilities were indeed stunning, his brain had a large number of abnormalities which meant that trying to extrapolate from his abilities to 'normal' functions would have been inappropriate. Neuropsychologists are very aware of this potential problem and it is for this reason that each research study needs to be extremely detailed and rigorous and is usually followed up by replication in other patients.

COMPARING TWO INDIVIDUAL BRAINS

One of the basic ways that scientific research moves forward is by the replication and extension of studies that have revealed important findings. In the case of cognitive neuropsychology, this is done by testing out theories suggested from one patient on another patient who is exhibiting the same or similar problems. If one of the aims is to map function onto physical brain areas (see Chapters 1 and 2) then comparison of the two patients needs to be done very carefully. Even if two patients show similar behavioural profiles (for example, the same type of reading problem), does that necessarily mean that their brains are the same and show the same size and extent of brain lesions? Even small differences in sizes of lesions can have a major impact on differences that may be too subtle to see at a superficial level but which may nonetheless have a great impact on task performance.

Bartley et al. (1997) carried out a study comparing the brains of identical twins with those of non-identical twins. Whilst finding that the brains of identical twins were much more similar in shape than those of non-identical pairs, they also found that the shapes of the individual gyri differed slightly between identical twins. Figure 3.6 shows three-dimensional images of my brain (AJ1) and that of my identical twin (AJ2). Without being a specialist in brain anatomy, you can see that although the two brains look similar (and more like one another than like a stranger who is the same age as us), our brains are far from *identical*. If this is the case for two genetically identical people, then two unrelated people are likely to have even more differences in their brains before they become damaged. So for example, if hypothetically a lesion of one cubic centimetre was made on two brains that are not identical, the particular brain structures destroyed in them would differ at least slightly. The impact that this is going to have on the cognitive problems exhibited can be either subtle or substantial.

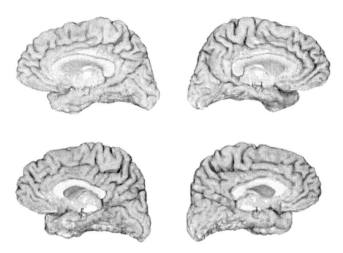

Figure 3.6   Brains of identical twins: my brain (bottom) and my identical twin's brain (top)

Even if all human brains were identical, natural brain damage or even neurosurgery does not result in 'clean lesions' which are restricted to distinct well-defined regions. For example, a blood vessel bursting may result in widespread damage affecting a number of different areas. If we think about research in language disorders as an example, researchers may be interested in production of spoken language which, as described above, is controlled by Broca's area in the frontal lobes. They could therefore study a patient who has had a stroke in this area. Although there may be a lesion in Broca's area, there may also be damage in adjacent cortical areas. The result is that as well as the difficulty in producing coherent speech, the patient may have a number of other cognitive problems either related to or unrelated to language. Therefore, the patient's speech problems could be because of damage to Broca's area only, or due to damage to the neighbouring areas only (because that interrupts the flow of information to Broca's area) or due to a combination of both. If this sort of issue can cause complications when studying one damaged brain, it is therefore not surprising that comparing two patients who may have differing damage that extends beyond Broca's area can greatly compound the problem. As a result, neuropsychologists need to be very careful and need to take into consideration *all* of the damage suffered by a patient or patients rather than just the areas of interest to their research. Again, this requires very thorough analysis of the patient's intact and impaired abilities.

Plasticity

The logic behind the subtractivity argument has been applied very successfully to create or support complex models of normal cognition. However, it is important to note that the logic needs to be applied with caution under certain circumstances due to the plasticity of the brain. Plasticity refers to the ability of the brain to repair itself both at the neuronal and even cognitive level. Rose & Johnson state that 'far from being fixed, unchangeable and static, we now know that the brain is a dynamic and interactive organ, constantly changing in terms of cellular activity, neural circuitry and transmitter chemistry in response to demands placed upon it' (1996: p. 14). For example, it is known from work on animal brains that the brain can recreate neurons lost due to lesions. Under some circumstances, the brain can also 'move' the function from one area of the brain to another if there is damage in the original area where that function is usually found. For example, it is known in babies that suffer severe strokes in the left hemisphere (which is normally where language is processed) that language can sometimes develop in the right hemisphere (Bates & Roe, 2001).

In the adult brain, this near-complete switch of language to the right hemisphere is not found. However, if even *some* cognitive functions can move to another intact part of the brain, then the above assumption of subtractivity cannot be applied to use findings from such patients to infer the workings of the *normal* cognitive system. This is because the assumption of subtractivity is based on the whole premise of *removing* sub-components rather than *moving* or *creating* new ones, since under normal circumstances this does not occur.

For example, it is possible to use the assumptions of associations and dissociations to work out a simplistic model of the cognitive system that has modules for problem solving, object recognition, face recognition, reading and memory (see Figure 3.7a).

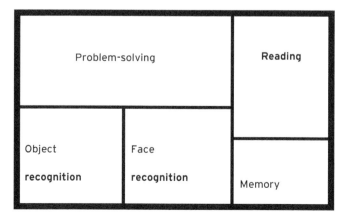

Figure 3.7a Hypothetical structure of the cognitive system sub-divided into major modules

Using the subtractivity assumption, it is possible to study healthy controls and patients who have suffered damage to the left hemisphere which results in different types of dyslexia (e.g. surface and phonological dyslexia) to sub-divide the overall reading system into a number of sub-sections such as A–H (see Figure 3.7b).

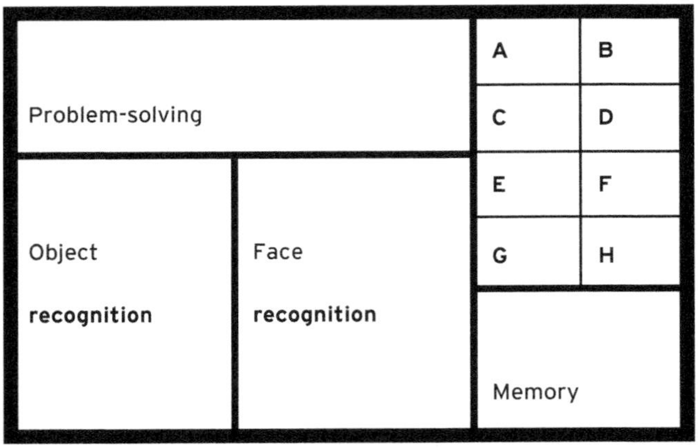

Figure 3.7b   Sub-division of the reading module into a number of separate components

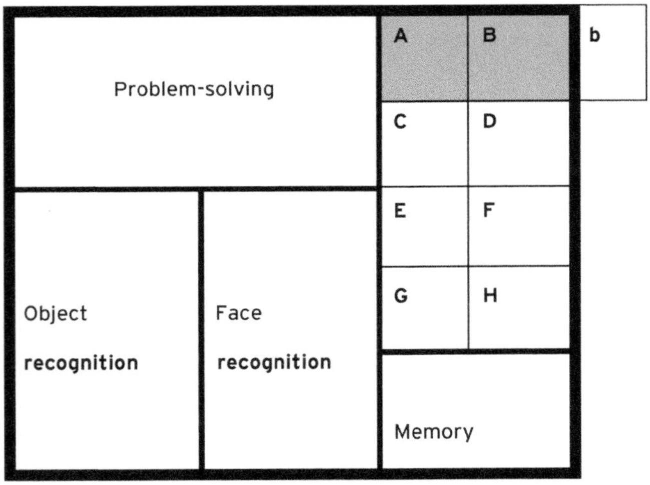

Figure 3.7c   Hypothetical use of a 'silent' reading system 'b' within the right hemisphere following damage to the parts of the brain dealing with reading components A and B

In deep dyslexia, however, it is suggested that following more extensive damage to this system which is thought to be largely in the left hemisphere (e.g. to A and B in Figure 3.7b), some aspects of reading occur using a 'silent' reading system (e.g. sub-component b) in the intact right hemisphere which ordinarily is not used (Coltheart et al., 1987; see Figure 3.7c). It is beyond the scope of this chapter to give a full account of the theory (see Chapter 10: Aphasia, Dyslexia & Language) but it is claimed that there is a complex interaction between this right hemisphere reading system and those aspects of reading that are still intact in the left hemisphere. This interaction is thought to be sub-optimal resulting in a cluster of consistent reading errors in deep dyslexic patients which include visual errors (e.g. reading WHILE as /white/), semantic errors (e.g. reading the visual input SWORD as /dagger/) and difficulties in reading words that are more 'abstract' than more visualisable 'concrete' words (e.g. having more problems reading JUSTICE than TABLE). This theory of deep dyslexia involving a right hemisphere reading system is one that is still under debate, but if it is even somewhat accurate, how representative of the normal reading system is it? Module 'b' does not tell us anything about the normal reading system that may be made up of modules A–H only. To date, there is very little evidence that the right hemisphere becomes involved in normal intact reading. As a result, because of the possibility of plasticity resulting in the formation of new modules, researchers need to apply caution when interpreting findings.

RESEARCH DECISIONS
Single Case Versus Group Studies

In standard experimental psychology, a large number of participants are studied to ensure generalisability, and an estimate of 'sampling error' is taken to extrapolate from the study participants to the general population. However, in neuropsychological research, this cannot always be possible since it is sometimes impossible to find more than a few patients with a rare condition. Even if it was possible to find a group of such patients, from the discussion on comparing two individual brains above, it is obvious that problems can arise due to the heterogeneity of brain damage across the group. The result is that a neuropsychologist is faced with the decision on whether to study a single patient in depth or to use a group of patients all with the same cognitive deficit. It is best to group the arguments by arguments for and against each approach and then look at the criteria that a researcher uses in their decision.

Arguments for Single Cases / Against Group Studies

Grouping of subjects may be legitimate in standard cognitive research where the assumption is that all subjects start off roughly equivalent, but this is not possible in neuropsychology for a range of reasons. One of the most important reasons is that at the start of a particular branch of research, almost by definition, most research begins with single cases. Paul Broca's seminal work on patient Tan was monumental in terms of showing how selective brain damage can affect very specific cognitive difficulties, and this started an explosion of replications by himself and other neurologists at the time. Similarly, Brenda Milner's work on patient HM (see Chapter 8: Amnesia & Memory) has been so important in the field of memory that the first paper (Scoville & Milner, 1957) has been cited a staggering 2500 times in other scientific articles; further, the insights on different aspects of this patient's memory impairments and preserved abilities set the agenda for more than half a century's work.

Tan and HM had cognitive disorders (aphasia and amnesia respectively), that can be caused by a number of different neurological disorders such as strokes, viruses and interruption of blood to the brain. Therefore, they are not uncommon disorders, with the result that it is possible to conduct group studies. However, there are some conditions such as prosopagnosia or Capgras syndrome (see Chapter 7: Prosopagnosia & Face Processing) which are extremely rare. As a result, it is impossible to gather a large group of patients with these conditions making a group study unfeasible; single case studies are therefore the best choice. Sometimes, a patient is seen who because of their particular circumstances is rare even if the condition itself might be relatively common. For example, Jansari et al. (2010) studied a patient with a particular form of accelerated forgetting (see Chapter 8: Amnesia & Memory) which up to that point had been documented only in patients who had temporal lobe epilepsy. A 'confound' in all of these previous studies is that a number of the drugs that are used to control some types of epilepsy have as a side effect memory problems. Therefore, in studying the particular accelerated forgetting in this group, it is unclear whether it is their condition (the epilepsy) or their medication that is causing the memory problem. However, Jansari et al.'s patient RY had no clinical diagnosis at the time that the study was initiated, therefore his accelerated forgetting could not have been the side effect of medication. Actually, as a result of the first set of studies with RY, it was discovered that he did indeed have a sub-clinical epilepsy that had been difficult to detect previously. Following the diagnosis, he was prescribed anti-epileptic medication and so a second study was conducted to look at whether this changed his memory performance. It was found that it didn't make any difference to his rate of forgetting; if the patients' medication in previous studies had been the *cause* of their forgetting, then RY would have been expected to get worse with the medication. Therefore, although in fact RY was not rare because he ultimately was in a relatively common group (patients with temporal lobe epilepsy), the timing of the studies before he had commenced medication made him rare.

Even if it is possible to gather a sizeable number of participants with the same cognitive disorder (for example, aphasia), the brain damage will vary across the group. For a start, as discussed above, before neurological damage the brain structure of any two individuals will be different; added to this, even if all of them had a stroke in the same cerebral artery, the extent of damage will have varied across the individuals. As a result, there will be variance in the types and extent of lesions. Given the heterogeneity among the group caused by differing types of brain damage, there may be important subtle differences in task performance between subjects within the same group. In standard research methodology (such as trying to work out whether females are better on a linguistic task than males), differences *between participants in a group* should be kept to a minimum to try to identify the differences *between the two groups*. Due to statistical principles, this allows averaging of the groups (e.g. the average female compared to the average male). However, in a neuropsychological study, this sort of averaging could mask (hide) subtle differences between two patients within the same group. Therefore, although a group of patients with aphasia performs differently to a control healthy group on a language-based task, there might be very subtle differences between two of the patients that could have very important implications for theories of language processing. Simply looking at the *average* of the group will hide these potentially important differences. As will be seen in some of the chapters (Chapter 4: Neglect & Attention; Chapter 5: Apraxia & Motor-Planning; Chapter 6: Visual Agnosia & Object Recognition; and Chapter 7: Prosopagnosia & Face Processing), it is sometimes the differences between individual patients that are the most revealing for theory building.

A related issue is that grouping subjects according to a syndrome (a cluster of symptoms) such as Broca's versus Wernicke's aphasics, which was the standard method in the early days of aphasia research (see Chapter 10) can be misleading. This is because although the patients may *share* some symptoms, the averaging and treatment of the individuals as a homogenous group can overlook many *differences* which may be the most revealing. The research in the 1940s and 1950s on aphasia suffered because of this, and eventually researchers had to find more fine-grained groupings to be able to explore the language difficulties more successfully.

Finally, there are those who say that it doesn't make sense to study many people if one very compelling case demonstrates an important point and might be the exception to the rule. So if we assume that the cognitive architecture is generally the same across us all, unless we *know* that someone is an 'alien among us', generalising from the one patient should suffice. Put simply, if I showed you one flying pig, how many more pigs would I need to show you to demonstrate that pigs could fly?! *Nature Neuroscience* uses the metaphor of finding a talking pig when discussing how important a case study needs to be in order to be accepted (cited in Medina & Fischer-Baum, 2017, p. 445). It should be remembered that the field of cognitive neuropsychology effectively traces its roots to the documentation of a single patient, Tan, while the work on the amnesic patient HM has been *the* bedrock for so many discoveries. As talking pigs go, they told us a lot…

Arguments against Single Case Studies / for Group Studies

As discussed above, due to the possibility of a patient being an 'alien among us' with a brain architecture that was unusual even before brain damage, there is a question of generalisability from a single individual to normal cognition. For example, the brains of patients with temporal lobe epilepsy may have developed non-conventionally due to their epilepsy and may therefore have created compensatory strategies not found in the intact brain.

In terms of resources, single case studies can take a substantial amount of time if the researchers want to look in great detail at a patient's abilities. Often experiments within a single case study are developed based on the findings from the initial experiments with the patient and so there is a stepwise evolving process in exploring particular issues. This method of developing a series of separate experiments – testing the patient and matched controls, and then based on these findings, spending time developing the next set of experiments – can mean that it can take a long time to get a coherent set of data. For example, it took us four years to collect the data for the nine experiments on our patient with prosopagnosia (Jansari et al., 2015: see Chapter 7); this makes one wonder how long it took Moscovitch et al. (1997) to conduct 19 experiments on their patient and matched controls! Further, given that one individual is the focus of all of this work, there is also the risk that if something happens to the patient, then the research can no longer continue; in a group study, it would be possible to replace a patient who was no longer available for study.

A possible concern with single case studies that can be avoided with group studies is that patient selection can sometimes be biased towards patients who fit into a particular theory – the result being that what is known as theory-driven research can be rampant because researchers are only studying the patients whose data goes along with their theoretical framework! Therefore, sometimes researchers find it very difficult to replicate the findings from other published research studies due to the original patient having been specifically chosen to prove a theory; as discussed in Chapter 2, the replication crisis is prevalent in psychology and, sometimes, single case research can contribute to that. With a group study where there are objective inclusion criteria for being part of the research (just as would occur for other areas of psychology), there is less chance of only selecting patients that fit one's theories.

How Do You Decide between Single and Group Studies?

With such a diversity of issues, how should a neuropsychologist decide which methodology to choose? The first consideration depends on resources. Some research institutions (for example, hospitals interested in research) have access to large groups of patients, whilst others only have limited numbers. A second consideration is the particular field of research, since patients with some types of deficit are extremely rare, while those with other problems are much more available. For example, Capgras syndrome (see Chapter 7), which results in a patient with a face-recognition problem feeling that his or her family have been replaced by imposters (e.g. Alexander et al., 1979), is *so* rare that it would be very difficult to find two patients to study at the same time. In contrast, Wernicke-Korsakoff syndrome, which is a cluster of deficits (the hallmark symptom being classical amnesia), is much more common, meaning that group studies are relatively feasible (e.g. Albert et al., 1979; Kopelman, 1989). Finally, the strictness of methodology and the vigour that is applied by researchers play a large part, because if all the caveats of studying single cases are borne in mind, and a patient is also tested very thoroughly, then a single case study can be the most informative approach available.

Recently, a new approach has been to combine the strengths of the two different approaches by studying 'case series'. In these designs, a group of patients or special participants is studied but their performance is analysed individually in addition to standard group analysis. This way, the richness of data that can come from studying an individual in depth is complemented by making a stronger statement about a group of individuals. For example, in the early days of research on synaesthesia (see Chapter 12), a lot of the research was on single cases, but there was growing understanding regarding the heterogeneity between individual synaesthetes. Therefore, Jansari et al. (2006) conducted a case series of three synaesthetes that demonstrated that each of them *did* in fact see 'coloured numbers' in their mind's eye when performing simple mathematical calculations, but also that the three of them differed from one another with variations in whether they were looking at the calculations visually or hearing them. This way, they were able to use the strength of case studies while avoiding some of the limitations by demonstrating that this was not occurring in only isolated individuals.

Overall, most fields have seen an evolution over time. For example, Broca's single case approach eventually led to group studies by many aphasiologists, and then more recently, respecting the subtle differences between individual patients, case series have become more popular. Therefore, it's not a case of 'Which is better?', but more so 'Which is better for this particular stage of this area of research?', 'How available are the types of research participants?' and 'What resources are available?'; it's perfectly possible to contribute to a research area with a single case study in a field where group studies are the norm as long as the research is conducted carefully.

DEVELOPMENTAL VERSUS ACQUIRED NEUROPSYCHOLOGICAL DISORDERS

Brain damage can occur at any time in someone's life – it could happen pre-natally in the womb, post-natally as a result of complications or due to a premature birth, during childhood due to accidents or during adulthood. To further complicate matters, the cognitive system may have problems not due to brain damage but because of a genetically inherited disorder.

A difficulty due to potentially genetic reasons is known as a developmental disorder, whereas one caused by physical brain damage is referred to as an acquired disorder. Therefore, a child who has always had a reading problem of a particular type could be classified as having developmental dyslexia, whereas someone who could read before brain damage but then shows impairment following a stroke would be classed as having acquired dyslexia.

Historically, more research has been carried out on acquired disorders than developmental ones for a number of reasons. One of these is that within cognitive neuropsychology, an attempt is being made to try to infer how the normal system works by looking at one that used to work normally but has now been damaged – this is the principle of subtractivity described above. An adult who used to be able to read normally who suffers brain damage that affects their reading has acquired dyslexia, and it is possible to use the subtractivity principle to hypothesise about the missing components as described above. However, since a developmental dyslexic's reading system may not have formed normally from the outset, making conclusions from examples of it about how an intact adult reading system works can be difficult.

Needless to say, the study of developmental disorders can still be extremely useful for understanding the problems that certain groups of young children and adolescents face in an attempt to find ways to help them; this is the field of developmental neuropsychology. In recent years, for example, dyslexia, autism and attention deficit hyperactivity disorder (ADHD) have been taken much more seriously, such that in some school systems (for example in the UK) children who have any of these conditions are given access to resources to support them with the difficulties they experience. As knowledge grows about how to study such groups, this area will develop greatly.

Due to the issue of plasticity mentioned above, *when* an individual suffers, their brain damage has important implications both theoretically and clinically. If damage occurs very early in life, then some level of neuronal repair and/or a certain amount of reorganisation may be possible. Damage later in life makes this unlikely, meaning that the same type of brain damage in childhood and adulthood can have very different results in the permanent problems that the patient may be left with. For example, some babies who are born very prematurely and whose lungs are not yet strong enough to circulate blood around the body sufficiently suffer damage to the brain because it is starved of oxygen for a brief but crucial period of time. In one such baby, the only damage caused was in a very discrete but important part of the hippocampus, an area that is vital for memory (Vargha-Khadem et al., 1997). Despite this, the baby grew up relatively normally and it was only at around the age of six that it was noticed that he had significant memory problems. Although he has quite severe problems with his memory, he is still able to have a job and look after himself to a certain degree. Adults who suffer the same brain damage to the hippocampus, however, have much greater difficulty in learning to cope because it is impossible for the brain to 'rewire' at that age and difficult to develop new coping strategies. For example, two very well-documented patients with severe amnesia, HM (Corkin, 2002) in North America and CW (Wilson & Wearing, 1995) in Britain, both had/have to live in care homes because of the impossibility of them living independent lives.

Chapter Summary

- If one cognitive ability is impaired in a patient (e.g. language) whilst leaving another intact (e.g. memory), these two abilities are said to dissociate and are governed by separate cognitive processes.
- It is possible to explain some patterns of observed behaviour with unitary systems rather than having to invoke two separate processes. In this simpler system, the more effortful aspects of processing (e.g. remembering events from many years ago) can be impaired whilst leaving more basic aspects (e.g. retaining five digits in memory for a minute) intact. If such an explanation is possible, researchers should adopt it.
- However, if two patients are found, one of whom is impaired on an ability A (e.g. ability to recognise emotion shown in a face) but has no problems with ability B (e.g. ability to recognise people) whilst another patient shows the reverse pattern (impaired on B but intact on A), these two abilities are said to show a double dissociation. A finding like this can be very strong evidence for the separation of cognitive processing.
- There are some caveats about the use of double dissociations that need to be borne in mind when interpreting data.
- Researchers need to be aware of the possibility that a patient may *not* be representative of the general population, and therefore to make statements about normal cognition it is important to replicate findings.
- Due to physical differences between any two brains and the fact that brain damage can often be diffuse rather than neatly localised, it is important to compare data from patients systematically both at the behavioural and neurological level.
- The assumption of subtractivity centres around the idea that what is observed in a patient is the effect of a whole cognitive system which has had certain modules (e.g. long-term memory) impaired or removed whilst leaving the rest of the system intact. By applying this assumption systematically and with care, neuropsychologists aim to construct an understanding of the entire intact system.
- Researchers need to be aware of the possibility of plasticity both neurally (regrowth of brain tissue if damage occurs *very* early in life) and cognitively ('movement' or adaptation of a function) following brain trauma.
- Due to the confounding and sometimes opposing factors of representativeness of single individuals and the heterogeneity of any two brains (as well as the extent of brain damage), whether to study single individuals or groups of patients is a very important research issue. There is no correct answer and there are many factors which determine the choice of methodology.
- Since brain damage can occur at any point in life and brain abnormalities can occur due to genetic factors as well, there is a difference between developmental disorders and those that are acquired following trauma. Applicability of methodologies and interpretation of results will therefore be determined by whether the behavioural problem is a developmental or acquired one.

Important Research Study

KF (Shallice & Warrington, 1970)

KF was involved in a motorcycle accident at the age of 19 and the resulting brain damage brought on epilepsy which he suffered for many years. This study was extremely important since Tim Shallice and Elizabeth Warrington were able to demonstrate that KF suffered from a very selective deficit in *only* his verbal STM; his STM for visual materials and his LTM were completely unaffected. This finding was seismic for a number of reasons. First, it demonstrated that it was possible to have impairments within STM but still transfer information into LTM; this is something that went against the way that the Modal Model was formulated. Second, it demonstrated that even the STM of the Modal Model was simplistic since there was no differentiation between different types of information, and yet the fact that KF could remember *visual* information within his STM but not *verbal* suggested that this part of memory was more complex than simply one store. Finally, this specific difference was what led to the development of the Baddeley & Hitch Working Memory Model which was able to explain how it was possible to have an impaired ability to remember words or numbers while still being able to remember visual information.

Important Researcher

Alfonso Caramazza

Alfonso Caramazza is an Italian neuropsychologist and neuroscientist based at Harvard University in the United States. His main areas of interest are the nature of language processing and conceptual representations in the brain. Besides his theoretical contributions in these areas, one of Alfonso's most important contributions is his defence of the single case study. Since in the rest of psychology, groups are usually used, the focus on a single individual seemed 'wrong' by many. In addition to this, with the growth of neuroimaging in the 1980s, many researchers went to 'the new kid on the block', abandoning work on neuropsychological patients. Therefore, Alfonso's strong defence of the single case study was extremely important at that time in history.

Questions for Reflection

- What is the cognitive neuropsychology jigsaw and why is it important for helping us understand intact healthy cognitive functions?
- Why are double dissociations such a powerful conceptual tool in neuropsychology?
- When deciding on the number of participants for a neuropsychological study, why is it not a simple case of 'single' or 'group'?
- Why are inferences about healthy cognitive systems easier to make from patients with acquired rather than developmental disorders?

Further Reading

- Medina, J., & Fischer-Baum, S. (2017). Single-case cognitive neuropsychology in the age of big data. *Cognitive Neuropsychology, 34*(7-8), 440–448.
- Caramazza, A. (1986). On drawing inferences about the structure of normal cognitive systems from the analysis of patterns of impaired performance: The case for single-patient studies. *Brain and Cognition, 5*(1), 41–66.
- Lambon Ralph, M. A., Patterson, K., & Plaut, D. C. (2011). Finite case series or infinite single case studies? Comments on 'Case series investigations in cognitive neuropsychology' by Schwartz & Dell (2010). *Cognitive Neuropsychology, 28*(7), 466–474.

4
NEGLECT & ATTENTION

Chapter Overview

This chapter will explore one of the most fundamental attributes that any living creature needs to have, which is the ability to pay attention to the world around it and then react to it accordingly. When there is dysfunction in this system, the consequences can be quite striking, resulting in a disorder called neglect, whereby it seems as if half of the world no longer exists to the individual. By studying patients with neglect, it is possible to build up a picture of the complexity involved in basic survival – how to represent all the sensory information around us in a spatial sense to allow us to make important decisions about how to interact with our environment, avoid danger, etc. As will be seen, given this rather fundamental role, neglect is one of the most intriguing disorders but also one that is so multifaceted that even neuropsychologists and neuroscientists are only just beginning to understand its complexity.

Chapter Outline

- Introduction: What is Neglect?
- The Main Symptoms of Neglect
- The Many Dimensions of Space
- Assessments of Neglect
- The Neuroanatomy of Neglect
- Theoretical Explanations of Neglect
- Object-Centred or Viewer-Centred Neglect?
- Future Directions for Neglect Research
- Chapter Summary

INTRODUCTION: WHAT IS NEGLECT?

Did you realise that every day, you are making a complicated journey into space – it's not outer space but it is space nonetheless! Whenever you cross a road, walk through a shopping area looking for a particular place to buy a sandwich, or arrive in a room where other people are sat in different places and you are looking for one of them, you are walking into space. If you can't do this, then you might get hit by a car as you cross the street, not notice the sandwich shop tucked between the clothes stores or see that your best friend is sat on a chair in the far corner of the room. While these examples are from the visual modality, similar issues apply to you not hearing the siren of an emergency services vehicle while you are driving or realising that someone is touching you on your arm to tell you something. Each of these errors could have a consequence for either physical or social survival.

As is obvious, space is a common dimension that is important across all our different perceptual systems. Your cognitive system needs to be able to prioritise the processing of the spatial location of the incoming sensory information relative to you, recognise what is in that space, and where necessary perform actions towards what is in the scene (which will be covered in Chapter 5 on Apraxia & Motor-Planning); this is basically the stuff of everyday survival, to see and to do. To be able to perform any of these functions successfully, you need to be able to *represent* what you see but also *where* it is relative to you so that you know what to do. Even those with healthy intact brains can fail to perceive and respond to information when attention is not directed to them. Sometimes when we are tired, distracted or overloaded with information, we all miss things that are there in front of us but which we are not paying attention to at the moment. Studying patients with neglect gives us an incredible window into how much attention we *are* paying to the world even if we are not consciously aware of it.

THE MAIN SYMPTOMS OF NEGLECT

Given the complexity of neglect, as will become obvious in this chapter, the symptoms that are presented can vary enormously. Overall, it is a syndrome that is defined as a failure or difficulty in perceiving, reporting or orienting to information or stimuli on the side of space opposite (contralesional) to the hemisphere that has suffered brain damage (known as the ipsilesional side). Since the majority of patients with neglect tend to have right hemisphere damage, this means that the right-hand side (RHS) of the body or space generally is known as the ipsilesional side and is usually attended to while the left-hand side (LHS) is known as the contralesional side and the one that is ignored. An important aspect of the condition is that none of the difficulties that are seen can be explained as being primarily sensory or motor in nature, and in addition they are not due to any intellectual difficulty. Therefore, although a patient might not notice a visual object that is on their contralesional side, there is no visual difficulty that can explain this, and while the patient may not voluntarily use their contralesional limbs, this is not caused by weakness or paralysis; finally, the deficit is not caused because of lack of understanding of instructions since they are usually perfectly capable of performing the same tasks on the ipsilesional side.

The most standard symptom is hemi-inattention which is more commonly known as hemispatial neglect, which is the lack of attention paid to information in the contralesional side of space. This can come in a variety of forms such as not turning to that side if someone approaches them or speaks from that side. Their eye gaze and orientation of their head tends to be towards the side ipsilesional to their brain injury and they will maintain this even if they eventually answer questions that are coming from their neglected contralesional side. The preference for one half of the world can even extend to personally relevant behaviour, eating only what is on the RHS of a plate with the plate then having to be rotated by someone else such that the uneaten food is now on the RHS for the patient to finish eating. In personal neglect, a patient might even only shave or put make-up on one side of the face. An interesting thing is that many patients who show these deficits are not aware they have a problem; this lack of awareness is known as anosognosia and is an intriguing demonstration of how the human mind can somehow create a world view that makes 'internal sense' (i.e. that everything is fine) despite very obvious external signs that they are not.

Another symptom that can be encountered is allesthesia which is reporting a physical sensation such as being touched on the contralesional side as having happened on the ipsilesional side; so a patient experiencing allesthesia would say that they were tapped on their right shoulder when someone touches them on the left shoulder. Visual allesthesia occurs when something that has been presented in the contralesional side is reported by the patient as having been seen in the opposite space. The intriguing observation here is that, unlike in hemispatial neglect, the properties of the stimulus *are* being registered, but they are being attributed to the intact side of space; this difference between the two symptoms suggests that conscious awareness is filtering through despite the incorrect localisation. In contrast, in somatosensory neglect the patient will ignore tactile, thermal or painful stimuli that are applied to the contralesional side of the body.

Two even more interesting symptoms involve the neglect of information only under certain situations. There are situations where a patient *will* notice and respond to information that is presented on the contralesional side if there is *nothing* on the ipsilesional side. However, if information is presented on both sides simultaneously, a patient can exhibit extinction whereby they now neglect the information in the contralesional side. This is obviously rather strange given that when presented on its own it will be noticed, which therefore demonstrates that at some level there is a 'competition' in terms of attention between the two visual spaces; this issue will be discussed further when exploring theories of what causes neglect. An even more extreme version of extinction is when it only occurs if the two stimuli are the same. For example, when Baylis et al. (1993) presented their neglect patients with stimuli in both visual fields, they only showed extinction when the two items were identical, a phenomenon known as repetition blindness (see Figure 4.1). Therefore, for example, if one visual field had a picture of a bottle and the other had a picture of a chair, then the patient was able to name both. However, if the photo of the bottle was shown in both visual fields, then the patient would only report the one on the ipsilesional side. Both extinction and repetition blindness are demonstrations that neglect is not as simple as ignoring half of all the information that is hitting the sensory systems, but that complex processing can occur and that the disorder is more at the level of conscious attention. Finally, a small subset of patients will also show somatoparaphrenia which is a delusional belief in which they think that the limb contralateral to a brain pathology, usually the left upper arm does not belong to them.

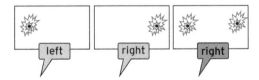

Figure 4.1   An example of extinction; when the task is to say where on the screen a visual stimulus is presented, if it appears *only* on the left *or* the right side of the midline then the response is correct but when it appears in *both* spaces, only the one on the right side is reported (Baylis et al., 1993)

From this short summary of the symptoms of mainly just visual neglect, it is obvious that the deficits are varied and complex. Importantly, they will not be shown by every patient and there may even be variance across time where some symptoms only appear in the very early acute stages after brain damage and others persist over a long period of time. For this reason, neglect should be seen as a syndrome with different patients showing different deficits which are all related at some level but nonetheless can differ markedly from one another. As will be seen later, part of this heterogeneity is likely to be due to the complex variations in patterns of brain damage between patients.

THE MANY DIMENSIONS OF SPACE

So far, most of the difficulties experienced by patients with neglect have been described using hemispaces, the half that is ipsilesional and that which is contralesional to the area of brain damage. Since a large proportion of the patients have right hemisphere damage, most examples of neglect have been about difficulties attending to the LHS of the world. However, careful study of patients has shown that there are many other dimensions along which neglect can occur. These many dimensions effectively demonstrate the complexity of the task of the attentional system.

An important dimension is where relative to a patient's physical space the information is coming from. Peri-personal space is that which is within physical reach of a person while extra-personal space is anything beyond that, and it has been found that this dimension can dissociate within a patient with difficulties in one but not the other. Although rare, some patients may even show altitudinal neglect where rather than the portion of space affected being along a horizontal axis (left and right), it is along a vertical axis.

Also, as seen above, while the most obvious forms of neglect are the highly visual ones, since the condition affects the attentional system, it can affect any sense that has a spatial dimension; therefore, there can be neglect for sounds or proprioception which may be less obvious but may well be affected in addition to the visual modality. In addition to the sensory input of information, patients may also show a deficit at the level of output of behaviour; motor neglect is the underutilisation of the contra-lesional limbs to perform actions or to interact with objects. Importantly, as stated above, this cannot be put down to a lack of understanding of what is required or paralysis or weakness of the limbs.

The origin of the information that is neglected can also vary. While the most obvious forms are perceptual, with the neglect being for information that is coming in through the sensory systems, the deficit can also occur for internally generated information. This representational neglect (see later) is for the mental images that we all use for making decisions about information that is not physically in front of us. The importance of this is that it demonstrates that neglect is not occurring at the level of 'shutting out' external information but may be happening at the level of how we construct an *internal model* of the world around.

Finally, while the left-right distinction sounds relatively straightforward, this itself can create yet another dimension; basically, the left or right of what? If the left side of a flower is not drawn, is that because it is that side of the flower or because it is on the left side of personal space? Egocentric neglect refers to the difficulty with information that is on left side of someone's perceptual world while allocentric neglect (also known as 'object-centred' neglect) is the difficulty with the LHS of each particular object irrespective of where it is in the visual scene (see Figure 4.2); this issue will be expanded further later in the chapter.

Figure 4.2 Egocentric neglect versus allocentric neglect in a visual copying task where a patient has to copy a line drawing; in the top panel, the patient is ignoring everything to the left of physical space (egocentric neglect), while in the lower panel, the patient has drawn most of the objects but emphasised the RHS, missing out details on the LHS of most of the objects in the scene (Rode et al., 2017)

Overall, it is obvious that neglect is a very complex topic. However, this should not come as a surprise given the central importance of our attentional system to everyday life. To have safe lives and to interact with the environment around us successfully, the cognitive system has to create a mental model of the world around us so that we can recognise things, decide which ones we want to move towards and which ones we want to move away from, work out how far or close they are from us so that we know what our physical system needs to do to interact with them, etc. This requires the information from a complex three-dimensional space around us to be processed and represented in a way that the other cognitive systems of visual recognition, hearing, language and motor systems can understand to allow us to take appropriate action. Given this complexity, it is little wonder that the attentional system can break down along so many dimensions.

ASSESSMENTS OF NEGLECT

Since there are a number of quite distinct symptoms that result from neglect, there are also a number of different tests that can help a clinician or researcher to determine whether a patient has the condition. As it is easier to control items that an individual sees and has to respond to, many of the most common tests are visually based; however, there are increasingly more non-visual tests as well.

Among the most frequently used visual tasks are cancellation, line bisection, copying and free drawing tasks. The simplest of these involves the participant being presented with an array of simple items such as lines that are randomly spread out. The participant is asked to put a line across (to cancel out) particular items – in the simplest case, to literally just put a line through any line that they see. A patient with hemispatial visual neglect of the left visual field (LVF) is likely to only cross out the lines that are towards the right of the array (see Figure 4.3a). The line bisection task is a bit more complex and usually involves the presentation of a horizontal line with the instruction to put a mark on the mid-point of this line. The typical response of someone with visual neglect is to put their mark towards the RHS of the midpoint. Different manipulations can be used of this task which can yield an idea of the extent of neglect but generally speaking it seems as if the individual can only see the right-hand half of the original line and then they put their bisection mark along this particular portion (see Figures 4.3b and 4.3c).

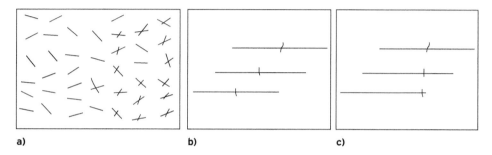

a)   b)   c)

Figure 4.3   a) Example of neglect patient's line cancellation performance; b) Normal line bisection; c) Highly impaired line bisection

Copying tasks are used a lot in neuropsychology when the visual system is involved since to copy something involves a number of different processes. The sensory information of what you are looking at needs to be accurately encoded. Next, this information needs to be bound together and perceived as separate parts of the visual scene; for example, rather than seeing just a big array of random colours and shapes, seeing instead that it is different items of furniture. Then a number of different processes are possible but in a simple drawing task, the internal perception (e.g. chair next to table) needs to be 'translated' into a series of hand movements to reproduce the same shapes. A typical response from a patient with visual neglect would be to draw mainly the RHS of each object as if they are ignoring the LHS despite it being in full sight.

Another popular visual task involves asking the individual to draw something from memory. With this type of task, it is possible to evaluate both what sort of 'mental images' an individual has within their cognitive system, as well as how they are able to reproduce this image. As seen earlier with the issue of representational neglect, some patients will only be able to report (or in this case draw) the RHS of an internally held visual image (see Figure 4.4). As can be seen, neglect does not result in a complete 'half and half' whereby there is a strict dividing line with exactly 50% of the object ignored. It is not understood why this would be the case, but certainly there is a lot of heterogeneity with some patients showing more extreme forms than others.

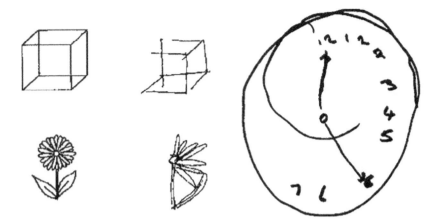

Figure 4.4   Examples of a patient's copying of visually presented line drawings of a cube and a flower, and their drawing from memory of a clock face (Reprinted from Handbook of Clinical Neurology, Husain, Masud., 359-372, Copyright (2008), with permission from Elsevier.)

While a majority of work is on *visual* neglect, it occurs in other modalities too, and it is possible to evaluate this depending on the particular modality. For example, for a patient who is showing a deficit in noticing sounds on the side contralesional to the brain damage, it is possible to evaluate this by playing them sounds via headphones with the sound coming randomly in one of the two ears or in both at the same time. A patient with auditory neglect will tend to ignore stimuli in their neglected side, or if they are showing extinction they will report the contralesional sound when it is played in isolation but only report the one on the ipsilesional side when sounds are presented in both ears. For a patient showing somatosensory neglect, there are a variety of tasks. Simple tasks can involve asking a patient to reach using their ipsilesional hand to touch a part of their own body on the contralesional side. A more advanced test, known as the 'fluff test', developed by Cocchini et al. (2001) involves attaching balls of cotton wool to points along the patient's arms, legs and trunk and requiring them to remove as many of them as possible. In both of these tests, the patient is likely to fail to reach across to the contralesional side or to miss picking items attached to that side of the body.

Generally speaking, while it is possible to see some very striking demonstrations of neglect using a variety of tests, it is important to realise that the results from such tests can be very variable. This is caused by a number of different factors. Since neglect is permanent in only a subset of patients, performance will be impacted by whether the patient is in the acute phase soon after their brain damage or in the chronic stage some time later. Similarly, due to the large heterogeneity in brain damage between patients (see later), unlike some of the other neuropsychological disorders, the areas of damage will determine the type of test that will prove challenging as well as the level of impairment that will be shown. Finally, there are factors such as motivation in the patient themselves which will mean that even within the space of a few days their performance will differ on the same test. As a result of these various factors, both a clinician and researcher need to be careful in any evaluation that they are performing; in situations where there is such variance and heterogeneity, the best thing, rather than relying on just one or two tests, is for a range of different tests to be used so that a consistent pattern can be established.

THE NEUROANATOMY OF NEGLECT

To determine the neuroanatomical basis of neglect, two seminal studies in this field by Heilman et al. (1982) and Vallar & Perani (1986) looked at the computerised tomography (CT) scans of 10 and 16 patients respectively who had all been diagnosed with the disorder. Using the 'lesion overlap' method whereby the common areas of brain damage are determined (see Chapter 2), the general consensus was that damage to the right hemisphere, and in particular the parietal lobes, caused neglect. Within the parietal lobe, the area most implicated is the inferior parietal lobe, and within that area, particularly two sub-divisions that are adjacent to one another, the right supramarginal gyrus and the angular gyrus (see Figure 4.5). There has been a lot of work with animals which has demonstrated that the parietal lobes are important for spatial localisation, and since neglect is essentially a disorder of mapping the spatial characteristics of the outside work into an internal model, this makes consistent sense.

Whilst there is general agreement about the importance of the inferior parietal areas in attention, as research has progressed, it has become clear that associating neglect solely with this region is probably simplistic. For a start, neuroimaging work with healthy individuals using a variety of different cognitive tasks has demonstrated that in addition to the parietal areas, parts of the frontal lobes become highly active during attentional tasks (e.g. Corbetta & Shulman, 2002). This immediately demonstrates that while damage

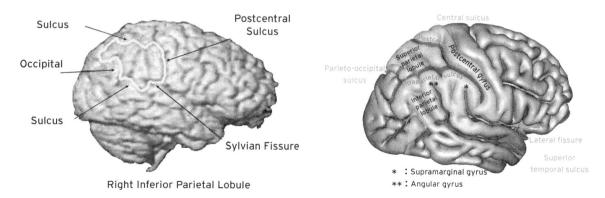

Figure 4.5 The right inferior parietal lobe and two sub-divisions, the supramarginal gyrus and the angular gyrus (BodyParts3D, © The Database Center for Life Science licensed under CC Attribution-Share Alike 2.1 Japan)

to one area may result in noticeable signs of a disorder, that in itself is not sufficient to localise the disorder or the cognitive ability to that area; as will be seen in Chapter 7 on memory, this has been the case for the neuroanatomical basis of amnesia. Further, as research methodologies have evolved, it has become obvious that there were a number of limitations to the earlier studies which include the particular neuroimaging methodologies used, the sample sizes of patients and the nature of the control participants.

In terms of neuroimaging, the CT (and MRI) scans used in the earlier studies in the field provide low resolution images. Since all of our brains (even those of identical twins!) are slightly different, trying to compare areas of brain damage between two people is actually quite difficult. Before automated systems for conducting lesion overlap were developed, researchers had to work out the area of damage from an individual patient's scans and then transfer it (literally using old fashioned tracing paper) onto a 'reference brain template'; then having done this for each patient individually, they could work out what the areas of maximum overlap were across all patients from this reference brain template. While these produced fantastic work that set the standard for years to come, they were open to human error as well as lacking in specific detail. However, nearly 40 years since Heilman et al.'s seminal study, the techniques for creating both high resolution brain scans as well as for evaluating level of overlap have gone through major revolutions resulting in much greater detail and precision. This has had a considerable impact in seeing the specific areas damaged rather than a sense of the general region of the brain.

Given that the major cause of neglect is stroke, even if this is the bursting of the same artery (usually the middle cerebral artery) in each person, the extent of damage will be different because of their individual biology, as well as how quickly they received treatment, since more brain tissue can die if the patient is left untreated. As a result of this heterogeneity, a study that has a relatively small sample is likely to capture less of the variability involved than a study that includes a large sample. Therefore, compared to the seminal studies in the field that had 10–16 patients, when a study is able to use 1281 patients such as that by Ringman et al. (2004), it is likely to get more reliable and replicable findings. Therefore, the size of the samples used has an enormous impact on the generalisability of the claims made.

Further, depending on the method that is being used, the types of control participants that are used is important. Are they healthy individuals with no brain damage? Or are the controls other patients with brain damage in areas away from the area of interest (for example, in this case patients who have intact parietal lobes)? Or are they patients with damage within the parietal lobes but who do not show signs of neglect; this last point is very important since not every patient with a lesion in the parietal lobes will show symptoms of neglect. To address these complexities, Karnath et al. (2004) studied 140 patients who had been admitted to a hospital over a seven-year period having suffered a right hemisphere stroke. Using neuropsychological assessment, 78 of these were classified as suffering from neglect while the remaining 62 did not show these signs. In addition to this choice of patients, they used a technique known as voxel-based statistical analysis to compare precise brain regions in the two groups. Using these advanced techniques, Karnath et al. found that the picture was much more complex than previously thought, and in fact they found that in addition to a number of deeper sub-cortical structures that other researchers have found to be damaged in neglect patients, the right superior temporal cortex (which sits directly above the inferior parietal lobule) was an area of significant damage.

The findings by Karnath et al. (2004) are a very nice demonstration of science evolving. Earlier studies had suggested that it was damage to just one area of the parietal lobes that was responsible for neglect but as researchers tried to replicate these findings, they saw that other structures could also be involved. Further, with the development of more refined neuroimaging and statistical techniques, greater precision has allowed the complex picture to emerge more clearly. Today it is well accepted that rather than just one area being involved in our attentional focus to the outside world, there is a network of areas involving both the parietal and temporal lobes, deeper subcortical structures and the frontal lobes that are responsible. Given the complexity of the task of the attentional system in taking in the sensory information from the outside three-dimensional world and creating an accurate representation within the brain that allows us to both understand and interact with this world, it is little surprise that an elaborate network is involved.

THEORETICAL EXPLANATIONS OF NEGLECT

The theoretical explanations for what causes neglect have varied, and at some levels reflect the complexity of the field as seen in the range of symptoms and multiple dimensions in which the disorder can manifest itself. There are four broad approaches which effectively go up the cognitive hierarchy through more refined processing. These levels are: 1) sensory intake; 2) attention; 3) representation of information; 4) spatial working memory.

Is Neglect Sensory Loss?

The simplest explanation for a patient not responding to information in half of the perceptual world would be that it is the result of loss of sensory stimulation from this area of space, so a form of 'amputation' of that visual (or auditory or proprioceptive) field. Indeed, brain damage can result in hemianopia which is the inability to see information in one of the two visual fields (see Figure 4.6). However, this can occur for both visual fields, left and right, and unlike neglect hemianopia tends to be largely *total* lack of response to information in that particular hemispace. Further, hemianopia can be explained by damage at different stages of the visual processing system as information is taken from the retina at the back of the eye through the brain to the occipital cortices at the back of the brain.

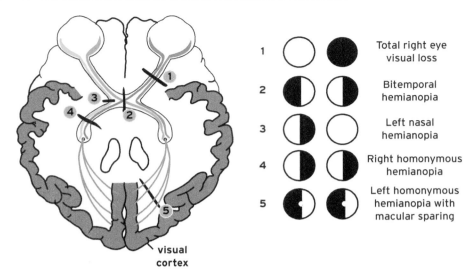

Figure 4.6 The visual pathways from the retina to the visual cortices showing different levels of visual defects depending on area of damage; these visual field defects are about sensory loss rather than attentional neglect

Source: Geeky Medics (geekymedics.com), Illustrator: Aisha Ali

A similar sensory explanation for neglect is very unlikely for a number of reasons. Using line bisection tasks, it has been shown that the errors that patients make are usually a proportion of the length of the line that is shown. If left hemianopia was involved, then the patient would only see the RHS of the line and would bisect this, resulting in their response always being three quarters of the way across. However, it is well established that the pattern of errors with line bisection are much more varied than this. Also, a patient who has a hemianopia tends to be aware of their impairment and compensates for it by turning their head towards the area that they know is a 'blind spot' for them; patients with neglect do not do this.

As described above, while some patients exhibit egocentric neglect, ignoring the LHS of the visual scene in front of them, some patients present with allocentric neglect with the LHS of each individual object being ignored *irrespective of which side of space* it is located. Further, it has been shown by Chattergee et al. (1992) that in letter cancellation tasks, a patient's performance is affected by the number of stimuli in the neglected side which suggests that the problem is more to do with attention than loss of sensory information (see below).

Is Neglect a Lack of Attention?

A number of theories have proposed that neglect occurs because of asymmetry in the way that the two cerebral hemispheres attend to external space. When taking electrical (EEG) recordings while healthy participants were presented with information in just one half of the visual space, Heilman & van den Abell (1980) observed that the left and right parietal lobes responded quite differently from one another. Based on these findings Heilman & Mesulam proposed that the left hemisphere controls attention to the opposite right hemi-space but that the right hemisphere can orient attention to *both* left and right hemispaces. As a result of this, left hemisphere damage does not have a major impact since the intact right hemisphere can attend to both halves of the world. However, right hemisphere damage leaves the intact left hemisphere solely in charge of attending to the right hemispace; as a result of this, due to the lack of attention to the left hemispace, the patient misses information that is presented here causing the focus to the right side of the world.

Following a number of findings that demonstrated that the asymmetry model was not sufficient, Kinsbourne (1987) proposed that in addition to each hemisphere attending to the contralateral visual field, the two hemispheres have a rivalry with each attempting to inhibit the other (see Figure 4.7). The consequence is much the same as above whereby left hemisphere damage results in reduced inhibition of the right hemisphere which therefore allows it to continue attending to both hemispaces. However, damage to the right hemisphere has a more substantial impact; not only is the attention that the right hemisphere gives to both hemispaces removed, but also the inhibition of the left hemisphere is taken away with the result that its focus on the right hemispace is in fact *enhanced*, resulting in the asymmetry observed in neglect.

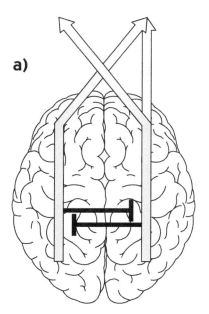 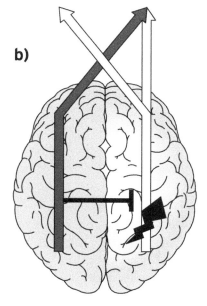

Figure 4.7 Cerebral asymmetry and rivalry to explain unilateral neglect. a) Arrows represent attention for the right hemispace from the left hemisphere but attention to both hemispaces from the right hemisphere; in addition, the vertical lines represent mutual inhibition by each hemisphere on its 'rival'. b) Right hemisphere brain damage removes the only attention that was directed towards the left hemispace, and in addition the loss of the inhibition towards the left hemisphere strengthens the attention that it is able to direct towards the right hemispace (Kinsbourne, 1987)

Kinsbourne's explanation of a strong attentional focus towards the right side of space has been supported by an elegant attentional switching paradigm developed by Posner et al. (1982). Participants have to fixate on a cross in the centre of a computer screen with two empty squares either side of it (see Figure 4.8). At some point following fixation, one of the two side positions is cued, for example with a small arrow above the fixation cross pointing in one of the two directions. Next, a stimulus appears in one of the two boxes and the participant has to make a response as quickly as possible when they notice this stimulus. The main manipulation in this study is the validity of the cue following fixation; a 'valid' cue is one which correctly draws attention to the box in which the target stimulus will appear while an 'invalid' cue is one which draws attention to the incorrect box. Posner et al. found that healthy participants were faster to respond during the valid condition than the invalid condition because the attentional focus had been drawn to it by the cue. By manipulating different elements of the paradigm, they proposed that moving attention from one area to another involves three processes; first we have to *disengage* our attention from its current focus, then we have to *shift* attention towards where we want to focus, then finally we have to *engage* in the new position by locking our attention there. Losier & Klein (2001) reviewed the research conducted in the previous 16 years using the cueing paradigm with patients with damage to either the right or left hemisphere. Their systematic analysis showed that the patients who had the most difficulty in this paradigm had right parietal damage. Further, they found that these patients had the most difficulty during the disengage stage of the paradigm when the invalid cue had driven attention towards the square on the RHS. This finding fits nicely into the Kinsbourne explanation, because according to that theory, the difficulty experienced is that right hemisphere brain damage has not only reduced or totally removed any attention towards the left hemispace, but the lack of inhibition towards the left hemisphere strengthens the attentional pull towards the right; the net result is that disengaging attention from this space is more difficult, increasing times to notice the target on the LHS or increasing errors.

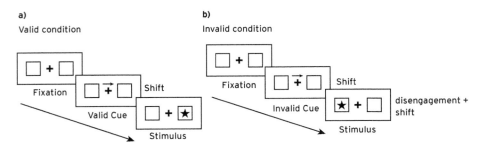

Figure 4.8   Cueing paradigm with three stages, 1) fixation, 2) cue and 3) stimulus for response under two different conditions; a) valid condition; b) invalid condition (Posner et al., 1982)

Further support for the 'attentional pull' theory has been provided by Eglin et al. (1994) who developed a visual search task which varied in difficulty. Participants had to search for targets amongst an array of distractors and what they found was that while both healthy and brain-damaged participants were slower as the task became more diffi-cult, there were particular problems for patients with right hemisphere lesions who had previously shown neglect on other tasks. For example, in Figure 4.9, if the task is to find a dark circle, then the array on the LHS is relatively easy since there is only one dark item; however, the array on the right is more difficult since there are five dark items, only one of which is a circle. Eglin et al. found that relative to healthy controls, as the number of distractors (e.g. the dark squares in this case) increased *on the ipsilesional side*, the right hemisphere patients began to experience significantly more difficulty. Using the Kinsborne and Posner explanations, it seems as if the distracting information on the ipsilesional (right) side is making it difficult to disengage attention from there with the result that it takes longer to detect the target in the contralesional side.

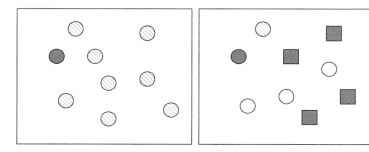

Figure 4.9 Example of 'easy' and 'difficult' search tasks as developed by Eglin et al. (1989). Searching for a dark circle in the left-hand array is easy since there is only one dark item, whereas in the array on the right, it is much more difficult because there are distractor items that are dark, but not circles

Is Neglect an Impaired Internal Representation?

Attentional accounts are useful for explaining perceptual neglect where the deficit is for attending to sensory information that is coming into the cognitive system from the LHS of the external world. However, given that some patients demonstrate allo-centric neglect with the LHS of each object being neglected irrespective of where in space it is located, such an explanation is not sufficient. The need for other explanations was highlighted by a wonderful, ingenious seminal study conducted by Bisiach & Luzzatti in 1978. They had two patients in the northern Italian city of Milan, and to evaluate whether or not their neglect was due to a deficit in percep-tual input or something more complex, they asked the patients to describe a very familiar scene from the centre of the city. The Piazza Del Duomo in Milan is a large square with a very imposing fourteenth-century cathedral at one end, a famous shopping arcade to one side and other commercial shops and restaurants on the other sides of the square. The two patients were asked to *imagine* standing on the steps of the cathedral looking out onto the square and then to describe what they saw 'in their mind's eye' as they looked out from that spot (point A in Figure 4.10). What they found was that the patients reported what would be seen on the RHS of the square if stood with their back to the cathedral (such as the famous shopping arcade) but described little of what was on the LHS. Now it is perfectly possible that maybe their memory and visual image of the square was only of this half of the square, because they had never really noticed anything on the other side of the square, or that it was too nondescript to remember! However, when the patients were told to imagine walking across the square to the opposite side, to turn round so that they were facing the cathedral and to describe what they saw (point B in Figure 4.10) they clearly described what would have been on the RHS from that particular perspective, this time not mentioning the shopping arcade or any of the other buildings they had previously described. Therefore, they were now 'seeing' everything that they had 'neglected' when they were imagining standing at the other end of the square. What this demonstrates is that the patients had intact knowledge of the whole square but when required to bring it up in their mind's eye, they were neglecting the contralesional side of their *mental image*. This therefore shows that neglect does not occur simply because of a deficit with external input but can

Figure 4.10 A schematic diagram of the Piazza del Duomo in Milan; Bisiach & Luzzatti asked their patients to imagine describe everything they saw while standing at point A on the steps of the cathedral looking out to the square, and then to do the same standing at the opposite end of the square at point B looking towards the cathedral. They found that when standing on point A, the patients described the side of the square to their right (in red) while when standing at point B, they described what they now saw to their right (in blue) (Bisiach & Luzzatti, 1978)

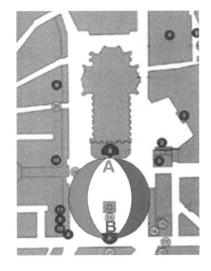

happen on *internally generated information*, and it was therefore termed representational neglect by Bisiach & Luzzatti. Similar findings have been seen with a French (Bartolomeo et al., 2005) patient who showed better responses to cities on the ispilesional side of an imagined map of France.

Bisiach et al. (1979) took this work one step further by showing that neglect can occur for information that is perceptually experienced but needs to be represented internally. They constructed cloud-like abstract shapes that were moved along behind a slit in a screen so that only a vertical segment was visible at any point; therefore, participants had to construct a mental image of the whole abstract shape by gradually piecing together the information they were seeing move behind the slit (see Figure 4.11). The experiment involved viewing two shapes, one after the other, and deciding whether or not they were the same. On some of the trials the shapes were the same, but on critical trials they differed slightly, with the difference being at one of the two extremes of the shape. What Bisiach et al. found was that compared to healthy controls, their 19 patients with right hemisphere brain damage performed significantly worse when the critical difference was on the left-hand extreme of the abstract shapes. This finding demonstrates two important issues. The first is allocentric neglect since the neglected information wasn't ever solely in the contralesional hemispace; it moved across the slit and therefore moved across both hemispaces. The second is that with the whole shape never having been visible, judgements could only be made by inspecting an image that was internally generated from the information gathered as it moved past the slit; therefore, this is yet another example of representational neglect.

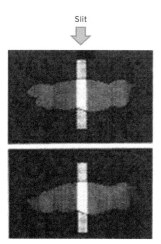

Slit

Figure 4.11 Bisiach et al.'s (1979) cloud slit experiment. Participants viewed abstract shapes move behind a narrow slit. On successive trials the shapes were either identical or had slight differences at one of the two extreme ends

Is Neglect Because of Impaired Spatial Working Memory?

Once information has gone through the cognitive hierarchy of sensory processing and internal representation, for it to be useful, since the world is not static and you need to make decisions based on what you are noticing, you need to be able to use the information in an active dynamic manner. Given that working memory (see Chapter 7) allows us to use the information we have in our current consciousness, Husain et al. (2001) looked at their neglect patient's ability to perform a visual search task. The task resembled a cancellation task where the patient had to look for particular targets in a visual array, but it was conducted on a computer screen, and rather than the patient crossing out targets, they simply had to look for them and move on to the next one; to evaluate their ability to perform the task Husain et al. tracked the patient's eye gaze. What they found was that not only did the patient tend to only search the right visual field (as happens in a letter cancellation task) but they repeatedly visited locations and targets that they had already found previously (see Figure 4.12). These 'revisiting behaviours' were interpreted as an inability to maintain spatial working memory.

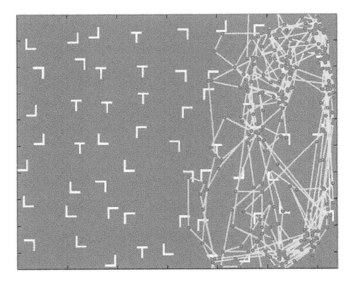

Figure 4.12 Husain et al.'s visual search task requiring a participant to search for as many Ts as possible in an array which includes Ls as distractors; the red dots are points where their patient's eyes fixated and the yellow lines are movements to the next position (Husain et al., 2001)

Pisella and Mattingley (2004) supported these results in a group study with eight right-hemisphere patients who all showed neglect; importantly, half of these patients had damage within the parietal cortex and half did not. They created a visual working memory task in which participants were shown a 4×4 matrix of squares with some of the

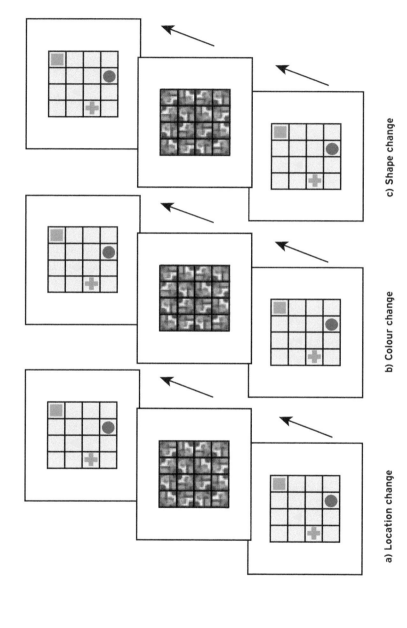

a) Location change **b) Colour change** **c) Shape change**

Figure 4.13 Pisella & Mattingley's visual search task requiring a participant to see a 4×4 matrix with different coloured shapes within it, then a random pattern followed by a test matrix that was either the same or changed; the change could be based on a) location, b) colour or c) shape (Pisella & Mattingley, 2004)

squares having objects (circles or crosses) in them (see Figure 4.13). After brief presentation of these, they were shown some random patterns followed by a new matrix similar to the first one and they simply had to decide whether or not the array looked different. Pisella et al. manipulated whether the change was based on the location of the objects, their colour or their shape – so a circle might change its position in the matrix, change from red to green, or change into a cross respectively. What they found was that while all their patients were poorer when the changes occurred in the contralesional side of the matrix, compared to the non-parietal patients, those with parietal lesions were particularly impaired when the location changed. This again suggests that the right parietal cortex is important for monitoring and maintaining spatial working memory.

So What Causes Neglect?

As is probably obvious, there are quite a few different explanations for what causes neglect, ranging from attentional to representational to active working memory deficits. However, it is important to note that given the sheer complexity of the disorder and that in fact it is a syndrome with a number of different symptoms, there is unlikely to be *one* explanation that can encompass all the different problems that a patient experiences. Instead, it's more of a 'horses for courses' issue where, depending on the particular errors that are being made, one explanation might be more appropriate than another. Therefore, for example, the spatial working memory explanation would not be sufficient to explain representational neglect. Also, the explanations do not need to be mutually incompatible. Given the complex network of brain structures and cognitive processes that are being revealed by the in-depth study of patients, it is becoming clear that with brain lesions that affect not just one very precise area but a number of adjacent areas, different aspects of the processing system will be affected, sometimes with multiple deficits being experienced.

OBJECT-CENTRED OR VIEWER-CENTRED NEGLECT?

As shown earlier, some forms of neglect are egocentric with the field of neglect being contralesional, so that for most patients who have right hemisphere damage, the LHS of the world is ignored. The other manifestation is allocentric, whereby it is the LHS of each stimulus or object that is missed. This issue has received considerable theoretical research using concepts from the object and face recognition literature (see Chapters 6 and 7). The way that an individual views an external object is known as viewer-centred while the standard 'typical' view of it is known as object-centred; for example, a chair can be viewed from above so that the legs are barely visible and that is known as the viewer-centred representation, while a standard side view of a chair in which all the legs and the back are clearly visible is known as the object-centred representation. Young et al. (1990) presented a neglect patient with 'chimeric' faces which had been created so that the left and the right halves were of different famous people. What they found was that the patient only named the face on the RHS. However, since this could be either allocentric or egocentric, they then presented two chimeras side by side and this time the patient named the face on the RHS for both chimeras; since an egocentric explanation would have suggested that the patient would ignore the chimera on the left, this demonstrates that the patient was missing the LHS of each face. This suggested that neglect is happening at the object-centred level.

Driver et al. (1992) took this one step further by presenting participants with a large red rectangle with a small green area at one of the two ends. Healthy participants report seeing a green shape with a contoured edge superimposed on a red background. In their experiment, participants were shown this stimulus and following that, were presented, *in isolation*, an outline probe which was the junction of the red and green in the rectangle and asked if the probe was the same as that seen in the target stimulus. Driver et al. predicted that if neglect is viewer-centred, then their patient would find the task easier if the green shape was on the RHS of the rectangle because it would fall within the hemispace that they paid more attention to. However, if neglect is object-centred, then the patient would find it easier if the shape was on the left-hand edge of the rectangle; this is because for the green object, the critical feature that is important in the task (the contoured edge) would be on the non-neglected side *of the object*. The results showed that whereas for healthy participants, performance was the same irrespective of laterality of the green shape, the neglect patient found the task much easier if the shape was on the LHS of space; when the critical difference was on the LHS of the green object, it was missed. They therefore concluded that neglect is happening at a level where the object has been segregated from its background and that it is therefore occurring at an object-centred level.

Although further researchers tried to argue for neglect happening at the viewer-centred level, Driver & Halligan (1991) countered this with another clever experiment. They created abstract shapes and from these put together pairs that were near identical but had one critical difference which was either on the LHS or RHS of the object (see Figure 4.14). When they presented the pairs with the 'axis of elongation' vertical so that the object looked like it was stood up, they got the standard neglect findings where the critical difference was missed if it was on the LHS. They then tilted the stimuli so that the critical difference was in the right hemispace. If neglect is occurring from a viewer-centred perspective, the patient should have been able to spot the difference. However, they found that a difference which was on the LHS of the object itself was still missed even when it fell in the patient's right hemispace. This therefore again demonstrates that neglect is occurring at the object-centred level. In a way, this is analogous to the representational neglect showing that a visual percept is created at the cognitive level and it is the LHS of this that is then somehow missed.

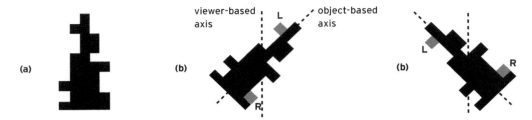

Figure 4.14 Driver & Halligan's stimuli; a) the axis of elongation is vertical; b) with the axis tilted to the right, a critical difference that could be on the LHS of the abstract shape is now in the right hemispace while a difference on the RHS is in the left hemispace; c) with the axis tilted to the left, an LHS difference is in the left hemispace and a right one within the right hemispace (Driver & Halligan, 1991)

What Happens to the Neglected Information?

An important question across neuropsychology and therefore also within neglect is what happens to the neglected information – is it totally lost or 'is it there somewhere'? There have been a number of investigations into this but possibly the most striking one was by Marshall & Halligan (1988), who presented their patient with drawings of two houses which were identical on the RHS but there was a fire emerging from the window on the LHS of one of the two houses (see Figure 4.15). When the patient was asked whether they could see any differences between the two houses, they said that there wasn't. However, when asked which house they would prefer to live in, despite having said that the houses were identical, they consistently chose the non-burning one! McGlinchey-Berroth et al. (1996) have also demonstrated that words that a patient neglected nonetheless impacted their decisions in subsequent trials in a semantic priming task.

Figure 4.15 Marshall & Halligan's housesn which one has flames coming out of a window on the LHS part of the building (Marshall & Halligan, 1988)

The findings from these studies demonstrate that 'ignored' does not necessarily mean 'lost forever'. Across neuropsychology there are many examples where 'implicit' or unconscious levels of awareness are demonstrated by patients for information that is not overtly available. These examples show the complexity of neglect and more generally amplify the fact that sensory processing and either verbal or behavioural responding to external stimuli are only part of the complexities of the human cognitive system with a huge amount that is not (yet) available for conscious inspection.

FUTURE DIRECTIONS FOR NEGLECT RESEARCH

It will have become obvious that neglect is both a complex and intriguing disorder. The complexity of the condition coupled with the different manifestations, with some symptoms resolving (disappearing) over time and others being more permanent, with even this dimension differing hugely between patients; this therefore makes overall evaluation of neglect difficult. In her review of the development of research in the field, Laurel Buxbaum (2006) has stressed how important the study of patients with neglect is for gaining insights into how we represent external objects in our cognitive realm, how our attention to both the outside world and our own physical selves functions and how this information is important for our spatio-motor processing (as seen in Chapter 5). To do this effectively, well-validated tests that are cross-validated with one another are needed; without these, the results from each study are only relevant to the patients that those specific tests are used on, and a comparison across studies becomes more difficult. If these tests can be computerised, then comparisons can become easier. For example, Bonato (2012) has shown that the difficulty of the assessment (known as task demands) can impact how impaired a patient can seem. By computerising paper-and-pencil tasks, it will be easier to validate and cross-reference between patients and studies. Finally, while there has been a focus on theories that explain neglect which shows a heavy spatial bias, it is important to explore the causes of the symptoms that are not lateralised simply to the left and right side of the world or of individual objects.

Chapter Summary

- Neglect is a very complex and heterogeneous problem which is unlikely to be a 'low-level' sensory issue.
- The condition is a syndrome with a number of different symptoms which will vary depending on the individual patient as well as site and extent of lesion.
- The best theories to explain neglect are ones that emphasise problems at the attentional level; from manipulations in complex experimental tasks, it seems that the neglect is operating at the object-centred level once a representation has been created internally from external stimuli.
- A stark demonstration of the object-centred level of neglect is found when there isn't even an external stimulus but the LHS of an image is ignored.

Important Research Study

The Milan Square / Piazza del Duomo Study (Bisiach & Rizzolatti, 1978)

The study on two patients *imagining* that they were standing in a famous square in the Italian city of Milan was very important since it demonstrated that the neglect that these (and by extension other) patients demonstrated for the LHS of the world was not to do with sensory processing. There was no external sensory information being presented since the patients just had to imagine what they saw in a place that, as locals of the city, they would have been to many times. The very clever 'thought experiment' demonstrated that neglect occurred at the level of the internal representation of information. The field of mental imagery is extremely complex since it is necessary to explain how we 'see' something that is not present; nonetheless, this study showed that when patients are neglecting half of the world, this is not due to poor sensory processing. This finding then led to studies with patients in other countries using similar variants of this experiment, and then to the 1979 cloud slit study by Bisiach et al. exploring how neglect even happened when a mental image had to be created 'online'. So if you ever go to the famous square in Milan think of how it has played an important part in our understanding of attentional processing.

Questions for Reflection

- Why is neglect more common after damage to the right hemisphere rather than the left hemisphere?
- How complete are the theories that attempt to explain neglect?

Go Further

- The theories covered here are useful for explaining neglect of the left side of the world; but not all neglect is just for that side of space and can have other dimensions too - explore those.
- How have scientists tried to explain the more complex symptoms of neglect such as extinction and repetition blindness?

Go Further

Dr Jansari's YouTube Videos

Confabulation, Capgras & Cotard's: The amazing insights from brain disorders (Parts 1 and 2)

Watch how Peggy has difficulties in copying drawings of a flower as well as drawing a flower from her memory (her mental image).

Further Reading

- Zebhauser, P. T., Vernet, M., Unterburger, E., & Brem, A. K. (2019). Visuospatial neglect: A theory-informed overview of current and emerging strategies and a systematic review on the therapeutic use of non-invasive brain stimulation. *Neuropsychology Review, 29*(4), 397–420.
- Husain, M., & Rorden, C. (2003). Non-spatially lateralized mechanisms in hemispatial neglect. *Nature Reviews Neuroscience, 4*(1), 26–36.
- Zorzi, M., Priftis, K., & Umiltà, C. (2002). Neglect disrupts the mental number line. *Nature, 417*(6885), 138–139.

5
APRAXIA & MOTOR-PLANNING

Chapter Overview

This chapter will explore a skill that you use every day all the time and which I am using right now as I tap away on my keyboard. To get through the world, we interact with objects by doing things to them – we touch them, pick them up, manipulate them in our hands, etc. Without this skill, we would not be able to feed ourselves, use everyday objects, use objects to protect ourselves if we were physically threatened, etc. Many of us have experienced difficulties in these skills because of an injury to an arm or a leg, and we know how it can compromise our lives so much. Some people who suffer a certain type of stroke can end up with either temporary or permanent paralysis which makes it difficult or impossible for them to use one or more of their limbs. However, there are people who aren't suffering from any form of paralysis or external damage to their limbs who still have difficulty interacting with everyday objects. These individuals suffer from a higher level problem that is not caused by external limb damage or damage to the motor areas of the brain, but is a more cognitive problem known as apraxia. By studying this sometimes difficult-to-spot disorder, neuropsychologists are able to understand how the brain creates motor programmes to allow us to go about our lives using everyday objects in our world.

Chapter Outline

- Introduction: What Is Apraxia?
- Apraxia and Everyday Functioning
- Subtypes of Apraxia
- The Neuroanatomy of Apraxia
- Heilman's Cortical Model of Ideomotor Limb Apraxia
- Chapter Summary

INTRODUCTION: WHAT IS APRAXIA?

Our movement can be compromised in a number of different ways and this is because of the complex processing chain that is involved. When we handle an object, important sensory information from our touch receptors, as well as information about the weight of the object from how much our hand and arm muscles have to work when we touch or try to pick it up, are conveyed to the brain. This, along with the visual information from our eyes, tells us what the object could be; so it could be a juicy apple or it could be a heavy metal object which has been cleverly made and painted to look like an apple. Once we have worked out what it is, we might decide what to do with it – pick it up to eat it or pick it up to weigh down papers on our desk.

The ways that your ability to interact with this object can be affected can vary enormously depending on the injury or damage that you have suffered. If there is 'peripheral' damage to your hands or to the nerves running from them to the brain or to the muscles in your arm, then it will obviously be impossible to pick up the object properly. However, even if all of this is intact, there are a number of different ways that damage within the more central system can affect performance. One of the most common problems is a stroke that affects the area of the brain that controls our motor movement known as the motor strip. Another cause is because of a rare neurodegenerative disorder known as motor neuron disease (MND) which affects the functioning of the nerve cells that are specialised for controlling the muscles around the body. This is a very difficult disorder in which the neurons weaken over time and therefore their ability to send the signals from the motor areas of the brain deteriorate over time. The most famous example of a sufferer of this is the physicist and cosmologist Stephen Hawking who was reduced to using muscles in his cheek because the nerves to those muscles were the last to deteriorate. Remarkably, he was able to have an exceptional academic career and even write books despite this incredible disability.

However, in 1890, a neurologist called Hugo Liepmann showed that it was possible for a patient to show difficulties in certain types of movements despite all of the physical architecture of the peripheral systems and the motor cortex being intact. His patient had suffered a stroke in the left hemisphere, and even after the type of weakness in the contralateral limbs known as paresis that is common with strokes had resolved, the patient was showing some very specific difficulties. He wasn't able to button a shirt or light a cigar even though he could perform simple gestures when asked to do so, could mime (pantomime) these gestures and carry out everyday actions spontaneously such as using a spoon while eating. Some important features of Liepmann's observations are that the difficulty the patient had with any of the movements could not have been due to not understanding the movements or actions requested of him; given that his stroke was in the left hemisphere (which you will see in Chapter 9 is highly important in language production as well as comprehension), a difficulty in understanding what was requested could simply have been due to a linguistic problem. However, the fact that he could perform simple gestures when requested demonstrates that his comprehension was intact. Further, the fact that he could use a spoon for eating demonstrates that the problem was not a simple motor or physical problem since using a spoon effectively requires motor control. Liepmann proposed the term apraxia to refer to the inability to carry out movements *in the absence of* primary motor, sensory or comprehension deficits.

Observing other patients, Liepmann found that such complex difficulties tended to occur in those with left hemisphere lesions but not those with right hemisphere lesions. From these observations, he proposed that to carry out a movement involved having an intention to do something (such as using an everyday object), then creating a 'motor plan' of how to do this, then for this plan to be executed through the motor system. In his model, information flows anteriorly (forwards) in the brain from posterior areas which understood *what* the external objects are (involving visual recognition in the occipital lobes) and *where* they are (involving the attentional system in the parietal lobes) towards the motor cortex (see Figure 5.1).

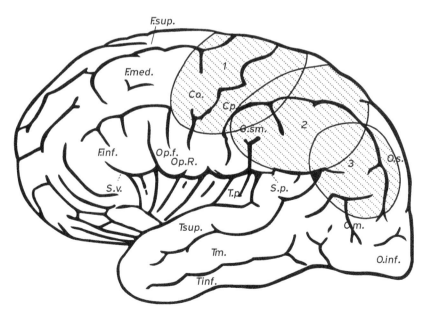

Figure 5.1   Liepmann's original model of information flowing from the occipital lobes (3) through the parietal lobes (2) towards the motor cortex (1) to allow us to interact with objects in our visual scene (Roby-Brami et al., 2012)

APRAXIA AND EVERYDAY FUNCTIONING

One of the reasons that clinicians are particularly interested in limb apraxia is the impact that it can have on everyday functioning. An important measure that is used by clinicians refers to everyday outcome following brain damage. This refers to the transition back towards the life that the individual had prior to their brain injury. There are various ways to evaluate this, but generally they address issues to do with getting back into the workplace, being able to engage in any leisure activities, the quality of their relationships and everyday life such as the ability to live independently, cooking or driving. Of course, the kind of life that each individual had before brain damage will differ from person to person, but clinicians are able to evaluate how close to their desired life outcomes their patient can get to.

More specifically, the presence and level of apraxia has been found to be a strong predictor of whether or not someone can return to work after a stroke (Saeki et al., 1995). Given that for many adults, their work/occupation can form a significant aspect of their sense of self, not being able to return to the work that they used to do before brain damage could have considerable impact on their overall mental health. Others have found that apraxia results in deficits in simulated activities of daily living, which are those actions that we perform on a regular basis such as making a cup of tea and washing dishes (e.g. Chestnut & Haaland, 2008; van Heugten et al., 1998).

SUBTYPES OF APRAXIA

Similar to a number of other neuropsychological disorders, apraxia has a number of sub-types which result in a variety of different difficulties. Further, this is a condition that, in addition to a form that is caused by brain damage, also has a developmental variant which individuals have from childhood. Known as developmental coordination difficulty (DCD), estimates suggest that 6% (so 1 in 16) children have this neurodevelopmental problem; there are some reports that indicate that there is a much higher prevalence of 10–20% of children. It seems that there may be an uneven gender distribution with males being four times more likely than females to have DCD. However, these are only estimates because with neurodevelopmental disorders it is quite possible for someone to go undiagnosed for a long time, if they have managed to find ways to cope with what they just thought were small weaknesses. They may only find out that they have the condition as an adult; for example, if you are not that great at playing football, then you might think that you are just not good at playing sports. But a formal assessment might find that you have DCD and, given the coordination involved in football, it is totally unsurprising that you weren't great at playing the game when you were younger. This is a major issue with neurodevelopmental disorders: many individuals may have difficulties in a variety of spheres (reading, writing, calculation, face recognition) but never realise that it is because of an undiagnosed issue. Research and awareness are important for ensuring that young people who may have neurodevelopmental disorders are diagnosed as early as possible so that they can be given whatever support is available, and also so that they do not have to endure any stigma that may be related to being poorer at a particular ability than other children their age.

While, as seen above, apraxia can have significant impacts on a brain-damaged person's life, due to the complexity of diagnosing the condition, there is little data available on its prevalence. Since the condition is usually brought on either by stroke or in the context of dementia, generally it tends to be diagnosed in the elderly population. Since the pioneering work of Liepmann, a number of different types of apraxia have been identified. Similar to the situation with neglect, apraxia is also somewhat complicated, and again this is because of the complexity of how we physically interact with the world and the movements that are required.

Researchers have identified three main types of movements which if impaired can result in apraxic difficulties; these can therefore be used in assessing the presence of apraxia. They are: gestures that involve using an object, which are known as 'transitive' – so for example hammering a nail or combing one's hair are transitive; 'intransitive' gestures that do not involve an object and which might typically be used for interpersonal communication such as waving your hand or giving a thumbs up signal to say that you agree with something; and 'meaningless' gestures which don't involve objects and do not serve any practical or social function such as curling your fist into a ball and putting that on your head.

A clinician or researcher can use different types of paradigms to assess the type and level of difficulty a patient is experiencing. A simple verbal command without the use of any objects could evaluate any of the different types of gestures; similarly, asking the patient to imitate what the assessor is doing would achieve the same result. Additionally, for transitive errors, an object such as a hammer can be presented with the request for them to show how they would use it. Using these methods, researchers have been able to identify a number of distinct sub-types of apraxia which may occur in isolation or in combination depending on the extent of brain damage that has been suffered.

The most obvious form of the disorder is ideomotor apraxia, which seems to be a breakdown within the production of the individual movements and is probably caused by a deficit in the sensorimotor programmes that allow an individual to start and control any motor activity. The result is that the timing, sequencing and spatial organisation of movements is impaired. For example, a combination of timing and spatial errors would result in a patient carving a turkey with poorly timed vertical movements (for example as if chopping an onion) rather than the coordinated horizontal movements that are more appropriate.

A more complex form is ideational apraxia where the individual actions themselves are intact but there is inappropriate use of objects and a failure in discriminating between gestures. The inappropriate use of objects cannot be due to a deficit as experienced by someone with ideomotor apraxia since the movements themselves are preserved.

As an example, Ochipa & Gonzalez Rothi (1989) reported a patient who had suffered a stroke affecting the right middle cerebral artery that had caused a combination of frontal, parietal and superior temporal lobe damage. The patient's auditory comprehension was intact, meaning that any difficulties with assessment could not be linguistic or auditory in origin. There was no visual agnosia since the patient could easily point to a particular named tool in an array of items. Nonetheless, the patient showed ideomotor apraxia in their inability to use the tools physically. Their impairments were at the conceptual level rather than in manipulation; while spatiotemporal movements in using objects was intact, the deficit was in terms of the actual function of the object. .

THE NEUROANATOMY OF APRAXIA

Similar to neglect, the neuroanatomical basis of apraxia is quite complex. The reason for this is that to use an object involves a chain of different processes. To use a hammer properly, it is necessary to visually recognise the object and if you are being instructed on what to do with it by a clinician, you need to understand what they are saying. To use the object, in addition to the name of the object, it will be important to know *how* to use it appropriately. Finally, the sequence of actions needs to be carried out appropriately; in this example, moving it up and down in a vertical plane to end at a particular point on the down-stroke. For this sequence, a number of different neurocognitive systems are involved, namely visual recognition (Chapter 6), verbal comprehension (Chapter 10), visual comprehension (this chapter) and motor sequencing. From the work that has been carried out on apraxia over the last few decades, it has become clear that apraxia is a deficit in the last of these systems.

What Versus Where

The first piece of the puzzle began in the 1960s when researchers (e.g. Schneider, 1967) started showing that the visual system was much more complex than a simple mapping of information from the peripheral visual system (the eyes and the retina) to the occipital lobes. In fact, it was becoming apparent that information was being sent to a number of different brain areas; depending on the particular animal species, there are up to ten regions, including subcortical regions that receive input from the retina. As a result of this, models involving cortical and subcortical pathways for visual processing started to become popular. These models suggested that while the cortical pathways were responsible for identifying objects, the subcortical routes were localising the object. However, in ground-breaking work by Ungerleider & Mishkin in 1982, this distinction was taken into the cortex when they suggested that the route starting in the occipital lobes and moving through the floor (or ventrum) of the brain is responsible for recognising an object, while a pathway going higher through the brain (the dorsal areas, as in the upper dorsal fin of a dolphin) is involved in showing us where an object is in the outside world. This distinction became known as the 'what' (ventral) versus 'where' (dorsal) pathways (see Figure 5.2a).

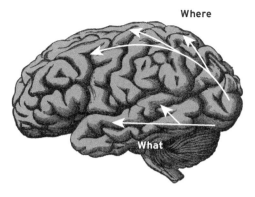

Figure 5.2a   The visual processing pathways proposed by Ungerleider & Mishkin (1982) with the ventral pathway recognising 'what' something is and the dorsal pathway localising 'where' it is

The Emergence of 'How To'

However, a decade after the work by Ungerleider & Mishkin (which had been largely informed by neurophysiological work in animals), it was cognitive neuropsychological work that demonstrated that even this distinction was not sufficient. Milner et al. (1991) carried out some remarkable work with a patient who had suffered bilateral occipital lobe damage from carbon monoxide poisoning. As a result, DF suffered from a very specific type of visual recognition difficulty known as visual shape agnosia. Like the seminal patient studied by Efron in 1868 (see Chapter 7), in addition to not being able to recognise objects, DF found even the simplest shape discrimination tasks (e.g. being able to tell apart two rectangles of different lengths) difficult.

Importantly, it wasn't what DF could *not* do but what she *could* do that was remarkable. This is one of the most powerful aspects of neuropsychology, whereby dissociations between what would seem like related abilities occur *in the same patient*, giving very strong evidence for the separation of physical or mental skills. If shown a straight line and asked to pretend that it was a slot like a mailbox, DF was unable to describe the slot or to match it to another line of a similar orientation – so this is what would be expected of her visual shape agnosia. However, if given a card and asked to imagine posting it through the same mailbox slit, DF's performance was flawless (see Figure 5.3). Also, for objects that she could not name (and therefore not show an ability to visually recognise), she was nonetheless able to reach out and move her fingers into the correct position to grasp the object.

Therefore, the difficulty that DF was demonstrating was related to the identity of an object at perceptual and semantic levels (the look and meaning of something) but her ability to know what action to perform with the same object was intact. Rather remarkably, at a similar time to the work by Milner & Goodale on DF, another group of researchers was documenting almost the exact opposite pattern of behaviour in patients who exhibited what was known as optic ataxia, a term that had been coined by a notable Hungarian neurologist Rudolph Bálint in 1909. Jeannerod & Rossetti (1993) have documented patients with lesions in the parietal lobes who effectively doubly dissociate from DF; they can give perceptual information about objects but have difficulty reaching out to objects placed in front of them, cannot make the 'mailing a postcard' type of movements that she could and can't make the appropriate changes in finger positions if trying to reach out to grasp objects. As a result of this beautiful double dissociation, Milner & Goodale suggested that the what/where system developed by Ungerleider & Mishkin needed to be refined to incorporate a 'how' system that was presumably also within the dorsal pathway given that this area was intact in DF (see Figure 5.2b).

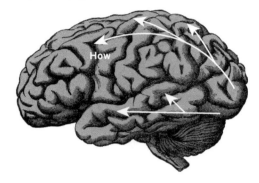

Figure 5.2b The development of the ventral/dorsal pathways model with the dorsal pathway processing information on how to work with an object in addition to localising it

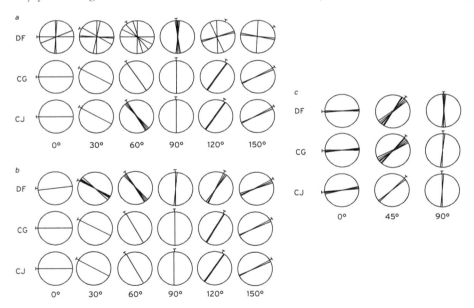

Figure 5.3 Examples from Milner & Goodale et al.'s (1991) work on DF showing her performance on a task which involved holding a card at an angle to match the orientation of a slot on an upright disc as if pretending to 'post' the card through the slot. Her performance, and that of two control participants is shown for three conditions: a) when the task was simply to rotate the card to match the orientation of the slot; b) when the task was to perform the action of reaching out to post the card; and c) when the task was to imagine the orientation of the slot with eyes closed. (Reprinted by permission from Springer Nature, A Neurological Dissassociation between Perceiving Objects and Grasping Them by M. A. Goodale et al., 1991)

The possibility that neural processing could be concerned with 'how to' do something was boosted by a number of neurophysiological studies conducted on monkeys in the 1990s. In Japan, a research team was conducting neurophysiological work which at some levels supported the 'what' and 'where' pathways, but there were neurons within the dorsal stream that didn't seem to be related to the object's location; this didn't fit in with the two system approach given that the dorsal pathway had been proposed as being responsible for working out 'where' an object was. The Japanese team found that these neurons seemed more responsive to information about the shape and size of the object that the monkey was grasping (Taira et al., 1990) even though it was not involved in recognising the object or localising it.

Meanwhile, another team in Italy under Giacomo Rizzolatti were taking recordings from electrodes that were placed in the premotor cortex to study how the brain processes information when performing actions. They found that there were cells that, compared to when the monkey was not doing anything, became active when the monkey had to reach out to grasp an object; therefore, these neurons were obviously involved in motor movement. However, intriguingly, they found (by accident it turns out!) that when the monkey was *observing* someone else (one of the experimenters) grasping the object, the same neurons became active (Rizzolatti et al., 1996). From this work, they suggested that some neurons hold motor representations of actions that *we are already familiar with* and these get played back when we observe others performing the same actions. They called these mirror neurons and they have been used to explain how we understand the actions of others, because if someone else performs an action that is 'recognised' by the mirror neurons, then we can comprehend what they are doing. Mirror neurons have been invoked to explain a number of different issues in human behaviour, some of which are not fully accepted, but nonetheless there is now general acceptance that they are involved in action perception.

Putting together these two pieces of evidence was vital for Milner & Goodale. The Japanese results helped to explain the fact that their patient DF was able to perform grasp movements for objects that she could not recognise – her ventral stream was damaged but her dorsal pathway which is responsible for such movements was intact. Further, the mirror neurons can be used to try to understand the problems that patients with apraxia can have in imitation of someone else's actions. Similar to the argument used in Chapter 3 about why a copying task is important for helping to see how much someone perceptually understands the information in front of them, an action imitation task requires that person to comprehend the action they are watching (e.g. using a brush to pretend to brush one's teeth) to try to replicate and imitate the action. Mirror neurons could be the neurophysiological pathway, and if these are damaged in the dorsal stream, then a patient will have difficulty copying someone else's actions.

The seminal findings above have been supported by further neuropsychological case studies demonstrating a dissociation between knowing the function of an object and how to physically manipulate it to use it appropriately. For example, Sirigu et al. (1991) documented a patient who had bilateral temporal lobe damage that left him with classic symptoms of agnosia, which in his case meant that he was unable to recognise living things such as animals and foods; by contrast, his recognition of man-made tools and objects was much better. However, they noticed that often when he named an object correctly, it was after the patient had been making gestures with his fingers as if he was trying to work out how to use the object. To explore how specific his understanding of the man-made items was, they created a task in which the patient was shown a series of common household objects and asked to describe them. They categorised his descriptions based on whether it described the functional use or the manipulation of the object. What was striking was that for many objects he was poor at giving an accurate description of their function, despite giving an appropriate description of how to manipulate them. For example, for an iron, his descriptions were 'Maybe you spread glue evenly with it' and 'You hold it in one hand and move it back and forth horizontally' while miming this correct action. Therefore, there is a clear distinction between impaired functional understanding and correct understanding of manipulation.

Contrasting with this, Buxbaum et al. (2000) explored the abilities of two patients with left parietal lobe damage who both showed severe apraxia. What they found was that the patients were unimpaired in demonstrating functional use of objects but had difficulties demonstrating an understanding of how to manipulate them. For example, if asked which of two objects out of a radio, record player and telephone served similar functions, then the patients were able to choose the first two items correctly since they both produce some sort of sound. However, if asked which two objects out of a piano, typewriter and oven were manipulated similarly, the patients were highly impaired, even though to healthy participants it is clear that the first two objects are manipulated by using fingers to press down on different components (the keys of the piano or of the typewriter). This elegant double dissociation with Sirigu et al.'s (1991) patient implies that the systems for understanding function and manipulation doubly dissociate from one another. The former seems to be based in the ventral stream in the temporal lobes (damaged in Sirigu et al.'s patient) while the latter is based in the dorsal stream in the parietal lobes (damaged in Buxbaum et al.'s patients).

Neuroimaging Evidence

The elegant work conducted by cognitive neuropsychologists and neurophysiologists has been nicely complemented by a number of studies that have supported the findings. In one of the first lesion overlap studies of its kind, Tranel et al. (1997) conducted a very large study with 116 patients with brain damage, who were presented photographs of famous people, common animals and everyday tools; the task was simply to give the name of the individual or the general name for the animal or tool. Using the correct and incorrect responses, they then grouped those patients who had particular difficulties in each of the three categories and next conducted a lesion overlap analysis to explore whether there were areas that were specifically associated with each type of knowledge.

What they found was that while the maximum overlap in brain damage for patients who couldn't recognise faces was in the right temporal pole, and that for those who had difficulties with animals it was in the right and left occipital regions, the area most affected in patients who could not name the tools was in the left temporal-parietal junction (see Figure 5.4).

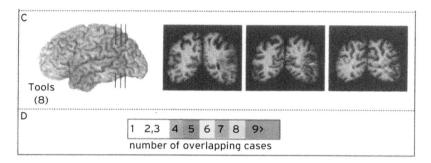

Figure 5.4   Lesion overlap findings from Tranel et al. (1997) showing that the area that was damaged most in patients who had difficulties with recognising tools was the junction of the temporal and parietal lobes in the left hemisphere (Reprinted from *Neuropsychologia*, 35 (10), Tranel, Daniel; Damasio, Hanna; Damasio, Antonio R, A neural basis for the retrieval of conceptual knowledge, pp. 1319–1327, Copyright (1997), with permission from Elsevier)

Next Chao & Martin (2000) used a similar design showing their participants different categories of information, but this time they studied neural responses in healthy participants by using fMRI. Their hypothesis was that if tools require different types of processing because they are relatively small objects that we manipulate with our hands, there would be a different neural signature to seeing such objects compared to viewing things that we don't manually manipulate. The four categories they used were tools, people, houses and animals. By comparing the brain activation when participants were viewing the 'non-manipulable' categories to the activation when participants were shown tools, Chao & Martin found that the left ventral premotor cortex and left posterior parietal cortex were activated (see Figure 5.5).

In the same year, Haaland et al. (2000) used a similar design to Tranel et al. (1997), looking at the lesion overlap in patients who had damage in different parts of the brain. The patients were assessed for ideomotor limb apraxia by asking participants to imitate five transitive actions (e.g. using their finger to brush to pretend brushing their teeth), give intransitive gestures (e.g. pretending to salute someone) and five meaningless gestures (such as touching their ear lobe with their index finger). Based on their performance on these actions, patients were then categorised as either having ideomotor limb apraxia or not having the condition. Next, using the lesion overlap methodology, they were able to see what the common areas of brain damage were. Haaland et al. (2000) found that the most common areas of damage were the middle frontal gyrus and intraparietal sulcus of the left hemisphere (see Figure 5.6).

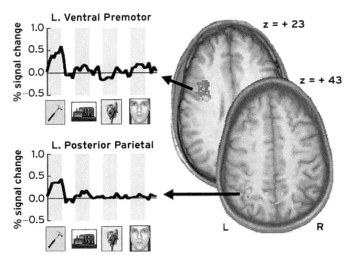

Figure 5.5 fMRI findings from Chao & Martin (2000) showing the selective activation of the left ventral premotor and left posterior parietal cortices in healthy participants viewing manipulable tools compared to other categories of visual objects (Reprinted from *NeuroImage*, *12*(4), Chao, L. L.; Martin, A., Representation of manipulable manmade objects in the dorsal stream, pp. 478–484, Copyright (2000), with permission from Elsevier)

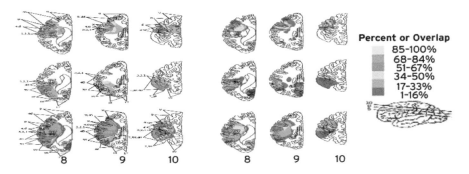

Figure 5.6 Lesion overlap findings from Haaland et al. (2000) showing that patients who demonstrated ideomotor limb apraxia tended to have brain damage in a left hemisphere network involving the frontal and parietal lobes (Reprinted from *Brain*, *123*(11), Haaland, Kathleen Y.; Harrington, Deborah L., Neural representations of skilled movement, Copyright (2000), with permission from Oxford University Press)

While the above studies involved the recognition of tools or the performance of actions, Pazzaglia et al. (2008) explored whether limb apraxia also affected the ability to understand actions performed by others. They did this by formally evaluating a group of patients with brain damage for presence or absence of limb apraxia using standardised tests. Next, they created a task in which an actor performed both transitive and intransitive tasks either correctly or incorrectly. For example, a correct transitive task would be holding and playing a guitar correctly and an incorrect one would be holding a flute in the same position and pretending to play it. An example of an intransitive task would be holding a thumb out to one side of the body and gesturing the way that a hitchhiker would try to get a car to give them a lift while an incorrect version of this would be holding the thumb out correctly but performing the gesture above the head. The actor was videoed performing all the actions and the films were shown to the patients without any sound so that this could not give any cues (such as the correct sound of the guitar being played); patients simply had to state whether or not the action being performed was correct. The results showed that the patients with limb apraxia performed significantly worse than the patients without the condition and that even within this impaired group, there were two subgroups (see Figure 5.7a). Further, Pazzaglia et al. performed lesion overlap analyses to work out the common areas for the groups of patients separately and then performed a *subtraction* analysis to work

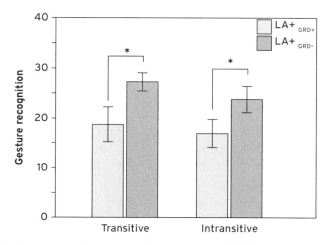

Figure 5.7a The behavioural findings by Pazzaglia et al. (2008) showing that within their group of patients with limb apraxia, there were two subgroups, one with a Gesture Recognition Deficit (LA+$_{GRD+}$) and one without (LA+$_{GRD-}$) (Reprinted from *The Journal of Neuroscience*, *28*(12), Pazzaglia, Mariella et al., Neural Underpinnings of Gesture Discrimination in Patients with Limb Apraxia, pp. 3030–3041, Copyright (2008) Society for Neuroscience)

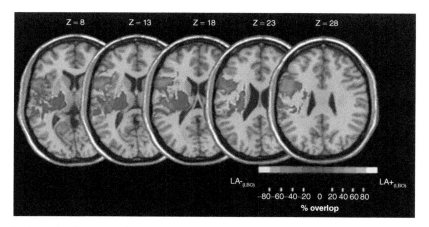

Figure 5.7b The lesion subtraction analysis by Pazzaglia et al. (2008) showing the areas that differed between their patients with (LA+) and without limb apraxia (LA-). (Reprinted from *The Journal of Neuroscience*, *28*(12), Pazzaglia, Mariella et al., Neural Underpinnings of Gesture Discrimination in Patients with Limb Apraxia, pp. 3030–3041, Copyright (2008) Society for Neuroscience)

out which brain regions *differed* between the patients with and without limb apraxia. What they found was that the crucial area was in the left inferior frontal gyrus, which is effectively at the end of the dorsal stream going from the occipital lobe through the parietal lobe and into the frontal lobe (see Figure 5.7b). Building on the seminal work by Rizzolatti et al. (1996) on mirror neurons in monkeys and their potential involvement in understanding the actions of others, a decade later, another Italian group were able to demonstrate a possible location that is crucial in humans for such processing.

In summary, research by cognitive neuropsychologists, neurophysiologists and neuroscientists has demonstrated that performing actions involves a complex system which has a number of different elements which can break down differentially. The breakdown can be for actions that involve objects, for gestures that carry meaning (such as waving goodbye to someone) or for meaningless gestures. Where objects are involved, double dissociations have demonstrated that the function of an object is processed separately from information on how to manipulate it; therefore, some patients with temporal lobe damage can sometimes demonstrate how to manipulate an object without knowing its function while some patients with parietal lobe damage can understand the function of an object but not know how to use it. These findings strongly suggest that we actually have not one but two visual recognition systems. The ventral stream through the temporal lobes seems to create and store abstract representations of what we see around us (see Figure 5.8 for the model developed by Buxbaum & Kalenine, 2010). This allows us to recognise these objects whenever we see them or use the representations to think about and interpret the world; importantly, this can be done 'offline' rather than 'in the moment'. The dorsal stream

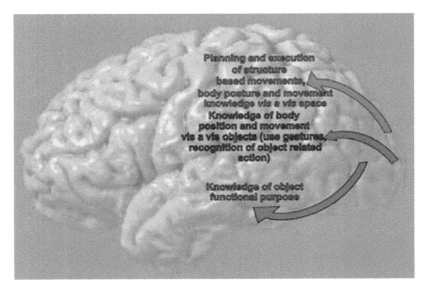

Figure 5.8 The development of the ventral/dorsal pathways model with the ventral pathway being involved in identifying the *function* of an object while the dorsal pathway processes information on *how* to use it as well as localising it (Buxbaum & Kalenine, 2010; Reprinted with permission of John Wiley & Sons)

on the other hand is very much in the moment, with the visual processing guiding the way we will act towards our *current* visual input and interact with objects or with others through our gestures. This involves rapid processing and being able to change or adapt our actions in real time moment-by-moment which can be crucial for survival.

HEILMAN'S CORTICAL MODEL OF IDEOMOTOR LIMB APRAXIA

As a result of the growing amount of evidence for the involvement of the parietal lobes in movement, a number of models have been proposed by Roy & Square (1985), Buxbaum (2001) and Gonzalez Rothi et al. (1991). The last of these came about through the work of one of the most important figures in this field, Kenneth Heilman, who along with his team in Florida, USA synthesised their own findings (Heilman et al., 1982) with those of other cognitive neuropsychologists. Observing the range of dissociations and double dissociations between patients, their model suggests that the basis for efficient production of meaningful actions is a set of visuokinesthetic engrams that are stored and processed within the parietal lobes, particularly in the left hemisphere. These engrams (which are effectively action programmes) allow us to perform movements that we are *already* familiar with very rapidly and efficiently.

These engrams can be thought of as the build-up of the actions that we have become familiar with through our lives whenever we learn a new action; as you will see in Chapter 8 (Amnesia & Memory), this is known as procedural memory. There is also an analogy with the 'face recognition units' that allow us to recognise faces of people that we have met before (see Chapter 7: Prosopagnosia & Face Processing). The visuokinesthetic engrams are fed forward from the parietal lobes to the premotor and motor areas for execution of the specific actions. While their earlier model was neuroanatomical, this was developed into a cognitive model by Gonzalez Rothi et al. (1991) (See Figure 5.9). As seen in Figure 5.8 this model has a pathway for visual gestural information that allows us to see the actions of others, the visual object recognition system (see Chapter 6) that allows us to recognise objects that we might want to manipulate and the verbal and auditory processing systems (see Chapter 10) which process the spoken words of others who might ask us to do something, or the written words that allow us to read instructions about actions that we need to perform. This aspect of the model is very progressive since it demonstrates that a particular cognitive system doesn't exist in isolation, but instead needs to interact with other cognitive systems that will be involved. Similarly, when we meet someone we know, in addition to the face recognition system understanding that this is a familiar face, this system also needs to interact with our memory system to remember the person's name and other biographical information about them (see Chapter 7) since this information is not 'in' the visual face but is stored in the general memory system.

Within the Gonzalez Rothi et al. (1991) model (see Figure 5.9), if you are asked to copy someone else's gesture, for example as if using a hammer to put a nail into a wall, this gesture is processed through the visual gestural system. Alternatively, if you are look-ing for a hammer to use, this is recognised through the object recognition system. Both of these routes then send information to the 'action input lexicon' which is where the visuokinesthetic engrams will be stored. If a programme exists for the action that is being performed by someone else, then this programme will be activated. Similarly, if there is a programme that is linked to the visual object that has just been recognised, the same programme can be activated. In a healthy brain, this information (stored in the parietal lobes) connects with the 'action output lexicon' and then to the motor systems that allow you to copy the other person's gesture or to use the hammer that you have just found.

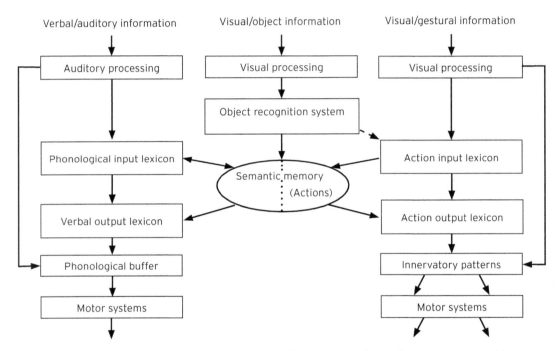

Figure 5.9 Cognitive model of limb apraxia (Gonzalez Rothi et al., 1991. Reprinted by permission of Taylor and Francis Ltd)

Apraxia can occur in at least two ways within this system. If the engrams in the action input lexicon are damaged then the patient will have difficulty performing gestures or even to discriminate between two gestures such as brushing teeth or flipping a coin. This is because the programmes for recognising the gestures in the action input lexicon are damaged and so the gestures that someone else is performing cannot be recognised. However, even if the engrams are intact, if the *link* which transfers the programme to the motor areas is broken (for example, the fibres connecting a particular part of the parietal lobes to the motor cortex), then it will be difficult for this patient to perform the gestures. However, since the programmes are intact, it *will* be possible for this second patient, unlike the first one, to discriminate between correctly and incorrectly performed gestures that *someone else* is performing. This is a nice example of how by comparing two patients and seeing what is common and also what is different between their abilities, it is possible to build up sections of a cognitive model to explain the steps in the processing of information. Then, as in the example above, it is possible to explain how the types of errors that a patient makes will depend on whether particular stores of information (such as the engrams) are destroyed by the brain damage, or whether the difficulty is that two parts of the system have become 'disconnected' from one another.

Chapter Summary

- Movement disorders can occur that are not due to peripheral nerve damage or damage to the motor strip that controls our ability to move our bodies; instead the movement disorder can occur at a cognitive level and is known as apraxia.
- Apraxia is not well understood and not researched as much as many of the other neuropsychological conditions; this may be because it is not easy to diagnose since it may initially just appear as if the patient is clumsy. Also, the disorders can sometimes be missed because of the presence of other more obvious disorders such as visual neglect and language difficulties. However, research shows that the presence of apraxia is strongly linked to everyday functioning and ability to return to work; therefore more research is necessary.
- The early taxonomy suggested a difference between the programming of the fine-tuned movements for handling objects (ideomotor apraxia) and the actual conceptual understanding of the movements themselves (ideational apraxia). There are other sub-types as well but there isn't full agreement on a taxonomy.
- The neuroanatomy of apraxia is complex because of the need to isolate the deficit; research points to the left parietal and posterior regions of the left frontal lobes as being central to movement planning.
- The most developed cognitive model of apraxia comes from Heilman and colleagues which involves motor programmes within the left parietal and frontal areas that are crucial for the smooth execution of movement.

Important Researcher: Kenneth Heilman

Kenneth Heilman is an American behavioural neurologist considered one of the fathers of modern-day neurology. His main contribution has been to the fields of visuospatial neglect and apraxia; he has developed influential models both for how we pay attention to the two halves of the visual world *unequally*, which explains why right hemisphere brain damage disproportionately affects patients, as well as a model to explain how we use motor programmes for the manipulation of objects. His work has influenced generations of neurologists and neuropsychologists in the States. A mark of his influence on the field is that he has written or edited 20 books, more than 115 chapters and more than a staggering 670 journal publications, with over 60,000 citations to his work.

Questions for Reflection

- Why from an evolutionary perspective does it make sense that the brain developed a system for storing information on how to manipulate tools and objects?
- What are the different components in the journey to understanding the anatomical basis of motor planning?

Go Further

- Apraxia encompasses more than simply ideational and ideomotor apraxia; explore what other forms there may be.
- Why might it be that patients have more problems when describing the movements or mimicking their use than when they can actually hold the object and use it?

Further Reading

- Park, J. E. (2017). Apraxia: review and update. *Journal of Clinical Neurology, 13*(4), 317-324.

6
VISUAL AGNOSIA & OBJECT RECOGNITION

Chapter Overview

This chapter will explore how information that is initially taken in through our eyes is processed through ever increasingly complex processes that make sense of what is seen to allow us to visually recognise what is in front of us, linking it with previous experience. This will demonstrate that object recognition is a very complex process that proceeds through a number of hierarchical steps and interacts with other aspects of the cognitive system such as memory and language.

Chapter Outline

- Introduction
- What Information Is Required in Visual Recognition?
- How Valid Is Lissauer's Dichotomy?
- What Is the Impairment in the Unusual Views Test?
- Is Perception Really Intact in Associative Agnosia?
- Chapter Summary

INTRODUCTION

When you see a banana, hear a cat meowing or a taste a nice wine or beer, how do you 'know' what it is that you are experiencing? This experience of 'knowing' is referred to as recognition and cognitive psychologists study different aspects of this process to understand how we experience the world. Many questions can arise during the process of recognition, and researchers endeavour to address these in systematic investigations. First, can your cognitive system even process the sight of the banana, the sound of the cat or the taste of the wine to a level that allows you to know that you have come across this before? Even if your sensory systems are able to do this, how can you *demonstrate* that you know what you are experiencing? If you were to draw the banana does that show you know what it is? Is miming how you peel a banana sufficient? Or what about being able to give a verbal definition of what a banana is to show your understanding? Or does recognition necessitate being able to say the word 'banana' when shown a slim curved yellow fruit? Finally, how are these processes affected by the sensory modality (visual, tactile, gustatory, olfactory or auditory) that is receiving the information? If you see something visually, could that be different from feeling it by hand, smelling it by your nose, tasting it with your tongue or even hearing it? So input modality may have an impact. Is a verbal response *necessary* to demonstrate understanding? What about miming how to use it or making an appropriate sound (e.g. pretending to bark to show that you understand what the cartoon of a dog is)? So output modality may have an effect.

Of course, it is immediately apparent that for some classes of information some of these senses will be more important than others; so for example, the 'sound of a banana' is not used often to recognise it and similarly the 'taste' of a cat's fur is not the usual way of recognising a household pet! However, these questions already demonstrate that we experience and interact with the world in many complex but quite modality-specific ways.

As a result of the complexity of the questions above and also because of the fact that for human beings, sight is possibly one of the most crucial senses, the visual object recognition system has received proportionately the most interest. This chapter will therefore focus on this vital system whilst acknowledging that other systems are very important. However, very similar parallel questions or issues will apply to each of the other modalities.

WHAT INFORMATION IS REQUIRED IN VISUAL RECOGNITION?

Visual recognition, like most cognitive abilities, happens in a number of stages. These stages involve quite distinct processes and can be affected in isolation as seen in cases of selective brain damage that result in extremely specific problems for the individual. Using the 'jigsaw' method of analysis (Chapter 3), it is possible to eventually piece together what the entire healthy system looks like.

The 'early' parts of the visual system lead from the retina, a photoreceptive screen at the back of the eye, to the back of the brain to the occipital lobes where visual recognition can begin (see Chapter 4 for a description of the early visual pathways including the retina and subsequent pathways). At this point, the information is quite raw and undergoes sensory processing to extract the most basic aspects of the visual image, including colour, detection of edges and movement. However, seeing 'yellowness' or 'curvedness' is not going to be sufficient to recognise the banana. At the next level, the information particularly regarding the edges needs to be 'grouped' so that it can be seen as one entity, and this needs to be combined with the colour (and possibly movement – see later). This process of grouping is known as perception and involves not simply 'seeing' the banana, but instead seeing it as a distinct object separate from all the other fruit in the bowl. Unless you had seen *this exact* banana before, this is a different one and for the sake of economy, the system has developed such that what you

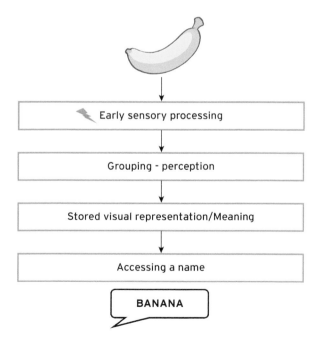

Figure 6.1 A basic model of object recognition taking information processing through a series of steps from initial sensory processing to naming what is seen

are seeing now is linked to a stored visual representation of other similar objects that you have encountered before (you will see this same issue in Chapter 7: Prosopagnosia & Face Processing). Without this facility to link what you are *currently* seeing with what you have *previously* experienced, every time you saw an object, you would need to 'learn' what it was from scratch. Having linked the banana in front of you with a visual representation of similar objects you have seen before, it is now possible to derive an understanding and extract a meaning for your current sensory experience. Finally, having a sense that this is a tropical fruit that has a solid but easy-to-peel skin, you are able to find the name for this object and say the word 'banana'. This series of steps for our basic model is illustrated in Figure 6.1. The remainder of this chapter will illustrate how cognitive neuropsychologists have added support to and then developed this basic model by the careful study of patients with visual recognition problems.

Early Visual Processing

Colour is known to be a specific attribute that is extracted from a visual scene separate from other aspects of information. An impairment in this process can result in a disorder known as achromatopsia and can occur following damage to an area of the occipital lobes known as V4. For example, Sacks & Wasserman (1987) described patient JI who had been involved in a motor vehicle accident. During an eye examination he was unable to distinguish between different colours or different letters, saying 'the letters appeared to be Greek letters. My vision was such that everything appeared to me as viewing a black and white television screen' (p. 2). Following this early problem with the letters, once the brain damage had reduced, he was left with good general visual acuity, seeing shapes and letters without any problem, but had lost the ability to judge colour either visually or even from a mental image. Subsequently, patients with achromotopsia have been documented by Bartolomeo et al. (1997) and von Arx et al. (2010). These patients' difficulty is almost the opposite to that suffered by patient PB (Zeki, 1998), whose brain damage left him virtually blind and he yet could still name colours that were seen or even imagined. The implication of these two very contrasting patterns is that colour is extracted from a visual scene separately from other aspects of information within the scene.

Even if a person can see shapes and colours, this is sometimes not sufficient to visually recognise the world. Patient LM suffered from damage to an area in the occipital lobes known as V5 which didn't affect her ability to judge colour, recognise objects or read. However, she complained of a difficulty in judging motion, saying that, for example, tea being poured into a cup looked like it was frozen in motion which also had the added effect that she couldn't judge when the cup was full because she could not see the level of the tea rising. A stark demonstration of the importance of processing motion for survival is that LM had difficulty in crossing streets with traffic because she could not see the movement of cars. This issue has since been partially replicated in patient WH by Huberle et al. (2012). Again, this impairment in judging motion contrasts with a famous case studied by Humphreys & Riddoch (2013) known as HJA. Unlike LM, HJA had difficulty recognising objects and people but yet he claimed that he could recognise his wife from particular movements and was better at recognising some animals when they were moving than when they were stationary.

In general, the different patterns of impairment and preserved abilities demonstrated by patients such as JI, PB, LM, WH and HJA allow us to develop our model in Figure 6.1 by splitting 'early sensory processing' into at least three parallel processes for extracting colour, movement and shape from a visual scene (see Figure 6.2).

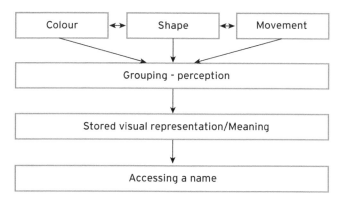

Figure 6.2 The model of object recognition expanded with colour, shape and movement separated

Object Recognition Problems

Following the early sensory stages, the recognition of an object can begin. Our understanding of the later stages has been helped incredibly by the seminal work of a German neurologist known as Heinrich Lissauer in 1888 (translated by Shallice & Jackson, 1988). Lissauer described the case of a patient that he referred to as Gottlieb L who began experiencing visual recognition problems after suffering a head injury when blown against a wooden fence during a heavy storm. Following physical recovery, many of the patient's visual and cognitive functions were left intact. These included general low-level visual abilities, colour naming and categorisation, verbal and numerical skills, visual memory for past events, drawing from memory and copying line drawings. Against this quite normal cognitive background, patient Gottlieb L had very significant difficulties in visually recognising objects. For example, when shown a pair of glasses, he named them as 'a lamp'; however, when he was allowed to touch and handle them, he named them correctly. Importantly, his ability to recognise objects by touch or by sound was also intact; this demonstrates that his object recognition difficulty was limited to the visual realm and was modality-specific.

From his meticulous observations and scientific analysis, Lissauer suggested that there were two major stages in object recognition. The first stage he hypothesised is known as 'apperception' – which involves creating a coherent percept of the object as a single entity –

and the second is known as 'association' – which involves attaching meaning to the percept. Using a German term 'seelenblindheit', meaning 'mindblindness', he then proposed that damage to these two stages resulted in 'apperceptive mindblindness' and 'associative mindblindness' respectively. Combining this with the term 'agnosia', popularised by the founder of psychoanalysis, Freud (1891), which means 'without knowledge', two terms that have endured for over a century were developed: apperceptive agnosia and associative agnosia. The chapter will now turn to the issue of whether this dichotomy suggested by Lissauer is valid and sufficient enough to explain healthy visual object recognition.

Apperceptive Agnosia

A classic case of apperceptive agnosia is patient Mr S described by Benson & Greenberg (1969). Mr S's recognition problems were so severe that he could not perform seemingly simple matching tasks, for example matching a triangle with another from an array of shapes, or copy simple everyday shapes and letters. It is important to note that the patient's visual acuity (which is the ability to distinguish shapes and the details of objects at a given distance), colour vision and other elements of sensory processing were within normal limits so his problem in carrying out these tasks cannot be put down to a problem at that 'early' level. Instead, it seems that following intact sensory analysis, Mr S was unable to group the information together to create a coherent visual image of what he was seeing. To see which of the shapes in the shape-matching test is the same as the target shape such as the triangle, it is necessary to see the triangle as more than just three lines but as having certain orientations relative to one another, certain points of conjunction, etc. Similarly, to copy the letter 'B' it is necessary to see more than two curved lines and one vertical line, but instead to see their orientations relative to one another and copy these accordingly. Without this ability to group the separate elements of the visual input, it will be very difficult to move forward in the recognition system.

During the 1980s, a number of researchers described more patients with similar problems using other tests that required construction of a coherent percept for successful recognition. For example, in Gollin's (1960) Incomplete Pictures Test, a series of degraded drawings is shown with each successive one having more visual information than the previous one (see Figure 6.3). While healthy controls are able to recognise the fish in the example by the second stimulus when there is still relatively little information available, a patient with apperceptive agnosia would need much more information and even then may fail to recognise the object. In the Ghent Overlapping Figures Test (Ghent, 1956), line drawings of a number of fruits are presented so that they are overlapping, and next to this a set of line drawings of fruits are presented separately; the task is for the participant to select which of the fruits are in the overlapped image. To complete this task, it is necessary to see the individual fruit in the overlapped image by separating them out visually from the other confusing information to then decide which of them is in the set of individual items. A patient with apperceptive agnosia would find the 'disambiguation' of the overlapping images difficult and therefore struggle to work out which of the fruits are in the main image.

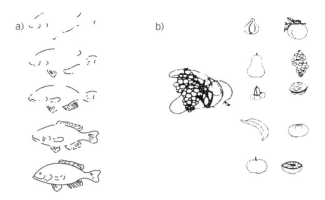

Figure 6.3   a) Gollin's Incomplete Pictures Test; b) Ghent's Overlapping Figures Test (Buttaro, 2018; Ghent, 1956) (Reprinted from Buttaro, M. (2011). "Gollin Figures". In Kreutzer, J.S.; DeLuca, J.; Caplan, B. (eds.). *Encyclopedia of Clinical Neuropsychology*. Springer, New York, NY. p. 1169, with permission)

Warrington & James (1988) developed a further test known as the 'Unusual Views Test' in which everyday common objects are shown from an unconventional angle or a more standard angle. In this test, all of the relevant information for recognition is present in the unconventional image but in order to name it, first of all a coherent image needs to be created and this then needs to be 'rotated' in the mind's eye to match against a more typical view. For example, the sunglasses shown from an obscure angle in Figure 6.4 need to be 'mentally rotated' to the more standard view before they can be recognised. Patients who are unable to do this are also classed as suffering from apperceptive agnosia.

Figure 6.4   Unusual Views Test – standard prototypical view of a pair of sunglasses and an 'unusual' view (adapted from Warrington, 1982)

In summary, apperceptive agnosia is a disorder which leaves an individual's intellectual abilities and visual acuity intact but results in significant impairments in visual recognition. The problem can be traced to difficulties in achieving a coherent percept of what is being seen, and this can be demonstrated by tests requiring copying of line drawings or naming of incomplete drawings and photographs of objects viewed from unusual angles.

Associative Agnosia

It is possible for an individual to have intact intellect and visual acuity, who can copy line drawings and who *passes* perceptual tests such as the Incomplete Pictures and the Unusual Views Test, but who nonetheless is unable to recognise objects; such an individual would be said to be suffering from associative agnosia. For example, Newcombe & Ratcliffe (1974) studied a patient MS who had suffered brain damage following a febrile illness and found that his copies of line drawings were very good reproductions of the original targets and were also easily recognisable for what they represented. However, faithful though his reproductions were, MS had significant problems naming the line drawings, only being able to name eight out of a set of 32 that he was shown *including* one that he was able to copy very well; according to Teuber, such patients experienced 'a normal percept, stripped of its meaning' (1968, cited in Farah, 2000a, p. 93).

One way of trying to conceptualise this is by looking at Figure 6.5. You would probably be able to describe visually and copy this figure without any problem. However, the object will probably not hold any meaning for you (it is in fact a 'greeble' which is part of a 'family' of individual characters artificially created by Gauthier & Tarr (1997) studying particular aspects of face recognition).

Figure 6.5   Example of a greeble (Gauthier & Tarr, 1997. Reprinted with permission from Elsevier)

Another classic example of an associative agnosic is patient FL who had suffered from cerebral atrophy probably due to alcoholism (Taylor & Warrington, 1971). On formal testing, his intellect and visual acuity seemed preserved and he passed a variety of perceptual tests such as copying line drawings, picking out two identical objects from an array and the Unusual Views Test; therefore, by passing these standard tests of perception, FL would not be classed as having apperceptive agnosia. However, when presented with 12 everyday objects, he was only able to name two of them. Taylor & Warrington found that as well as not being able to name the objects, FL also didn't seem to 'understand' them. For example, when he was given a key, he didn't know what to do with it and when taken outside while it was raining, he didn't know what to do with an umbrella that was closed. To formally test their intuition that the patient had difficulty understanding the *meaning* of objects, Warrington (1982) developed a test known as the 'Matching by Function Test' (see Figure 6.6).

Figure 6.6   Warrington's (1982) Matching by Function Test; the participant has to decide which of the upper two images is the same object as the one in the lower image, something that cannot be done simply through perceptual information but through understanding what the object represents.

Here, two visually dissimilar objects, such as a walking cane and an open umbrella, are presented above a third object (a closed umbrella) that visually resembles one of them but is functionally the same as the other. The participant has to decide which of the first two items serves the same function as the third. If the decision is being made purely on visual similarity, then the choice would be the walking cane whereas if the patient 'understood' what the object was (without needing to even name it), then the choice would be the open umbrella. On this test, FL scored 9 out of 20 which is below chance, which suggests that he could not extract the meaning of the objects. This is the classic interpretation of associative agnosia; despite intact perceptual abilities, the individual is unable to attach meaning to what they see and it is this that impairs their ability to recognise and name once-common objects.

Summary of Lissauer's Classic Model of Object Recognition

From the above discussion, it is possible to see that visual perception proceeds via a number of different processes that take information gathered by the retina and then in a series of successive stages attempts to link it with existing stored knowledge. One of the most influential theories of recognition proposed by Lissauer (1888) suggests that once initial sensory analysis is complete, there are two distinct stages, and damage to either one of these can result in object recognition impairments. Apperceptive agnosia results from difficulties in achieving a coherent internal representation of each object, known as a percept, from the information provided by earlier intact sensory stages. Associative agnosia on the other hand results from difficulties in deriving meaning from the coherent percept produced by earlier sensory and perceptual levels (Figure 6.7).

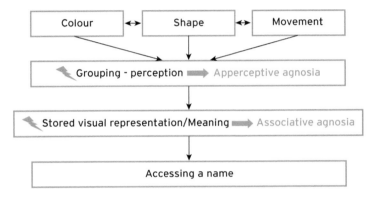

Figure 6.7   Expanding the model with breakdown at different levels resulting in apperceptive and associative agnosia

HOW VALID IS LISSAUER'S DICHOTOMY?

The above discussion has shown that Lissauer's original dichotomy between two main stages of visual object recognition is generally supported by the evidence from patients with specific forms of brain damage. Whilst at an initial level, this dichotomy is extremely useful, there are a number of reasons for questioning this strict two-stage model. These are:

1   Fractionations within apperceptive agnosia.
2   The usefulness of the Unusual Views Test for helping to understand the stages involved in object recognition.
3   The validity of the claim that perception is intact in associative agnosia.
4   Fractionations within associative agnosia.

By exploring these issues it will become possible to develop the model of object recognition further.

Fractionations Within Apperceptive Agnosia

An assumption made by the simple two-stage model is that the perceptual stage is one distinct stage; and therefore the prediction is that all patients should pass or fail the *same* tests. However, Kartsounis & Warrington (1991) have shown that this may be oversimplified. Their patient (FRG), who had suffered from partial cortical blindness attributable to cortical degeneration, passed all standard tests of visual acuity and shape discrimination implying that his initial sensory abilities were intact. However, he could not do 'figure/ground segmentation' which requires the ability to see some level of three-dimensionality in a simple line drawing. For example, in Figure 6.8, there is an impression of a 'see-through' triangle in front of a rectangle. FRG described this as 'a triangle in the middle and a straight line across the top' (Kartsounis & Warringon, 1991, p. 475). This contrasts with groups of right hemisphere patients who can visually segment such diagrams but fail the standard Unusual Views Test. Since both the figure/ground segmentation and matching of unusual views would be considered to be perceptual tasks, the fact that there is a dissociation in performance by different patients between the tasks implies that the perceptual stage is more than a single unitary stage.

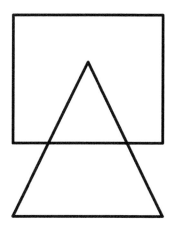

Figure 6.8   Figure/ground segmentation from Kartsounis & Warrington (1991) (Reprinted with permission from Elsevier)

The Unusual Views Test

While the Unusual Views Test has proven to be very useful in demonstrating the problems of some patients, the utility of the test for 'diagnosing' apperceptive agnosia has been questioned for two reasons. The first is the generalisability of Warrington & Taylor's (1973) original findings, and the second is the theoretical explanation that is suggested for the observed impairment.

How Generalisable Are the Findings from the Test?

Farah (2000b) has criticised the findings from Warrington & Taylor's (1973) highly influential study for three reasons. First, she claims that many patients who fail this test don't have recognition problems in everyday life and only show impairments in this artificial laboratory task. As a diagnostic tool it therefore does not predict how patients are performing in the real world. This suggests that the test might lack ecological validity which refers to the correspondence between performance on a test in the clinic and what happens in the real world (see Chapter 9 on Executive Functions for a further explanation of this important concept). Second, Farah questioned how the patients who have problems in matching *unusual* views perform on matching *different* views of the objects. She said that even healthy controls take longer to identify objects from unusual views and therefore it is possible that the Unusual Views Test is simply picking up a generic 'visual problem solving' issue rather than a specific visual recognition one. Finally, from an anatomical perspective, she has questioned whether Warrington & Taylor's (1973) participants are representative of patients with object recognition problems. The patients in their 1973 study had largely parietal lobe lesions whereas more recent work using neuroimaging has strongly suggested that object recognition occurs along more ventral pathways in the brain (those that run along the base of the brain) involving the occipital and temporal lobes. As is obvious, this issue is complex and the debate is not yet resolved.

WHAT IS THE IMPAIRMENT IN THE UNUSUAL VIEWS TEST?

Even if it is agreed that the Unusual Views Test *is* tapping something important within the object recognition system, there has been some debate on what that actual ability is. Warrington & Taylor (1973) suggested that most objects have distinctive features that are used in recognising them; for example, the prongs of a fork are very distinctive and important in recognising examples of this item. According to the 'distinctive features' account, unusual or rotated views minimise or obscure the features that are visible, thereby impairing successful recognition.

An alternative account is based on a model that is derived from computational modelling of vision rather than cognitive neuropsychology. David Marr's influential work (e.g. Marr, 1976; Marr & Nishihara, 1978) was based on trying to work out the different levels of computations that would be required for a machine to recognise an object. The model was very complex and beyond the scope of what is possible to describe here, but at the heart of it were a number of stages that corresponded to different levels of visual processing (see Figure 6.9 for a very simplified version). The first stage of the model involved the creation of what is known as a 'Raw Primal Sketch' by the extraction of low-level information about edges of objects, bars of continuous light, conjunctions of edges, etc. This raw information was then further processed to what was known as the '2½D sketch' by deriving depth cues, segmenting the foreground from the background, etc. This was known as the 2½D sketch because it was based on only one perspective, the one that the viewer was observing from; Warrington & Taylor later referred to this as the 'viewer-centred representation' since the only information that can be used to recognise this object depends on the angle from which it is viewed. The next stage in Marr's model was the full '3D sketch' which was derived by accessing a *previously stored* three-dimensional description that matched the 2½D sketch. Warrington & Taylor (1973) referred to this as the 'object-centred representation' since this image does not depend on the angle that the object is being viewed from. You will see in Chapter 7 on Face Processing that there is an analogous process whereby some patients have difficulty in seeing that two different images of a face taken from different angles are of the same person.

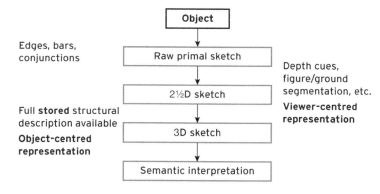

Figure 6.9   Marr's model of vision (1976)

One of the critical aspects of Marr's model is the transformation from the 2½D to 3D sketch. This requires assigning what is known as a 'principal axis' to the 2½D sketch and refers to a plane of symmetry which is usually the longest axis of an object. For example, when viewing a chair from the front, this would be down the middle of the chair from top to bottom. If this principal axis can be 'extracted' from the 2½D sketch then an *internal transformation or rotation* is possible which allows the system to match what is seen in a 3D image *already stored* in the system. This latter 3D image will have been stored from all previous experiences of that class of objects, and the goal of visual recognition is to match the *current* experience with something that has been processed, understood and stored in the past. Within Marr's model of vision, these images are all stored independent of the observer's perspective and can be rotated in three dimensions in the mind's eye; this makes the transformation from the 2½D to 3D sketch crucial for successful object recognition. Once the 3D sketch has been accessed, the final stages within the model involve accessing semantic information about the image (e.g. man-made object, used for sitting on, usually has a back and four legs) and then a name (e.g. chair).

The above series of steps allow successful recognition if the principal axis can be derived for an object. However, it is suggested that when an object is viewed from an unusual viewpoint, this becomes more difficult. For example, in Figure 6.4, it is more difficult to work out the axis of symmetry in the lower image than in the upper image. The impact of this is that it is easier to rotate the upper image to match a stored 3D image than performing the same transformation on the lower one, making recognition of the former as a pair of sunglasses more straightforward. The importance of this formulation is that, using the neuropsychological data (e.g. Warrington & Taylor, 1973) that a class of right hemisphere patients has significant difficulties with the Unusual Views Test, it is suggested that the main cognitive impact of this form of brain damage is impairing the ability to derive the axis to allow the necessary mental rotation to occur.

Therefore, two quite different accounts have been put forward for the failure of some patients on the Unusual Views Test, one based on distinctive features having become obscured and the other on the impact of mental rotation. To resolve this debate, Humphreys & Riddoch (1984) attempted to evaluate which of these two stances was correct. Their rationale was that if distinctive features are more important, manipulating the extent to which these are minimised should systematically affect recognition; therefore, if these are more difficult to see, then it will make recognition more difficult. If, however, the principal axis is important, then manipulating the ease with which this can be derived will impact recognition abilities. Their study involved a three-item matching task and the participant simply had to say which of two test items was the same as a target item that was presented above them. In the 'minimal feature' condition, the axis of symmetry was kept constant while the main features in one of the two target images were obscured. Therefore, in Figure 6.10a, the upper cue image is a saw shown from a standard view. Its principal axis of symmetry is in the plane of the page. The correct target item is the lower right one which has maintained the same principal axis but which has obscured the distinctive teeth of the saw. The other condition was known as the 'foreshortened' condition in which the perspective was manipulated; the result was that while an important feature was still visible, the axis of symmetry had been changed. Therefore, in the example in Figure 6.10b, the upper image's distinctive feature is the twisted end section which is clearly visible in the lower right target item. However, it is not possible to rotate around the axis of symmetry of the target item because it has been 'foreshortened' and is not the longest axis as seen in the upper cue item.

Humphreys & Riddoch (1984) compared the performance of five patients with right hemisphere damage with their classic patient HJA (see below) who had suffered bilateral occipital lobe damage. Their results were rather surprising: whereas the right hemisphere patients found the foreshortened condition difficult (similar to Warrington &

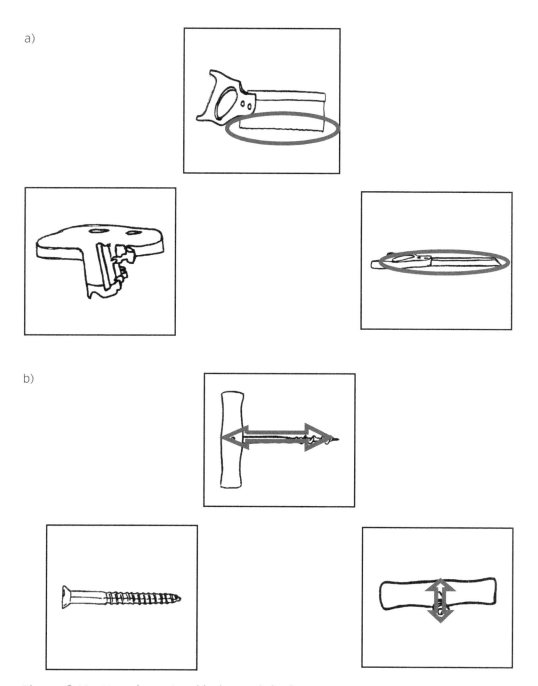

Figure 6.10 Humphreys & Riddoch stimuli for features versus axes (1984): a) the 'minimal features' condition, and b) the 'foreshortened' condition.

Taylor's (1973) study) without any problem with the minimal feature condition, HJA's performance was the opposite. As long as featural information was present, he had no difficulties with the mental rotations required in the foreshortened condition but he had great difficulties in the minimal features condition. From this converse pattern of findings, Humphreys & Riddoch (1984) concluded that *both* distinctive features and what they referred to as 'view normalisation' are required for successful object recognition. This was later incorporated into their model of visual object recognition, but for now, it is possible to further develop our model from Figure 6.7 to accommodate these findings (see Figure 6.11). Within this model, distinctive features as suggested by Warrington and colleagues are important at the perceptual level to allow access to the stored visual representations. HJA's brain damage seemed to impact his ability to find these in objects, thereby contributing to his severe object agnosia. A further stage of mentally rotating or normalising the view created by the perceptual stage is required if an object is seen from an unusual angle. Right hemisphere damage seems to impact this ability resulting in difficulty accessing the higher level information about the object that is currently being viewed.

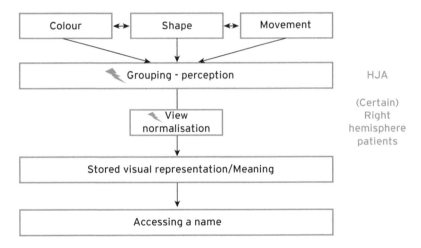

Figure 6.11   The model expanded to incorporate the Humphreys & Riddoch (1984) findings of view normalisation to accommodate the difficulties of patient HJA and certain right hemisphere patients

IS PERCEPTION REALLY INTACT IN ASSOCIATIVE AGNOSIA?

According to earlier views, if a patient passes the standard tests of visual perception but has difficulty recognising objects, they should be classified as having associative agnosia. But the suggestion that passing these standard tests implies intact perception has been questioned for a number of reasons.

Type of Visual Input Affects Recognition

Banich (2004) points out that the *type* of visual input to a patient's system can have an impact on their recognition. According to her, clinically, patients show a hierarchy of difficulty such that line drawings prove most problematic, colour photographs less so and real objects even less so. If patients with associative agnosia have intact perception, this difference as a function of input should not occur. However, since across these three types of input there is increasing perceptual information (colour, depth, three-dimensionality, etc.), the implication is that the patients *are* experiencing some level of perceptual impairment. This issue is a difficult one to resolve, however, because it could be argued that these patients should not have been categorised as suffering from associative agnosia in the first place. Farah (2004) has pointed out that terms such as apperceptive and associative agnosia can be used at a clinical level to describe particular patterns of performance or more rigidly when attempting to incorporate findings into a theoretical framework.

Method of Performance on Apperceptive Tests Can Be Abnormal

One argument used above is that if a patient such as MS (Newcombe & Ratcliffe, 1974) can copy line drawings well, then their perceptual abilities must be intact. However, just because someone's 'final performance' looks good, does that necessarily mean that the *method* that they used is normal? It is therefore sometimes important to look at a number of other aspects of performance apart from just the final performance. This can include the amount of time it took to complete the task, the strategy that the individual used, etc.

Figure 6.12 HJA's line drawings of St Paul's Cathedral and three everyday objects (Humphreys & Riddoch, 2013) (Copyright (1987) from To see but not to see: a case study of visual agnosia by Humphreys, Glyn W. Reproduced by permission of Taylor and Francis Group, LLC, a division of Informa plc)

A classic example is the case of HJA who has been mentioned a number of times. In their very detailed analysis of HJA's visual recognition problems following a bilateral occipital lobe stroke, Humphreys & Riddoch (2013) show examples of HJA's copies of an etching of St Paul's Cathedral in London and three everyday objects (Figure 6.12). The copies of the line drawings are extremely good and yet HJA was unable to name any of these items; this pattern of performance would ordinarily categorise his deficit as associative agnosia.

However, the copy of the etching of St Paul's Cathedral, while excellent, took him six hours to complete! Also, whereas normal drawing of such an image would usually involve drawing the overall outer shapes and then filling in the smaller detail, HJA drew using a slavish line-by-line method. He concentrated on a small section of each image that he was copying and faithfully reproduced that portion before moving onto another part of the same image. Both the time that it took and more importantly the manner in which he drew suggest that, in fact, HJA was not perceiving the world normally. The implication of this is that a diagnosis based on passing standard tests of apperceptive agnosia (e.g. in this case whether an individual can copy a line drawing) might be a bit simplistic and calls into question the sharp boundary between the two major forms of agnosia originally suggested by Lissauer (Figure 6.7).

If tests of perception imply that neither apperceptive nor associative agnosia can adequately explain HJA's impairment, what form of visual recognition problem did he have? From his slow slavish line-by-line drawing it is obvious that HJA could see the individual elements of objects. Also, the way that he did not actually copy the overall outer shape of an object before filling in the details begs the question of how he was perceiving the *global*

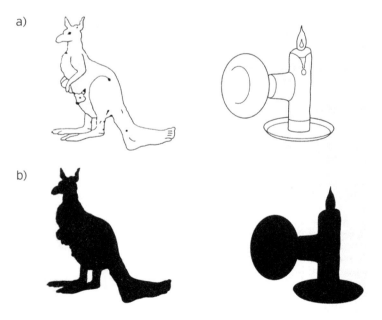

Figure 6.13   Object Decision Task (Humphreys & Riddoch, 2013): a) Line drawings; b) Silhouettes (Reprinted with permission from Oxford University Press)

form of objects. To assess this, Humphreys & Riddoch (2013) created an 'Object Decision Task' in which participants were presented drawings of objects half of which were created by combining elements of two 'real' objects to create a 'non-object'. For example, in Figure 6.13, one non-object has been created by combining the head and body of a kangaroo with a human foot while the other is a door-knob attached to a candle.

Participants were presented the real objects and non-objects in two conditions, as full line drawings (Figure 6.13a) and also as silhouettes (Figure 6.13b); the task was simply to decide whether the image was or was not of a real object. The results showed that while healthy controls found the decision easier for the line drawings than the silhouettes, HJA showed the reverse pattern – he found it more difficult to make judgments on the full line drawings than the silhouettes. Humphreys & Riddoch (2013) interpreted this set of results by saying that drawings have local features that *individually* make sense since they are part of real objects. Therefore, the head, body, front arms and long flat back legs all look appropriate for a particular animal, in this case a kangaroo, whilst the part of the foot in Figure 6.13a also looks appropriate for a human foot. The fact that HJA found the line drawings more difficult suggests that he was basing his decisions on local information to interpret the world – he saw parts of an animal that make sense and, as he moved around the drawing, he eventually also saw the foot which itself belongs to a real object as well, with the result that he classified some of the non-objects as real objects. Silhouettes, on the other hand, don't have the local information so the decision had to be made on the overall shape. In HJA's case, there were no local features to distract him and at some level, he must have had enough overall global knowledge of what a kangaroo or a candle look like to work out whether or not the silhouettes conform to these representations. The fact that his *stored representations* of objects were intact was seen by the fact that his drawings from memory of everyday objects were extremely accurate.

The intriguing set of results from the Object Decision Task led Humphreys & Riddoch (2013) to propose that at the level of perception, there have to be at least two separate processes. The first of these establishes the global form of a stimulus and this corresponds to the 'Grouping' in Figure 6.11; it seems that HJA does not have problems at this level. The next stage involves individual internal features being 'bound' together into an integrated whole – without this process, it is not possible to match against stored representations within the system. HJA's deficit was at this level, and this resulted in the slavish line-by-line drawings in Figure 6.12 since he was not able to integrate the information he saw into a coherent whole to draw the outer shapes first before filling in the smaller detail. Similarly, in the Object Decision Task, the two halves of each of the non-objects are 'real' in themselves, and since he is not able to integrate these into a coherent whole, he performs badly. Humphreys & Riddoch (2013) therefore suggested that HJA suffered from a particular perceptual problem that they termed integrative agnosia. This form of agnosia has since been replicated by Butter & Trobe (1994) with their patient SM. By incorporating this into the model from Figure 6.11, we therefore arrive at a more comprehensive model (Figure 6.14).

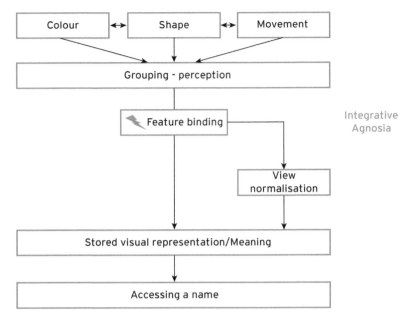

Figure 6.14　Developing the model further to incorporate integrative agnosia

Fractionations Within Associative Agnosia

Following successful completion of the various stages of perception above, is recognition guaranteed? Again, here we find that the system is more complex than originally proposed (e.g. Figure 6.7). Two relevant issues are:

1　Are visual structure and meaning of an object separate?
2　Is our knowledge of all classes of information held together or are different categories of objects processed differentially?

Visual Structure Versus Meaning

A possible definition of associative agnosia would be the ability to pass all the standard tests of perception (copying, drawing, unusual views, etc.) but failure to recognise visually. A patient with this problem would also be bad at *miming* the use of the object; for example, when shown an intact banana, not being able to mime peeling the skin before eating it. This shows that the deficit is in *visual* recognition. However, some patients can demonstrate their understanding of the object if they process it through another modality, for example, if given it in their hands to feel through tactile perception. Presumably, from an evolutionary perspective, it would make sense if the different types of information about the world were stored in a coherent fashion so that the sight, smell and taste of a banana were held together. This would mean that seeing a banana might prepare biological processes to get ready for the taste of one, or the sound of a lion might conjure up the sight of one and what the consequences would be of running into one. From this line of reasoning, if, as has been demonstrated, for some patients it is possible to recognise the object through one system (the tactile one) but not another (the visual one in this case) then the implication is that information being conveyed by each of these sensory modalities must be separate from the system that understands that information. The latter system is known as the semantic system, and patients who are unable to recognise an object visually but can do so through tactile perception must have a deficit at a stage preceding this system; this is because the semantic system itself must be intact if it is possible to access information within it through touch, taste, etc. This system is known as the structural description system which holds a visual representation of all objects and roughly corresponds to the 3D sketch in Marr's model of vision (Figure 6.9). The existence of this system is demonstrated quite clearly when comparing HJA with another patient, Dennis, also studied by Riddoch & Humphreys (1993). Both had severe object recognition difficulties but both could *copy* line drawings well implying intact perceptual stages. However, whereas HJA could draw very well *from memory*, Dennis had significant problems. While his *copies* of a giraffe and penguin were easily recognisable for what they were, his *drawings from memory* of a giraffe and owl held almost no resemblance at all to reality.

From these contrasting abilities, it seems that HJA has intact internal representations that allow him to draw from memory very well; his difficulty is in accessing these representations due to the problems at earlier stages centring mainly around the binding of individual features. Dennis on the other hand passes all the perceptual tests since for him all these levels seem intact, but his internal representations for objects seem to be severely damaged. The result is that however good the visual input is, for example from a picture of a cat, since his internal representation of cats is damaged, a match cannot occur and he has difficulty naming the animal. When you see a cup, the perceptual stages process this information to arrive at a coherent image and this needs to be matched against the stored representations within this structural description system to allow successful visual recognition.

In the case of visual object agnosia, the central semantic system is usually intact, but in other forms of cognitive deficit, it can become progressively impaired. For example, in semantic dementia, which is usually associated with ageing, individuals slowly lose their understanding of common objects. This degradation is not due to problems in the visual recognition system, as discussed above, but due to more central processes related to the semantic system itself.

Is There Just One Semantic System or Are There Many?

In the 1980s and 1990s, as patients with different levels of object recognition difficulties were being documented, groups of researchers, first of all in the UK and then in Europe and the US, started documenting how patients with agnosia were showing differential problems depending on the semantic category that the object belonged to. The seminal study in the field was by Elizabeth Warrington and Tim Shallice in London, who studied four patients who had all suffered brain damage from herpes simplex encephalitis (HSE). They found that all of these patients were fine at naming photographs of non-living objects (and body parts) but had great difficulties identifying the photographs of living things (Warrington & Shallice, 1984). The most striking case was patient JBR who was able to identify 90% of non-living objects but only 6% of living things; as an example, his description of a photograph of a compass was 'tools for telling direction you are going in', while for a photo of a snail he offered 'an insect animal' and for a parrot simply 'don't know' (Warrington & Shallice, 1984, p. 838).

This has been replicated in a large number of studies with a number of different patients, and the results suggest that even if there is a stage of stored visual representations (see Figure 6.14), it must be more complex than a single generic associative stage as originally suggested by Lissauer. A single stage would make it difficult to explain why these patients had more difficulties with some aspects of recognition than others. The implication of this was that the semantic system was differentiated along categorical lines with the biggest distinction being between living and non-living things; if there were *at least* two different semantic systems, then it would be possible for patients like JBR's brain damage to severely affect the functioning of the one specialised for recognition of living things but leaving visual processing of non-living things unaffected.

Although there were a number of studies from different researchers around the world, including a patient with a very specific difficulty with fruits and vegetables (Sartori & Job, 1988) replicating these findings, during the early 90s, there were a number of studies that argued that what was seen in these studies was an 'artefact'; in other words, that although the patients may have performed better on one category than another, this was caused by other simpler factors rather than because of a complex semantic system. Funnell & Sheridan (1992) worked with a patient who, following a road accident, had an impaired semantic memory. In their first experiment, they saw that when the patient was asked to name photos or define words, she showed a category-specific impairment, but also that there was an effect of how familiar she had been with specific items. This is important because if you are not familiar with an aardvark, seeing a photo of this animal would mean that you would not be able to name it; this would not be because you have a recognition problem but because you don't often see this animal in your everyday life. In their second experiment, they ensured that the photographs used in both categories were of similar familiarity so if they had some highly unfamiliar items in one category, they made sure that there were equally unfamiliar photos in the other. When they did this, they found no difference in recognition between the two categories. Their conclusion was that the reason that the earlier studies had found the category-specific finding was simply an artefact of not controlling for familiarity of test items.

In a similar vein, Stewart et al. (1992) tested a patient who like JBR had survived HSE. While the patient initially showed a category-specific effect similar to JBR, they argued that objects from the living world tend to be more visually complex than those from the non-living world. Therefore, for example, there is more visual complexity when looking at an elephant than when looking at a chair. In addition, similar to the thinking of Funnell & Sheridan (1992), they decided to make sure that the names of the items were similar in terms of familiarity – again, 'aardvark' is less often used than 'chair' in the English language. It is possible to work out the word frequency of a word which is a measure of how often a particular word is used in a language; a word such as 'chair' would have a high frequency whereas 'aardvark' would have a much lower one. Stewart et al. (1992) therefore did control for visual complexity and word frequency in addition to visual familiarity, and found that the category-specific effect in their patient disappeared.

Therefore, the results of a few studies which controlled for important experimental variables such as word frequency and visual familiarity and complexity seemed to suggest that the findings during the 1980s were simply an artefact of the testing methods and procedures. However, this argument was greatly weakened when the case of CW was documented by Sacchett & Humphreys (1992), who presented with the *opposite*

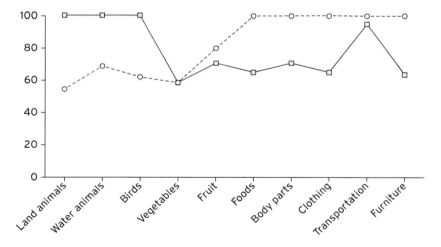

Figure 6.15 Performance accuracy on an object recognition task demonstrating a double dissociation between two patients on recognition of living and non-living things on the same stimuli studied by Hillis & Caramazza (1991) (Reprinted from Hillis, Argyle E., & Caramazza, Alfonso (1991) Category-specific naming and comprehension impairment: A double dissociation. *Brain*, 114 (5), 2081–2094 by permission of Oxford University Press)

difficulty to patient JBR and those who had been documented by researchers, arguing that the category-specific deficit was an artefact. CW had greater difficulty naming non-living objects and body parts but was unimpaired on naming living things. It is important to note that this double dissociation is specific down to the inclusion of body parts – JBR was poor at living things *apart from body parts* while CW was poor at non-living things *and body parts*. It could be argued that CW was tested by different people in a different lab at a different time to JBR and therefore there are various difficulties to suggesting that this is a full double dissociation. However, this argument is weakened by the fact that Hillis & Caramazza (1991) demonstrated a double dissociation on two of their patients who were tested using the same stimuli (see Figure 6.15).

Beyond Category Specificity

While the debate on whether the semantic system was categorically specific has continued, a number of studies have revealed even more complex dimensions! For example, McCarthy & Warrington (1988) reported the case of patient TOB had no problems with identifying non-living things from either pictures or words; however, while TOB had difficulty identifying living things from words, he was fine at identifying the same objects from pictures. From this work, they argued that the semantic system must be modality-specific to some degree to allow such a pattern of results.

It is possible to argue that a photograph of an object is always going to be easier to recognise than a word which is, after all, just a 'code' to represent that object – so seeing a cat gives you sensory information about the cat in a way that seeing the letters C-A-T doesn't. However, McCarthy & Warrington (1986) and Warrington & McCarthy (1994) documented two patients (FRA and DRS respectively) who showed intact understanding of objects when given either a word or a description of it; by contrast, both were bad at naming the visual objects. Even when they were asked to mime information about the object in case the issue was simply related to word-finding, they had difficulties, therefore suggesting that there was a modality-specific issue. Neither FRA nor DRS showed signs of having apperceptive agnosia so a deficit at a more basic visual level could be ruled out.

Overall Evaluation

Overall, it is obvious that the recognition of objects is a very complex process which clearly happens in a number of stages. While Lissauer suggested that there were two main stages, it has become clear that there are more. In addition, it seems that there are some stages which might involve parallel processes that result in the double dissociation that Humphreys & Riddoch (1984) found with the Unusual Views Test and the various dissociations found both at the level of category-specificity and modality-specificity. However, it is difficult to derive a universally accepted model for a number of reasons. Part of this is because there are few standardised tests in the field, although the Birmingham Object Recognition Battery (BORB: Riddoch & Humphreys, 1993) was a good step in the right direction. Such tests can mean that all researchers are 'speaking the same language' when they describe the deficits of their patients. However, as research in the general field of object recognition in healthy individuals has moved on substantially since the BORB was published, there will be factors that it does not include. A further issue is the rarity of patients with selective agnosia; as with face-recognition disorders, compared to some of the more common deficits (such as with language or memory), it is only when researchers who are well versed in a field come across appropriate patients that it is possible to move the field forward. However, as has been seen with the initial documentation by Lissauer and then the work by Warrington and her colleagues followed by the next generation of researchers, this field is advancing slowly but surely.

Chapter Summary

- Object recognition is a very complex process that occurs by information being processed through successive stages. The initial stages involve analysis *in parallel* of colour, shape and movement; we know that these forms of information are processed in parallel because each of these attributes can be affected *selectively* leaving the others intact.
- Following this initial analysis, there are a number of *sequential* stages. Lissauer (1888) created a two-stage model involving creating an internal percept of what is being looked at followed by associating meaning to this. This model was backed by seeing the pattern of patients with different types of brain damage using tests that involve perception or understanding the meaning or use of an object.
- Since the mid-1980s, fine-grained analysis of some patients' impairments has revealed that the two-stage model was perhaps too simplistic. Since then, to accommodate these findings, more refined models have been developed.
- Due to the rarity of sufficient cases of selective object agnosia that can be studied in detail there is still no full consensus on a comprehensive model.

Important Researcher

Elizabeth Warrington

Elizabeth Warrington is one of the most important neuropsychologists in the world, whose paper with Tim Shallice in 1970 on a patient with a selective short-term memory deficit (see Chapter 8) was one of the foundation stones for the birth of cognitive neuropsychology. As Head of the Department of Neuropsychology at the world famous National Hospital for Neurology and Neurosurgery in London, Elizabeth has had a profound impact on international neuropsychology. Her collaborations with Tim Shallice, Alan Baddeley and Rosaleen McCarthy on a wide variety of areas, but particularly memory and conceptual understanding such as object recognition, have been the stuff of textbooks for decades. Her work on patient JBR and other patients with herpes simplex encephalitis opened up a whole debate on the structure of the semantic system. Related to this, one of her main interests has been dementia and, in 1975, she identified and codified a new form, semantic dementia.

Important Study

HJA (Humphreys & Riddoch, 2013)

HJA was a remarkable patient that Glyn Humphreys and Jane Riddoch studied for many years. He was a gentle mild-mannered man who suffered a stroke at the age of 61 and was subsequently left with both object agnosia and prosopagnosia. Glyn and Jane worked with him for many years until he passed away, demonstrating that as with some other important cases in the literature, amazing findings come about because of a relationship and in fact collaboration between the patient and the researcher(s); this is a relationship of mutual respect, generosity and desire to inform science. HJA was one of the few neuropsychological patients to have a whole book written about him (the wonderful *To See But Not To See*) which details some of the beautiful detailed work that Glyn and Jane conducted with him. This work demonstrates how it is possible to initially classify a patient with a disorder (agnosia), but then by doing fine-grained analysis this classification can be further fine-tuned (in HJA's case, 'integrative agnosia'), which helps the researchers understand the patient's deficits and then hold that up as a mirror to inform how the healthy intact system functions.

Questions for Reflection

- How valid is Lissauer's original distinction between apperceptive and associative agnosia?
- Is the semantic system organised along categorical lines?
- Did HJA suffer from apperceptive, associative or integrative agnosia? Exploring this question will demonstrate how it is possible to use data in different ways to understand overall function and how interpretations or cognitive models can change as more research is carried out, sometimes on the same patient.

Go Further

- The semantic system can't make a 'conscious decision' on whether something that is seen visually is living or non-living in terms of how it processes information. However, it may be that to recognise an object as a fruit requires a lot of sensory information such as its colour, shape and smell, whereas to recognise a chair, the functional information about it is going to be more important. Further still, for small manipulable tools, even more fine-grained information on how to handle it would be useful. Given that this sensory, functional or motor information is processed in different parts of the brain, perhaps that is why damage to different parts of the brain affects the recognition of specific categories of information. Explore this further through the work of McCarthy & Warrington, Farah & McClelland, and Humphreys & Riddoch.

Go Further

Dr Jansari's YouTube Videos
Why do we know less about the human brain than the dark side of the moon? (Parts 1 and 2).

Watch these videos to be introduced to Philip who, following a motor vehicle accident, has been left with severe agnosia that affects his ability to recognise living things.

Further Reading

- Humphreys, G. W., & Riddoch, M. J. (2013). *To See but Not See: A Case Study of Visual Agnosia*. Psychology Press.
- Farah, M. J. (1996). The living/non-living dissociation is not an artefact. *Cognitive Neuropsychology, 13*(1), 137-154.
- McCarthy, R. A., & Warrington, E. K. (1988). Evidence for modality-specific meaning systems in the brain. *Nature, 334*(4), 428-429.
- Warrington, E. K., & McCarthy, R. A. (1994). Multiple meaning systems in the brain: A case for visual semantics. *Neuropsychologia, 32*(12), 1465-1473.

7
PROSOPAGNOSIA & FACE PROCESSING

Chapter Overview

This chapter will explore a cognitive ability that is vital for us as a social species, face processing. How do we see 'an object' in the outside world and from seeing that object derive all sorts of related information that allows us to socially interact or even to avoid that 'object'? Is the way that we see a human face different to how we see other visual objects, and if so, why?

Chapter Outline

- Introduction
- Historical Background
- What's in a Face? Different Information Derived From a Face
- Fractionation of Prosopagnosia
- Main Research Questions in Prosopagnosia
- Models of Face Processing
- Covert Recognition of Faces
- Delusional Misidentification: Capgras Syndrome
- Extremes of Face Recognition in the Healthy Population
- Chapter Summary

INTRODUCTION

One of the most important skills for *social* survival is the ability to recognise other individuals that we encounter. When we see another person, we need to work out whether or not we have seen that person before. Even if we have never seen that person before, we can derive a lot of information from their face that can help us decide whether this person is friendly looking to approach or whether they look dangerous and should be avoided. If we do recognise the person, then we will probably have thoughts in our minds about previous encounters which again tell us whether we want to talk to the person or to avoid them; and most of this information is not 'in' the face that we are looking at but requires interaction with the general cognitive system so that we can recall memories, conversations and emotions.

The complexity of such a system is made very clear when encountering someone who has difficulty recognising another individual who they should be familiar with. As will become apparent in this chapter, this difficulty can vary enormously between different people and, by careful analysis of their errors, we are able to develop complex models of how intact face recognition occurs.

HISTORICAL BACKGROUND

As with many disorders studied by neuropsychologists, the first people to describe problems in visually processing faces were neurologists. For example, Charcot (1883) and Wilbrand (1892) described patients that they were treating and provided some of the first reports of face-processing problems. Due to the rarity of the condition, our understanding of it has developed possibly more slowly than that of some of the more common conditions, such as amnesia (Chapter 8) or aphasia (Chapter 10). In 1947 a German neurologist called Joachim Bodamer studied a series of cases that exhibited conditions similar to those that had been historically documented. He was the first to use the Greek roots for face (*prosopon*) and lack of knowledge (*agnosia*) to propose a new term 'prosopagnosia', which therefore literally means 'lack of knowledge of faces'. A term that came into common usage in the late twentieth century, particularly for use with individuals who suffer a developmental version of the condition (see later) is face-blindness. While this latter term is used a lot, especially for those who have the developmental variant of the condition, many feel that it is inappropriate because of the suggestion that the sufferer is 'blind' – as will become obvious, individuals with prosopagnosia are definitely not blind!

WHAT'S IN A FACE? DIFFERENT INFORMATION DERIVED FROM A FACE

When looking at a human face, we are able to extract a lot of information from it. Much of this information extraction happens in *parallel* (meaning simultaneously) while some occurs *in series* (meaning in a series of stages where one has to be completed to move on to the next stage); we know this because of the presence of dissociations and double dissociations (see Chapter 3) that have been well documented in patients.

Expression Analysis and Identity Recognition

Two very important types of information we are interested in when looking at a face are *who* someone is and how they are *feeling*: this is because as a very social species we want to interact with the person we like or make sure we avoid them if we've had negative experiences with them! Figure 7.1 shows images of four faces, and if you were asked which of the other three faces was of the *same person* as the one in the top left, you would hopefully choose the one in the bottom right. If you were asked which face shows the *same emotion* as the one in the top left, you would choose the top right one instead. To do this task, you've had to perform two different forms of facial processing: 1) extracting unique identity; and 2) understanding emotional expression.

We know that these two aspects of a face are processed separately because of a number of double dissociations. For example, while patients HJA (Humphreys et al., 1993) and DY (Jansari et al., 2015) were both able to tell what emotion a face showed, they had profound difficulties in recognising familiar and famous faces. Conversely, patient SM (Adolphs et al., 1994) didn't have problems in recognising people (and therefore did not have prosopagnosia) but had enormous difficulties in decoding their emotions.

Figure 7.1 Different information extracted from a face: two people showing two different emotions each.

Lip Reading and Emotional Expression Analysis

Have you ever been watching a live TV broadcast where there is a slight delay between the sound and the picture? Even though the sound can be clear, it can feel strange. The reason for this is that although you are not aware of it, when you are looking at someone speaking, you are *automatically* able to read lips, and the 'disconnect' on the faulty live broadcast between the lip movements and the sound feels odd! We know this because of a remarkable illusion known as the McGurk Effect described by McGurk & MacDonald (1976). Participants are shown a video in which they see an actor *mouthing* the syllable /*ba*/ while simultaneously being played the sound /*ga*/. When asked what sound they *hear*, healthy brain-intact participants consistently do *not* report the auditory stimulus (/*ga*/) but say that they hear the sound /*da*/. This illusion demonstrates that when we 'hear' someone speaking, if we are looking at their face, even though we are not aware of it, we are actually also lip reading.

Campbell et al. (1986) studied a patient known as D who suffered from prosopagnosia and was also unable to judge expressions from faces. However, D was able to imitate the facial expressions of someone else; therefore, similar to the copying tasks described in Chapter 4 (Neglect & Attention), Chapter 5 (Apraxia & Motor-Planning) and Chapter 6 (Visual Agnosia & Object Recognition), this shows that her problem was not a perceptual one – she was able to visually see the information in someone's face and reproduce it with her own facial muscles. Her problem was in analysing and understanding the expressions. What Campbell et al. (1986) found was that despite having a problem in analysing this information (a lot of which comes from the mouth area, in addition to the eyes), D was also susceptible to the McGurk Effect and therefore was able to lip read. However, their other patient, T, who had no problems in facial recognition or in recognising emotions was not susceptible to the illusion (saying that she heard the sound /*ga*/) and was therefore incapable of lip reading. This double dissociation between patients D and T demonstrate quite strongly that information about facial emotions and lip-movements is processed in parallel. In summary, a number of different aspects of face processing doubly dissociate from one another. In addition to those described here, other dissociations do exist and overall they demonstrate the richness of information that can be derived *in parallel* from a face. The consequence of this information all being extracted simultaneously from a face is that different forms of brain damage can selectively impair processing of one or more of these forms of information while leaving the others intact.

FRACTIONATION OF PROSOPAGNOSIA

As different neurologists and then researchers began to document cases of prosopagnosia, it became apparent from the detailed descriptions of what the patients could and could not do that there was a lot of heterogeneity between them. Over time it became clear that these differences represented related face-recognition disorders which fractionated from one another. When thinking about face-recognition problems, it is useful to think of the difference between the 'presentation', which is the observable difficulty, and the underlying cognitive deficit. Imagine having a group of individuals lined up all of whom say 'I don't know' when you ask them who is in a photo of one of the most famous people in the world, such as Queen Elizabeth II of Great Britain. Although the observable problem *appears* to be the same for all the individuals, the *reason* for each failure to recognise the Queen could differ greatly. What this would demonstrate is that the process of recognising a person is complex and probably involves a number of components, with each of our individuals having a difficulty at a different part of this system. So, using the jigsaw analogy (see Chapter 3) and by studying each person in detail, we can build up an understanding of the overall system.

Generally speaking, there are three main points at which a problem can arise. These involve successive stages whereby failure at one stage means that it is impossible to get to the next stage and the ultimate goal of recognising someone. As an overall framework, it is useful to consider what is happening when you 'recognise' a person who is in front of you and are able to provide a name for them. The process involves:

- decoding the visual information
- putting this information together to 'know' that it is a human face
- and then finally knowing that *this* face is one that you have encountered before.

These stages are supported by the Bruce & Young (1986) model that will be explained in more detail later in the chapter. Deficits in face processing can arise at each of these three stages resulting in what might superficially seem like *one* condition, but in fact demonstrates the existence of many subcomponents.

Impaired Visual Analysis

The first stage of face recognition is the same as that which is involved in everyday object recognition (see Chapter 6). If an individual is not able to visually analyse a scene and unable to separate out objects using information about edges and shapes, then it will be impossible for the more complex subsequent stages to have sufficient information to function. A famous example is the real-life music teacher in Oliver Sacks's book *The Man Who Mistook His Wife for a Hat* (Sacks, 1985).

From the experimental literature, one of the earliest well-documented cases is that of patient JAF studied by Warrington (1986). This patient had good enough visual acuity to be able to read small newspaper print, so there was no generic sensory problem. However, JAF was unable to recognise even herself in a mirror and said that what she saw didn't look like a face. Using an assessment known as the Efron Shape Matching Test it was demonstrated that JAF's primary problem was an inability to discriminate shapes. Since, at the most basic level, the human face is a series of shapes for the different features, an inability to process shapes made it impossible for the patient to recognise faces. It should be noted that this is therefore a *general* problem rather than one specific to face processing since the patient's visual deficit was not limited to faces.

Impaired Perceptual Analysis

The primary visual abilities allow you to see the individual bits of the jigsaw, but these are meaningless unless they can be put together to see the overall image being displayed. As seen in Chapter 6 (Visual Agnosia & Object Recognition) perception is the skill that brings this information together, integrating it to allow you to see the image as a distinct entity. The main way that this is tested is by seeing whether someone can 'manipulate' the image that is being presented in front of them – if someone is able to create an independent coherent image by integrating the individual bits of the visual jigsaw, they should be able to then answer questions about how that image would look under different conditions. An early test developed by De Renzi et al. (1968) involved seeing images of two faces taken from different viewing angles with the task being to decide whether or not it is the same person in the two images (see Figure 7.2).

Figure 7.2   Example of a trial in De Renzi et al's (1968) same-different matching test (Reprinted from Ennio De Renzi, Giuseppe & Scotti, Hans Spinnler, Perceptual and associative disorders of visual recognition, Neurology 19(7), 634, https://n.neurology.org/content/19/7/634)

Looking at Figure 7.2, in order to answer the question, it is necessary to create an internal image of the face on the left, then 'mentally rotate' it to work out whether or not it is the same as that on the right. Similarly, the Face-Matching Task developed by Benton & Van Allen (1968) presents one face and six faces below it taken under different lighting conditions with the task being to work out which of these matches the target face.

Patient S studied by Bodamer (1947) was able to pick out individual features such as a nose on a face and could distinguish faces from other visual stimuli. Therefore, he could do the visual analysis, see the individual shapes, etc. However, he said that all faces looked like flat oval plates with dark eyes and didn't look familiar to him; as a demonstration of how extreme his problem was, he wasn't even able to recognise his own mother. So, what we see in S's case is that different information can be seen and understood *individually* but cannot be *integrated*. Following the taxonomy developed by Lissauer (see Chapter 6: Visual Agnosia & Object Recognition), some researchers refer to a difficulty at this stage of face recognition as apperceptive prosopagnosia.

Impaired Face Recognition

Even if the integration of information is possible, does that mean that recognition is going to be possible? Bruyer et al. (1983) studied patient W who had suffered brain damage which left him with bilateral occipital lobe lesions. After physical recovery, he was able to pick out a picture of a face from an array of other pictures, to copy line drawings of faces, to work out gender & facial expressions and was good at matching unfamiliar faces, pictures of faces from different angles, etc. This demonstrates that he was able to get through the first two stages of face processing, the visual analysis and the visual perception. Despite this, W was bad at recognising individuals even a year after his stroke. When he was shown videos of himself and people that he should have known, such as the health professionals working with him, but with no identifying characteristics (by putting hoods on the faces so that identifying hairstyles could be hidden), he said all faces were unfamiliar. Importantly, however, if he was allowed other information on the individuals shown such as their voice, he performed better. This discrepancy between not being able to recognise the individuals from their faces but performing much better with other information such as their hairstyles and especially their voices suggested very strongly that W's difficulty was in accessing stored visual representations of people from the face. Again, following Lissauer's taxonomy, some researchers refer to a difficulty at this stage of face recognition as associative prosopagnosia.

MAIN RESEARCH QUESTIONS IN PROSOPAGNOSIA

There are a number of important research questions that emerge from the consistent documentation of patients who are unable to recognise other human faces. First, is prosopagnosia simply a form of amnesia? Second, are human faces treated specially by the brain? Finally, if *and only if*, we decide that faces are special, what are the cognitive mechanisms involved in face recognition?

Is Prosopagnosia Simply a Form of Amnesia?

Patients with classical memory problems (see Chapter 8) are unable to recognise people that they have just met a few minutes before. Therefore, it is tempting to wonder whether someone who cannot recognise a familiar face is simply showing signs of amnesia. However, this is very unlikely for a number of reasons. First, patients with amnesia (such as the famous patient HM – see Chapter 8) can have problems with face recognition, but this is due to a problem in the memory system not in the face-processing system. Any cues about the person such as their voice, or any information about the person such as their job, etc. often result in no improvement in recognition. However, individuals with prosopagnosia can greatly benefit from non-facial cues. For example, as discussed above, Bruyer et al.'s (1983) patient W was unable to recognise faces if the hair was covered but if he was allowed to see someone's hair or hear their voice, he was much better at recognising the person. This demonstrates that the patient *does* have intact 'understanding' about someone but was simply unable to recognise the person *by looking at* the 'internal elements' of the face.

Are Faces Special?

Given the evidence that non-face cues can help someone with prosopagnosia to recognise a person, it is tempting to think that there must be something visually special about the human face. Further evidence that the processing of faces is different from that of other classes of objects comes from two sources – studies with neurologically intact healthy individuals and studies on patients with brain damage.

Evidence from Healthy Individuals

Face Inversion Effect

In a landmark study (Yin, 1969), presented photographs of objects that tended to only be viewed in one orientation in two conditions, either upright (the standard orientation) or inverted (see Figures 7.3a and 7.3b). What he found was that although recognition decreased for most objects when viewed inverted, there was a *disproportionate* impact on the recognition of human faces – turning human faces upside down dramatically impairs our face recognition. This very robust finding has become known as the Face Inversion Effect (FIE).

To explain the FIE it has been suggested that there are two main types of visual processing, *featural* and *configural*, which are used differentially for different types of visual recognition. Featural processing is similar to doing a jigsaw, adding up the individual elements of a visual scene. Configural processing involves 'seeing the whole' as one entity. It is thought that featural processing is used to recognise most of the visual world – so a chair that you are looking at is actually initially seen as four vertical thin elements with a wide horizontal section at the top of these elements and then possibly another wide vertical section rising up from one edge of the horizontal section – these elements are put together, to see, in turn, the legs, the seat and the back of the chair. When trying to recognise a human face, however, we do not perform this piecemeal method of adding up the information from the left eye, the right eye, the nose, etc. Instead, it is suggested that using configural processing we see the face as *one* unit; please note that the terms holistic processing and gestalt processing are also used by different authors and although there are subtle differences between them, for the sake of simplicity, only the term configural will be used here. This process may have been developed by the brain through evolutionary pressures because of the special importance of the faces of other humans.

Importantly, to explain the FIE, configural processing is thought to be an automatic process which occurs without any conscious control, *and* it is dedicated to faces that are viewed *upright*. As a result, when looking at a familiar face in its normal upright orientation, recognition happens both *automatically* and rapidly. However, if the face is viewed upside down, given that configural processing is specialised for upright faces *only*, it can no longer work. Therefore, the cognitive system has to revert to using featural processing to try to recognise

Figure 7.3a   How easy is it to recognise these two famous images when inverted?

the face. Since we are not used to trying to recognise faces in this piecemeal manner, either accuracy drops or the time to name the individual is greatly increased, resulting in the FIE.

Figure 7.3b The same images as in Figure 7.3a – the Face Inversion Effect is finding that inverting Barack Obama's photo makes a bigger difference in recognising the image than inverting the photo of the Taj Mahal in India

Composite Face Effect

To further demonstrate the importance of configural processing in face recognition, Young et al. (1987) devised an ingenious study in which participants were presented 'composite pictures' of famous people. These facial composites were created with the top half of one person (such as the famous American actress Marilyn Monroe) and the bottom half of someone (such as the first ever female Prime Minister of Great Britain, Margaret Thatcher). These composites were presented in two conditions – in the 'misaligned' one the two halves of the faces were not lined up while in the 'aligned' one they were so that, at least at first glance, the image looked like a whole intact face (see Figure 7.4 for a modern day example).

Figure 7.4 An example of the Face Composite Effect – the top half of each image is that of Barack Obama while the lower half is of Will Smith, but it seems easier to recognise the former American president in the image on the right.

Source: McKone, E. et al. (2013) Importance of the Inverted Control in Measuring Holistic Face Processing with the Composite Effect and Part-Whole Effect. *Frontiers in Psychology*, 4.

The participant was told that the stimulus they were about to view consisted of two different people and that their task was always simply to name the top half. What Young et al. (1987) found was that participants found the task of naming the top halves much more difficult in the aligned condition than the misaligned condition; this became known as the Composite Face Effect (CFE). Further, they found that when the composites were turned upside down, participants actually became more accurate at naming the same target! Young et al. interpreted the CFE by suggesting that creating the aligned composite face produces a new configuration which the participant does not have conscious control of; it happens automatically and so the halves cannot be seen independently even though they have been told that the image is made up of two different individuals. As a result, they have to mentally tease apart the image (probably) using featural processing to isolate the top half to name the face. However, as seen in the Face Inversion Effect earlier, when the composites are turned upside down, since holistic processing is disrupted, there is no such composite and paradoxically, the top half of the face becomes easier to recognise.

In a further demonstration of the impact of inversion and configural processing not working upside down, Thompson (1980) / Bartlett & Searcy (1993) presented participants with two images of the face of Margaret Thatcher upside down. The two images were identical apart from the eye and mouth regions having been turned upside down in one of the two. Thompson (1980) found that when the two images were presented upside down, participants found it difficult to tell what the difference was (see Figure 7.5).

Figure 7.5 The Thatcher Illusion

However, when the same images are seen upright, the 'grotesqueness' of one of them is very obvious (see Figure 7.5). The explanation was that in the inverted condition, configural processing cannot be used and so featural processing has to be used to compare each of the local elements. Since the information in the two images is exactly the same with the only difference being the way that that eyes and mouth sections are shown, it becomes difficult to differentiate the two faces. However, upright configural processing can see the whole in a way that is impossible when inverted.

In summary, the observations from the Face Inversion Effect, the Composite Face Effect and the Thatcher Illusion all demonstrate that the brain may be treating human faces differently from other classes of objects.

Evidence from Brain-Damaged Patients

Some neuropsychologists have suggested that the fact that, generally speaking, an individual with prosopagnosia is still able to recognise other visual objects in their everyday life is a strong demonstration that faces are treated specially by the brain. This line of argument is based on the idea that the brain damage has 'knocked out' or selectively affected the area that is specialised for face recognition, leaving the parts that are involved in recognising other objects fully intact. Whilst persuasive, not everyone agrees with this account!

Damasio (1985) suggested that faces were not special because some patients with face recognition problems also have problems with other classes of objects, especially when the objects can be visually confusable. As an example, Bornstein et al. (1969) described a patient who following right-hemisphere brain damage was unable to recognise once-familiar faces. Importantly, although the patient had been brought up on a farm and had been excellent at identifying animal faces, they now also had a profound difficulty in recognising the faces of different animals.

One way to look at this argument is by remembering that when we are asked to name an object such as a particular vegetable that is slender and orange in colour, the answer 'carrot' could be correct. When we look at the face of a famous actor who died tragically, the answer 'Marilyn Monroe' might be correct. However, these two responses are quite different. In the first of the two, we are being asked to name the *category* that the particular item in front of us belongs to, whereas in the second, we are *not* being asked to name the category (human face) but instead the particular individual example that we are looking at. If we 'knew' different carrots individually and had been asked to name *this* particular carrot as 'Charlie' and the one next to it as 'Chris' and the one next to that as 'Colin', then the comparison of the two tasks is possible. But given that in one task we are asking for the name of a category and in the other the name of the particular example, the suggestion that the inability to name a familiar face demonstrates the special nature of faces is weakened.

Could face recognition therefore just be at the top of a hierarchy of the recognition system and therefore *faces* just happen to be the most difficult stimulus to discriminate or recognise? This issue has been tackled in several ways using evidence from patients with brain damage.

Are Faces Simply at the Top of a Unitary Object Recognition Hierarchy?

There are a number of lines of argument *against* the idea that face recognition is simply part of an object recognition hierarchy – these are within-category object recognition studies, double dissociations and the specificity of prosopagnosia to human faces. To address the within-category specificity argument, Jansari et al. (2015) developed a task to assess the specificity of the problem demonstrated by their patient DY who had profound difficulties in familiar face recognition. Using four types of non-face objects (football shirts, cars, national flags and famous buildings), they presented 20 examples of each category for naming. If DY's face-recognition problem was simply because he was required to make a within-category discrimination for faces, then the prediction would be that he should have also found this task difficult. The results showed that DY was always within normal limits for all categories (see Figure 7.6). Therefore, he could easily

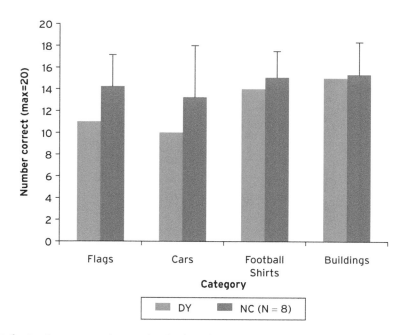

Figure 7.6   Performance of an individual with prosopagnosia (DY) and health controls (NC) demonstrating within-category discrimination (Jansari et al., 2015)

discriminate *between* exemplars from these categories which weakens the argument that prosopagnosia is simply a within-category recognition problem.

The suggestion that faces are just a more complex visual object relies on the finding that often, patients with prosopagnosia don't have difficulties recognising everyday objects. For example, McCarthy & Warrington (1986), Hécaen et al. (1974) and Jansari et al. (2015) all present such patients who had profound difficulties with recognising human faces but who showed no particular problems with non-face objects. So, are faces simply at the top of a 'difficulty' hierarchy?

However, a double dissociation between object agnosia (see Chapter 6: Visual Agnosia & Object Recognition) and prosopagnosia suggests that there are differential processes involved in the recognition of the two classes of information. For example, both Ferro & Santos (1984) and Behrmann et al. (1994) describe patients with preserved face recognition ability but with very impaired object recognition which could be demonstrated in different ways. In a fascinating study, Moscovitch et al. (1997) explored the specificity of their object agnostic CK's difficulty by showing him some paintings by the Renaissance artist Achimboldo, which at first glance to healthy individuals look like odd fantasy faces but which are actually composed of everyday natural entities. For example, a painting known as Rudolfo is composed of common fruits and vegetables (see Figure 7.7). CK had no difficulty describing the face-like image as 'a happy-looking man, facing to the right with the eyes looking slightly in the other direction. The cheeks are red and he has a large nose. He also seems to have some bags under his eyes' (Moscovitch et al., 1997, p. 589). However, he had profound difficulties naming the fruits that had been used to create the face. This profound demonstration of a patient who can do facial processing while having a difficulty recognising the fruits within the same visual image, along with the cases of patients with prosopagnosia for whom recognition of the fruits would be straightforward, provides a clear double dissociation between object and face recognition.

One final line of argument for the special nature of human faces comes from exploring the specificity of prosopagnosia. If human faces were not special, then the prediction would be that any individual with prosopagnosia should have problems with all faces since all animal faces are made up of the same components which are also in the same general configuration, i.e. two eyes above a nose which is above a mouth. However, McNeil & Warrington (1993) report the bizarre case of a patient, WJ, who following a stroke became prosopagnosic. After the stroke, WJ ended up becoming a farmer and acquired a flock of 36 sheep. Relative to his difficulty with learning to remember unfamiliar human faces, WJ's ability to recognise both individual sheep in his own flock as well as the ability to learn and remember the faces of unfamiliar sheep stood in stark contrast to that of control participants who had extensive experience of working with sheep. WJ's ability to learn to encode and remember the faces of individual sheep while being unable to do the same for both once-familiar and novel human faces demonstrates that not only are faces treated specially by the brain, but that it treats human faces particularly specially.

Figure 7.7   Vertumnus and Portrait of Rudolf II von Habsburg by Arcimboldo (1591), used by Moscovitch et al. (1997) to investigate face-processing in a patient with selective agnosia (Image courtesy of Skokloster Castle)

Are Faces Special? Configural Processing in Patients with Brain Damage

So far, the research outlined has looked primarily at whether there are special mechanisms for face processing in healthy individuals and for looking at specific dissociations in those with brain injury. A number of researchers have looked directly at the issue of the mechanisms in patients with brain injury by devising paradigms that specifically manipulate whether featural or holistic processing can be used in the recognition of faces.

Jansari et al. (2015) had seen that their patient DY was able use the features in faces to sometimes recognise familiar people. For example, when seeing a photograph of the famous American actress Marilyn Monroe, he was able to name her; importantly, however, he took seven seconds to recognise one of the most famous photographs ever taken before the arrival of the internet. Another example is that they had noticed that when DY was shown an (older) photograph of me when I had a goatee beard and

Figure 7.8 The photograph of Ashok Jansari used by Jansari et al. (2015) and a portrait painting of the singer George Michael

gold earring (see Figure 7.8), DY confidently stated that he thought the photo was of the singer George Michael! In both cases, it seems that DY was piecing together the features that he could see to arrive at a *hypothesis* of who it could be. In the former case, he was successful, but in the latter, although he was able to *see* the individual features of the face (the goatee, the gold earring and the darker skin, since George Michael was Greek while I am Indian; see Figure 7.8) his hypothesis of who it could be was quite wrong!

To formally test this explanation, Jansari et al. investigated the issue by using a paradigm originally developed by Moscovitch et al. (1997) for their patient CK who was unable to recognise everyday objects but was unimpaired on human face recognition. Since cognitive psychologists had already hypothesised that faces are largely recognised using configural processing while other objects have to be recognised featurally (see above), Moscovitch et al. suggested that CK's dissociation came about because his ability to engage in configural processing was intact while his featural processing was compromised. To evaluate this directly, they used photographs of famous individuals who CK had no problem in recognising and presented them in two conditions. In the 'intact' condition, the original photograph was shown while in the 'fractured' condition, the same image was cut into segments isolating different facial features such as the eyes and mouth but presenting them such that the relative positions of the features were maintained – therefore, the segments containing the eyes were presented vertically above that which contained the nose, and this was above the segment that contained the mouth. Moscovitch et al. hypothesised that in this fractured condition (as opposed to the intact one), configural processing could no longer be used and so the recognition system would have to revert to the featural one that was usually used for recognising non-face objects. Since CK was unable to recognise such stimuli, the prediction was that even though the same visual information was available in both sets of sets of stimuli, when CK was forced to use featural processing, his performance would be greatly impaired. Indeed, the results showed that CK's performance in the fractured condition fell by six standard deviations only recognising 40% of the same faces that he had recognised when they were intact.

Given that their patient DY presented a double dissociation with CK, that is, he is able to recognise everyday objects but can't recognise faces, Jansari et al. (2015) speculated that DY's configural processing system was compromised but the featural one was intact. They adapted Moscovitch et al.'s paradigm by asking DY's wife for the names of the few celebrities that he did manage to consistently recognise – when on TV, for example – and creating intact and fractured versions of photos of these people (see Figure 7.9 for a modern day example; please note that this image was not used in the study itself).

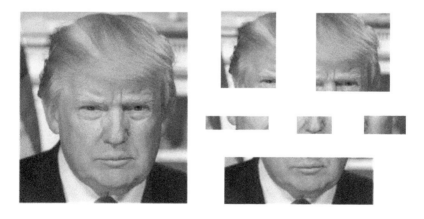

Figure 7.9 Examples of Intact and Fractured images of a famous individual (Donald Trump) – it is possible to use configural processing to recognise the image on the right but this is not possible for the image on the left and therefore featural processing is needed.

Jansari et al. (2015) found that in terms of accuracy, whereas CK's performance fell to 40% once the faces were fractured, there was no difference in DY's recognition ability between the two conditions. Not only was there no difference in accuracy, by measuring the time it took participants to correctly name a face, they found that whereas age and IQ-matched control participants took about twice as long to name a face in the fractured condition than in the intact condition, DY actually took *longer* in the intact condition (see Figure 7.10). This double dissociation between CK and DY using the same paradigm whereby the former found the intact condition easier, while the latter found the fractured condition easier, is further evidence for the special nature of human faces.

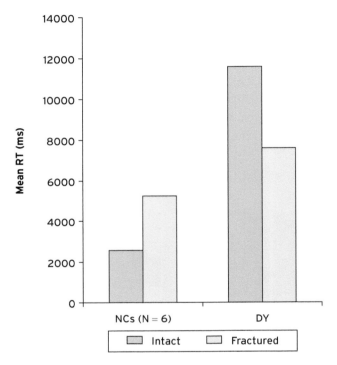

Figure 7.10   Mean response times for prosopagnosic patient DY and matched controls (NCs) on a face-fracturing paradigm (Jansari et al., 2015)

MODELS OF FACE PROCESSING

Given the weight of evidence that suggests that faces are treated in a special manner by the brain, various models have been proposed to explain how faces are recognised within an intact system. Possibly the most influential model was developed in the UK by Vicki Bruce & Andy Young (Bruce & Young, 1986). This model brought together the everyday mistakes made by healthy individuals when recognising people that are familiar and also the mistakes made by people with brain damage. For example, using a diary study in which students were asked to record instances of having difficulties in recognising someone on their university campus, the research-ers were able to note that their errors fell into different categories and also that there were specific combinations of errors (Bruce & Young, 1986). These combinations showed that unlike double dissociations which demonstrate that cognitive processes work in parallel, certain processes worked in 'series' where it was only possible to proceed to some stages when earlier stages had been completed. For example, it would be possible to know that someone is familiar and know that they work in the campus canteen without knowing their name, but it would be impossible for some-one to say, 'That woman's name is Antoinette but I don't recognise her, and I don't know anything about her'! This implies that first you recognise whether you know someone, then you recall some information about them and then finally you recall their name.

Within the Bruce & Young (1986) model it is possible to explain both the double dissociations found in individuals with prosopagnosia and the combinations of errors

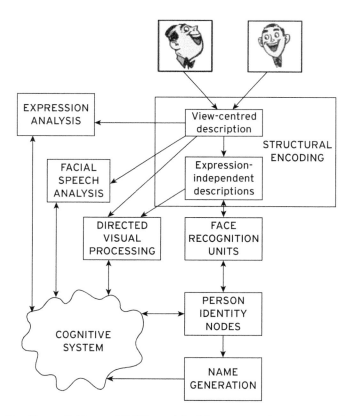

Figure 7.11   The Bruce & Young (1986) model of face processing (Reprinted from *Vision Research*, *41*(9), Andrew J Calder, A. Mike Burton, Paul Miller, Andrew W Young & Shigeru Akamatsu, A principal component analysis of facial expressions, 1179–1208, Copyright (2001), with permission from Elsevier)

made by healthy individuals (see Figure 7.11). When a face is first seen, the 'structural encoding' stage creates a coherent representation of it which is specific to the viewing angle. At this point four parallel processes can occur. Directed visual processing allows that image to be manipulated in the mind's eye to allow imagining what the face looks like from different angles; facial speech analysis allows lip reading to occur; expression analysis allows understanding of emotions; and activation of the face recognition units (FRUs) occurs if the face is familiar.

We know that these processes occur in parallel because of the double dissociations between different patients outlined earlier. The FRUs are effectively your memory bank of faces that you have seen before and are simply visual representations of faces that you have encountered. When the information from your eyes has been processed through a number of stages described earlier (sensation, perception, etc.) eventually you have an image of what you're seeing *right now*. Your visual and memory system then see if this image *matches* a stored FRU. If it does, that representation gets activated. Once an FRU gets activated, then you get a feeling of familiarity; however, this simply means that you know that this face is familiar. Next the person identity node (PIN) needs to be activated successfully; this is where your information about the person lies and is effectively the semantic or knowledge part of the cognitive system. Importantly, at this point, the information is abstract and not specifically derived from the face itself. Finally, if there is sufficient activation then the name generation stage allows you to recall the name of the person you are seeing.

The Bruce & Young (1986) model can neatly explain many of the issues encountered in the chapter so far. A difficulty at the structural encoding stage would result in apperceptive prosopagnosia (impaired perception), while if the patient could get through this stage but still have difficulties then they would have associative prosopagnosia (intact perception but impaired recognition). The parallel nature of the four processes that occur after structural encoding help to explain the double dissociations found between emotional recognition, lip reading and face recognition. Finally, the serial nature of the processes that allow us to recognise familiar faces via the FRUs helps to explain the temporary difficulties that we can all have sometimes if tired and knowing that someone is familiar but not knowing their name or even who they might be despite 'knowing' that you have seen that person before; this is sometimes known as the 'tip of the tongue' phenomenon whereby you know you know the answer but can't quite find it *right now*. It is beyond the scope of this chapter to go into detail, but this serial nature also helps to explain why in degenerative disorders such as dementia, the breakdown of recognition happens in a way that parallels the effects of normal tiredness but in an exaggerated and unfortunately permanent fashion. Initially the sufferer will forget the names of familiar people, then they will start confusing one familiar person such as their son for another such as their husband (when processing at the PINs becomes inefficient) and then eventually, when the FRUs are affected, lack of recognition sets in.

COVERT RECOGNITION OF FACES

One of the themes that has emerged through neuropsychology has been that while patients show profound impairments in a particular cognitive domain when tested *explicitly*, sometimes they will show intact knowledge at an implicit or unconscious level. The same is very much the case in the field of prosopagnosia. For example, Bruyer et al. (1983) studied a patient known as Mr W who had profound difficulties recognising faces and even said that when he looked in a mirror, he thought he looked odd and as if it was another person. However, Bruyer et al. had seen that rather than having absolutely no knowledge of once familiar faces, occasionally Mr W showed some residual knowledge which depending on the task *occasionally* resulted in correct recognition. To test whether this residual information was a systematic pattern, Bruyer et al. devised a clever task where they presented pairs of stimuli with a visual element (a face) and a verbal element (a name) in each pair. They manipulated whether or not the face or the name was famous and additionally whether or not the famous faces were paired with the correct names. Using a modern-day example, it would be like putting the face of Brad Pitt with the verbal label 'Brad Pitt' (correct pairing) or putting it with the verbal label 'Tom Cruise' (incorrect pairing). It is important to note that they will have used famous celebrities that the patient will not have been able to name if just shown a photo of the face. The results showed that Mr W was able to learn face-name associations that were correct faster than incorrect ones, even for those faces that he could not *explicitly* recognise; so for example, when shown the picture of Brad Pitt, not being able to name him but nonetheless learning to pair that photo with the label 'Brad Pitt' faster than to the label 'Tom Cruise'. What this suggests is that there was some residual information about the identity of a face which *interfered* with trying to associate that face with an incorrect name label. Bruyer et al. were the first to suggest that at least with some patients there can be *implicit* or *covert* levels of recognition in prosopagnosia.

Using a different approach, Tranel & Damasio (1985) measured 'skin conductance response' (SCR) which is a measure of autonomic arousal over which we have no conscious control. They presented two individuals with prosopagnosia a combination of photographs of both people who should have been familiar (family members, famous people, members of the medical team) and unfamiliar people. Despite not recognising the faces that should have been familiar to them, both patients showed large differences in SCRs depending on whether they were looking at familiar or unfamiliar faces even though they claimed no familiarity with any of the faces. These results therefore demonstrate *biological* mechanisms/underpinnings for recognition that do not reach conscious awareness.

De Haan et al. (1987) took the field further by expanding on Bruyer et al.'s (1983) study. They devised a study in which participants were presented with pictures of faces and a name attached to the face in a kind of speech-bubble; the participant's task was simply to state whether or not the *name* was that of a politician (see Figure 7.12 for a modern day example).

Figure 7.12   Examples using De Haan et al's (1975) method of pairing a famous name with three faces, one that belongs to the name, one from the same professional category and the final one from a different category.

It is important to note that the response here was based on the *verbal label* (the name inside the speech bubble) rather than on the face it was attached to. The study was designed so that there were three conditions. In the SAME condition, the name was that of the person in the photo itself, in the RELATED condition the face was of a politician but not the one named and in the UNRELATED condition, the face was of a celebrity from a different category such as a TV presenter – the crucial comparison was between the RELATED AND UNRELATED conditions. De Haan et al. found that *healthy control participants* were significantly slower in the UNRELATED condition even though neither of the faces matched the name inside the speech bubble. What this demonstrates is that despite the instructions having been to make a decision about the *name* inside the speech bubble, some information from the face that it was visually attached to was affecting participants' responses – the *professional category* of the face (TV presenter) was somehow affecting the judgement about the name which demonstrates the *automaticity* of the access to semantic information if a face is recognised. De Haan et al. found that a prosopagnosic patient, PH, showed the same interference effect despite not being able to recognise the 'interfering faces'. Interestingly, the learning of face-name pairings was quicker even for faces of people he had met since his accident. The implication is that his ability to set down new descriptions of people – FRUs – of people is preserved, but explicit access to them is disrupted. It is important to note that this type of covert recognition is not found in all patients.

An important consequence of the research on covert recognition is that the 1986 version of Bruce & Young's model is unable to explain these findings since there is no mechanism for unconscious levels of processing being intact while conscious levels are affected. The result of this was that using connectionist modelling (see Chapter 1) that was becoming popular at the time, Burton et al. (1990) developed the Interactive Activation and Competition (IAC) Model. In this model, rather than the linear stepwise progression from the FRUs to the PINs followed by name generation units (NRUs), the links between these different parts of the system were a bit more complex with the PINs being the centre of activity; additionally, a new type of representation known as semantic information units (SIUs) were added which had generic information that was common across different groups of people (e.g. being an actor or politician, or being known for playing a particular sport). Importantly, activation could happen in both directions, so for example, rather than the unidirectional flow of information from the FRUs to the PINs, information could also flow in the opposite direction (see Figure 7.13). Using this model, Burton et al. (1990) were able to explain how the type of covert recognition found in patients like PH found by De Haan et al. (1987) was possible.

Interestingly, the model made predictions about other types of face-recognition errors that should be found in some types of patients that had not yet been documented.

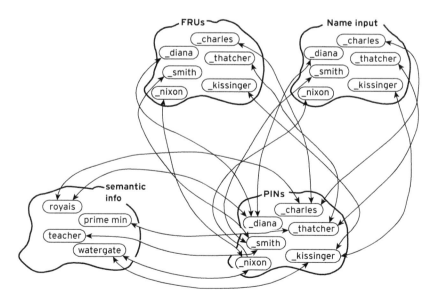

Figure 7.13   Part of the Interactive Activation and Competition Model developed by Burton et al. (1990) (Reprinted from *British Journal of Psychology, 81*(3), A. Mike Burton, Vicki Bruce & Robert A. Johnston, Understanding face recognition with an interactive activation model, Copyright (2011), with permission from John Wiley & Sons)

In an ingenious experiment, De Haan et al. (1991) tested a patient, ME, who could say that the photograph or name of a famous person was familiar but not provide any more information than this. The IAC Model would explain this as saying that ME's SIUs could not be accessed so the names and faces themselves can look familiar without providing any further information about them. However, given that the PINs, FRUs and NRUs were linked to one another, it was predicted that ME should be able to match faces and names *without being able to provide any semantic information about them* – this is because the SIUs are not needed for the FRUs and NRUs to be connected through the PINs. This is exactly what De Haan et al. (1991) found with their patient. This was a very powerful finding because not only did it show that the model was able to explain the *existing* literature but it also made *new predictions* which turned out to be accurate. An important point to consider here is that this demonstrates quite nicely the evolution of science. First, disparate findings about face recognition from both healthy individuals and those with brain damage were brought together into one model by Bruce & Young (1986). Then, demonstrations of covert recognition showed that this model could not fully explain face recognition (e.g. De Haan et al., 1987). Next, to address these problems, Burton et al. (1990) refined the Bruce & Young model (1986) model creating the IAC Model which could explain covert recognition. Finally, this new model predicted patterns of impairment in patients that had never been seen before, but which were then later found to be accurate by De Haan et al. (1991).

DELUSIONAL MISIDENTIFICATION: CAPGRAS SYNDROME

Finally, a strange disorder that is almost a double dissociation with the covert recognition found in some patients with prosopagnosia is known as Capgras syndrome, in which the patient thinks that familiar people have been 'duplicated' and replaced by imposters. Initially, this disorder was thought to be a psychological reaction to an emotional trauma and was first documented in 1923 by Joseph Capgras, a French psychiatrist and a colleague Jean Reboul-Lachaux in the case of an oddly named patient known as 'Madame Macabre'; the patient complained that her husband and other people she knew had been replaced by lookalikes (Capgras & Reboul-Lachaux, 1923). Given the genesis of this description by a psychiatrist, the psychodynamic explanation was the most prominent, and indeed even today, when it is seen, it is usually seen in the context of psychiatric units. For example, a study of 364 admissions to an acute psychiatric hospital in Taiwan found that 2.5% of the patients showed signs of Capgras (Huang et al., 1999). Using a retrospective approach, a London study examined records of 250,000 individuals who had been referred for diverse mental health difficulties and found that 84 of these met the criteria for Capgras.

However, Alexander et al. (1979) were the first to demonstrate that there may be an organic basis to the strange delusion. They documented the case of a 44-year-old man who had suffered a subdural hematoma, which is the collection of blood between the surface of the brain and the overlying skull due to some sort of head injury. Following surgery to treat this serious condition, the man was left with bilateral frontal lobe and extensive right hemisphere damage. More than two years after this incident, although most of his initial cognitive difficulties had resolved, he was convinced that he had two families each with five children in them and that the names of the wives and the number of children in the two families was exactly the same, the only difference being that the children in one family were one year older than those in the other. He claimed that he had not seen the 'original' family since his brain damage and despite not having seen his 'first wife' since that incident, he still had good feelings for her! In conversation, he was able to admit that the idea of one family that was identical to the one that was physically there with him was implausible but he maintained his belief in this being the case.

Given this case of Capgras syndrome brought on by organic brain damage, purely psychodynamic explanations cannot suffice. In an attempt to bring together the findings from covert recognition in prosopagnosia and Capgras syndrome, Ellis & Lewis (2001) used a model first proposed by Bauer (1984) who was one of the first to demonstrate covert recognition using SCR. Bauer suggested that face recognition involved two distinct pathways, one that is conscious and is based on the physical properties of the visual image that is seen; the second is unconscious and is based more on an emotional response to the face. The conscious pathway from the occipital lobes through the temporal lobes is known as the ventral route, while the unconscious pathway runs through older structures of the brain that are related to emotional processing (see Figure 7.14a).

Ellis & Lewis (2001 suggested, using this model, that covert recognition in prosopagnosia was caused by damage to the ventral conscious recognition pathway, with the dorsal unconscious pathway being intact (Figure 7.14b). The result of this is that a patient may claim not to recognise their relative from a photograph but may nonetheless show a change in SCR when looking at the face. As a double dissociation with this, Capgras syndrome was explained as damage to the dorsal pathway with the ventral pathway intact (Figure 7.14c). The consequence of this is that in a patient such as the one documented by Alexander et al. (1979), the ventral pathway allowed the face recognition system to go through to activating FRUs (see the Bruce & Young (1986) model above) when he saw his wife and children. The PINs and name generation stages would also be activated so that this information became conscious when he saw his family. However, due to the damage in the dorsal pathway, the emotional recognition that usually occurs (without any conscious awareness) when we see a loved one was not getting triggered in the patient. As noted by Alexander et al. (1979) the patient had frontal lobe damage which is vital since this area evaluates information on a moment-by-moment basis (see Chapter 9: Executive Functions); the contradiction between the information from the ventral and dorsal pathways, one saying that the people in front of him are his family while the other is not producing an emotional reaction, leads to the erroneous conclusion that these individuals are not in fact his family and have been replaced by lookalikes!

a)

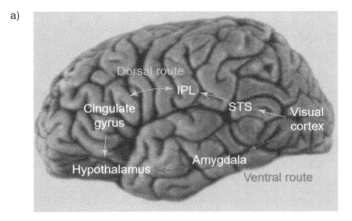

b)

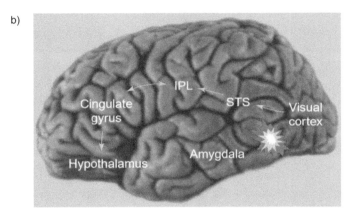

c)

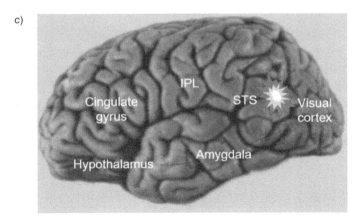

Figure 7.14 Neuroanatomical account of different aspects of face-processing: a) Bauer's (1984) original model of two separate routes, one for conscious processing (the ventral route) and one for unconscious autonomic processing (the dorsal route); b) an explanation of covert recognition in prosopagnosia caused by damage to the ventral route; c) an explanation of Capgras Syndrome caused by damage to the dorsal route (Ellis & Lewis, 2001) (Reprinted from *Trends in Cognitive Sciences*, 5(4), Ellis, Hadyn D and Michael B. Lewis, Capgras delusion: A window on face recognition, pp.149–156, Copyright (2001), with permission from Elsevier.)

This organic explanation of Capgras syndrome and how it is a mirror to covert recognition is quite compelling, especially since it is now recognised that the delusion can also occur in a number of conditions besides traumatic brain injury. For instance, it is sometimes reported in a number of neurodegenerative disorders such as dementia with Lewy bodies and Parkinson's disease. Since these conditions involve a gradual dysfunction in different parts of the brain, it is plausible that this could include parts of the dorsal pathway, thereby bringing about Capgras syndrome.

To incorporate the findings from both covert recognition and Capgras syndrome, Breen et al. (2000) expanded the Bruce & Young (1986) model. In the same year, Haxby et al. (2000) presented a more neurobiological version of the model in which they proposed specific cortical areas as the centres for the various cognitive processes outlined in the cognitive models (see Figure 7.15). It should be noted that while visually these latter models may look different, ultimately, they are simply developments of the seminal Bruce & Young (1986) model, proposed to incorporate new findings and to move towards the specification of neural locations for specific parts of the model.

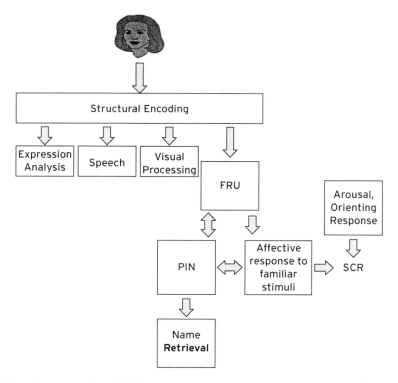

Figure 7.15a Breen et al.'s (2000) adaptation of the Bruce & Young (1986) model to incorporate the possibility of covert recognition in patients with prosopagnosia (Reprinted with permission from Taylor & Francis)

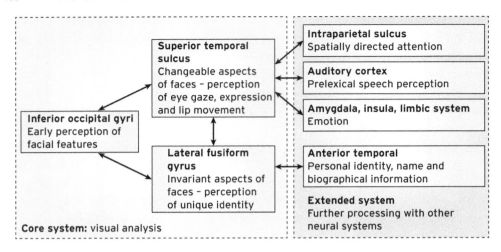

Figure 7.15b The neurobiological model of face recognition developed by Haxby et al. (2000) (Reprinted with permission from Elsevier)

EXTREMES OF FACE RECOGNITION IN THE HEALTHY POPULATION

The examples that have been dealt with so far to understand face recognition all refer to patients who have acquired prosopagnosia (AP) following brain injury. However, over the past 20 years, researchers in the field have become increasingly interested in studying a more common condition: developmental prosopagnosia (DP); it is estimated that DP affects about 2% of the population (Bowles et al., 2009). As opposed to people who have acquired the condition, and therefore had intact face recognition abilities prior to the injury, individuals with DP have failed to ever develop these abilities in the absence of any type of lesion or traumatic event. The presence of an identifiable brain lesion, along with a marked and clear *change* in cognitive functioning following the event, makes it possible to diagnose AP in a formal way. However, the same cannot be said about DP. The fact that most people realise they struggle with face recognition only in adulthood, suggesting lack of insight into their abilities, and the extensive use of compensatory strategies that allow these individuals to get by and adapt to most situations despite these difficulties, makes diagnosing the condition a major challenge. For example, recognising your colleague who sits right across your desk every day and who never changes hairstyle doesn't make you good at recognising faces. Contextual information allows you to recognise the *person*, not the face. Now let's imagine you had developmental prosopagnosia. If one day your colleague shows up with new glasses, a completely different hairstyle and without his badge, you might be able to recognise him only the moment you hear his voice, or he approaches his desk. Not having a number of contextual cues to aid your recognition and having to rely on his face would make it difficult for you to associate that person's identity with the colleague you are used to working with side by side on a daily basis.

There are people, in contrast, who seem to lie on the opposite extreme of the face recognition spectrum: so-called super-recognisers who have exceptionally good face recognition abilities (Russell et al., 2009). Imagine that you are taking the bus to go to university just as you do every day. You notice someone is staring, as if he's trying to figure out where you've met before, but you recognise him immediately; you know you've met that person, only once, two years ago at a party. Now that's not common, most of us would probably be in the other person's shoes, maybe having a vague sense of familiarity but struggling to remember the identity and the exact situation in which we met that single individual years ago.

As with many cognitive abilities, across the population, face recognition seems to show a bell-shaped distribution with some people at the very high end (super-recognisers) and some at the very low end (people with developmental prosopagnosia), and most other people in the middle of this spectrum. For example, Davis et al. (2018) used a test of unfamiliar face memory developed by Russell et al. (2009) known as the Cambridge Face Memory Test Plus (CFMT+). They found that the distribution of scores was normally distributed with many people scoring 70–80 (out of the maximum of 102) with fewer and fewer people attaining scores that were higher or lower than this central tendency (see Figure 7.16). Interestingly, at a societal level, studies have demonstrated how identifying people with these superior face recognition abilities can have important real-life implications, such as recognising suspects in a police investigation from blurry images in CCTV footage (Davis et al., 2018). Most of us would recognise our colleague even if we met him at a bar without his badge, but most of us would also struggle to immediately identify a person we met on a single occasion a number of years ago. The models and different facets of face recognition discussed across the chapter represent solid ground to move forward in the field and learn more about such a complex skill which has been demonstrated to be selective and one that impacts human beings on a number of levels from the cognitive, emotional, and relational to the societal.

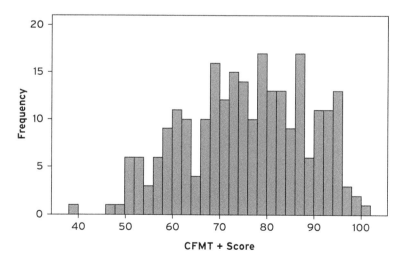

Figure 7.16 Frequency distribution of scores on the Cambridge Face Memory Test Plus (Davis et al., 2018) (Reprinted with permission from John Wiley and Sons Ltd)

Chapter Summary

- Face recognition is a complex process with problems occurring at three main points: analysis, perception and recognition. Problems at the different levels map onto two general forms of face-recognition problems similar to those found in object recognition, apperceptive agnosia and associative agnosia.
- We extract many different types of information from a face including emotional expression, lip reading to help us understand what someone is saying, and the identity of the individual if they are familiar to us. Many of these processes doubly dissociate from one another.
- The fact that individuals with prosopagnosia can recognise someone from their voice, a verbal description of them and sometimes even from hair, shows that the difficulty is not related to memory but specific to being able to process the face.
- Research suggests that faces are visually processed differently from other classes of objects, the former using configural processing and the latter featural processing. This is supported by a number of phenomena such as the Face Inversion Effect and the Composite Face Effect in healthy controls as well as detailed work with patients with prosopagnosia.
- The various findings from both healthy individuals and those with brain damage have been brought together in complex models of face recognition.
- Some individuals with prosopagnosia show covert recognition, and these findings are being used to refine existing models.

Important Researcher

Andy Young

Andy Young is a British neuropsychologist who has spent a lot of his career exploring different aspects of face processing. Along with Vicki Bruce, he created the Bruce & Young face recognition model in 1986 which brought together a lot of data on both how healthy controls and patients with brain damage analyse and recognise different aspects of a face. Andy's Face Composite paradigm is a classic in face processing, demonstrating the automaticity of a configural processing system dedicated specifically to facial stimuli; this paradigm has been adapted countless times by other researchers. Further, along with Freda Newcombe and Edward De Haan, he elegantly demonstrated that patients who cannot consciously or explicitly recognise faces can show behavioural indices of unconscious recognition. This then drove a new area of research, as well as demonstrating that the 1986 model had limitations. However, a strength of the theorising that went into that model is that all subsequent models of face processing are effectively hybrids of the model that Andy first helped to develop more than 35 years ago.

Questions for Reflection

- Are faces just visual objects or are they processed *at least to some levels* using different mechanisms?

- How has our understanding of healthy face recognition evolved through the documentation of patients with different types of recognition difficulties?
- Could developmental prosopagnosia simply be at the lower end of a 'normal' face recognition spectrum rather than a 'condition' in its own right?

Go Further

- While it is true that some individuals with prosopagnosia show covert recognition, not all patients do. Why is that? Work by Andy Young and colleagues has shown that you can dissociate behavioural covert recognition (such as the face-name associations) from the more biological form (such as the galvanic skin response differences). They've suggested that there are different pathways and that only if these are intact will a patient show these forms. See if you can explore this area.
- Many patients with prosopagnosia also have difficulties in route-finding known as topographic agnosia; they can easily get lost even in familiar surroundings. As described in Chapter 3, when there is an association of symptoms like this, it could be for a number of reasons – maybe the two functions (face recognition and spatial navigation) are just neighbours in the brain so brain damage may 'knock out' both abilities, but in fact they are separate skills; or maybe there is something that the two of them share at a processing level? If you think about it, when given the directions to find a place in an unfamiliar location, it is not the *number* of lefts and rights that is important but the *combination* and *order* of these relative to one another. Does that sound a bit like configural processing...?
- Both research on patients with brain damage and healthy controls has heavily implicated the fusiform gyrus for face recognition to the point that it is often referred to as the 'fusiform face area'. However, that might be jumping the gun. There is some research that has shown that when chess grandmasters look at a board in play, their fusiform gyrus becomes active. Is it possible that this area is not actually specialised for faces but for the configural processing that sees patterns – most of us would just see random chess pieces on a board but the grandmasters seem to be seeing patterns since to them it is not where individual pieces are but how they relate to one another that matters. So do we need to change our thinking about the special nature of faces?

Go Further

Dr Jansari's YouTube Videos
Dr Ashok Jansari on the BBC talking about prosopagnosia

This five minute clip on the BBC shows a patient with profound prosopagnosia and looks at how this impacts him at a personal level as well as what we might learn from patients like this.

Who are you? Interview with someone with prosopagnosia (face blindness)

This is an interview with a patient talking candidly about what it means for him not to be able to recognise his wife or his daughters, the impact it has on him emotionally and how he finds a way to cope in his everyday life.

Confabulation, Capgras & Cotard's: The amazing insights from brain disorders (Parts 1 and 2)

See how a patient with Capgras syndrome tells a woman that she is really nice and looks just like his mother and that she really should meet his mother – the woman he was saying this to *was* his mother.

Further Reading

- Young, A. W. (2016). *Facial Expression Recognition: Selected Works of Andy Young.* Psychology Press.
- Bruce, V., & Young, A. (2013). *Face Perception*. Psychology Press.
- Palermo, R., et al. (2017). Do people have insight into their face recognition abilities? *Quarterly Journal of Experimental Psychology, 70*(2), 218-233.
- Rossion, B. (2018). Humans are visual experts at unfamiliar face recognition. *Trends in Cognitive Sciences, 22*(6), 471-472.
- De Heering, A., Rossion, B., & Maurer, D. (2012). Developmental changes in face recognition during childhood: Evidence from upright and inverted faces. *Cognitive Development, 27*(1), 17-27.

8
AMNESIA & MEMORY

Chapter Overview

This chapter will explore possibly one of the most important cognitive skills we use virtually on a minute-by-minute basis, memory. This ability allows us to take in new information, process it in the light of what we might already know, store it for later use to respond to it if necessary and to recall the information often many years later. By studying patients with damage to different facets of memory, we are able to develop complex models of the multiplicity of human memory.

Chapter Outline

INTRODUCTION

What is a bicycle? When was the last time that you rode a bicycle? How do you ride a bicycle? These questions rely on the assumption that you have encountered bicycles before and are therefore testing stored knowledge otherwise known as memory. A particularly important question that relates to memory is whether these three questions require access to just one store of knowledge or a number of different stores. If it is decided that more than one store of knowledge is required, then we will have to decide that there are 'multiple memory systems'. One of the ways to investigate this issue is to explore the problems experienced by patients with a variety of memory problems. This chapter will begin with a brief overview of the various causes of memory problems. Then, starting with a very simple cognitive experiment, it will be shown how there are at least two different forms of memory and then use this finding to expand our knowledge of the multiple memory systems.

CAUSES AND TYPES OF MEMORY PROBLEMS

Memory is one of the most complex cognitive skills and part of this is because of the content of a memory. When you think about a holiday that you went on, you will probably 'see' some of your experiences, you might 'hear' music that was playing at the time, you might 'taste' food that you ate at the time, you might 'feel' the warmth of the temperature where you went and you might even experience a 'smell' of the place you were in. What is happening is that you are 'playing back' parts of the *original* events and that playing back is the act of remembering. Each of those original constituents to your experiences, the sight, sound, taste, feel and smell of what you did on your holiday were initially experienced by your five different senses. At the time, the experiences will have been processed in early sensory areas, for example, as in Chapter 6 (Visual Agnosia & Object Recognition), in the visual areas within the occipital lobes, the auditory areas for what you heard, etc. These individual sensations will have needed to be *combined* so that you had *one coherent* experience. The act of remembering the holiday is an *attempt* to play back this combination and effectively to try to *re-experience* the event.

As should be obvious, a number of different areas of the brain are involved in initially experiencing something and then in combining all of the information to create a conscious (or even unconscious) knowledge of the event. As a result of the complexity of this process, there are many different causes and types of memory problems. Figure 8.1 attempts to demonstrate this complexity. At the most basic, a memory problem can be caused by emotional or psychological difficulties, or it can be caused by physical damage to the brain; these are known as psychogenic and organic causes respectively. While psychiatrists deal with psychogenic cases of amnesia, cognitive neuropsychologists deal largely with organic amnesia. This can either be time-limited (or transient) or it can be permanent with little or no improvement following damage. Transient amnesia can be brought about by some forms of epilepsy (known as transient global amnesia and transient epileptic amnesia), through an extreme treatment for some forms of mental illness known as electro-convulsive therapy or as a consequence of almost any form of injury to the brain known as post-traumatic amnesia; the time course of each of these types of memory problems varies, but importantly it is for a limited period of time.

The more severe form of memory problems that are permanent can be differentiated by whether the difficulty is unchanging or whether it gets worse over time. If the memory problems worsen over time, this will be due to a degenerative neurological disorder such as senile dementia of the Alzheimer's type (SDAT), Pick's disease, Huntingdon's disease and AIDS; it should be noted that in these conditions, the memory problem is part of a larger group of problems that the patient will be suffering from. Therefore, for example, while the general public sees SDAT as a memory disorder, the memory difficulty is actually only one of the first and most obvious signs of the disease with other cognitive problems becoming more apparent as the disease progresses. Within the permanent stable group of problems, the difficulty can be specific to certain types of material or it can be global. While loss of understanding of objects and faces (as seen in Chapters 6 and 7) or of places (known as topographic agnosia) is limited to specific types of knowledge, some forms of brain damage have more widespread impacts. These global and stable memory problems encompass most types of material and can be brought about by a large variety of causes. These include disorders such as Wernicke-Korsakoff syndrome, herpes simplex encephalitis, generic closed head injuries, anoxia (interruption of oxygen to the brain), strokes, aneurysms, complications caused by the growth of tumours, surgery such as lobectomy or following carbon monoxide poisoning. In the last decade, there has also been a growing understanding that repeated small head injuries cause multiple small lesions that can lead to memory problems which are effectively a form of dementia. This condition, known as chronic traumatic encephalopathy (CTE) is degenerative, worsening over time. This was highlighted in the Hollywood film *Concussion* which is the true story of how a Nigerian pathologist working in the United States noticed that a number of former American football players who had been behaving very erratically before they died had many micro lesions in their brains. He was able to suggest that these were caused by the continual small injuries that the brain was experiencing as a result of the constant forces on the head experienced over many years from taking up the sport as a child through to playing at a serious professional level. Recently, high profile cases have shown the same issues in the original English football (soccer) and rugby as well as Australian Rules Football (e.g. Yuan & Wang, 2018).

Finally, during the global pandemic that started in early 2020 due to the SARS-CoV-2 virus (which became colloquially known as 'Covid'), while the original symptoms were mainly respiratory and many people who contracted it recovered fully, there was a subset that did not make a full recovery and instead suffered from what is known as 'Long Covid'. One of the symptoms of Long Covid is subtle but persistent memory problems. At the moment, this has been documented in self reports by Søraas et al. (2021) but it will probably take a few years to see whether the difficulties experienced by these individuals in 2020 and 2021 will fade away or will be permanent problems.

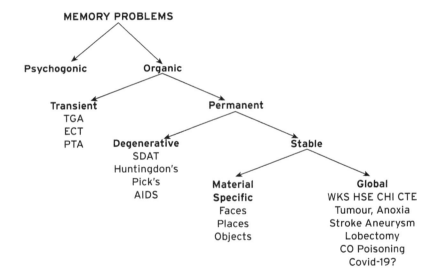

Figure 8.1   Types and causes of memory problems

As is obvious from Figure 8.1, a memory problem can vary on a number of different dimensions, namely cause (psychogenic or organic), duration of problem (transient or permanent), prognosis over time (degenerative or stable) and type of information affected (specific to certain classes of information or global to all types). The causes of each of these different sub-types of difficulty vary enormously which makes understanding memory extremely complex. Different researchers study specific levels of this complex system. For example, researchers studying Alzheimer's disease study how different cognitive functions (such as language and memory) deteriorate at different time points and with varying time courses; this knowledge will hopefully eventually help with managing and helping patients in the future who are diagnosed with the disease. However, to understand human memory in isolation, it is better to study the impairments of patients whose difficulty is limited to that cognitive function alone. Therefore, for the remainder of this chapter, patients who have permanent stable and global memory difficulties that have an organic origin will be considered.

THE SERIAL POSITION CURVE AND THE MODAL MODEL OF MEMORY

To understand the importance of some of the seminal findings from patients with brain damage, it is useful to first look at one of the most classic memory tasks that has helped in the understanding of human memory. In this task, developed by Murdock (1962), participants are presented with a number of words at a fixed pace and then straight after the last word, they can be asked to recall all the words they can remember in any order. By looking at how many people remember the first word in the list, the second word, etc. it is possible to plot a graph of the overall recall of each word as a function of its original position in the list. The resulting shape of the graph, known as a serial position curve, is a classic 'U shape' (see Figure 8.2).

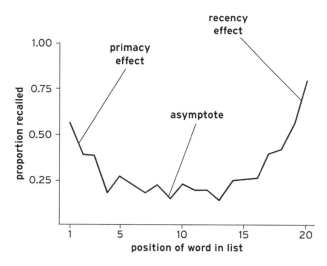

Figure 8.2   The serial position curve with three classical components (Capitani et al., 1992. Reprinted with permission from Elsevier)

There are three parts to this curve which are known as primacy (good recall for the earliest items in the list), recency (good recall for the most recent items) and asymptote (poorer recall for items in the middle of the list). It is possible to do different variations of the experiment such as increasing the speed of presentation of words, or presenting a distracting task after the last word and asking for recall a minute later to investigate the impact on these three components. What is found is that different manipulations affect the primacy and recency components *separately*; in effect there is a double dissociation (see Chapter 3), implying that primacy and recency are caused by different processes. As a result of these findings, it has been suggested that while recency reflects retrieval from some sort of short-term memory, primacy and asymptote reflects retrieval from a longer-term memory.

Findings such as the serial position curve led to the development of the multi-store or Modal Model of memory (Atkinson & Shiffrin, 1968). Before this model, the American psychologist William James had talked about 'primary' and 'secondary' memories; the former referred to information that we hold in our consciousness which only lasts for a few seconds and the latter to information which can last for an unlimited time and can be brought to our consciousness when it needs to be used. Atkinson & Shiffrin built on these early thoughts as well as the primacy and recency effects in the free recall task to propose a model in which information is processed in a serial manner, meaning that information needs to go through one stage before it goes onto the next (see Figure 8.3).

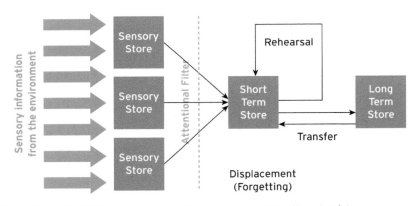

Figure 8.3　The Modal Model proposed by Atkinson & Shiffrin (1968)

According to Atkinson & Shiffrin, information comes in from our five senses and is held very temporarily (e.g. for 200 ms) in sensory stores before it is either processed further or discarded. A system known as attention filters out what is important and passes that through to the short-term store (STS). The STS has a limited capacity and holds only a finite number of items. There is debate on what this number is, but according to Miller (1956) the capacity of the STS is the 'magic number 7 plus or minus 2' so that most people hold between 5 and 9 items. Given this limited capacity and the fact that the sensory stores are constantly feeding information through the attentional filter as new information is coming in, what has been placed in the STS can only stay there temporarily. According to Atkinson & Shiffrin, unless something is done with this new sensory information, it is 'displaced' or forgotten. However, if this information is processed in some way such as repeating it over and over again (a process known as rehearsal) then it is possible that it might be moved into the long-term store (LTS). The duration that information can be held in this store is said to be unlimited; in other words information could remain in the LTS or LTM[1] for a lifetime, making it a potential store for all the information one has ever learnt; of course it is impossible to test the full capacity of LTM but we know that people who live to very old ages who do not suffer from dementia can recall memories from their childhoods 80 or 90 years ago. According to the Modal Model, the recency portion of the serial position curve reflects what is currently held in STM while the primacy portion reflects early items that have been transferred to LTM as a result of some form of conscious or unconscious rehearsal.

The Case of HM

Arguably, the most momentous event in the history of research on human memory was a neurosurgery that was carried out in Montreal in 1953 on a young man called Henry Molaison (Scoville & Milner, 1957). HM (as the young man became known), suffered extremely severe intractable epilepsy. Epilepsy is a very complex condition and there are many different types of epilepsy, but a simplistic explanation would be that it is

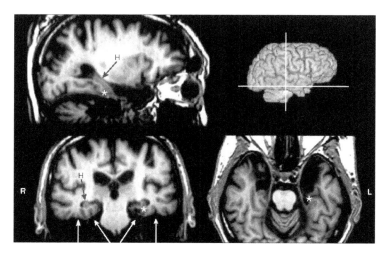

Figure 8.4 Different images of HM's brain; in the lower right image which is a view looking down onto the brain from above, the areas of black on the 'medial' parts of the temporal lobes are the areas from which damaged brain tissue was removed during the surgery (Corkin, 2002. Reprinted with permission from Springer Nature BV)

---

[1]Please note that while Atkinson & Shiffrin used the terms STS and LTS, the terms STM (short-term memory) and LTM (long-term memory) are more commonly used and so these will be used for the rest of this chapter.

an electrical storm generated by damaged nerve cells. Normally functioning cells will only fire when stimulated by other cells in a clear ordered pattern. In contrast, damaged cells produce 'unprogrammed' electrical activity that causes a sort of avalanche effect spreading to connected brain regions. The resulting 'storm' disrupts the activity that the brain is currently engaged in resulting in a seizure. How this happens is not very well understood, but in many cases the seizure can be somewhat controlled by anti-epileptic medication. In HM's case, however, medication was not effective, and despite treatment he continued to suffer from the most severe forms of attacks known as 'grand mal' seizures. From research on animals, it had been discovered that if the area of the brain creating the storm known as the epileptic focus was removed, then the likelihood of further seizures was greatly reduced. In 1953, having localised the seizures to the medial (more central) parts of the temporal lobes, the neurosurgeon William Scoville performed a bilateral medial temporal lobectomy on HM. Figure 8.4 shows scans of HM's brain taken in 1998 showing the areas that were removed from his temporal lobes and which then filled up with fluid.

Surgery was very effective in reducing seizures for HM; however, Brenda Milner, a clinical neuropsychologist (who had studied at Cambridge University with one of the fathers of experimental psychology, Oliver Zangwill, and for her PhD at McGill University with one of the fathers of neuropsychology, Donald Hebb), realised that from that point onwards HM was no longer able to create new memories. Further work on other patients demonstrated that if a patient underwent a unilateral temporal lobectomy, the consequences on memory were less severe. HM's inability to lay down new long-term memories was caused because both medial temporal lobes, particularly a structure known as the hippocampus, had been removed. This severe difficulty in creating *new* long-term memories is known as amnesia.

In contrast to the severe long-term memory problems, Milner (2003) showed that the number of digits that HM could remember in their correct order (a task known as digit span) was identical to that of matched healthy controls. In later research on amnesia, giants of British neuropsychology Alan Baddeley & Elizabeth Warrington (1970) conducted the classic free recall task to look at the serial position curve of a group of patients with amnesia. What they found was that although the primacy and asymptote portions of the curve were significantly different to those of matched control participants, the recency portion was indistinguishable between the two groups (see Figure 8.5). Putting these two findings together, since digit span was thought to represent the capacity of the STM and recency was thought to be the outpourings of this store, the fact that these seemed intact in patients with amnesia suggested that STM for them was unimpaired. This explanation, coming from cognitive neuropsychology, greatly strengthened Atkinson & Shiffrin's (1968) Modal Model (from standard cognitive psychology) because it suggested that STM is separate from LTM. Using this framework, it was hypothesised that the primary deficit in patients with amnesia is an impairment in transferring information from the intact STM to LTM resulting from the brain damage.

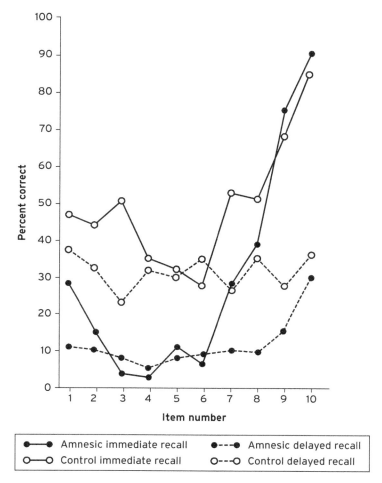

Figure 8.5 The performance of patients with amnesia and matched healthy controls on a serial position memory experiment (Baddeley & Warrington, 1970); the crucial lines are for 'immediate recall' showing that while the amnesic patients have poor recall of the early items, their recall of the last few items (recency) is identical to that of controls (Reprinted with permission from Elsevier).

KF and the Double Dissociation

One of the important aspects of the Modal Model is its serial nature, whereby information first comes into the sensory stores, then some is filtered into the STM and then some of that passes into the LTM. A strong prediction of this 'directional flow' (effectively left to right in Figure 8.3) is that if a patient has an impairment in STM, then he or she should have difficulty in transferring information to LTM. This prediction was put to the test when Shallice & Warrington (1970) studied a patient known as KF who had suffered a closed head injury from a motorcycle accident. When KF was tested clinically, it was found that his primary deficit was a very reduced digit span; whilst normal span would be about 7 (reflecting Miller's (1967) magic number), KF's was only 2. According to the

Modal Model, this reduced digit span is a sign of a deficient STM and since information has to be processed here to transfer to LTM, this latter store should also be affected. However, despite this severely reduced digit span, KF was actually found to have an intact ability to lay down new long-term memories. This counter-intuitive result (plus further aspects of KF's profile which will be expanded on below), greatly weakened the Modal Model as it was originally proposed.

Also, this presentation of an impaired STM but intact LTM provides a classic double dissociation with the case of patients with amnesia who have an intact STM but deficient LTM. The consequence of this double dissociation is that some researchers concentrate solely on studying STM while others concentrate solely on LTM (Figure 8.6).

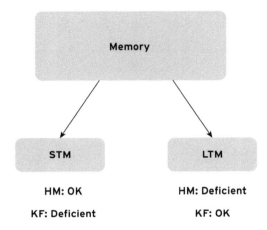

Figure 8.6 The double dissociation between HM and KF allows a separation of STM and LTM into parallel systems

WORKING MEMORY

In addition to the fact that KF's dissociation proved problematic for the unidirectional and serial nature of memory, another issue was the specificity of his memory problem. In their landmark study, Shallice & Warrington (1970) found that KF's short-term memory abilities differed depending on the type of material that he was presented. Using different subtests of the Wechsler Adult Intelligence Scale (WAIS) that are specifically designed to test short-term memory abilities, Shallice & Warrington found that while KF was very impaired on the tests that required verbal memory, his performance on the subtests that were more visually based was completely normal. For example, one of the subtests known as Picture Completion requires the participant to work out what part is missing from a picture of an object; this task only requires visual processing and therefore it is possible to see how specific an individual's problems are. While the normal score is 10, KF achieved a score of 13. With this dissociation between poor performance on verbally based information and intact performance on visually based information, this seminal study demonstrated that short-term memory was much more complex than the original Modal Model had suggested.

While the case of KF was difficult to explain using the Modal Model, a framework being developed in the UK by two British cognitive psychologists was able to do so. Alan Baddeley & Graham Hitch developed the Working Memory Model (1977), which was based largely on standard cognitive psychology looking at different issues in memory with mainly university undergraduates. Using a number of clever manipulations, they were able to demonstrate three very important effects in verbal memory. The Phonological Similarity Effect showed that when trying to hold information in STM, if the individual items sound similar to one another (for example, CAT, MAT, BAT), then there is a reduction in overall memory (Baddeley, 1966; Conrad, 1964). This suggested that the 'code' that is used in our memory for verbal information is based on the sound of the information rather than its actual meaning. The Word Length Effect showed that we generally find shorter words (for example, DOG, PEN, COT) easier to remember than longer words (for example, UNIVERSITY, ALUMINIUM, DECADENCE; Baddeley et al., 1975). This important finding gave an explanation for how much we can hold in our STM if we are given unrelated information to remember. Within the model, it is assumed that there is a 'holding process' known as the Articulatory Loop which is akin to an old-fashioned audiotape through which we play verbal-based information. Finally, the Unattended Speech Effect showed that verbal-based material (such as conversations happening close to you or the lyrics from music) can *automatically* enter your cognitive system and can impair performance on tasks that require concentration.

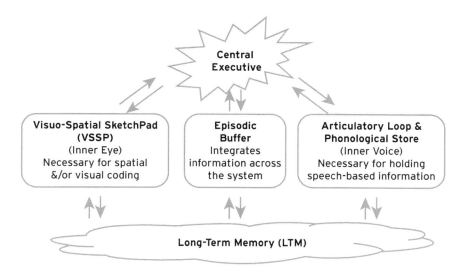

Figure 8.7   Baddeley & Hitch's (1977) Working Memory Model

Using data like this, Baddeley & Hitch proposed that our STM abilities involve (initially three but now) four different components. In this system, there are separate STM structures for each of the senses; the main two that have been documented are those for auditory-verbal information (known as the Phonological Store) and for visual information (known as the Visuo-Spatial Sketch Pad: VSSP). In addition to these modality-specific systems, there is one for managing the information across all of STM (known as the Central Executive: see Chapter 9) and an intermediate system for coordinating communication between information in LTM, the Central Executive and the modality-specific systems known as the Episodic Buffer (see Figure 8.7). There has now been more than 45 years of research on the Working Memory Model with new findings from healthy individuals, patients with brain damage and neuroimaging studies that are revealing how we bring in and *work with* new information that we experience and how we integrate it with what we already have stored in our LTM.

Figure 8.8   a) Examples of sculptures created by Wilson, Baddeley & Young's patient LE before and then after her brain damage; b) LE's line drawings from memory of a bird, a camel and an aeroplane respectively (Wilson et al., 1999) (Reprinted from Wilson, Barbara A., Baddeley, Alan D. et al., LE, A person who lost her `mind's eye. *Neurocase*, 5(2), Copyright (1999), reprinted by permission of Taylor & Francis)

In addition to patients like KF who have a problem in the verbally based Phonological Store, although rare, patients have been described whose impairments demonstrate a double dissociation with his presentation of difficulties. For example, Wilson et al. (1999) documented a patient, LE, who had suffered a rare form of brain damage from an autoimmune disorder which had severely affected her STM. Despite the brain damage, LE's verbal memory on the same tests that KF did poorly on was entirely unaffected. However, her free recall and recognition of visual information that she was presented were extremely poor. Of course, we know that there is general variation in the population in all cognitive abilities (just as there is variation in our ability to run 100 metres or cook a meal) which would mean that we would expect some people naturally to do worse than others in a drawing task. However, in LE's case, the fact that she used to be a successful artist and sculptor (see Figure 8.8a for an example of her previous work) but was incapable of drawing from memory everyday things like a bird or a plane (see Figure 8.8b for examples, of this) following her brain damage implies that her visual STM has been severely impaired. In the Working Memory Model, LE's impairment would be in the functioning of the VSSP.

More recently, Jansari et al. (2004) have demonstrated that it is possible to have intact functioning of both the Phonological Store and the VSSP but nonetheless have impairments in STM. Their patient AN had a horrific accident at university in which he fell about 20 feet onto his head and nearly died. Remarkably, although a coma had to be induced to save his life, AN made a recovery and apart from a few sensory problems (loss of taste and some visual problems) he was left with hardly any cognitive issues, and after a year of recovery was able to return to university, complete his studies and get the highest grade possible! However, AN did complain of problems in memory where he could easily lose the thread of a conversation, especially if more than one person was talking at the same time. Given the earlier work on KF and LE, Jansari et al. conducted similar tests to evaluate AN's Phonological Store and VSSP; surprisingly AN performed very well on all the tests implying that neither of the subsidiary sensory-specific systems was impaired.

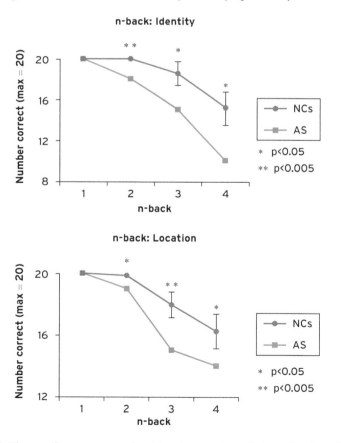

Figure 8.9 a) The performance on the Identity version of the n-back task by Jansari et al.'s (2004) patient AS; b) AS's performance on the Location version of the task

As a result of this, they then performed a task that is known to require the Central Executive known as the 'n-back' task. Whereas a digit span task requires taking in information and simply repeating whatever has been heard, and therefore tests the ability to *store* information, the n-back involves storing *and processing* information. For example, a verbal task might involve seeing a string of non-consecutive letters (e.g. R-G-Y-T-N-C…) in the middle of a computer screen one after the other which need to be held in memory; then at some point, without warning, the screen will have an instruction such as 'What letter was three back?' and the task is to say which letter was 'three letters ago' from the point of the instruction. Therefore, if it came after the letter C, the answer is Y but if it came after the letter T, the answer is R. This is a much more complex task that requires the Central Executive to 'juggle' the storage of information with the processing of the order of the words so that when the instruction is given, it is possible to review the order to find the correct answer. Jansari et al. found that while AN was perfectly OK on 1-back (the last letter) he was significantly impaired at any longer processing lengths (see Figure 8.9a). Further, when they did a version of the task which required visual information about different locations on the computer screen, again, while AN was perfectly OK with 1-back, he was significantly impaired at longer lengths (see Figure 8.9b). They therefore concluded that while AN's Phonological Store was intact for *storing* information, when a task involves *processing* and the Central Executive has to manage this activity, the system cannot cope. At an everyday level, if one person is talking to AN, he is able to track the conversation but with two people talking at the same time, switching between the two voices becomes necessary and at that point AN notices problems.

THE STRUCTURE OF LONG-TERM MEMORY
Procedural versus Declarative Memory

When thinking about any knowledge that was acquired more than a few minutes ago (i.e. something from LTM), an important distinction is the knowledge of a skill compared to knowledge of a fact. Philosophers such as Ryle (1949) had discussed the difference between knowing 'how' to do something (e.g. how to ride a bicycle) compared to knowing 'what' about something (e.g. being able to describe a bicycle or relating a story about the last time you rode one). This distinction was adopted by neuropsychologists including Neal Cohen and Larry Squire in 1981. They suggested that LTM was composed of two major types of memory systems which they referred to as procedural memory (for skill-based knowledge) and declarative (for fact-based knowledge). A very important reason for proposing this distinction came from studies looking at patients with amnesia. Data from these studies suggested that despite not being able to remember particular events that occurred after the onset of their amnesia, patients were still able to learn new skills. A famous example is a study by Corkin (1968) involving what is known as a 'mirror-drawing' task. In this task (see Figure 8.10a), the participant is presented with a drawing of a star with a smaller star within it. The objective is to draw a line between these (to create a third medium-sized star) while trying to avoid touching the inner or outer star.

a)

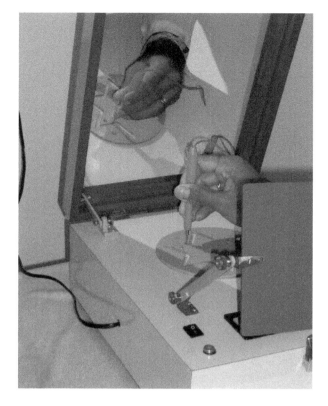

b)

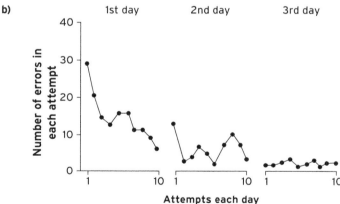

Figure 8.10   a) A photo of the author (AJ) doing a mirror-drawing task b) HM's performance as the number of errors on successive attempts on three consecutive days attempting the mirror drawing task (Corkin, 1968. Reprinted with permission from Cambridge University Press)

To make the task fiendishly difficult, the participant is not allowed to see his or her hand but is only able to look in a mirror at their reflection to guide their movements. It is generally found that as people repeat the task, their performance improves. One way to measure this 'learning' is to see the number of times that the participant's line crosses either the inner or outer lines – a perfect performance would result in never crossing the lines and therefore zero errors. During the first day on the task, HM improved greatly from about 30 errors to about 5; by the third day, he barely made any errors and had effectively 'learnt' the task (Figure 8.10b). However, when asked whether he had ever done the task before, HM stated that he had never seen it before! According to our latest distinction within LTM, HM displayed an intact procedural memory but his ability to create new declarative memories (including the knowledge of having completed the task before) had been severely compromised. Skill-based memory like this can be demonstrated using a range of tasks including the ability to see 'closure pictures' (Crovitz et al., 1981) and solving the Tower of Hanoi problem (Cohen, 1984). As a result of such findings, it is possible to develop the 'memory tree' further by splitting LTM into procedural and declarative memory (see Figure 8.11).

The finding that amnesic patients display intact procedural memory and the ability to learn *new* skills is very robust and is a vital ingredient in attempts to create rehabilitation regimes for such individuals (see Chapter 11). If procedural memory is intact in amnesia, then the major impairment must lie within declarative memory which will now be explored.

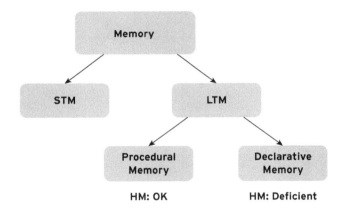

Figure 8.11   LTM is split into procedural memory and declarative memory

Retrograde versus Anterograde Amnesia

Research shows that although in patients like HM declarative memory had indeed been severely affected by brain damage, the damage is not total. In fact, the damage can be selective and there are two main dimensions. One of these refers to *when* the information was learnt and the other refers to the actual content of the information. In virtually every case of memory loss the forgetting is seldom absolute covering *all* time periods; one very important dimension being *when* the material was originally learnt. The reference point used is the point at which the individual sustained brain damage known as the amnesic episode; the time periods before and after the brain damage are referred to as the 'pre-morbid' and the 'post-morbid' periods respectively. Difficulty in remembering events that occurred in the pre-morbid period is known as retrograde amnesia while an impairment in learning or retaining new information in the post-morbid period is known as anterograde amnesia (see Figure 8.12).

Retrograde Versus Anterograde Amnesia

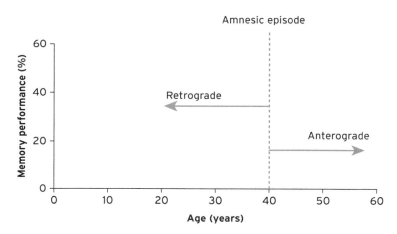

Figure 8.12 Schematic depiction of retrograde and anterograde amnesia for a hypothetical 60 year old patient who suffered brain damage at the age of 40. If you were looking at a patient's memory performance from different points in their life (for example, their memory of autobiographical events), the retrograde period is any time before the amnesic episode while the anterograde period is anything following this episode

Anterograde amnesia is the central feature of what is called 'the amnesic syndrome' which is a constellation of symptoms that together define clinical amnesia. Different patients can have varying levels of retrograde amnesia but to be classed as suffering from classical amnesia, there must be a significant impairment in creating *new* long-term memories, i.e. anterograde amnesia. It is important to point out that a common mistake is to call any sort of memory problem 'amnesia'; by the definition above, formally, it must include a severe anterograde amnesia.

A very important point here is that rarely would either a clinician or a researcher see a patient who has got *total* retrograde and *total* anterograde amnesia since the extent of these will be determined by a large number of factors such as the site and amount of brain damage. In textbooks, like this one, for most neuropsychological examples, the most extreme cases are presented for illustrative purposes but in the 'real world' there are greater shades of grey!

As an example, HM's amnesic episode was the temporal lobectomy and the retrograde amnesia refers to difficulty remembering events prior to the surgery, whereas his anterograde amnesia is clearly seen in his inability to remember any significant event from that point onwards. In the case of a famous British patient called Clive Wearing (Wilson & Wearing, 1995), the amnesic episode was a virus known as herpes simplex encephalitis (HSE) which can be very dangerous if not detected quickly enough and can cause extensive brain damage, or worse still, death. One of the major areas that HSE can destroy is the medial temporal lobes and scans showed that Clive had damage in these areas; so although the two cases are caused by different aetiologies, HM through a surgical procedure and Clive through the virus, the resultant brain damage overlaps a lot. Both HM and Clive had different degrees of retrograde amnesia but were both virtually incapable of creating new long-term memories.

Another form of brain damage that affects memory is known as Wernicke-Korsakoff syndrome (WKS) which is usually related to complications caused by severe and extensive alcoholism. The damage in WKS is in slightly different structures to the medial temporal lobe cases, in areas known as the diencephalon and mammillary bodies (see Figure 8.13). Despite the area of brain damage being different, the anterograde amnesia of patients with WKS is very similar to that of patients like HM and Clive. However, the retrograde amnesia is slightly different; it is usually more severe and shows what is referred to as a negative temporal gradient whereby memory for events just before the onset of the WKS is extremely poor and then gets progressively better as one delves further back into the patient's life.

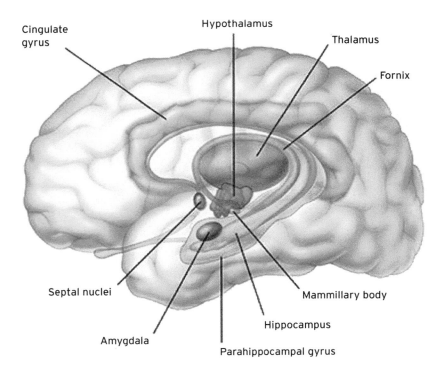

Figure 8.13   Diagram to show some of the central 'mid-brain' structures that are involved directly or indirectly in memory (Garrett & Hough, 2017)

An even more complex form of memory problem is known as focal retrograde amnesia (FRA) where the patient shows almost the opposite pattern of memory problem to the cases just described. For example, patient DH studied by Hunkin et al. (1995) had suffered a head injury following a motorcycle accident, and after recovering it was found that he had a very dense retrograde amnesia, being virtually incapable of remembering any events from his life before the accident. In contrast to this, his ability to learn new things was unaffected allowing him to lead a relatively normal life unlike people like HM and Clive. It should be noted that, given the definition of the amnesic syndrome above, a patient with FRA is *not* considered to be suffering from classical amnesia because he showed very little sign of anterograde amnesia.

Having covered the time periods that are relevant to problems within declarative memory, now we will turn to the actual content of this memory store.

Episodic versus Semantic Memory

One of the greatest thinkers in the field of memory research is Endel Tulving. Evaluating the pattern of intact and impaired abilities in amnesics, Tulving (1972) suggested that all declarative knowledge could be categorised as either episodic or semantic. Episodic memory refers to the ability to remember specific events such as the last time that you rode a bicycle. Semantic memory on the other hand refers to knowing facts such as what a bicycle is. Tulving (1972) suggested that the fundamental problem in amnesia was a difficulty in laying down new episodic memories while semantic memory was left unaffected by the brain damage. One of the main reasons that Tulving suggested this distinction was that the general intelligence of patients with amnesia seemed to be

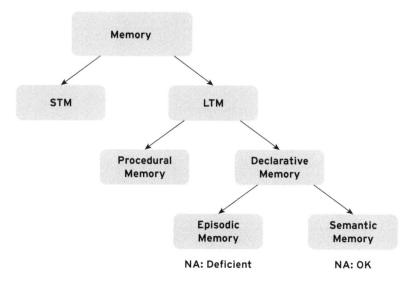

Figure 8.14 Declarative memory splits into episodic and semantic

relatively intact. For example, patient NA studied by Squire & Moore (1979), who was classified as densely amnesic, scored 103 on the Wechsler Adult Intelligence Scale (WAIS) which among its items includes many factually based questions; this test is developed so that the average across the population is 100 and therefore NA's score is totally normal. In contrast to this, NA, like many other amnesics, had very poor autobiographical memory which is one of the most important aspects of episodic memory; autobiographical memory is memory for events that occurred in one's life such as holidays, birthdays and other personal events. Consistently it is found that after a brief period, many amnesics have great difficulty recalling these events from their lives. Tulving's distinction between episodic and semantic memory therefore seems to be supported (see Figure 8.14).

Is Semantic Memory Really Intact in Amnesia?

While Tulving's distinction between episodic and semantic memory was plausible especially because of the way that it explained the clinical picture of patients with amnesia, since the initial research in this area, two lines of evidence have been put forward that imply that the distinction may not be as clear as originally suggested. One argument is about the point in time that the semantic information was first learnt and the other is about the difference between an episodic memory and a semantic one.

One of the original assumptions in Tulving's explanation was that the semantic system is intact in classical amnesia; the evidence for this was that amnesic patients' linguistic and intellectual skills were unimpaired (for example, see the case of NA on pp. 191–192). However, this is probably an oversimplification. Although this unimpaired knowledge is being tested *now* in the post-morbid period, a large majority of it was laid down many years ago in the pre-morbid period, for example, at school and in early adulthood; so patients will have learnt that the capital of France is Paris and that a hippopotamus is a big heavy African animal early in life before they had their brain damage. We saw above that even in patients with dense anterograde amnesia, retrograde amnesia is seldom complete and patients can often remember from earlier parts of their life. Therefore, testing a patient's knowledge from a time from which we know the patient can access memories is not a fair test of what their semantic memory is like *now*.

Butters & Brandt (1985) addressed this in a rather unique study on a university professor who had become amnesic following WKS. Before he became amnesic, the patient, known as PZ, had written an autobiography which was therefore a written record of at least some of his episodic and semantic knowledge at that time. To test whether PZ's semantic memory was intact (as Tulving would have predicted), they presented him with names of academics that he had written about in his book. PZ was asked to give some factual information about each name to demonstrate what he knew about each of these people; this factual information about the academics would be considered semantic memory since PZ wasn't asked for any event-based (episodic) memories of the people. Butters & Brandt (1985) found that compared to matched control participants (who were other professors working in the same field), PZ performed very poorly. This showed that although the names of the academics had been part of his knowledge store at the time of writing the book, his understanding of them at the time of testing in the post-morbid period was greatly impaired. This implies that PZ's semantic system, just like his episodic memory system, had been damaged by the WKS.

The second line of evidence against Tulving's original suggestion is that if the semantic system is intact, then it should be possible to add new facts to the store. As a comparison, remember that when it was suggested that LTM was composed of two different types of memory, procedural and declarative, one important aspect was that procedural memory was proposed to be intact in amnesia; in addition to skills that had been acquired *before* the onset of amnesia being unimpaired, it was found that new skills could be learnt *after* the onset. To address whether in a similar manner the ability to create new semantic memories was unimpaired in HM, Gabrieli et al. (1988) tested HM's knowledge of words that had come into general American English usage since his temporal lobectomy in 1953. They presented him with words like *filofax* and *space shuttle* and asked him to give a definition to evaluate his understanding. It was found that compared to matched controls, HM was significantly impaired. Therefore, unlike his ability to learn new skills that showed that his procedural memory was intact, it seemed that HM's semantic system was not functioning well enough to learn new facts.

When Is a Memory Episodic and When Is It Semantic?

The above two strong arguments have suggested that perhaps episodic and semantic memory are not as distinctly separate as Tulving had originally hypothesised. One way to try to understand why there isn't a clear distinction is to ask the question 'when is a memory episodic and when is it semantic?' To most people the knowledge that Paris is the capital of France is a semantic 'fact'. However, if I was to ask you what the capital of the Pacific nation Tonga is, the likelihood is that you would not know. If I then told you that the capital is Nuku'alofa you would have learned something; the result is that later when I asked you for the capital of Tonga you could give me the correct answer. At this point, is your knowledge episodic or semantic? One way to think about it is to ask 'How do you know something?' so if I was to ask you how you knew that Paris was the capital of France, you would state that it was a fact that you have known for a very long time. However, for the Nuku'alofa example, you are likely to say 'because you have just told me that it is the capital of Tonga'. This latter explanation refers to time-based information and an event occurring, that of me telling you the answer, so in fact, using our definition above, it is an episodic memory. It is very likely that at one point you didn't know that Paris was the capital of France, then learnt it and came across it so many times that it *eventually* became a fact for you.

Marigold Linton (1982) addressed the relationship between episodic and semantic memory in a very interesting study of her own autobiographical memory by meticulously making records of daily events for a period of six years. At the end of this period, she systematically tested her memory of the events. What she found was that if during this six year period she had started doing something for the *first time ever*, her memories for the first few occurrences were very clear with strong 'episodic' detail. For example, she became part of a committee during this period which involved travelling to a new city for the board meetings, and she found that her memory for the first few of these was very clear with vivid detail. However, as she started repeating these once-new events, her recall of these subsequent repetitions (for example, the fifth or sixth board meeting) became quite generic, almost factual, i.e. quite 'semantic'. From this, Linton suggested that when a new event is experienced, recall for it tends to have more of an episodic aspect than semantic, but then with constant repetition, later events of the same type tend to be largely semantic in nature. Another important figure in the field, Laird Cermak (1984), later went on to refer to this shift or change that occurs in the nature of a memory as the semanticisation of memory (see Figure 8.15).

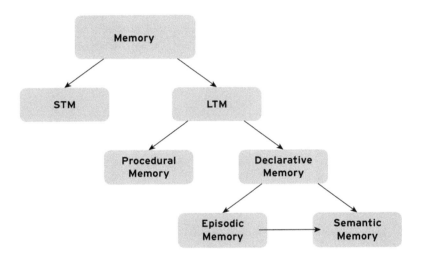

Figure 8.15   The semanticisation of episodic memory into semantic memory

IMPLICIT VERSUS EXPLICIT MEMORY

A final important distinction relevant to the multiplicity of human memory is the level of consciousness involved in the process of remembering information. Consciousness used to be an issue that was only the realm of philosophers such as Descartes (1649) and Leibniz (1916). However, the neurologist Claparéde (1911) tried out something rather bizarre to see if his patients' behaviour would change even if they did not consciously remember learning something previously. He conducted an informal experiment (that would be difficult to get through an ethics committee today!) in which he concealed a small pin in his hand so that it produced a small pain when he shook hands with one of his amnesic patients. Later Claparéde saw that the patient would avoid shaking hands with him again even though he or she could not remember why; since the uncomfortable experience before was the only reason for this change in behaviour, it implied that at some level, the patient had a memory of what had happened.

Many years later, the issue of consciousness was used by cognitive psychologists such as Schacter (1987) to differentiate between different types of memory *testing*. He proposed that any test that required the subject to recall a specific learning episode (and therefore the information that was learnt) consciously should be called explicit memory. As a student, you will take many explicit memory tests in your studies. For example, when you have to write a paper about a topic in an exam, this is an example of 'free recall'; when you have to choose from an answer to a question from a list of possibilities such as in a multiple choice question exam, this is an example of 'recognition'; finally, if you are trying to fill in a cross-word based on information that you had learned in a lecture and where you have already been given the first few letters as a clue, that is an example of 'cued recall'. The common theme across all of these examples is that you are required to consciously remember something that you 'know you know' and which you will hopefully have come across in your revision. Any test which does *not* require any specific reference to the previous learning episode is testing your recall indirectly and is said to be accessing your implicit memory. At a general level, the word explicit can be synonymous with conscious or overt while the word implicit can be synonymous with unconscious or covert.

There are different ways in which it is possible to demonstrate implicit memory in patients with amnesia. At a physiological level for example, Verfaellie et al. (1991) studied

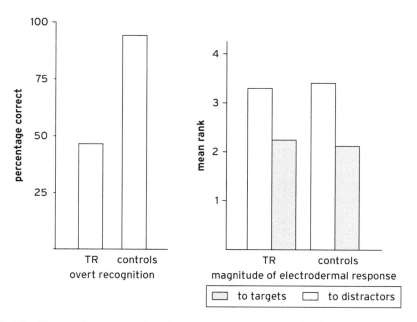

Figure 8.16 The performance of patient TR on overt (or explicit) recognition and his covert recognition (Verfaellie et al., 1991. Reprinted with permission from Academic Press)

memory in an amnesic patient TR using both explicit and implicit methods. They presented the patient and matched controls a group of words to learn; half an hour later they did a standard recognition test, which using the explanation above would be classed as a test of explicit memory. They found that TR was significantly impaired relative to the controls. However, they also tested his galvanic skin response (GSR) while he was viewing the words in the recognition test; the GSR is not under conscious control and therefore it is classed as an implicit measure. What Verfaellie et al. (1991) found was that on this physiological measure, TR's response to target words differed to that for distractor items in exactly the same way as seen in healthy controls (see Figure 8.16). This demonstrates that there is a biological signature of having encountered the information before, so even though the patient is not consciously aware, there is unconscious or implicit recognition.

An even more powerful demonstration is through the use of a repetition priming paradigm which is the change in response to an item (word, object, etc.) as a result of having previously encountered it. In an example of such an experiment, participants could be presented with a list of words to read and simply asked to say whether or not they liked the word. Half an hour after this study phase, participants could be presented with word stems comprising the first three letters of words and asked simply to fill in the fragment with 'the first word that comes to mind'. Some of these stems could be completed using words that had been encountered earlier (for example, the stem MAR___ could be completed as MARKET if this had been one of the studied items), while others were stems for words that had not been presented. Using this paradigm Graf et al. (1984) were able to show that while patients with different types of amnesia performed poorly in a free recall task where they were asked to explicitly remember the words that they had learnt, they performed the same as matched controls on the stem completion task (see Figure 8.17 with patients in black bars and controls in white bars).

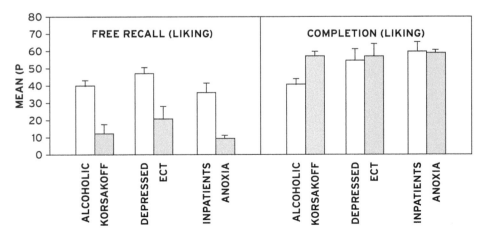

Figure 8.17   The performance of different groups of patients on free recall and stem completion memory tasks (Graf et al., 1984. Copyright © 1984, American Psychological Association)

Both the physiological paradigms using methods such as GSR and the cognitive methods using word stem completion are powerful demonstrations that while an individual with amnesia may not be able to explicitly recall information they have learnt, often it is possible to demonstrate implicit levels of recognition; this is important since it can then be harnessed possibly for rehabilitation.

This would then allow us to expand the memory tree to what is shown in Figure 8.18. Please note that implicit and explicit memory are not different *types* of memory but instead different *processes* to access the same information. Therefore, it is possible to find the word MARKET by either an explicit process of trying to remember hearing it earlier *or* implicitly without thinking about the learning episode; the information that is being retrieved is the same but it is the process by which it is found that differs, and while explicit memory is impaired in people with amnesia, implicit access may be possible.

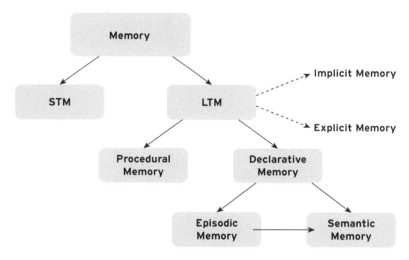

Figure 8.18   Implicit and explicit memory as processes that can be used to access long-term memory

The Role of the Hippocampus

Ever since the seminal work on HM and subsequent studies on patients with HSE, it became very clear that the hippocampus was important for the ability to retain information about our experiences, a kind of 'memory central'. As a result of this, a number of strands of research have explored *why* this area is important, so let's turn to that issue.

Memory as a Basis for Imagining the Future

While the fantastic work in the 1970s and 1980s was instrumental for helping us understand the different divisions in human memory, a different approach has been more prominent since then. Overall, this approach has asked the question 'What is memory for?'

Tulving and his colleagues had noticed that one of the patients that they had documented in a number of studies who had very poor episodic memory for his past *in addition* had difficulties in imagining the *future*. Having seen this in one patient, as good scientists, they began to look at other classically amnesic patients and they found that they too had difficulties in imagining a future event such as 'Tell me what you might be doing for your next birthday?' Although this sounds a bit sci-fi in that none of us knows what the future actually holds, in fact, it makes intuitive sense. As a finely tuned species, for survival, we also need to think about the future, anticipate what might happen, consider different alternatives, maybe change plans, etc. If we weren't able to do this, then we could constantly just be 'stumbling' from one moment to the next. Therefore, an ability to imagine our future ends up sounding like a very important survival skill. Although unrelated, as you will see in Chapter 9 on Executive Functions, one of our most important skills is being able to remember to do things in the future – call your mother at a particular time, give a friend the money you owe them when they arrive, etc.

With Tulving having made this suggestion, one of his PhD students, Dan Schacter, who has since become one of the most prominent memory researchers in the world, has spent the last decade or so at Harvard in Boston demonstrating how vital the central part of the temporal lobes, namely the hippocampus, is for allowing us to do this 'mental time travel' not only into the past to remember events that we have experienced, but also into the future to imagine what may happen.

The Hippocampus for Creating Scenes

While the work in Boston was suggesting that the central role of the hippocampus was the ability to time travel, a very different approach was taken by researchers in London led by Eleanor Maguire. She and her team did a fascinating study into the function of the hippocampus by studying, of all things, London taxi drivers! As a chance finding in a study on patients with damage in the hippocampus, they noticed that one/some of their control participants had abnormally *large* hippocampi. By delving into this chance finding and then investigating groups of taxi drivers, they found that in general taxi drivers in London had larger hippocampi compared to non-taxi drivers who were from similar demographics. Not only this, but they demonstrated that as a novice trainee taxi driver started learning the extensive 'Knowledge' (an in-depth study of a large number of specific London street routes and all places of interest which takes on average 3–4 years to complete), the hippocampus grew with greater knowledge. This work earned Eleanor Maguire the wonderful IgNobel Prize for science that first of all makes us laugh but then makes us think.

Maguire's work was extremely important since it fitted in with one of the most seminal tasks developed for studying spatial navigation and memory. Richard Morris in Edinburgh developed a water maze task which is a circular tank with water that covers a platform that cannot be seen from the surface that experimental rats or mice had to try to swim towards. By manipulating the visual cues on the walls around the tank, Morris and his colleagues demonstrated that the rodents were very likely using these cues to help navigate towards the platform and were able to do so irrespective of where they were placed in the tank after they had learnt the original task. Importantly, Morris et al. (1982) then demonstrated that experimental animals that had had their hippocampi lesioned were no longer able to find the platform that they had been able to before. This suggested that the spatial learning and memory that flowed from it must have been dependent, to some level at least, on the hippocampus. A final piece of the puzzle came about when Hassabis et al. (2007) found that patients with bilateral hippocampal damage were unable to imagine fictitious scenes that were atemporal in that they were not meant to be set in the past, present or the future. Figure 8.19 shows an example from one of their patients describing sitting on a sandy beach. Comparing the patient's attempt with that of a healthy control shows a stark difference in level of detail and coherence of the visual scene.

Cue: *"Imagine you are lying on a white sandy beach in a beautiful tropical bay"*

P03: As for seeing I can't really, apart from just sky. I can hear the sound of seagulls and of the sea...um... I can feel the grains of sand between my fingers...um... I can hear one of those ship's hooters [laughter]...um... that's about it. *Are you actually seeing this in your mind's eye?* No, the only thing I can see is blue. *So if you look around what can you see?* Really all I can see is the colour of the blue sky and the white sand, the rest of it, the sounds and things, obviously I'm just hearing. *Can you see anything else?* No, it's like I'm kind of floating...

Control: It's very hot and the sun is beating down on me. The sand underneath me is almost unbearably hot. I can hear the sounds of small wavelets lapping on the beach. The sea is a gorgeous aquamarine colour. Behind me is a row of palm trees and I can hear rustling every so often in the slight breeze. To my left the beach curves round and becomes a point. And on the point there are a couple of buildings, wooden buildings, maybe someone's hut or a bar of some sort. The other end of the beach, looking the other way, ends in big brown rocks. There's no one else around. Out to sea is a fishing boat. It's quite an old creaking looking boat, chugging past on its small engine. It has a cabin in the middle and pile of nets in the back of the boat. There's a guy in the front and I wave at him and he waves back...[continues]...

Figure 8.19 The performance of a patient (P03) with amnesia and a control participant being asked to imagine fictitious events in the future in Hassabis et al.'s (2007) study (Copyright © 2007, National Academy of Sciences, USA)

Putting all of these different strands together, Maguire and her colleagues came up with the Scene Construction Theory (SCT) which states that the central role of the hippocampus is to generate atemporal scenes. These provide the bedrock for both episodic memory of the past as well as imagined events in the future. However, in addition to this, this scene construction forms the basis of spatial navigation as seen in the water maze and the taxi drivers; in these situations, memory *per se* is not the important cognitive activity, but instead navigating around the world, which in pre-history when we were hunter-gatherers on the African savannah will have been crucial. As is obvious, the

SCT is quite powerful since the Boston theory of the hippocampus being important for a form of time travel either into the past or the future cannot explain why patients with hippocampal damage are unable to describe a scene such as sitting on a sandy beach which doesn't require either of these forms of travel. The SCT can not only explain this but can be used to explain a range of other findings such as spatial navigation; by being able to explain findings at a more general level, the theory gives more explanatory power, making it more powerful.

IS THERE ONE FORM OF AMNESIA OR MANY FORMS?

Going back to Figure 8.1, it is clear that memory problems can come about from a variety of different causes and have manifestations that differ along a number of dimensions. Having earlier defined classical amnesia as the permanent difficulty in creating new long-term memories (see above), an important question is whether there is only one form of brain damage that can bring this about or if in fact there are a number of different amnesias, each caused by damage to different sites in the brain. There has been a complicated history in this debate which isn't yet fully resolved.

Initially, the weight of evidence suggested that amnesia was caused by damage to the medial temporal lobe (MTL) structures. This was due to a large body of evidence, the most famous of which was the seminal work on HM who had had areas of his MTLs, particularly his hippocampi, removed. In addition to this, patients who have survived HSE, such as Clive Wearing, tend to have extensive damage to the MTLs. Finally, there are patients who have damage to very specific areas of only the hippocampus such as patient RB whose lesions, following ischemia (interruption of blood flow to the brain), were restricted to only an area known as the CA1 field of the hippocampus (Zola-Morgan et al., 1986).

While this evidence is very neat, it cannot explain the fact that another major type of amnesia can be caused by WKS. The damage in such patients is not hippocampal but in the mammillary bodies of the diencephalon. Between the 1970s and 1990s, there was extensive work by Albert et al. (1979) and Cohen & Squire (1981) in the States and Alan Parkin at Sussex University in Brighton, UK to demonstrate that MTL and WKS were two different forms of amnesia. It is beyond the scope of this textbook to go into details but the evidence seemed relatively strong that *at least at some level* the two sites of damage caused different manifestations of memory problems which superficially looked very similar but which on closer scrutiny demonstrated differences.

To complicate matters further John Aggleton in Cardiff has conducted a series of very elegant studies that have demonstrated that damage to another area known as the fornix can produce amnesia (Aggleton et al., 2000). More recently, using work with animals, he has shown that yet another area, known as the retrosplenial cortex, is important in the formation of memories and therefore damage to this area can also cause 'an' amnesia.

So what does this mean? Are there at least four different types of amnesia caused by MTL damage, WKS or lesions in the fornix or retrosplenial cortex? Possibly… but following Occam's Razor – that we should not needlessly multiply our explanations when a simpler explanation could suffice – a possibility is that there is only *one amnesia* but with different manifestations depending on the site of damage. This explanation is made highly plausible by the fact that all four of these structures are linked because of rich connections between them. Certainly the hippocampus, thalamus and mammillary bodies are all linked in a very old neural system known as the Papez circuit and this system itself has strong connections to the retrosplenial circuit (see Figure 8.13). Given this rich interconnectedness between each of these structures which are processing different aspects of our current experience, it becomes plausible that damage to *any* of the major structures will disrupt neural processing of that event and therefore impair the representations that are laid down. If these representations are poor at the point of encoding, then a difficulty in recreating the original memory is an obvious consequence.

While there is no clear answer on whether there are many forms of amnesia or just one, a more holistic explanation as suggested by Aggleton and colleagues is very compelling. It is the job of researchers to test this theory by investigating the performance of patients with different lesions within this system. Further, theories like the SCT will need to explain why damage to areas outside the hippocampus cause a memory problem, given that central to that framework is the role of the hippocampus to create atemporal scenes.

ACCELERATED LONG-TERM FORGETTING

The amnesic syndrome is defined (see above) as a constellation of problems which includes a deficiency in laying down new long-term memories; this latter crucial element is usually assessed by presenting an individual information, testing them straight away (to ensure that they have paid attention and the information has gone into STM) and then testing them at a delay, usually around half an hour to see whether the information has been transferred to LTM. Depending on the difficulty of the task, most people will perform slightly worse 30 minutes after hearing something compared to immediately after the event; however, patients with classical amnesia will show a severe impairment, often having forgotten everything. This might initially suggest that 'passing' a memory test means that an individual has no memory problem. However, Kapur et al. (1997) documented the case of a patient with temporal lobe epilepsy who performed normally on standard clinical tests of memory, but compared to matched controls was densely amnesic 40 days later. They suggested that this was evidence that the consolidation process – that at a neurobiological level strengthens connections between neurons and is central to learning and memory – was more complex than originally thought. They suggested that instead of this being a 'one-off' process moving information from STM to

LTM in one single consolidation stage, that there were multiple stages to this that may take days, weeks or months.

Since Kapur et al.'s (1997) documentation of long-term amnesia which then became known as accelerated long-term forgetting (ALF), there has been growing interest in the area. There are multiple reasons for this interest, partially because it allows clinicians and researchers to understand groups of patients who in the past didn't fit the category of amnesia that patients with temporal lobe damage demonstrated. Many patients with temporal lobe epilepsy fall into this category, and this is possibly because the seizures that they experience (similar to what HM will have experienced before his temporal lobectomy) interrupt the consolidation processes that are thought to start in the hippocampus. Importantly, while this has been shown in adults with transient epileptic amnesia (for example, Butler et al., 2007), accelerated long-term forgetting has also been shown in children with epilepsy by Gascoigne et al. (2019).

In addition to adults with epilepsy, accelerated long-term forgetting has also been found in older participants who complained of memory problems but who performed normally on standard tests by Manes et al. (2008). This is an important group because while it is well known that part of healthy ageing is a small deterioration of memory (my 83-year-old mother's memory is not what it used to be when she was 50 for example), statistically, it is known that those who complain of everyday memory problems are at greater risk of developing what is known as mild cognitive impairment (MCI) and perhaps progressing to one of the most common forms of dementia, Alzheimer's disease. Given this risk and the fact that such older participants perform *normally* on the tests that are currently used by clinicians, an important aim of researchers has become the need to develop more sensitive tests to capture those at risk of dementia in the future.

Jansari and colleagues have addressed this issue after documenting accelerated long-term forgetting in a patient with subclinical epilepsy. Using a task that involved learning and then recalling fictitious stories at a number of different intervals, Jansari et al. (2010) showed that their patient RY was significantly impaired within a day of first learning stories despite having passed the standard clinical tests (see Figure 2.9). While at an experimental level it is interesting to know that such forgetting can be objectively measured, from a clinical perspective, it is not useful since in most clinical practices, if a patient sees a neuropsychologist for evaluation, they would see them once for maybe up to two hours but either never again or only again after a very long delay. Therefore, a test that requires a patient to learn stories and be tested on them the following day could not be used clinically for pragmatic reasons. To address this, McGibbon & Jansari (2013) developed the Verbal Associative Learning & Memory Test (VALMT) which involves learning pairs of unconnected words (for example, TABLE-SHAWL) and then at a number of delays giving the first word of the pair and testing for recall of its pair. They found that on this new task, RY, who had only shown an impairment on the story recall task, now was impaired within 55 minutes of learning new information (see Figure 8.20).

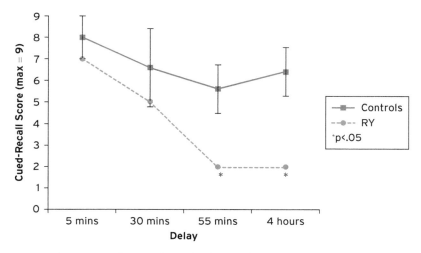

Figure 8.20   Performance of RY and matched controls on the Verbal Associative Learning & Memory Test demonstrating his impaired memory within 55 minutes of learning new information (McGibbon & Jansari, 2013)

Given that societally, it will be necessary to find ways to diagnose dementia earlier than has been possible, VALMT is now being used to explore memory in older populations. It has been found that when healthy elderly individuals who *currently* have no diagnosis for any cognitive impairment were classified as 'Fast' or 'Slow' depending on how quickly they initially learnt the word pairs on VALMT, there was a striking difference in their memory performance (McGibbon et al., 2022). While the Fast group showed very little forgetting and were quite similar in their 'forgetting curve' to a Younger group, the Slow Elderly showed catastrophic forgetting that was similar to that of patient RY (see Figure 8.21). Importantly, the performance of the Fast and Slow Elderly was indistinguishable on one of the standard memory tests that is used regularly by clinicians. Depending on whether these results can be replicated, there is a possibility that VALMT is detecting a *preclinical signature* of dementia in that performance on it might allow prediction of who is at risk of developing the condition. If this was the case then it may be possible to put support mechanisms in place for these individuals even before the obvious signs of the disorder become apparent. Finally, Jansari & McGibbon (2022) have shown that VALMT differentiated between a group of participants who engaged in recreational sports that involved head contact (football, rugby, American football, etc.) and those who didn't. Given the increasing understanding that CTE can be caused by small repeated knocks to the head as can occur in contact sports, and the fact that a sizeable proportion of professionals from these sports develop early onset dementia, this implies that VALMT may be able to pick up the subtle effects of these repeated non-concussive head injuries. Since many people begin to play sports during childhood and it is known that the brain is constantly developing during childhood and adolescence (see Figure 9.4), it is important to consider the impact that the repeated head injuries have on this forming brain.

It is interesting to note how the work that started with patients like HM in 1957 has evolved into understanding the complexities of human memory and then how some of this can be applied to groups (the healthy elderly and people who engage in contact sports) that would not ordinarily be seen within the umbrella of neuropsychology.

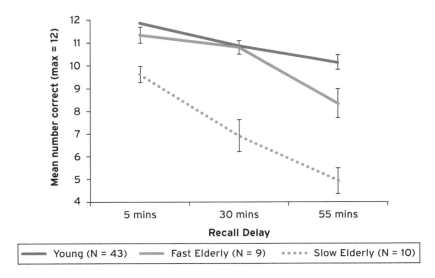

Figure 8.21   Performance on VALMT of Young and healthy Elderly participants who had been separated into those who learnt the word pairs in the task quickly and those who were slower (McGibbon et al., 2022)

Chapter Summary

- Memory is a complex skill that brings together a lot of sensory information, and for survival some of this needs to be filtered out by the process of attention and the remainder moved to a temporary short-term store. Depending on various factors, some of this then gets transferred to a more permanent long-term store.
- Various models for the functioning of these stores have been put forward, the two most prominent ones being the Modal Model and the Working Memory Model. These have highlighted various properties, particularly of the short-term store.
- Research on patients with various memory disorders, particularly amnesia, has shown that long-term memory is complex with double dissociations demonstrating a difference between procedural and declarative memory as well as episodic and semantic memory. There is also a difference between implicit and explicit memory processes.
- Recently, research has focused on the role of the hippocampus, with two prominent theories suggesting that it is for imagining the future or for creating the visual scenes that allow us to navigate around the world.

- More recently, research has begun to explore the issue of accelerated forgetting whereby individuals pass the standard tests of memory but nonetheless show catastrophic forgetting. This work is being applied to areas that are not traditionally seen within this area, namely the early diagnosis of dementia and the impact of closed head injuries through contact sports.

Important Researchers

Brenda Milner, Endel Tulving and Alan Baddeley

In a field as big as memory it is unsurprising that it's impossible to choose *one* important researcher. These three individuals have all made monumental contributions to the field.

Brenda Milner is a British-Canadian neuropsychologist who did her PhD with the famous Donald Hebb who did seminal work on the formation of synapses. It was Brenda's insights into the impact of a bilateral temporal lobectomy that resulted in the monumental findings on memory and amnesia with patient HM. She worked with HM for many years as did her students including Suzanne Corkin, also a very prominent memory researcher. Remarkably, at the age of 103, Brenda was still working!

Endel Tulving is an Estonian-born Canadian experimental psychologist who some refer to as the Godfather of memory research – if something is said about memory, then Endel probably said it first! He is famous for differentiating between episodic and semantic memory and also coming up with the 'encoding specificity principle' regarding the fact that the environment we are in has an impact on how we store information. He wrote a book in 1983, *Elements of Episodic Memory*, which has been cited over 3000 times, and many of his students, such as Dan Schacter, have gone on to become greats of the field.

Alan Baddeley is a British psychologist who along with his PhD student Graham Hitch developed the Working Memory Model to elaborate on the structure of short-term memory. This model has endured for over 50 years which is a testament to Alan's precise thinking which allows the model to explain so many different aspects of everyday working memory. Recent work by another of his students, Susan Gathercole, has looked at how evaluating working memory in school children can be extremely useful for helping them improve in their studies, demonstrating that the model is not just explanatory but has real-world consequences. Rather nicely, Alan and Graham still work together over 50 years since developing their model.

Important Research Study

HM

Henry Gustav Molaison is possibly the most famous patient in the history of cognitive neuropsychology. Students often cite Phineas Gage and Tan rather than HM but the fact is that psychology, let alone neuropsychology, hadn't even been *born* when those two patients were documented by *neurologists*. Henry suffered a head injury before the age of 10 from an accident while riding his bicycle and as with a number of other patients (see KF in Chapter 3) developed epilepsy. Having localised Henry's epilepsy to his medial temporal lobes, neurosurgeon William

Beecher Scoville suggested removing these damaged parts of the brain that were causing the seizures in a surgery that was experimental. Given the intense severity of his seizures, the family consented to it, and indeed the surgery in 1953 greatly reduced his seizures. However, for the next 55 years, he was not able to lay down any meaningful long-term memories. The remarkable Brenda Milner noticed that the surgery had left Henry with intact STM but his LTM was severely affected, and so began the systematic studies that lasted for half a century, first by herself, then by her student Suzanne Corkin and then her students. He was referred to as HM to protect his identity and his name was only made public after his death.

Questions for Reflection

- Is there only one human memory or more than one?
- Is amnesia one condition or is it a number of deficits?

Go Further

- What is the actual deficit in amnesia - is it how the information is encoded, stored or retrieved? This issue has been debated for decades and the prevailing thought is that it is a problem in consolidation (storage).
- Given the complexity of the different aspects of memory, it is unsurprising that many different parts of the brain are involved - so where is STM and is it in a very different place from LTM? What about procedural memory?
- Why, even among healthy individuals, is there such a massive spectrum of memory abilities? How can we all get a bit better?

Go Further

Dr Jansari's YouTube Videos
Memory, forgetting & dementia: What is human memory and why do we forget? (Parts 1 and 2)

'What did I just read? I don't know, I can't remember' – is what anybody without a memory would say. Technically it's a bit more complicated than that, but you get the gist. Memory is a crucial part of our existence, for what is life if not a collection of memories. This video reviews how neuropsychologists are developing an understanding of the complexity of human memory, what we can do to help those with different forms of memory problems and the efforts that are being made to try to diagnose dementia.

How can we improve our memory? Insights from a cognitive neuropsychologist

It seems only fitting that for you to retain any of the information you just read, you should probably know how to remember. This video goes over the best ways to reduce the chances of you forgetting something.

Further Reading

- Schacter, D. L. (2002). *The Seven Sins of Memory: How the Mind Forgets and Remembers*. HMH.
- Wearing, D. (2005). *Forever Today: A Memoir of Love and Amnesia*. Random House.
- Maguire, E. A., Gadian, D. G., Johnsrude, I. S., Good, C. D., Ashburner, J., Frackowiak, R. S., & Frith, C. D. (2000). Navigation-related structural change in the hippocampi of taxi drivers. *Proceedings of the National Academy of Sciences, 97*(8), 4398–4403.
- Ekstrom, A. D., Spiers, H. J., Bohbot, V. D., & Rosenbaum, R. S. (2018). *Human Spatial Navigation*. Princeton University Press.
- Parkin, A. J. (2013). *Memory and Amnesia: An Introduction*. Psychology Press.

9
EXECUTIVE FUNCTIONS

Chapter Overview

This chapter will explore the skills that you use every day almost on a moment-by-moment basis. Generally speaking, the posterior two-thirds of the brain process your current experiences and feed this information forward to the front of the brain. The front of the brain is able to hold onto the information that you have been listening to, seeing right at this moment or feeling, and then use this to decide what to do in the next minute, next hour or next day. It is effectively the manager of the brain that co-ordinates and makes all our higher level decisions. As will become obvious, any difficulties with this part of the brain will have important consequences.

Chapter Outline

INTRODUCTION: HISTORICAL BACKGROUND

A pivotal event in neuropsychology (which only gained its true importance many years later) happened in 1848 during a bizarre incident at the construction site of an American railroad. One of the workers, Phineas Gage (see Figure 9.1) accidentally set off an explosion that resulted in a tamping iron about an inch in diameter shooting up through his lower cheek and out of the top of his head, flying 20 ft in the air before landing. Amazingly, the heat of the bar cauterised and therefore sealed the hole that it made in Phineas Gage's head. Not only did he survive, he was actually able to walk away from the scene and talk quite easily. Initially, it seemed that this accident had had no major harmful effects. However, with time, this amiable reliable man became quite unreliable, made very bad judgements (e.g. he managed to ruin himself financially) and seemed to lack social skills. A neurologist, Harlow (1868), who worked with Gage suggested that the damage to his brain had disrupted the ability to plan and to maintain socially accepted behaviour.

Figure 9.1 Phineas Gage holding the tamping iron that went through his face

At the time, it was not possible for Harlow to investigate his ideas, but almost 150 years later a patient, EVR, underwent surgery to remove a tumour from an area in the frontal lobes just above the left eye. Due to the fact that neurosurgery involves intrusive procedures that cannot be avoided, a certain amount of brain damage is left by the surgery if the tumour is not on the surface of the brain. Since EVR's tumour was very deep in his frontal lobes, he was left with unavoidable brain damage at the base of his left frontal lobe. Following recovery, the neurologists working with him noticed an identical change in behaviour that was seen in Phineas Gage: EVR became totally immersed in mundane tasks and entered into risky business ventures, thereby bankrupting himself which ultimately led to him losing his job (Damasio, 2006).

Seeing the similarity between EVR and how Phineas Gage had been described, Hanna Damasio tried to recreate the damage that must have occurred to Phineas Gage's brain. Using Phineas Gage's skull and the original iron bar (both kept in the Harvard Medical Museum in Boston) she recreated the original shape of his brain prior to the accident. Then using a sophisticated brain-imaging system, computer simulations 'shot' the iron bar through Phineas Gage's simulated brain to determine what exact parts had been damaged in the accident (see Figure 9.2). The findings showed that the damage Phineas Gage had sustained was in the same location as EVR's. By studying EVR, it became possible to confirm the preliminary evaluation that Harlow had made of the cognitive deficits suffered by Phineas Gage, despite him having died over a hundred years before (Damasio et al., 1994). Having done this, Antonio Damasio went on to create a sophisticated model of the functions of the frontal lobes which formed the basis for his book, *Descartes' Error* (Damasio, 2006). Although the main import of this study is a historical one, it shows clearly how a behavioural description of an individual from 150 years ago and clinical, experimental and brain imaging work on a current patient can be used to help develop models of cognitive functioning.

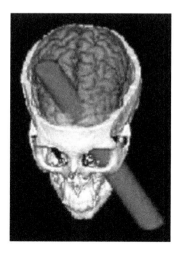

Figure 9.2   Reconstruction of the damage to Phineas Gage's brain

EVOLUTION AND DEVELOPMENT OF THE FRONTAL LOBES

To understand why the damage to Phineas Gage and EVR caused such catastrophic changes in behaviour it is useful to look at both the evolution and development of the brain particularly with the frontal lobes. Although there are different ways to measure the size, volume and density of different brain areas, it is fairly well accepted that compared to most other animal species, the human prefrontal cortex is proportionately the largest. For example, while in a squirrel monkey the frontal lobes take up about one twentieth of the brain (5%) moving through the animal hierarchy to the chimpanzee, this increases to a quarter of the brain; the human frontal lobes take up a third of the brain (see Figure 9.3). Similarly, it has been found using complex analysis by Smaers et al. (2017) that in the great apes and humans, the expansion within the frontal lobes has been significantly greater than the expansion in other more posterior parts of the brain. Therefore, compared to other animals and to our own evolutionary ancestors, the frontal lobes seem to be of central importance.

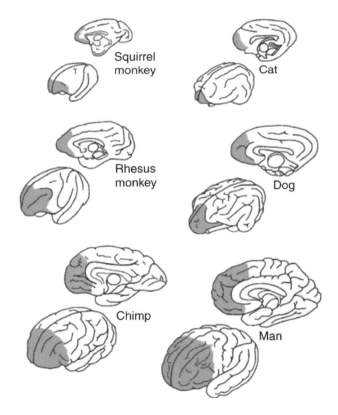

Figure 9.3 Proportion of the brain taken up by the frontal lobes (in blue) across different species (Reprinted from: The Prefrontal Cortex; Anatomy, Physiology and Neuropsychology of the Frontal Lobe (2nd edn). By Joaquin M. Fuster. New York: Raven Press. 1989. 255 pp. *The British Journal of Psychiatry, 155*(4), 579–579)

In a very important longitudinal study, Gogtay et al. (2004) tracked the development of the brains of a group of children for up to ten years, scanning their brains every two years. Using sophisticated computer models to understand the patterns that were emerging and extrapolating these patterns, they were able to demonstrate that as a child is developing, although there is constant change across the brain, this change is not uniform with some areas developing much faster than others (see Figure 9.4). Importantly, Gogtay et al. found that areas of the brain that are older from an evolution-ary perspective matured quite early, with newer areas maturing later. They also found that, generally, the 'axis' of development was from more posterior areas of the brain moving forwards. Both these findings point to the fact that today, our frontal lobes are the last to fully mature with some estimates suggesting that the human brain isn't fully 'cooked' until the early to mid-20s ☺.

At the other end of the age spectrum, while the relationship is complex, it is well accepted that healthy ageing, unrelated to any degenerative disorders such as demen-tia, nonetheless involves a weakening of the executive functions. This became known as the *frontal lobe hypothesis*, which suggests that this deterioration of executive func-tions is caused by the atrophy (shrinkage) of some parts of the frontal lobes (e.g. Moscovitch & Winocur, 1992).

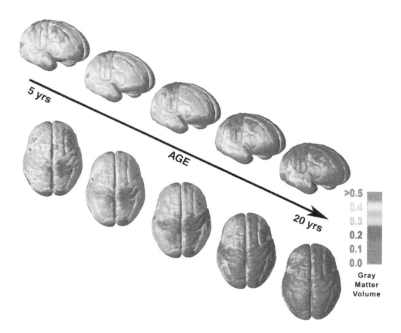

Figure 9.4   Gogtay et al.'s images of the child's developing brain with the frontal regions reaching full maturity last (Copyright © 2004, National Academy of Sciences, USA)

ASSESSMENT OF EXECUTIVE FUNCTIONS: TRADITIONAL CLINICAL ASSESSMENTS

Given the complexity of difficulties associated with frontal lobe development or dysfunction and models of executive functions (see below), it isn't surprising that there is a large number of assessments that clinicians and researchers have used for decades. Amongst the most common are the Stroop Test, the Verbal Fluency Test, the Trail Making Test Form B (TMT-B) and the Wisconsin Card Sorting Test (WCST) (see Figure 9.5), with each evaluating different aspects of executive functions. The Stroop Test relies on the automaticity of our reading system and usually involves one condition where the names of colours are written in that particular colour (for example, the word RED written in red ink). A different condition would involve the same words but written in an 'incongruent' colour, i.e. different to the word itself (for example, the word RED written in blue ink: see Figure 9.5a). The task would be, in each condition, to name *the colour of the ink* rather than reading the word itself. In the first 'congruent' condition, this would be easy since the colour of the ink is red and the word itself is RED; however, in the incongruent condition, the correct answer is 'blue' (the colour of the ink) and therefore the word RED itself has to be ignored. Usually most people find the second condition much harder and therefore more errors are made and/or it takes much longer to go through a list of such items. The *difference* between the congruent and incongruent conditions gives a measure of *automaticity*.

Green   Red   **BluePurple   Blue   Purple**

Blue   Purple   **Red   Green   Purple   Green**

Figure 9.5a   Stroop test example

Source: Fitness queen04, 'Stroop Effect Memory test.png', published under creative commons attribution-share alike 3.0 unported license on Wikimedia Commons

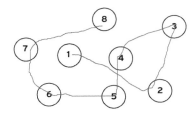

Figure 9.5b   Trail Making Test Form B (TMT-B)

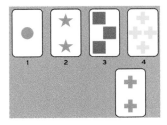

Figure 9.5c   Wisconsin Card Sorting Test (WCST)

Source: Grant & Berg (1948)

The Verbal Fluency Test is relatively simple requiring a participant to produce as many words as possible in a minute for each of three categories. The simplest version involves producing words beginning with the letters F, A and then S for a minute each, while another version could be words from three different categories such as animals, vegetables and items of furniture. There are a number of scores that can be used by a clinician or researcher, such as number of correctly produced words. Since a participant has to come up with as many different words in a minute as possible, this test shows the *flexibility* of the cognitive system for producing new items given certain constraints without being stuck saying the same items repeatedly.

The TMT-B is a relatively simple paper-and-pencil task in which a series of circles are presented on a sheet of paper in a random configuration, each with the one figure in it, either a letter or a number from A to L and 1 to 13. The task is to draw a line joining the circles alternating in ascending letters and digits; therefore, the participant should draw a line from the circle with the A to the circle with a 1 and then from that one to the circle with a B followed by the circle with a 2, etc. (see Figure 9.5b). Since this task requires alternating between two different organised sets of information (letters and numbers), it requires *visual attention* and *task switching* which is vital for survival in everyday life to allow us to cope with change.

The WCST is one of the most complex executive tasks and involves sorting a set of cards into piles like you would sort regular playing cards. For the latter, you could put all the 2s together, all the Jacks together and all the Aces together. In the WCST, the cards have got different quantities (one to four) of one of a number of shapes (circles, squares, etc.), that are in one of four colours (see Figure 9.5c). The participant has to sort these cards, one at a time, into piles according to a rule that the person assessing knows but that *they do not tell the participant who instead has to guess* – the assessor simply says 'yes' or 'no' after each sorting attempt and the participant has to show the ability to respond to the feedback that they are receiving and to change their sorting strategy. Even when the participant works out what the sorting rule is, after a set number of correct responses, the assessor then changes the sorting rule; so for example, the rule they had in mind might have been 'colour' but after four successful sorts, they change to 'shape'. At this point, the participant needs to understand that a rule that *was* working for a while no longer works. There are quite a few different scores that can be extracted from performance on the WCST but one major one is the number of correct categories that are sorted since that demonstrates the ability to take feedback from the external world (in this case the assessor saying 'yes' or 'no' to whether they have got the sorting rule correct). Another important measure comes from how the participant changes their behaviour once the assessor changes category; so for example, if 'colour' had been the correct one and after four correct sorts, the assessor says 'no', the participant needs to guess the new sorting rule. Some individuals get 'stuck' and cannot move out of the rule that they have been sorting on and continue with the rule that has been correct but is no longer correct. This is known as perseveration which is a classic sign of an executive problem.

Tests such as the Stroop, Verbal Fluency Test, TMT-B and WCST have been used for decades by clinicians and researchers, both to assess patients with behavioural problems and to scientifically understand the functioning of the frontal lobes. For example, the

WCST had been used in over 600 scientific published papers by 2004. However, as we will see later, the fact that tests have been used many times and are part of the arsenal that is employed by a clinician in their assessment of patients does not necessarily guarantee that the results or conclusions based on performance are reliable or valid.

MODELS OF EXECUTIVE FUNCTIONS

Since the 1970s, as models of our cognitive behaviour have developed and been refined and our ability to understand the problems demonstrated by patients with brain damage has improved, it has been possible for different groups of scientists to start to try to map out how our ability to manage our higher order abilities occurs. Although there are a number of different models each with a different focus, four main models will be discussed here since they are amongst the most prominent and therefore influential.

Baddeley & Hitch's Central Executive

As demonstrated in Chapter 8, weaknesses within Atkinson & Shiffrin's Modal Model led to the development of the Working Memory Model by Baddeley & Hitch to explain findings such as a patient with brain damage having an impairment within STM but still being able to create new long-term memories. While the modality-specific systems (the Articulatory Loop (AL) and the Visuo-Spatial Sketchpad (VSSP) being the main ones) handled processing of information that was initially encountered through one of the senses (hearing or vision for example), they hypothesised that there was a central processor that, amongst other things, co-ordinated information flow between these systems. An easy example is that while you are *looking* at these words visually, you can probably hear an 'inner voice' that is saying out these words so that your experience is of *hearing* the words. You probably don't remember when you were a toddler who was first learning to read letters, but there was a time when what feels automatic to you (reading visually presented words) was actually quite a challenge and this skill had to be learnt. At that point, your reading system was developing and the system that was coordinating between your visual system and your inner voice to 'sound out' the letters and words to thereby develop your reading system was this 'translation' system known as the Central Executive.

The Central Executive was thought to cover a number of different activities, and in fact the earliest evidence came from Baddeley & Hitch (1976), who hypothesised that if STM did indeed have a limited capacity (for example, 7±2 items), and this capacity is taken up with trying to hold onto a set of numbers for a memory task, then an individual should not be able to perform a *secondary* task such as an abstract reasoning task. What they found, however, was that although participants' time for performing the secondary task increased as the number of words to remember for the primary task increased, there was no impact on accuracy. What this implied was that the cognitive system could perform two tasks *simultaneously*. This led to the development of dual-task paradigms, which involve one primary task being performed at the same time as a secondary task, to explore the limits of the cognitive system and, particularly in this case, the Central Executive. Baddeley et al. (1997) went on to use this method to demonstrate that patients with frontal lobe lesions who showed everyday executive deficits were impaired when two unrelated tasks were combined despite being able to perform each task separately. This gave further strength to the possibility of the Central Executive being located within the frontal lobes.

With there being clear evidence for a 'managerial' system, the Central Executive is thought to perform a number of different tasks. These involve: 1) The co-ordination of activity of the primary sensory systems. As described above, the AL and the VSSP are the most obvious primary systems but there is nothing to say that we don't have primary systems for our other major sensory systems since we also have memory for smell, taste and proprioception (touch). 2) The co-ordination of retrieval strategies from long-term memory, since as described in Chapter 8, information about what you did on your last birthday, what the capital of Mongolia is and what Einstein's famous equation is are all held in a longer-term store that needs to be accessed when we need this information. 3) The selection of attention which allows the cognitive system to focus on the most relevant information, since at any one time we are experiencing multiple forms of information.

Although Baddeley did not have a specific model of the Central Executive, work was being carried out during the 1980s and 1990s on patients with different forms of brain damage and psychopathology who were showing difficulties in overall management of behaviour. One particular model, also being developed in the UK, helped him suggest how we could conceptualise these managerial functions (see Supervisory Attentional System below).

Norman & Shallice's Supervisory Attentional System

Norman & Shallice took as the shell of their model the thinking of the great Russian Alexandra Luria, who is known widely as the father of modern neuropsychological assessment. Luria had suggested that there are three general levels of brain function almost like layers of an onion. The deepest and innermost level is the brain stem which is responsible for general arousal for basic survival. The second layer is responsible for taking in information from the environment as well as from the rest of the body, processing it and storing it; this layer is found in the temporal, occipital and parietal lobes. The highest level is responsible for coordinating and regulating moment-to-moment behaviour and this is found in the newest part of the brain, the frontal lobes.

Norman & Shallice took Luria's thinking one step further by suggesting what the functional units were within this three-layer system. Within their model, the fundamental elements were 'programmes' for actions or thoughts, known as schemas that an individual has learnt over time. Although they did not explicitly state this, these schemas are probably equivalent to the procedural memory that was referred to in Chapter 8. For example, there would be a programme for how to change gears in a car, one for how to comb your hair, another one for how to use the keyboard on a laptop and another one for how to write a text on the screen of a smartphone; similarly, there would be 'scripts' of what to think when asked a question about favourite pastimes, make a decision when someone offers you two different options for a train journey, etc. Each of these programmes or scripts is a separate schema for that particular action or thought. These schemas are activated either by the output of recently activated schemas (so effectively the last thing that was done) or environmental conditions that the individual is going through; these conditions are either external from the sensory information that is being experienced, or internal from thoughts or personal needs. It is thought that there is an enormous but finite number of schemas (potentially all the physical things that one can do or can think) and that these are arranged in some sort of hierarchy. So for example, something relatively simple such as how to tie shoelaces is a low-level action schema, whereas how to do statistical analysis for a complex research study would be a high-level schema.

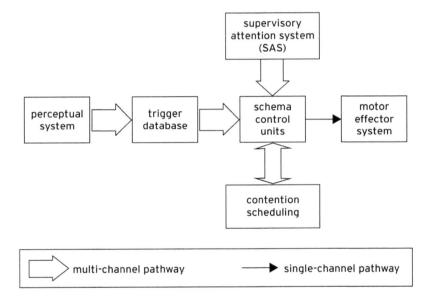

Figure 9.6   Norman & Shallice's (1986) Supervisory Attentional System (Reprinted with permission from Springer Nature)

Figure 9.6 shows a representation of Norman & Shallice's model. Information from the external environment comes in through the senses and is processed by the perceptual system (eyes, ears, etc.) which then goes to a trigger database which is the set of thoughts and actions that you are experiencing *at this precise moment*. This is obviously a combination of the information that is coming in from the outside world as well as the output of what you have just been doing or thinking. This combination of external sensory information and your current internal state is the pool of information that will trigger one of the schemas. If this happens efficiently, then the output from a particular schema for what you need to do *right now* is chosen and this then activates a set of responses through the motor system. As an example, if you are driving a car, currently the schema for driving a car at a steady speed is active and this allows your legs and arms to control your car as necessary. As the traffic starts thinning out, this information is being processed by the perceptual system which is being fed into the trigger database. This is also being activated by your internal thoughts about needing to get home by a particular time; the combination of seeing that the traffic is decreasing and the thought that you need to get home soon makes you decide to accelerate your speed. This is a *change* from what you are doing at the moment and so a new schema needs to be activated; once this new schema is activated, the motor effector system makes this happen by changing the gear with one hand or simply by pressing your foot on the accelerator.

So far it is possible to understand what happens under 'normal' conditions but we are constantly having to alter our behaviour because of changing circumstances or because of an emergency. The SAS deals with this by having two separate control systems known as contention scheduling and the supervisory attentional system (SAS). Contention scheduling ensures that the correct schema is activated from the information in the trigger database and once this has happened, other schemas that could potentially be initiated are inhibited. For example, while driving, it is necessary to look in the mirrors to check for traffic that is coming up from behind. Under other circumstances, looking in a mirror is used to make sure that you look OK or that your hair isn't a mess, etc. However, while driving, when monitoring the state of the traffic on the road, a glance in a mirror should *not* activate the schema for tidying one's hair and this is prevented by the contention scheduling.

The SAS comes into action when a big change is needed or there is an emergency. It monitors what someone is currently doing, allows planning of actions for the future and for thinking about how to solve novel situations for which there isn't an existing schema, as well as being vigilant for any danger. Taking the driving example, although the current schema might have you accelerating to get home quickly, if a cat or a child runs into the road, the SAS would immediately come in to *stop* the current schema and to activate the schema for doing an emergency brake. In essence, the contention scheduling allows you to continue doing routine activities while the SAS becomes active when a change is required.

Stuss & Benson's Three Process Model

About 20 years after Norman & Shallice suggested their model, a group of researchers in Toronto, Canada at the Rotman Research Institute at Baycrest Centre, who had been researching the deficits that patients with frontal lobe damage demonstrate, came at the issue from a slightly different angle. They hypothesised that there wasn't *one* frontal lobe function, and therefore rather than creating a model that tried to explain everything within this one system, they instead started looking at the *processes* that were involved in the types of tasks that patients showed consistent difficulties in. They created their own set of tests that they called ROBBIA – the ROtman-Baycrest Battery for the Integration of Attention (Stuss et al., 2005). In addition to testing their patients on the ROBBIA, they also tested them on traditional tests such as the Stroop and the WCST to see if similar processes were involved.

By studying many patients using this large range of tasks, rather than imposing a 'top-down' model that they then tried to support with evidence, they let the evidence inform them what the model should be – in traditional research we call this 'bottom-up', where the data tells you the answers. From their extensive analysis of both the types of errors patients were showing and the areas of the brain where they showed brain damage, they suggested that there are four general functions within the frontal lobes which they named Energisation, Executive, Emotion/Behavioural Regulation and Metacognition; interestingly, only the second of these was seen to be what is cognitively seen as 'executive functions'.

Within this framework, there are two types of executive functions, *task setting* and *monitoring*. Task setting is brought into play when a conditional 'if-then' process is involved, so for example, in the Stroop, the task would be '*If* the word you see is a word you know, *then* ignore the word and just name the colour of the ink it is written in'. This task setting also involves 'adjustment of contention scheduling' (Stuss, 2011, p. 760) since, using the Norman & Shallice framework, this involves being able to move from one pre-programmed task to another. Patients who had errors in task setting tended to have damage in the left dorsolateral areas of the prefrontal cortex (PFC) or lDLPFC (see Figure 9.7). The other executive function, monitoring, requires keeping track of one's performance, particularly under conditions where speed is important. Patients who made errors in such tests tended to have damage in the right dorsolateral areas of the PFC or rDLPFC.

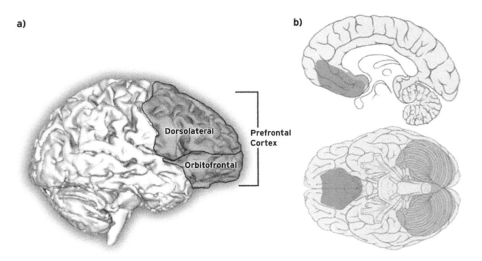

Figure 9.7   Three major areas of the frontal lobes implicated in executive functions: a) the dorsolateral and orbitofrontal, and b) the ventromedial prefrontal cortices

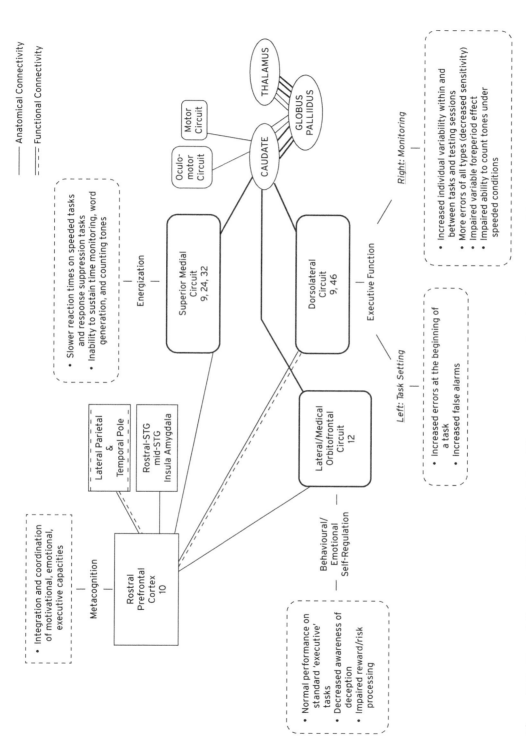

Figure 9.8 Stuss & Benson's (1986) model of the different processes within the distinct parts of the frontal lobes and their connectivity to each other as well as to other parts of the brain (Reprinted with permission from Cambridge University Press)

Within the Stuss & Benson model, the three other functions within the frontal lobes are related to but not integral to the executive functions. Energisation is the process of initiating (starting) and sustaining any cognitive or behavioural response. This is required in a range of tasks such as those that need you to suppress behaviour (e.g. Stroop) or to keep going and create new information such as in the Verbal Fluency FAS task. Their patients who had difficulties with these tasks tended to have damage in the dorsomedial areas of the frontal lobe also known as the dorsomedial prefrontal cortex or DMPFC (see Figure 9.7). Emotional regulation involves integrating the motivational, reward/risk, emotional and social aspects of behaviours to allow us to perform a task fully. Eslinger & Damasio's famous patient EVR is a classic example of such a patient since he could pass the standard executive tasks but was unable to make ordinary everyday decisions. These patients tend to have damage to what is known as the ventromedial areas of the frontal lobes or VMPFC. The final function of the frontal lobes is integrating and coordinating the activities of the other functions to allow us to perform the types of complex and/or novel tasks that we take on effortlessly every day. The overall activities of this function are rather complex and difficult to quantify but the Toronto group found that patients who had damage in the polar (or tip) area of the frontal lobes, also known as the rostral areas, tended to have these much higher order deficits that could not be simplified into one of the other more primary functions.

While this model is more complex than the SAS model and there are many aspects that need more clarification and detail, this is unsurprising given that in science we start with simple models and then develop them by doing further research. One of the attractive things about this model is that aspects of the SAS model can be seen here, since the tasks that are being energised, set or monitored are effectively the schemas from the earlier model, and these functions are an attempt to differentiate between the different types of control processes that Norman & Shallice referred to as the supervisory attentional system and contention scheduling. Further, this model (see Figure 9.8) attempts to locate the various processes to specific brain regions which are known to be anatomically connected to one another.

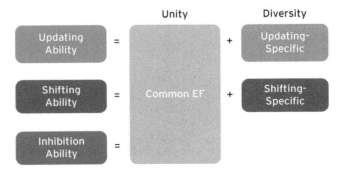

Figure 9.9   A diagrammatic representation of Miyake's Unity-Diversity model of executive functions

Miyake's Unity-Diversity Model

A model that is quite different from the three models above is that by Miyake & Friedman which, like the Stuss & Benson one, separates out executive functions into a number of different overall functions. However, unlike the Norman & Shallice and Stuss & Benson models, and to a lesser extent the Baddeley & Hitch model, which are based on observations of patients with brain damage, Miyake & Friedman's work is based on individual differences found in the general population. Their work involved the performance of large samples of twins, pre-adolescent children and older adults on a range of cognitive tasks. Overall, they observed three abilities that are commonly thought of as executive functions. These are: 1) *Updating* which is the constant monitoring and then rapid addition or deletion of contents of one's current working memory; 2) *Shifting* which allows the flexible switching between tasks or mental sets of information; and 3) *Inhibition* which is the conscious overriding of habitual or powerful responses because of what is currently necessary. By statistical analysis of large sets of data, they observed two important things. One was that performance between these three observable abilities correlate with one another; given this, they concluded that there must be *one* underlying executive function that is common to all three observable abilities which they refer to as the 'common executive function (EF)' that is used in *all* tasks at this level. They also found that when statistically they had accounted for this Common EF, there was still a significant impact of processes that were specific to Updating and Shifting; so in other words, there was no inhibition-specific process.

As a result of this statistical analysis, the Miyake & Friedman (2012) model (see Figure 9.9) allows for both a unified central ability which is the Common EF as well as two specific and diverse abilities, namely Updating and Shifting. The attraction of this model is that it accepts that there may be a generalised central ability irrespective of what you do; while not central to this debate, this suggestion is similar to the idea of a generalised intelligence or *g* which goes beyond specific types of intelligence (e.g. verbal, visual, kinaesthetic, emotional). However, at the same time, it allows for very specific abilities that result in the individual differences between us all, such that one person might be good at tasks involving one function such as Updating but poor at another such as Shifting, while another person may have exactly the opposite pattern. Needless to say, while attractive, the proof of this model will be in how it not only explains the data on individual differences in healthy individuals that were used for deriving the model, but also on how the model is able to explain the range of differences seen as a result of different types of executive dysfunction brought on by different conditions (see below).

Having reviewed four of the prominent models that have been put forward for explaining executive functions, it is unsurprising that there are both commonalities and differences. Table 9.1 summarises some of the main criteria that could be used to evaluate the models, and it is clear that each has its strengths and weaknesses, but possibly, on balance, from a neuropsychological perspective, the Stuss & Benson model is the most compelling.

Table 9.1 Comparison of four models of executive function based on the criteria of evidence base, cognitive specificity, anatomical specificity and level of testability

Model	Evidence base	Cognitive Specificity	Anatomical Specificity	Testability
Baddeley & Hitch's Central Executive	Some: • Dual task paradigms • Healthy controls and patients with brain damage/ dysfunction	A little:	Very little	Not easy since concepts are not well defined enough
Norman & Shallice's Supervisory Attentional System	Some: • Largely patients with brain damage/ dysfunction • Older adults	Some	A little	Not easy since concepts are not well defined enough
Stuss & Benson's Three Process Model	Strong: • Patients with different types of frontal lobe damage	A lot: • Processes clearly defined	A lot: • Three different processes localised to specific frontal locations	Very testable due to specificity of both the cognitive processes and the anatomical localisation of these processes
Miyake's Unity-Diversity Model	Strong: • Identical twins • Adolescents with ADHD • Older adults	A lot: • Combination of separate processes and also a unified process used across all tasks	Not much	Quite testable

PROBLEMS IN ASSESSMENT AND THEORISING: ECOLOGICAL VALIDITY

The models and then the assessments that have flowed out of the four frameworks reviewed above have been relatively successful in helping both clinicians diagnose the difficulties of their patients and for researchers to refine their understanding of how the frontal lobes allow us to manage our complex everyday behaviour. However, as is probably clear, there are a few obvious issues that emerge. First, while each of the models is compelling and can explain how you function in quite specific situations, none of them is comprehensive enough to explain how you go about all the different things you do on a daily basis; for example, they suffice for explaining how you make a decision under pressure (monitoring within the Stuss system) or how you have to stop what you are doing and do something totally different (activating the supervisory attentional system in the Norman & Shallice model) but these are relatively specific. Therefore, at the moment, there is a limit to the explanatory power of the models.

The second and in some ways related problem is that numerous studies have found that the assessments that have come out of these theoretical frameworks are not sufficient to explain the range of difficulties demonstrated by patients. One of the most classic examples of the problems with current assessments is that the well-known patient EVR, who has very severe problems in his decision-making abilities, performs almost flawlessly on the WCST, a test that is sometimes seen as a 'golden test' of executive functions. Given that his difficulties are well-documented and not even subtle, it seems rather bizarre that he should do so well on a test that is used every day by clinicians around the world. Over time, more and more clinicians have seen that they have patients who have obvious problems in managing their everyday lives, and yet on many clinical tests look unimpaired.

This issue was highlighted strongly by Shallice & Burgess (1991) who had been told by people who worked in neuropsychological rehabilitation centres that, like EVR, they had clients who on paper looked unimpaired (such as good performance on the WCST) but who had major problems in the types of activities of daily living that such centres are trying to help improve. So for example, when taken out to do a classic everyday task, shopping, these clients showed major difficulties in managing this task efficiently, something that presumably they will have been able to do with ease before their brain damage. Therefore, Shallice & Burgess selected research patients who all performed in the unimpaired range on the WCST and took them shopping! They gave the participants a few broad rules (about being efficient in the way that they used their time and not visiting a shop more than once) and observed their behaviour. What they found was that in this naturalistic sort of setting where patients weren't bound by the strict rules of a laboratory test, they performed very differently to matched healthy controls – the route that they took to perform their list of tasks around the shopping centre was often disorganised, they visited a shop more than once, they visited shops that were not on their to-do list, etc. Just visually in Figure 9.10, comparing the route of the healthy control participant on the left with that of the patient with frontal lobe damage on the right, it is obvious that the route taken is more haphazard and there are visits to shops that were not on the original list.

Findings like the Shallice & Burgess 'Multiple Errands Task' led researchers (e.g. Chaytor & Schmitter-Edgecombe, 2003) to question the traditional tests and call for tests to have more 'ecological validity'. Generally speaking, this refers to tests being more realistic and the results being more predictive of everyday behaviour outside of the clinic. Two general principles that are important are verisimilitude and veridicality. Verisimilitude refers to how much the cognitive demands of a test resemble what is required in a real everyday environment. Veridicality refers to how much performance on the test matches everyday functioning, which in this case would be measures such as clinician ratings of functioning, ratings by the individual's family members of their behaviour at home and

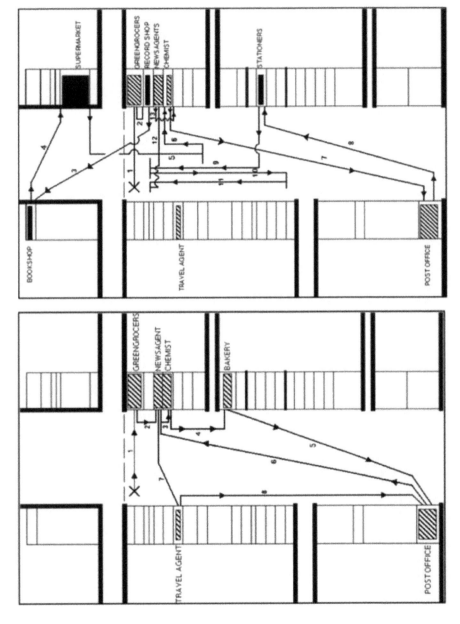

Figure 9.10 Diagrammatic representations from Burgess et al. (2006) of two examples of the routes taken by a healthy control (left-hand side) and an individual with brain damage (right-hand side) on the Shallice & Burgess (1991) shopping task (Reprinted from Burgess, P. W et al. Copyright (2008). On the role of rostral prefrontal cortex (area 10) in prospective memory. In M. Kliegel, M. A. McDaniel, & G. O. Einstein (Eds.), *Prospective Memory: Cognitive, Neuroscience, Developmental, and Applied Perspectives* (pp. 235–260). With permission of Taylor & Francis Group/Lawrence Erlbaum Associates)

employment status, as these will all be related to the cognitive and emotional abilities following brain damage. As an analogy in a different realm, my eyesight is appalling and I've had to wear glasses since before I was ten. When I go to the opticians, they will ask me how to read a series of letters on a board that is far away with the letters getting smaller and smaller. While I don't go around the outside world looking at boards of letters that are getting smaller and smaller, the demands on my eyes match what I need to do outside the opticians every day – I need to read letters that are on a computer screen, on labels in the supermarket, signs in the train station, etc. which are all different sizes and different distances from my eyes. Therefore, the tests that the opticians are doing demonstrate verisimilitude. Their assessment of my eyesight and the 'rehabilitation' they suggest, which is a pair of glasses or contact lenses that allow me to see things in my everyday life outside the optician's testing room, demonstrates veridicality.

As demonstrated by the case of the performance of EVR and the Shallice & Burgess shopping centre patients, tests like the WCST lack some levels of verisimilitude and veridicality. The demands of the WCST (see earlier) are quite abstract and only map onto very specific aspects of everyday life but not to a very common task such as going shopping; there is therefore low verisimilitude. The fact that both EVR and the shopping centre patients do so poorly in everyday tasks while passing the WCST demonstrates that results from it do not correlate with the real-life behaviour that clinicians are trying to predict with their assessments; there is therefore low veridicality.

THE DEVELOPMENT OF ECOLOGICALLY VALID TESTS OF EXECUTIVE FUNCTIONS

In response to this lack of sensitivity of existing tests, researchers and clinicians have attempted to develop more ecologically valid tests. Early ecologically valid tasks, similar to the shopping task, tended to involve performance in the 'real world'. For example, Chevignard et al. (2010) developed a task for assessing the functioning of children following traumatic brain injury which required them to follow simple recipes to bake a chocolate cake and to make a fruit cocktail. By observing performance on these tasks, they were able to predict what sort of difficulties the children would have in their everyday lives.

While such paradigms have strong ecological validity, they require intensive resources (for example, a kitchen or access to a shopping centre) and are difficult to replicate across clinics or research centres. Therefore, a new generation of paradigms turned to using virtual reality (VR) to overcome these issues – by using computer-based tasks (either immersive VR or non-immersive VR) it is possible to create complex and taxing situations without putting the participant in danger, and this also allows replication across different clinics, research centres or populations. Corti et al. (2021) have summarised the range of such tasks from shopping to removing furniture from a house to performing everyday errands, comparing them on a range of criteria.

One of these tasks is the Jansari assessment of Executive Functions (JEF©) developed by Jansari et al. (2014) and involves a participant pretending to work in a standard business office as a temporary worker. They did this because they were working with adults with brain injury who were attending a vocational rehabilitation centre where they were learning new skills to try to get back into the workplace, and often the work placements were in offices working as a clerical assistant. JEF© was designed so that eight different aspects of executive behaviours that clinicians repeatedly see as problematic following frontal lobe brain damage could be assessed; these are the ability to prioritise, to plan, to select from a range of options, to think adaptively if an original action could not be completed, to think creatively when your usual range of actions is not possible, and three forms of 'prospective memory', which is being able to do something in the future based on whether it is triggered by a time (e.g. call your mother in half an hour), an event (e.g. when the postal van arrives, make sure that you give the driver the big parcel that needs to be sent out), or an action that you yourself are currently engaged in (e.g. if you break something, make sure that you make a note of it in the office log book).

In their first study, Jansari et al. tested a group of individuals with brain damage and compared them to a group of healthy controls who were matched for age and gender in a real-world version of the task where participants were brought into the research centre where they physically moved around office spaces to complete the task. Their results showed that although the individuals with brain damage performed in the 'unimpaired' range on a number of standard clinical tasks, they were significantly impaired on the real-world version of JEF©.

Following the first study, Jansari et al. created a replica of their real-world office space in a non-immersive virtual environment that resembles a standard computer game; Figure 9.11 shows a screenshot of this environment with the participant moving around using the arrow keys and moving objects by clicking on them to pick them up and then placing them in a new location. Jansari et al. then replicated their earlier study with a larger group of patients and controls and found that this new VR version was able to detect the executive difficulties of individuals with brain damage in much the same way as the real-world version. Since then, Jansari and colleagues have used JEF© to reveal the difficulties of patients like EVR, who had had surgical removal of frontal lobe tumours (Denmark et al., 2019: see Figure 9.12), the negative impacts of recreational substances on otherwise healthy individuals (C. Montgomery and colleagues, 2010, 2011, 2012; Jansari et al., 2013), the positive impact of caffeine (Soar et al., 2016) and the executive difficulties experienced by people with bipolar disorder (Hørlyck et al., 2021). They have also gone on to create a children's version – JEF-C© – in which the child is told that it is their birthday and that their parents are trusting them to run their own birthday party while they go out for the day; the child has to get the house ready, welcome their guests, decide on what they will eat during the party, etc. The original version of JEF-C© was able to demonstrate the improvement of executive functions in healthy children as a function of age (Jansari et al., 2012), has been translated into other languages including Hebrew (Orkin Simon et al., 2020) and has been used to reveal the executive difficulties of children with brain damage using a French translation (Gilboa et al., 2019). Given the success of these virtual environments in revealing the complexity of executive functions and the difficulties that brain damage or neuropsychiatric disorders can produce, coupled with improved technology, the next decade is likely to see a great expansion in our understanding of this complex ability.

One of the important differences between JEF© and the standard clinical tasks is that the latter tend to test executive functions separately; therefore, there are tests of planning, others for prospective memory and yet others for making selections. However, the analogy that Jansari et al. suggested was that this was like a musical conductor rehearsing the violins as a group, then the woodwind instruments as a separate group, then the percussion instruments in another group, and after these three separate rehearsals, expecting all of the different parts of the orchestra to perform together in harmony at a concert without ever having played together! As is probably obvious from the models of executive functions, these skills are highly complex, requiring the use of many lower-level cognitive skills simultaneously; therefore, testing them each in isolation is not challenging the patient in the way that a real-world task such as the shopping task, the cooking task or JEF© require.

Further, it is becoming increasingly apparent that while the models reviewed earlier are good for attempting to understand the complexity of executive functions, perhaps they are too abstract to help in the development of clinical assessments that can help for effective management of patients following brain damage. Therefore, it is important to differentiate between assessments and model formation, since certainly in the area of executive functions (maybe unlike in the case of the more primary cognitive functions

Figure 9.11   Screenshot from the virtual version of the Jansari assessment of Executive Functions (JEF©) showing the environment within which the participant navigates

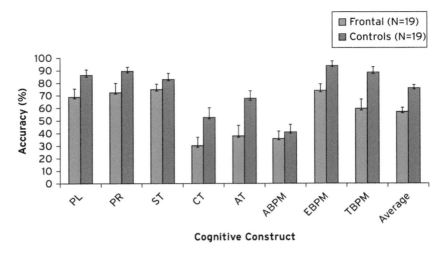

Figure 9.12   Performance of patients with frontal lobe lesions (following surgical removal of tumours) compared to matched controls on the Jansari assessment of Executive Functions (JEF©) (Denmark et al., 2017)

such as vision and memory) the two don't seem to go hand in glove, with the models not necessarily leading to the development of ecologically valid tests. However, ultimately, both need careful control so that assessments have good experimental control with ecologically valid results while models have good demonstrable clinical utility.

THE OMNIPRESENCE OF THE FRONTAL LOBES AND EXECUTIVE FUNCTIONS

As is clear from this chapter, damage to the frontal lobes can result in very significant behavioural difficulties; even in healthy development, the frontal lobes are the last to mature and possibly the first to start deteriorating as we age. Their centrality to healthy cognitive and mental lives is seen in the fact that they are also implicated in many conditions beyond brain damage. Most neurodevelopmental disorders that often first become apparent in childhood, including dyslexia, attention deficit hyperactivity disorder (ADHD), autistic spectrum condition (ASC) and developmental coordination difficulty (DCD, also known as dyspraxia), all involve executive problems.

In addition, the field of neuropsychiatry is beginning to demonstrate that there are cognitive difficulties, particularly executive deficits, in a whole range of conditions including schizophrenia, bipolar disorder, obsessive compulsive disorder and eating disorders. In addition, research in the field of addiction is revealing that a central aspect of the challenge faced by sufferers is a loss of (executive) control over once pleasurable activities. Further, given the lack of maturity of the frontal lobes until the mid-20s (see above), there is growing understanding of why substance use and misuse during adolescence is particularly dangerous and may create difficulties that are irreversible. Finally, one of the most important processes that we all experienced as new-born babies was developing an attachment to our caregivers, particularly to our mothers. While it has become clear that any difficulties in this process can lead to emotional and behavioural difficulties for the child, new research is beginning to demonstrate that at least part of this is because of weakened executive skills. Research is now beginning to explore whether there is a causal link between the insecure attachment and the compromised higher level cognitive abilities.

A WORD OF CAUTION: FRONTAL LOBOLOGY

It is obvious from the content of this chapter that executive functions are implicated in a number of abilities that seem to be related to the complexities of everyday life. These abilities allow us to manage our moment-to-moment behaviour, plan for later today and for next month, to multitask and to problem solve in a manner that does not seem to be possible for other animals. These abilities can be compromised by being not old enough or moving into older age, acquired brain injury, having a neurodevelopmental disorder, substance misuse and being prone to a range of neuropsychiatric disorders.

Given this huge complexity of the frontal lobes and executive functions, and therefore their omnipresence across many aspects of human behaviour, there can sometimes be a tendency to attribute *all* complex functions to the frontal lobes or to sub-divisions within it. For example, a simple search for research studies on the ventro-medial prefrontal cortex (VMPFC) produces an enormous amount of work that suggests that this one area of the brain is involved in everything from theory of mind to memory to decision-making to emotional-processing to social cognition to psychopathy in children – basically, the VMPFC is very busy! The problem with this, however, is that it then becomes difficult to work out what the actual function is – as was seen in Chapter 8 on Memory, there is fierce debate on what the hippocampus does with at least two major theories centred around formation of memories; however, for different areas of the frontal lobes such as the VMPFC, there is an enormous heterogeneity. This has led some, such as David (1992), to suggest that 'the frontal lobes do everything/nothing' (p. 244) because if so many functions are attributed to one particular area of the brain, then in a way, we lose specificity of function. In an aptly entitled review 'The elusive nature of executive functions', Jurado & Rosselli (2007) attempt to summarise some of the complexity and consequent confusion that is involved in trying to establish the precise nature of these higher order abilities. Therefore, it is important for researchers and clinicians to begin to see whether in fact all of these different functions are 'housed' in one area of the brain or whether there are more 'elemental' processes that all the suggested functions share. The next decade is likely to be an extremely busy time for research into the complexity of our executive functions.

Chapter Summary

- The human frontal lobes take up a larger part of the human brain than all other animal species; they are also the last to develop, such that while other parts of the brain are fully functional by puberty, the frontal lobes are not fully mature until the mid-20s.
- Damage to the frontal lobes results in difficulties in a broad set of decision-making and control behaviours that are collectively known as the executive functions.
- Assessment of executive functions is carried out with a wide range of tests; however, there is sometimes a discrepancy between the findings from these assessments and an individual's everyday behaviour, demonstrating a lack of ecological validity.
- There are a number of models of executive functions that try to encompass the main difficulties that are observed in patients with frontal lobe damage.
- A new generation of more ecologically valid assessments have been developed, some of which are using virtual reality; these assessments seem to mirror the everyday difficulties of patients more closely than the traditional older tests.

Important Researcher

Donald Stuss

Donald Stuss was a Canadian neuropsychologist who studied the frontal lobes of the human brain, and directed the Rotman Research Institute at Baycrest from 1989 until 2009 and the Ontario Brain Institute from 2011 until 2016. He had a remarkable and distinguished scientific career and yet began rather unconventionally. He did a stint as a seminarian training to be a priest and also as a high school teacher; while he didn't follow these career paths they obviously provided a way of working with people and also a way of teaching that benefited many individuals, from the patients he worked with to the students he mentored. Donald's major contribution to the field was our understanding of the functioning of the frontal lobes and developing a framework for understanding the complex functioning of this part of the brain, and out of that framework developing an assessment battery. From his enormous amount of work, he co-authored two books: *The Frontal Lobes* (1986) and *Principles of Frontal Lobe Function* (2013).

Important Research Study

EVR (Eslinger & Damasio, 1985)

Before coming to the attention of neurologists, EVR was described by everyone around him as a role model; happily married, head accountant for a company and an active member of the local community. At the age of 35, he was diagnosed with a tumour that was affecting both frontal lobes. Following surgery to remove the tumour, EVR's general cognition was largely unaffected with both his IQ and memory being in the superior or very superior range. Despite this, EVR's behaviour changed dramatically, and within a few years he had become divorced from his wife of 17 years, got married again a month later and divorced again two years later. He made very bad financial decisions resulting in becoming bankrupt and having to live with his parents; the most straightforward everyday things such as washing in the morning for work or deciding which restaurant to go to for a meal would take him literally hours. I was fortunate enough to work with him during my postdoctoral fellowship with Antonio Damasio in Iowa, and EVR is a highly articulate man who could charm the birds out of the trees. However, a man who used to run the accounts for a company is now left highly impaired at the simplest decision-making tasks and actually has to live in a care home as a result. Working with EVR gave Antonio amazing insights into the role of the frontal lobes in decision-making, from which he developed the **somatic marker hypothesis**. This theory is beautifully articulated in his bestselling popular science book *Descartes' Error*, in which he argues against the rationalist view that logic is the only important thing for decision-making, and that our emotions (that come from our body or 'soma') are central; losing this, as can happen with the type of brain damage that EVR suffered, results in purely logical decisions that can result in major errors. Hanna Damasio used Brainvox (see Chapter 2) to virtually shoot a tamping iron through Phineas Gage's skull (kept in a medical museum in Boston) to work out which parts of his brain would have been damaged in that fateful accident in 1848; by doing so, she showed that the two patients separated by 150 years of history but with very similar behavioural profiles had suffered very similar brain damage (see Figure 9.2).

Questions for Reflection

- Is there one executive function or many?
- How do the various models of executive functions differ from one another?
- What is ecological validity and why is it particularly important in research on executive functions?

Go Further

- The frontal lobes are intimately linked to control of behaviour and therefore any issue regarding addiction has a 'frontal component'; a big issue is how to understand this component in the hope that it will be possible to help treat the various forms of addiction that result in such personal and societal costs.
- Given the enormous role that the frontal lobes play in human behaviour, many mental health issues such as depression, anxiety and schizophrenia are strongly influenced by the executive functions, so if you are interested in these areas, there is a big research base that you can explore.

Go Further

Dr Jansari's YouTube Videos

The brains of the brain: Why is the prefrontal cortex involved in just about everything?

What is it that separates us from animals? If you were thinking it was our clothes, you'd be wrong; instead it is the front of our brains called the prefrontal cortex. A lot of our understanding about this area has come from brain-damaged individuals as well as people with conditions such as ASC and ADHD, and from the impact of recreational drugs. This video gives an overview of this complexity by looking at what researchers and clinicians have found by studying a large spectrum of different groups of participants.

Are head injuries during childhood related to later criminality?

Can a head injury really make you more likely to commit a crime? The answer is... maybe. Studies have shown that the rate of head injuries in prison populations is *eight* times what is found in the general public and that most of these injuries occur during childhood. This video explores why this might be the case, and what could possibly be done to tackle this.

Neurobiology of addiction: Brain structure & function

The word addiction usually conjures up images of illegal drugs or alcohol, but really it describes the loss of control over a once-enjoyable activity such as eating, shopping, sex, or even skydiving. This video reviews addiction from psychological and neuropsychological perspectives including: 1) How does the pursuit of pleasure result in a behaviour that can take over someone's life, often eventually just being continued to stave off displeasure? 2) Why is adolescence such a difficult period when addiction can set in and potentially cause irreversible damage? 3) What are scientists discovering about individual differences and why are some people more prone to addiction than others? 4) What might be the ingredients of a successful rehabilitation programme?

Further Reading

- Damásio, A. (1994). *Descartes' Error: Emotion, Reason, and the Human Brain*. Putnam.
- David, A. S. (1992). Frontal lobology: Psychiatry's new pseudoscience. *The British Journal of Psychiatry, 161*(2), 244-248.
- Stuss, D. (2013). *Principles of Frontal Lobe Functions*. Oxford University Press.

10
APHASIA, DYSLEXIA & LANGUAGE

ASHOK JANSARI & ANISHA DESAI

Chapter Overview

This chapter will explore probably the most studied aspect within neuropsychology, our ability to communicate. There has been a rich history in this area since the middle of the nineteenth century which has resulted in an evolution of complex models of how we communicate verbally and through writing. This research has demonstrated that language is far from an automatic process that we learn as children but can be disrupted in multiple ways revealing the intricacy of an ability that at some levels separates us from the rest of the animal kingdom.

Chapter Outline

- Introduction
- Nineteenth Century Neurologists and Box and Arrow Models
- The Demise of the Neurobiological Models
- Cognitive Neuropsychological Models of Language
- Chapter Summary

INTRODUCTION

If I am thirsty and need my mother to give me water, I first of all need to have the thought or desire to have water, then I need to work out how I will communicate this with my mother, then if I have decided to ask for it verbally, I need to form a sentence. To do this I need to find the words for that sentence followed by the motor programmes that allow my mouth to utter the sounds that will allow her to understand what I mean when I say /*Please could I have some water?*/ and know what she can do to help me. Similarly, if my mother needs some water, if she makes similar sounds with her mouth, which will sound different to the sounds that I myself make, I need to be able to work out that what she is saying is not one continuous sound but in fact a number of separate sounds, where each one ends and the next begins (in this case six individual utterances), what each individual sound means and then what the particular string means before I can realise that my mother needs me to pass her some water. Taken further, I could convey the same information to someone else but by writing it down using a code in the form of symbols that has developed through the centuries in which individual lines and shapes denote individual letters, sounds or ideas and then groups of these characters, when combined, create words that have meaning and when these words are put into a string, carry a particular meaning.

If asked, most people would think of language simply as our ability to speak. However, speaking (or speech) is just one mode which allows us to express our linguistic abilities to communicate with others. Therefore, someone who loses their speech does not necessarily lose their language or ability to communicate. It merely means that they lose their ability to communicate using the spoken modality. This demonstrates therefore that rather than being a single ability, language is a complex system that is used in many different ways to communicate. While research is beginning to demonstrate that animals have forms of communication that can have some complexity, at the moment at least, it seems as if the sheer complexity of human language makes us unique within the entire animal kingdom.

This complex system allows us to use symbols (letters, sounds and words) and rules (grammar and syntax) to organise and convey information between individuals. As in the example of asking my mother for water, we use words to describe, direct and instruct; we also use them to express and explain our thoughts, our feelings, our choices, likes, dislikes, to retell stories and to interact and socialise with one another. Equally, we use language to understand others' descriptions, instructions, expressions, thoughts and feelings, etc. We also adapt our use of language and selection of words in a multitude of ways depending on the context. We generally talk differently to people in authority (e.g. a policeman, a judge or maybe even a lecturer) than how we would with our friends or family; often we have completely different vocabularies for the two. But how do we know to do that?

And not only do we do this in one language; many can do it in several languages and interchange between different language systems – there are over 7000 known living languages in the world today. Some people will move between different languages within the same conversation seamlessly. In India, for example, the two national languages are Hindi and English, and each state has its own regional language. In large urban centres such as Mumbai, there is a big migrant population from many neighbouring states. The result is that an urban professional may switch between two to four languages in quick succession. How are they all organised in the same way in the brain to elicit the similar outputs or behaviours across the majority of humans? How does the brain store, compute and use these multiple systems? How do we adapt this intricate system? And how is this information processed if writing a word, saying the word, talking about the the meaning of the word or talking about a specific word; for example, I can talk *write* the word 'cat' in English or I could write it in Italian, I can write it in my mother tongue Gujarati, I can *say* the word, I can *describe* what I mean by this word or I could be describing my beloved cat Rover (see Figure 10.1) In the rapidly evolving technological world, we are seeing how e-communication has resulted in us even using small images that we refer to as emoticons to convey meaning; in a sense, where written language is concerned, it almost feels as if we have gone back to where we started more than 4000 years ago (see Figure 10.2) with small images conveying meaning ☺.

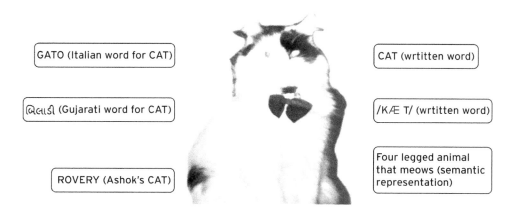

Figure 10.1   The use of symbols for representing information about the world, in this case, a cat

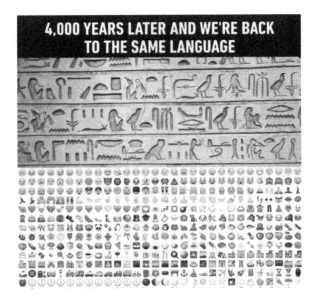

Figure 10.2 Egyptian hieroglyphics used 4000 years ago and some of the emoticons used today, both symbols that are used to convey meaning (Reproduced with permission from Kaa Memes)

Given the complexity of language, when it fails, it affects not only the person's ability to speak or communicate, but also affects them on cognitive, emotional, behavioural and social levels. As the field is enormous, this chapter will only be able to deal with two elements that most of us use on a constant basis: our ability to produce language and our ability to read written language.

NINETEENTH CENTURY NEUROLOGISTS AND BOX AND ARROW MODELS

Up until the nineteenth century, it was believed language was distributed across the brain. However, as described in Chapter 1, in the mid-1800s a giant shift in thinking was made when areas of the brain were identified and linked with specific language processes. Following Paul Broca's seminal work in 1861 on his patient Tan, it was seen that there were at least two different aspects to language, since Tan could *receive and understand* language but could not *create speech*, so this was the first dissociation that was documented. Following Tan's death, Broca completed an autopsy of his brain, and found a lesion on the surface of the left frontal lobe. The same was found in a number of patients that Broca studied subsequently and therefore the idea that this area was required for speech production became a cornerstone of our understanding of language (see Chapter 1).

Broca suggested that this area held 'motor images' for the words that we are able to physically say, and therefore, in addition to being known as Broca's aphasia, at different points in history, a disorder in being able to speak fluently has been known as motor aphasia. It is interesting to note that the motor images of words that one can say are analogous to the visuokinesthetic engrams which are the physical movement actions that someone is able to perform (Chapter 5).

Later, in 1874, Carl Wernicke working in what is now modern-day Germany found the complete opposite pattern to that seen in Tan in two of his patients. This time, these patients had no difficulty with their articulation (motor movements of their speech muscles) but they spoke rapidly and their speech was often nonsensical. Furthermore, they were also unable to comprehend the speech of others; therefore, this was effectively a double dissociation with Tan who had been able to comprehend but not speak. A post-mortem of Wernicke's patients revealed damage in the posterior left temporal region of the brain which subsequently became known as Wernicke's area (see Figure 10.3). It was suggested that this area was able to recognise the spoken word forms that a person hears as well as provide the spoken word forms when you are speaking yourself. As the disorder involves bringing in sensory information from the outside world (hearing what someone is saying) and recognising it, in addition to Wernicke's aphasia, a difficulty in comprehension was also sometimes known as sensory aphasia. It is interesting to note that the 'sensory images' of sounds are analogous to the face recognition units for faces that someone has encountered before (Chapter 7).

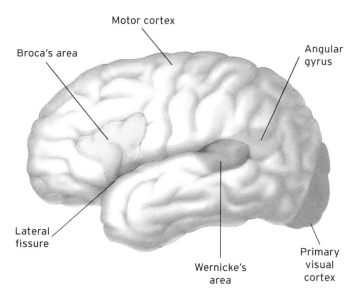

Figure 10.3 Broca's and Wernicke's areas identified in the brain in the late 1800s (Garrett & Hough, 2017)

Following the documentation of many similar cases by other neurologists, by the end of the nineteenth century, these two regions of the brain, Broca's and Wernicke's areas, became accepted as critical for speech production and speech comprehension respectively. More importantly it demonstrated that understanding and producing language were two distinct processes that appeared to occur in two separate areas of the brain. Importantly, the two areas of the brain are anatomically linked through a fibre tract known as the arcuate fasciculus, so given the obvious link between being able to hear and comprehend what someone says to you and your own ability to speak back to them, Wernicke proposed that damage to this would *disconnect* the two areas from one another. In addition to not being able to communicate information between the two areas, Wernicke predicted that this damage would result in a third type of language problem or aphasia. The patient would be able to receive and comprehend speech because Wernicke's area was intact and the patient would also be able to create speech since Broca's area was intact. However, the patient would not be able to *repeat* what someone else said to them because to do this requires communication between hearing what someone says, understanding what they said (within Wernicke's area) and finding the words to copy the heard sound and then getting the speech mechanism to actually say the word (within Broca's area). This requires communication between the two areas (via the arcuate fasciculus) so damage to this linking network would make repetition impossible. Indeed, Wernicke's prediction proved to be correct, and thus a pattern that allows a patient to comprehend and create language but not to repeat what is said to them is known as conduction aphasia; see Figure 10.4 for a box and arrow model to explain the condition.

While Broca and Wernicke wrote about their work in their native French and German languages, one of Wernicke's compatriots, Ludwig Lichtheim, published a paper in 1885 in English which may have been an important game changer. Writing in English made his work accessible to a much wider audience and, more importantly, he took Wernicke's ideas and presented them as abstract diagrams; these original diagrams only had arrows

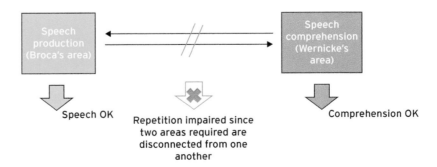

Figure 10.4 A box and arrow model explaining conduction aphasia as a disconnection between the two intact centres for speech and comprehension

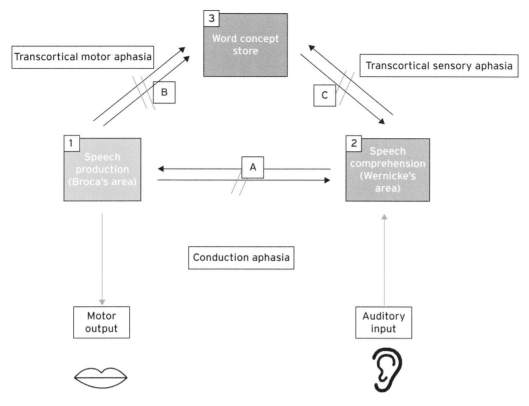

Figure 10.5   A representation of the Lichtheim-Wernicke model of language input and output showing three important centres and pathways between them which help to explain five different forms of language disorders

linking different anatomical structures but this idea caught on and subsequent thinkers started adding boxes to these diagrams. Over time, this evolved into the 'box and arrow' movement that made this field take over. Indeed Graves (1997) has shown how many of the great neurologists and then subsequently cognitive neuropsychologists owe their beautiful formulations of cognitive functions to the Wernicke-Lichtheim model. This includes Geschwind's models in language (see later), the dual-route reading model in language (see later), Lissauer's model of object recognition (Chapter 6), Liepmann's and Heilman's models of apraxia (Chapter 5) and the Bruce & Young model of face recognition (Chapter 7).

While Lichtheim's model simply brought together Wernicke's ideas in a visual form, it was important for two reasons. First of all, he added a system for word meaning to the model which holds the concepts that we understand (kind of our dictionary of words). Second, similar to how Wernicke was able to predict the existence of conduction aphasia when he suggested the link between the speech and comprehension areas, Lichtheim's model was able to predict several new syndromes in addition to the three types of aphasia that had already been documented; please see Figure 10.5 in which 'centres' holding information have been given the numbers 1, 2 and 3 respectively and then the pathways that connect these centres have been given the letters A, B and C. Within this Lichtheim-Wernicke model, transcortical motor aphasia occurs when there is damage between the area that holds the word concepts and Broca's area. The result is that with the arcuate fasciculus (pathway A) between Broca's area (1) and Wernicke's area (2) intact, it is possible to repeat words; however, due to damage to pathway B, *spontaneous speech* is poor since it is necessary to have fluid and constant access to the word store to speak continuously and fluently. Transcortical sensory aphasia is caused by a disconnection between the word concept area and the 'sensory images' in Wernicke's area in pathway C. The result is that with pathway A intact, spontaneous speech is OK but the damage to pathway C makes both comprehension and repetition of what is heard difficult.

The Lichtheim-Wernicke model became extremely influential and was *the* methodology in researching language disorders (as well as other cognitive issues as described above) for a number of decades. Indeed, a century after Broca's initial work, one of the most important influential neurologists of the twentieth century, Norman Geschwind, who coined the term behavioural neurology, used evidence from brain-damaged patients and neuro-imaging to add more detail to this model. His work showed that the angular gyrus, an area at the front of the parietal lobes (see Figure 10.6), is involved in transferring information from the visual areas to Wernicke's area to allow us to 'translate' the squiggles that you see on a page or screen into a sound that you 'hear' and understand in your mind. In addition, he identified Heschl's gyrus, an area within the auditory cortex (see Figure 10.6), as being involved in the transfer of sounds to Wernicke's area where meaning can be extracted to allow us to comprehend what we are hearing.

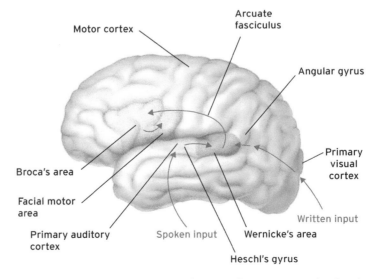

Figure 10.6 Heschl's gyrus and its relationship to other areas involved in language (Garrett & Hough, 2017).

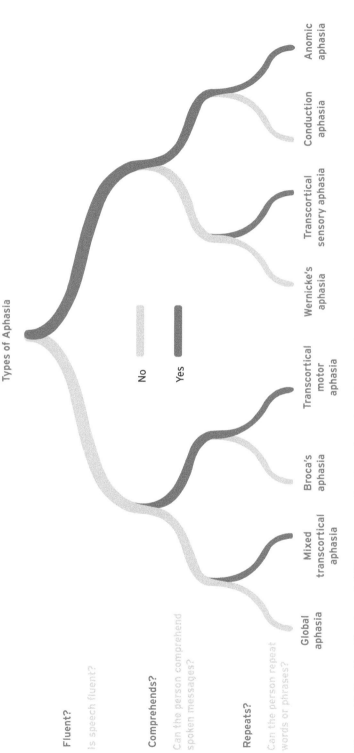

Figure 10.7 Classification of different types of aphasia based on fluency of speech, comprehension of spoken language and ability to repeat words or phrases

Source: Aphasia Definitions from Aphasia.org

Eventually, through the work of many researchers and clinicians, a system was developed for how to classify patients with language disorders (see Figure 10.7). A key divide in this system is whether speech production is fluent or non-fluent; further dimensions are to do with comprehension of spoken language and the ability to repeat words. This classification enables the explanation of aphasias where a patient has suffered damage to several cortical areas which therefore give rise to 'mixed' or 'global' aphasia that does not neatly fit into one of the five types described above. Using this approach of identifying the major areas of preserved and impaired abilities eventually led to the development of the most comprehensive assessment tool for language disorders, the Boston Diagnostic Aphasia Examination (BDAE; Goodglass et al., 2001).

THE DEMISE OF THE NEUROBIOLOGICAL MODELS

The legacy of the nineteenth and twentieth century diagram-makers in moving our understanding of language processes forward is unquestionable. However, there are a number of reasons that eventually this approach proved unsatisfactory. There are likely four different factors for this. As language was the first cognitive function to be documented and then systematically codified by neurologists, there has been a lot more development of the field than with many other aspects of cognition; given that clinical observations are happening around the world by different people trained in different systems, there has possibly been a lack of a common language (if you will pardon the pun!) for how to document and talk about the disorders. Second, due to the system of arteries that feed different parts of the brain, damage that affects the language areas is not uncommon, especially in older age. As a result, at least clinically, many more cases are seen of language disorders, and this allows more research and documentation than for example, cases of pure prosopagnosia (Chapter 7) which is incredibly rare. This is coupled with the third reason which is that as outlined at the beginning of this chapter, language is an incredibly complex system and there will therefore be multiple ways in which it can break down. Finally, all of the research and theorising before Geschwind was conducted before the information processing revolution (see Chapter 1). This way of seeing cognitive functions and the new field of cognitive neuropsychology freed researchers from the prevailing methodology, giving them a new method for thinking about language.

Two of the most important figures in the field of cognitive neuropsychology, Andy Ellis and Andy Young, outline four reasons why the above factors led to the demise of the box-and-arrow methodology (Ellis & Young, 1988). The first was that the models seemed to be limited to helping explain disorders that affect the comprehension, production and repetition of *single* words. Given that language is an incredibly complex system with words being placed in specific orders based on grammatical and syntactic rules even to make the most basic sentence such as 'The cat is looking bored', the models were limited. The second weakness was that boxes represented centres for different types of information, such as Broca's area containing the motor images for speech and the arcuate fasciculus transferring information about what is heard (and comprehended) from Wernicke's area to Broca's area to allow one to repeat what you hear. However, there was no explanation of the *processes* that were involved in this complex step. Students of cognitive psychology will know that a similar argument was made about the early Modal Model of memory (Chapter 8) since it outlined stores but it didn't explain the processes that were involved that moved information from short-term to long-term memory; this eventually led to the Levels of Processing approach (Craik & Lockhart, 1972) which did exactly this. Therefore, there was a 'shelf-life' for box-and-arrow models before more explanatory detail became necessary.

The third reason outlined by Ellis & Young (1988) is that the models, probably because of their origins within neurology, were focused on explaining *impairments* in patients. Therefore, modifications were only made to the models when a yet undocumented type of language problem was discovered; there was no attempt to see if the models also explained intact language. The danger of this is that the models evolved simply by the addition of new arrows and boxes; as Ellis & Young say 'a theory that can "explain" any patient who comes along simply by redrawing a diagram is unfalsifiable' (1988, p. 13). In scientific philosophy, a theory that is unfalsifiable is by extension a theory that explains everything, and a theory that explains everything doesn't explain anything…

The final difficulty that Ellis & Young (1988) pointed out is a complex conceptual one but one that has important implications. They point out that the diagram-makers ended up creating a 'two for one' whereby they had a theory about concepts (sound images, word concepts, etc.) and the way that these were connected, and they overlaid this on top of a neuroanatomical theory whereby the centres were in special regions of the brain. The problem with this is that if function X was thought to be located in brain location 123 and we found a patient ABC who had damage in region 123 but her symptoms were *not* X, how would we interpret this? Would we decide that it was because the explanation of what happened at 123 was wrong (so the concepts thought to exist there such as X were wrong) OR that in fact, the model was totally correct but just that the positioning of X, Y, Z and all the other functions was incorrect and that is why patient ABC is not showing the expected problems? With a 'two for one' theory, it is impossible to disentangle these possibilities.

Issues with Mapping Brain to Behaviour

Applying some of the issues to language processing specifically, it is possible to understand why a new way of thinking was required. Given the fourth point made by Ellis & Young (1988), since Broca's area is so central to speech production, it would be predicted that damage to this area would always lead to speech problems. However, Dronkers and her colleagues (e.g. Dronkers et al., 2000) have found that only 85% of patients who have what would be classified as Broca's aphasia have damage in Broca's area and that only 50–60% of patients who have damage in this area show the classical speech problems. Similarly, they found that only 65% of patients with Wernicke's aphasia had damage in the area classically associated with Wernicke's comprehension area, while only 30% of patients with damage in this area showed the classic comprehension difficulties. Similarly, in a study of 134 stroke survivors who had relatively circumscribed (meaning clear and limited) left frontal lobe lesions, Gajardo-Vidal et al. (2021) didn't find a one-to-one mapping. In fact, they found that long-term speech production impairments were actually related to damage to white matter tracts (see Chapter 2).

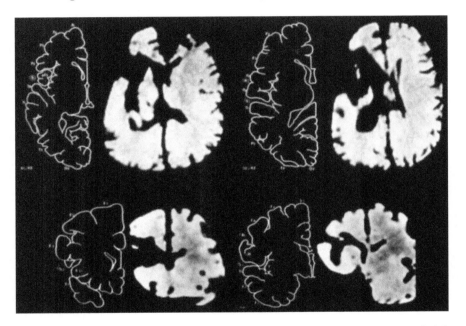

Figure 10.8 Diagrams produced in the nineteenth century of patient Tan's brain (left-hand side in each pair of images) next to CT scans of the brain in the late twentieth century, demonstrating that the damage suffered was not simply on the lateral surface as originally suggested by Paul Broca, but extended into deeper parts of the left hemisphere (Dronkers et al., 2007) (Reprinted from Dronkers, N. F., Plaisant, O., Iba-Zizen, M. T., & Cabanis, E. A. (2007). Paul Broca's historic cases: High resolution MR imaging of the brains of Leborgne and Lelong. *Brain, 130*(5), 1432–1441, with permission of Oxford University Press)

Interestingly, this last finding then goes along with a remarkable study by Dronkers et al. (2007) in which they scanned Tan's brain, which has been kept in a museum in Paris. It is important to note that Broca studied Tan's brain at post-mortem and also that understanding of brain anatomy has progressed hugely in the 160 years since Tan passed away. Dronkers et al. (2007) found that Tan's brain damage was much more extensive than damage simply to the area that became known as Broca's area. As can be seen in Figure 10.8, the damage to the left hemisphere extended from the lateral (outer) surface into more medial regions. This damage, similar to that in the patients studied by Gajardo-Vidal et al. (2021), will have affected white matter tracts. Putting these two pieces of evidence together and using Ellis et al.'s (1988) fourth point above, the interpretation of the damage to the surface of Broca's area resulting in the speech production problems experienced by Tan may have been over-simplistic.

In addition to the issues around the two areas discovered by Broca and Wernicke, more recent research has also demonstrated that other areas are involved. For example, the cerebellum – at the back of the head, which is literally at the other end of the brain from the 'classic language areas' – has been shown to be involved in aspects of linguistic processing both in terms of reading and writing (e.g. Starowicz-Filip et al., 2017). Similarly, other research has demonstrated that whereas there had been so much focus on the left hemisphere, the right hemisphere is actually involved in quite a number of broader aspects of language including intonation, rate of speech production, non-verbal communication (pragmatics) and non-literal language (such as use of idioms and metaphors).

In summary, while the early neurobiological models of language were instrumental in initiating a fascinating area of research, they proved limited. The idea of quite 'language centric' localised areas each with very specific modular roles has proven to be quite simplistic. As with most other cognitive functions, the strictly localised view of functions is no longer considered appropriate. This is because modern understanding of the brain shows that there are multiple networks that interconnect many different regions which are involved in a particular skill. Using my example of asking my mother for a glass of water, there is my physical thirst, my decision to ask someone else, me being able to see that the water is near my mother, me forming the request at an abstract level, the construction of the sequence of words that are needed for me to ask, the search for the motor programmes for the words and using an intonation that makes it clear that I am asking for something rather than simply making a statement; even this series of steps misses out many micro steps. It is no wonder then that when using modern neuroimaging techniques that not only look at the physical structures but which also look at the physical connections between non-adjacent brain areas, that there is a rich *network* involved in me making this simple request. For example, Figure 10.8 shows networks that were established by Del Gaizo et al. (2017) when they studied the brains of 92 survivors of left hemisphere strokes using complex techniques known as structural connectome lesion symptom mapping (CLSM) and connectome dynamics lesion symptom mapping (CDLSM). You don't need to be a specialist in neuroanatomy to see that the picture is quite a bit more complex than that which had prevailed for a long time (see Figure 10.3).

Given that the prevailing neurobiological models of language were not sufficient, a change was required. In fact, a Kuhnian paradigm shift was required! In scientific

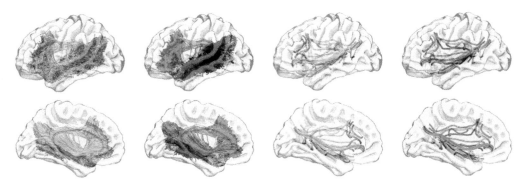

Figure 10.9 Complex brain networks involved in language established by Del Gaizo et al. (2017) after analysis of 92 survivors of left hemisphere strokes

philosophy, this is when a fundamental shift in thinking and methodology is required. A classic example is that the ancient view of the solar system saw all the other planets and the Sun orbiting around the Earth at the centre. This view was popularised most by the Egyptian astronomer Ptolemy in the second century CE. Subsequently, for 14 centuries, whenever astronomers came up with a new discovery, they had to make additions to the Ptolemaic view of the solar system; this usually involved complex maths to explain how a particular planet could have a certain number of moons, be a certain distance from the Earth, etc. However, a Polish astronomer in the beginning of the sixteenth century, Copernicus, challenged this view saying that the insistence on keeping the Earth at the centre of the solar system was over-complicating matters. He proposed a very different view, one in which the Sun was at the centre and all the planets including the Earth orbited that star; at the time, since from a theological point of view, having the Earth (as created by an Abrahamic God) at the centre of all creation was vital, Copernicus's views were considered heresy and he was actually excommunicated from the Church! However, soon after this monumental Kuhnian paradigm shift looking at the solar system in a completely different way, subsequent astronomers and physicists were able to show that indeed Copernicus was correct. In a similar way, while for a century after Broca's important work with Tan, the neurobiological box-and-arrow model sufficed, it seemed that the time was ripe for language to go through its own Kuhnian paradigm shift...

COGNITIVE NEUROPSYCHOLOGICAL MODELS OF LANGUAGE

The Kuhnian paradigm shift came at the end of the 1960s and 1970s with the cognitive revolution (see Chapter 1). Interestingly, part of this revolution started from the field of language with the work of two Goliaths of neuropsychology, John Marshall and Freda Newcombe. Newcombe's PhD research was on the effects of wounds during World War II caused by small pieces of shrapnel entering the brains of soldiers which left them with very selective forms of brain damage that had not been documented before. This work, which was eventually published as a book entitled *Missile Wounds of the Brain: A Study of Psychological Deficits* (Newcombe, 1969), became a sort of bible for the field for many years to come. Through her collaboration with Marshall, the two of them started a new methodology which along with work happening in memory and attention (see Chapter 1) laid the foundations for cognitive neuropsychology. While neuropsychology had effectively started with the studies of single individuals by the likes of Broca and Wernicke, as the field developed, over time, the main methodology for research was the study of groups of patients; from a research perspective, that makes perfect sense since it is possible to generalise findings in case they are only relevant to a few unusual individuals (see Chapter 3 for a discussion on this issue).

Marshall & Newcombe (1966) studied a patient GR who had sustained a gunshot wound to the left hemisphere in 1944 and two decades later was showing a bizarre reading error. For example, when shown the word ANTIQUE he would say */vase/*, or when shown the word CANARY would say */parrot/*! Rather than doing what those following the neurobiological model had been doing for a number of decades and make a statement about the part of the brain damaged in GR as being involved in a particular function, Marshall & Newcombe instead used this error to try to infer how the *healthy intact* brain might function to allow correct reading of these words as */antique/* and */canary/* (see later for an explanation). They gave the term deep dyslexia to this type of reading error whereby an individual provides a word that is *semantically* related to the target word. Marshall & Newcombe followed this seminal paper with an even more important one seven years later in which they described six patients, two of whom had deep dyslexia and two each with forms of reading problems that until then had also not been documented (Marshall & Newcombe, 1973). The patients with what they termed visual dyslexia showed errors whereby what they said visually looked like the word written down; for example, ROB was read as */robe/* or POD was read as */pad/*. Patients were classified as showing surface dyslexia if they made errors in *irregularly spelt* words, those in which the word cannot be made up simply by 'adding up' the constituent elements of the written word; for example, in British English pronunciation, BROAD should *not* rhyme with the word ROAD and ROUTE should *not* rhyme with OUT.

While the work carried out by Marshall & Newcombe was half a century ago (yes!), the remarkable thing is the legacy that it created. As will be seen in the remainder of the chapter, their work led to an extremely influential model of language production and reading that is still relevant today. In addition, while there are differences between acquired and developmental versions of cognitive disorders (see Chapter 3), this model has been used in the development of assessments for language disorders, and in addition is even used in understanding the difficulties of children (and adults) with developmental reading disorders. Finally, the methodology they developed of using dysfunction to inform intact function, which can then in a reciprocal manner help in the assessment of other patients, and then to formulate methods of rehabilitation to help these individuals (see Chapter 1) has become central to most fields in cognitive neuropsychology.

The Dual Route Model of Reading

Following the early work on the acquired dyslexias, a number of notable psycholinguists including Karalyn Patterson and Max Coltheart developed the ideas of Marshall & Newcombe further by studying individuals with variants of the three types of dyslexia that had been documented. The model by Kay et al. (1996), known as the Dual Route Model, is the currently accepted theoretical model in explaining how single words are understood, processed and produced. Central to this model is the fact that there are two independent routes, one which involves the 'sounding out' of the constituent parts of a word (just as we did when we were young children learning to read), and the other a kind of 'matching' against a dictionary called the lexicon of all the words that you are already familiar with (see Figure 10.10). For example, the made-up word (known as a non-word) YAMCAT would be possible for you to read even though you have never seen it before because you are able to use grapheme-to-phoneme conversion (GPC) rules that you've learnt through your life – you learnt how to sound out the strings of letters AM and AT and then were able to add letters to both of these strings to know how to say YAM and CAT when you first *saw* those strings. Now, without ever seeing YAMCAT before, you use your (GPC) rules to be able to say /*yamcat*/.

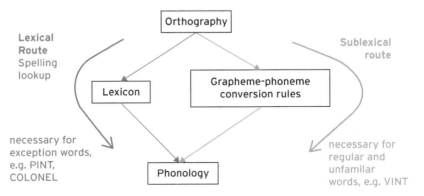

Figure 10.10 The central elements of the Dual Route Model of reading with a lexical route going through the lexicon, which holds the words that an individual currently knows, and the sublexical route which involves converting letter strings to sounds using grapheme-to-phoneme conversion

Importantly, even in healthy brain-intact individuals, there will be differences in reading which can be explained by the Dual Route Model. This is because the lexical route is relatively fast since it does not require breaking down a string of letters into 'manageable' bits that you can then sound out using the GPC rules that you have learnt through life. It is a more automatic process of seeing a word that you have seen and pronounced before; this automaticity is much more rapid than the GPC route. A skilled reader will be someone who has seen and learnt the pronunciations (and probably the meanings) of many words and will have a larger lexicon than someone who doesn't read often; as a result their reading will be faster and more efficient since they will not need to resort to the GPC route. An important element is that irregular words, which are defined as those for which standard GPC rules cannot work, can *only* be read using the lexical route. These words (which are also sometimes referred to as exception words) don't follow the standard GPC rules for various reasons. For example, using the GPC rules the word PINT could be broken down to IN, then putting the letter P in front of that and then adding a /t/ sound at the end. Using this method, the word PINT would rhyme with the words HINT and MINT; however, that would be a regularisation error. Similarly, all words that have come into the English usage from other languages such as COLONEL, BOUQUET and DÉTENTE do not follow the GPC rules *of English* (they may well do for their languages of origin). Therefore, for both irregular words and many non-English words, the *only* method for pronunciation is by becoming familiar with the word (using memory) until it becomes part of the lexicon.

As an aside, this property of the English language is used for some 'rough and ready' tests of intelligence. While formal tests of intelligence are long and complex, it is possible to get an *estimate* of someone's intellectual abilities by doing a simple reading test! Two such tests are the National Adult Reading Test (NART: Nelson & Williams, 1991) and the WTAR (Holdnack, 2001), which involve a participant reading a list of single words that are all irregularly spelt. The participant simply has to read aloud the words and the number of *correct pronunciations* is scored. The rationale is that they will only be able to pronounce the words if they already exist in their lexicon, which can only happen if they have come across the word before and *at least* know the pronunciation. The score of correctly pronounced words can then be converted using a table to derive an estimate of IQ. When an individual has suffered brain damage, unless this has affected their language abilities, it is possible to get an estimate of their intellectual capacities *before* the brain damage by using the NART or WTAR; in this case it is known as their pre-morbid IQ. Since their intellectual abilities can be compromised by the brain damage, by comparing their *current* IQ using more formal tests of IQ with this pre-morbid IQ, it is possible to get an idea of the severity of the brain damage (see Chapter 2).

The central elements described above are within a much more comprehensive model which brings together spoken language, naming of visually presented words and reading print (see Figure 10.11). This is important because this model can be used to understand and explain the types of reading errors originally documented by Marshall & Newcombe (1973) but also the types of general word retrieval problems that patients can have when speaking or writing.

Deep Dyslexia

As described above in the case of GR (Marshall & Newcombe, 1966), the most striking feature of deep dyslexia is that a patient makes semantic errors producing a word that is related in meaning to the target word but visually looks totally different, for example, reading SWORD as /*dagger*/. Additionally, there are a number of other features including the inability to read non-words (see above), visual errors and an

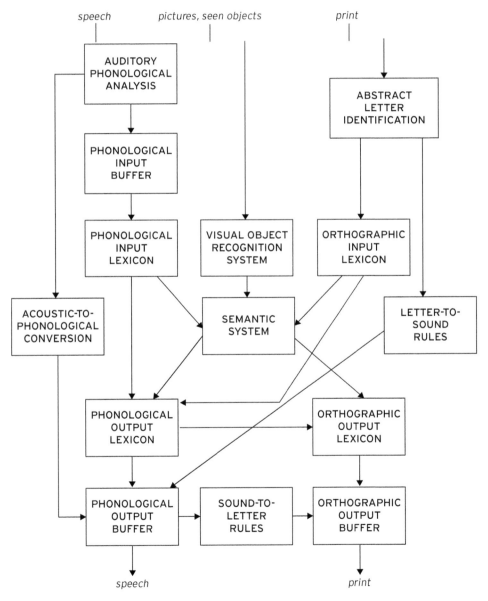

Figure 10.11   The Dual Route Model of word retrieval by Kay et al. (1996)
(Copyright © 1993, American Psychological Association)

effect of concreteness. A visual error involves reading a word that looks physically like the target word, for example, reading THING as /*think*/ or SKATE as /*scale*/. This problem probably derives from errors within the 'abstract letter identification', whereby individual letters are misread and therefore the output to the 'orthographic input lexicon' is wrong – with just one or two letters being misidentified, this would produce the types of visual errors that are sometimes reported. Concreteness refers to the difference between concrete words, which are those that refer to physical things that can be visualised or imagined (e.g. a cat or a chair), and abstract words, which refer to concepts that are more difficult to imagine (e.g. love or harmony); this property can also be referred to as imageability (see Chapter 6). A number of models have been proposed for explaining how deep dyslexia comes about which include the possibility that a more 'primitive' system in the right hemisphere is used when the major left hemisphere language areas are damaged. However, at present, while the deficit is very obvious in patients, a well-accepted explanation is yet to be proposed.

Phonological Dyslexia

The hallmark of phonological dyslexia is the inability to read non-words aloud. For example, Funnell (1983) worked with a man who suffered brain damage at the age of 58. His reading of real words was relatively intact with the main problems being with the words of low frequency. Compared to this, he failed to correctly read out a single one of 20 non-words that he was presented with; if he attempted reading one of these, despite having been told that they were all made-up non-words, he always produced a real word. For example, for the non-word COBE he said /*comb*/ and for PLOON he said /*spoon*/. In addition to this, when he was given 12 letters to read, he wasn't able to give the syllabic sound of any of them and yet when he was presented the sounds of these letters, he was able to repeat the sound perfectly. What this demonstrates is that he had the knowledge of the sounds but could not *translate* them from print to sound; in the case of non-words, similarly, he couldn't translate these strings of letters into sound. The fact that he was able to read real words without any problems demonstrated that he was able to use the orthographic input lexicon which holds the visual forms of words that someone *currently* knows to either derive the meaning of the word via the semantic system or to simply say the word without thinking about its meaning using the 'phonological output lexicon', which holds the sound patterns of words that we are familiar with; this can then send information to the 'phonological output buffer' which creates the actual sounds (see Figure 10.12a). For words that have not been encountered before, there is no representation in the orthographic input lexicon, and in healthy individuals, the Letter-To-Sound Rules need to be activated to read such letter strings. Therefore, by this sort of careful analysis of WB's pattern of intact and impaired reading, Funnell (1983) was able to conclude that this was the system that was impaired in the patient.

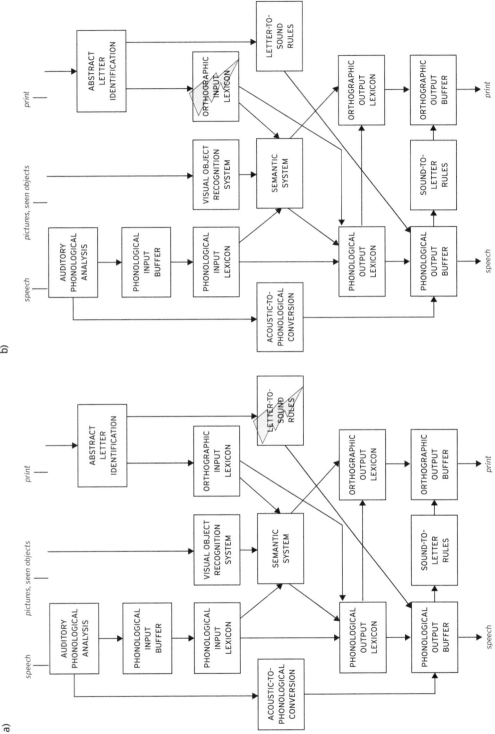

Figure 10.12 a) The locus of WB's phonological dyslexia as documented by Funnell (1983); b) The locus of KT's surface dyslexia as documented by McCarthy & Warrington (1986) (Both adapted from Kay, Lesser & Coltheart, 1992)

Surface Dyslexia

The most striking sign of surface dyslexia is a difficulty in reading words that do not follow traditional pronunciation rules. Some languages (such as Italian, Spanish and German) are classed as phonetic, since you will know from the spelling of a word how to pronounce it and vice versa. For example, I (AJ) speak fairly good Italian and have been learning Spanish; the result is that even for Italian and Spanish words *that I have never seen before* I can read the word out loud and get the pronunciation more or less correct. However, English is an irregular language in which while there are general rules, there are also many irregularities. Therefore, as described above, someone who is not familiar with an irregular word will read it incorrectly. The same will happen with someone who suffers from surface dyslexia. McCarthy & Warrington (1986) documented the case of KT, a 54-year-old patient who was showing specific language problems, and so they looked specifically at the issue of regularity by using six separate sets of word lists that had been carefully created with equal numbers of words that were regularly spelt or irregularly spelt; two of the sets had a third list that was classed as 'very irregular'. They found that the patient's ability to read correctly varied enormously across the lists with the number of correct pronunciations of the irregular and very irregular words sometimes being a third or a quarter of that for the regular words. The locus of the patient's deficit is likely to have been in the orthographic input lexicon which allows an individual to read out words that they are *already* familiar with (see Figure 10.12b). As a result, the patient can only use the phonological route using the letter-to-sound rules to translate what they see into a sound; for words like ABDOMINAL or STATE these rules suffice but for a word like COLONEL they don't, so a patient is likely to say */kollonel/*. Unlike a patient with phonological dyslexia like WB, however, a patient with surface dyslexia like KT will have no problems reading non-words like COBE or PLOON; therefore, there is a double dissociation between these two reading problems.

The Dual Route Model and Developmental Dyslexia

As explained in Chapter 3, it is important to remember that there are differences between acquired and developmental versions of various cognitive disorders. Most students will have heard of dyslexia before studying neuropsychology, but that will have been developmental dyslexia that can be diagnosed at school rather than acquired dyslexia which has been the main focus of this chapter. As outlined above, the Dual Route Model has come about because of the documentation and evaluation of adults who have suffered brain damage to a previously functioning language system. However, research has demonstrated that children with reading disorders tend to use the sub-lexical route, sometimes reading slowly letter-by-letter rather than using the faster lexical route. Overall, although Marshall did not originally develop his model for explaining developmental dyslexia, it has been shown (for example, by Castle et al., 2006) that in fact it is possible to apply the framework very well to understanding the reading disorders found in children. Indeed, Brunsdon et al. (2002) have demonstrated how the model can be used in rehabilitation for improving reading in a ten-year-old child, TJ, with developmental dyslexia. They used a treatment programme that had previously been used with an adult with acquired dyslexia which involved reading, writing and copying target words in a repeated fashion over a period of weeks and testing TJ periodically as well as four weeks and four months after this training. Compared to TJ's reading abilities before the programme (known as the baseline), there was a clear incremental improvement with each week of training. Importantly, the fact that the improvement wasn't simply because of the one-to-one attention that TJ was receiving and practice he was doing was seen in his performance a month then four months later (see Figure 10.13).

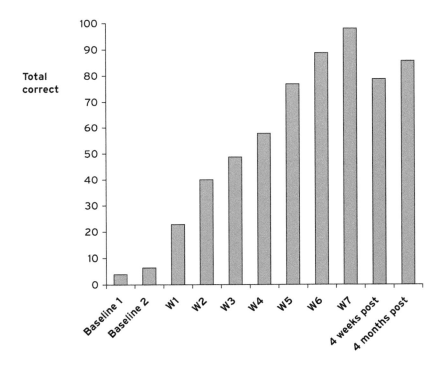

Figure 10.13   The number of words correctly recalled by a ten-year-old child, TJ, with developmental dyslexia before (baseline), during and after weekly training to improve his reading skills (Brunsdon et al., 2002. Reprinted with permission from Taylor and Francis Ltd)

Overall Evaluation of Dual Route Model

The Dual Route Model has been extremely useful in helping to understand a number of different types of reading problems whilst giving an insight into the complexity of the intact system. It is important to note that while the three main forms of dyslexia have been presented as discrete conditions, in fact, it is seldom the case that a patient fits neatly into just one of these boxes. Just as with any other neuropsychological condition, since nature doesn't create 'clean lesions' that only affect a very small area of brain, the damage can be widespread; as a result, given the complexity of the language networks (see Figure 10.9), a number of different levels of the system can be affected at the same time. Therefore, a patient may show a combination of the above problems if the brain regions involved in the specific cognitive processes are all damaged. Further, the deficits will also not be 'all-or-none' such that a patient with surface dyslexia for example, will not have difficulty with *every single* irregularly spelt word with some words posing fewer problems for them. A neuropsychologist would therefore be interested in what the factors beyond regularity of spelling are that affect the level of difficulty that a patient experiences.

In addition, while the three main forms of dyslexia have been covered, there are other types of reading problems that, because of space, have not been dealt with, including patients who can only read by sounding out each letter individually and those who know the meaning of a word but can't find the word itself (known as anomia). In addition to these reading problems, as seen in the model (see Figure 10.11), there is a route for writing which has not been discussed here; deficits in this part of the system lead to a complex set of writing disorders known as dysgraphia.

While there are major strengths to the Dual Route Model, there are a number of limitations. At the moment at least, it is a useful explanatory framework for the production and reading of single words as well as of the naming of objects. However, importantly, there is no mechanism within the model for understanding how we put words together to form sentences. Beyond that, grammar and syntax within these sentences can greatly change how the same set of words in different orders can change the intended meaning. Further still, the intonation of speech (the sing-song patterns) can make a difference whereby a set of words can either be a statement or it can be a command or a question. Further still, language is dynamic so we *change* our way of speaking and even the words we use depending on the *context* within which we are speaking; these can vary depending on whether we are with a group of friends or at a formal work meeting which will impact what we say or how to interpret what others are saying.

Finally, the model has been developed from the work of some fantastic neuropsychologists primarily in the UK, and is based on English-speaking patients with brain damage. Given that some languages are much more phonetic than others (see above), some of the elements of the model may not be as relevant in other languages, for example, ones in which *all* words are phonetically spelt. Further still, the model works for explaining reading difficulties in languages that have scripts where a grapheme represents a phoneme (known as *segmental* scripts); however, what about other writing systems that employ *ideogrammatic*, *pictographic* and *logographic* elements like Chinese or Ancient Egyptian? Next, do the language processes work the same between people who only speak one language and those who speak more than one? With the latter, is the semantic system of both authors of this chapter (AJ and AD), who are fully bilingual in English and our mother tongue Gujarati from north-west India, the same or do we have separate semantic systems for each of our languages? We both grew up bilingual and one of us (AJ) has gone on to learn Italian in his 30s followed by Spanish more recently. Irrespective of the level of fluency that is achieved, does the age at which someone learns the second (third or fourth) language impact how the semantic system is formed and develops? All these issues need to be addressed for us to eventually be able to understand the language difficulties of patients with brain damage as well as to understand how our major communication skill(s) function.

Chapter Summary

- Language is an extremely complex skill that is not simply about speaking but a number of different forms of communication.
- In the nineteenth century, a number of neurologists working with patients who had developed language problems following brain damage began theorising about how different parts of the brain were involved in specific linguistic abilities. The box-and-arrow models that emerged from this movement were very influential for almost a century as understanding of the role of the brain in language evolved.
- Eventually in the late 1960s and 1970s, the rise of cognitive psychology gave a new way of thinking, particularly through the work of John Marshall and Freda Newcombe who documented three very different types of reading problems and explained them using an information-processing approach.
- The Dual Route Model of language was developed out of this influential work and has gone on to explain a number of complex issues within reading and also language production and writing (the latter not covered here).
- While the Dual Route Model is very impressive for explaining a range of issues, there are levels of language that it cannot explain, and this has driven forward research.

Important Researcher

Max Coltheart

Max Coltheart (1939-) is an Australian cognitive scientist who specialises in cognitive neuropsychology and cognitive neuropsychiatry. Working in the UK with a group of British neuropsychologists, he is seen as one of the founders of cognitive neuropsychology as a distinct field. He is known for creating the 'dual-route' reading theory in the late 1970s and the two-factor theory of delusional belief in the 2000s (see Chapter 7). Max has been at the heart of an important debate over what can be learnt about cognition through functional neuroimaging studies which has had an important impact on the way that some forms of cognitive neuropsychology have formed (see Chapters 1 and 2). Max has won numerous awards and was also instrumental in the founding of MACCS (the Maquarie Centre for Cognitive Science) in Sydney, Australia, which is a premier research institute that has produced generations of international researchers.

Important Research Study

GR (Marshall & Newcombe, 1966)

In terms of the DNA of cognitive neuropsychology as a field distinct from the neurobiological models of human behaviour and the new field of cognitive neuropsychology, this paper was *the* birth of the field. In it, two remarkable British neuropsychologists, John Marshall and Freda Newcombe, carried out a forensic analysis of patient GR's reading problems and used the new language of cognitive psychology to suggest how these *errors* allowed us to gain insight into *intact* reading processes. Previously, the neurobiological models tried to pinpoint what the disorder said about what the damaged part of the brain was involved in (neurobiological models) or tried to create information processing models which could sometimes be divorced from how healthy or brain-damaged patients performed. The particular deficit that GR demonstrated was deep dyslexia which had never been documented before; this paper was followed up by another one in which two more deficits, phonological and surface dyslexia, were documented in other patients. Together, these findings laid the foundations for the Dual Route Model which has endured for half a century. So while GR's deep dyslexia is not particularly rare, like HM, it was the seismic shift in our thinking of reading in this case that makes this study so important.

Questions for Reflection

- Even if the way that the nineteenth century diagram-makers saw language eventually became outdated, in what ways was it important?
- Why is the Dual Route Model so influential in our thinking about language both for those with acquired dyslexia and children with developmental dyslexia?

Go Further

- Language is obviously very complicated and goes well beyond single word reading – explore how other issues are being researched by scientists to turn the single words into the rich communication that we all engage in effortlessly every day.
- Think about how language might be changing with modern technology, such as rapid communication with abbreviations (e.g. lol!). Will this pose challenges for clinicians who are trying to understand the language deficits of a 'modern person' who might have developed language in this era or do you think it would not matter?

Further Reading

- Tremblay, P., & Dick, A. S. (2016). Broca and Wernicke are dead, or moving past the classic model of language neurobiology. *Brain and Language, 162*: 60-71.

11
COGNITIVE NEUROPSYCHOLOGICAL REHABILITATION

JWALA NARAYANAN & ASHOK JANSARI

Chapter Overview

This chapter will explore an important and exciting area of neuropsychology. As outlined in Chapter 1, one of the main reasons for studying and understanding the brain is so we can help patients with a brain injury. This chapter will take you through how patients are helped to return to their lives following their brain injury. The chapter describes what is known as the holistic approach to neuropsychological rehabilitation with a focus on the latest developments in cognitive rehabilitation and technology.

Chapter Outline

- Introduction
- History of Neuropsychological Rehabilitation
- What Is Cognitive Rehabilitation? And What Is It Not?
- The Rehabilitation Process
- Rehabilitation of Different Cognitive Domains
- Assistive Technology
- Chapter Summary

INTRODUCTION

While the rest of this book has explored how the study of individuals with brain damage informs us about the functioning of intact cognitive systems as well as the possible assessment of patients, this chapter will take a different focus – how can we help patients to adjust to a new life following their brain damage. Neuropsychological rehabilitation involves the attempt to lessen the cognitive, behavioural, emotional and psychosocial disorders caused by the brain injury. Whilst the focus of this chapter is cognitive rehabilitation, it is important to emphasise the need to understand cognitive deficits in the context of the patient. As you will see, focusing solely on improving cognition may not necessarily have a positive impact on everyday living and quality of life. When a person has a brain injury it leads to a significant change in the overall life of that person but also sometimes of their family. Even a small injury can have a big impact depending on the area of damage. Having difficulties in cognitive abilities that we used to take for granted such as not visually recognising your family members, not being able to remember what someone just said to you, not being able to keep focused on a task or making decisions, or being unable to read a simple newspaper, can have far-reaching consequences. Some of these skills might be important in everyday living whether at home or at work; some of these are necessary to maintain our relationships with family, friends or colleagues since they are used to the individual being able to do these things. In this way, a neuropsychological disorder can very much be a 'hidden disability'; as with any disability, this can lead to emotional difficulties especially since the person has to adjust to a new life where they cannot take those cognitive skills for granted any more.

As a consequence of the complexity and range of difficulties that an individual may face, neuropsychological rehabilitation has evolved to be a 'holistic' process with the patient and family being central to the planning and setting of goals of the rehabilitation process. It is holistic in the sense that the process takes into account the patient's life before the brain injury, the present limitations or opportunities in their lives including family, financial, work support and any disability caused by the brain injury. This forms the context within which patients are encouraged to focus on goals for rehabilitation that are most valued by them. It is important to differentiate rehabilitation from treatment and recovery. In fields outside cognitive neuropsychology, treatment may include medication, surgery or other therapies to recover to the pre-injury state. For example, if my knee started hurting while running, my treatment could involve a range of possibilities including hot and cold treatments around the muscles, massage, ultrasound treatment and possibly even surgery. While this may all take time depending on the level of injury, unless I had caused extremely serious damage, the aim would be to eventually get me back to being able to run; indeed, one of us (AJ) had just this following knee surgery and managed to run a half marathon years later. Unfortunately, this level of return to pre-treatment levels is seldom possible when an individual has a severe cognitive disorder.

Cognitive neuropsychological rehabilitation focuses on helping patients reach their *optimum* capability to lead a life of *independence and dignity*; within this aim, trying to recover the full level of performance of a cognitive function (e.g. memory or face recognition) is not the aim, but instead assisting the individual to *adjust* to their new life with the aid of strategies where possible while also addressing emotional adjustment. Neuropsychological rehabilitation can be considered any time after a brain injury: it could be in the acute phase (usually within three to six months of the event) or even many years after someone has had a brain injury. Although the field of rehabilitation following brain injury dates back to the early twentieth century, current rehabilitation practice is still built on some of the foundational work carried out by the pioneers of the field.

HISTORY OF NEUROPSYCHOLOGICAL REHABILITATION

The field of neuropsychological rehabilitation developed around the time of World War I. Interestingly, different individuals across the world made efforts towards cognitive and neuropsychological rehabilitation around the same time (Boake, 1991). There were two main factors that drove the need and then growth of efforts at rehabilitation. The first factor was that because of the advancement in warfare, particularly the types of bullets that were being developed, many soldiers were surviving bullet wounds to the head if their trajectories missed deeper brain structures that were vital for survival. Coupled with this, there had been a general evolution within medical care. The twentieth century therefore saw an increase in gunshot wound survivors due to improved medical treatment, sophisticated rifles with smaller bullets and better helmets. Rehabilitation hospitals were created for soldiers with brain injuries returning from war. These 'schools for soldiers' offered psychological assessments and rehabilitation strategies that are still used in current practice.

Two early pioneers were Walter Poppelreuter and Kurt Goldstein; both were German-trained neurologists, with the latter having studied under the great Carl Wernicke. Poppelreuter published the first book in brain injury rehabilitation in which he described the classic experimental methods to understand visual disturbance and how retraining exercises can influence the brain recovery process. He also described the importance of vocational rehabilitation as part of the rehabilitation programme; this is a structured programme to help a patient retain a job or find a new job that they are able to carry out given their disabilities. Goldstein's work made specific recommendations for speech, reading and writing, but importantly, he also argued that rehabilitation of brain injury required much more than retraining exercises for specific cognitive abilities. His work formed the basis of holistic approaches to neuropsychological rehabilitation (Prigatano, 1999) that is still in practice to date.

Around the time of World War II, Alexander Romanovich Luria, often known as the father of neuropsychological assessment, led a research team at an army hospital in understanding compensatory methods for patients with brain injury. Luria's work on understanding brain function and possible remediation methods for deficits was derived from the numerous patients with brain injuries he was exposed to. Luria practised and propagated the philosophy that psychological research must be carried out for the betterment of patients and that the person must always be seen in their social context (Luria, 1979).

Another influential neuropsychologist, Oliver Zangwill, worked with World War II brain injury patients in Edinburgh in the UK. He emphasised the need for re-education for people with brain injury to be able to cope with their disabilities. He referred to three main approaches: compensation, substitution and direct retraining. Compensation meant reorganising of function to minimise a disability; an example of this may include a patient who is unable to regain complete recovery in a lower limb, even after physiotherapy, and may have to rely on a crutch to compensate for his inability to balance on both limbs while walking. Substitution was learning a new way of doing something due to the damage to the brain, for instance lip reading for people who are deaf. Finally, direct retraining, considered as the highest form of training, involved repeated practice or training of a lost ability, like physiotherapy may do for a weak limb; however this may not always be possible, particularly in people with cognitive disorders.

In the USA, Louis Granich and Joseph Wepman were known for their work in people with language difficulties. John Aita, another well-known neurologist around the same time, set up a unit for men presenting with penetrating injuries to the brain, stressing that mere neurological evaluation, neurosurgical interventions and referrals to physiotherapy did not suffice for men with brain injury. The unit was an interdisciplinary care team for post-acute head injury rehabilitation involving a range of professionals such that a social service worker, an occupational therapist, a physiotherapist, a ward nurse and a psychologist met once a week to discuss each patient individually to tailor a programme of support for that person which looked holistically at the patient rather than each of their needs being seen separately. This interdisciplinary framework is still followed in many rehabilitation facilities around the world (Wilson et al., 2017).

Therefore, due to formative issues related to types of bullets, improved healthcare, the young age of soldiers who were left with specific disabilities but who could nonetheless have a chance of a productive life post-injury and the efforts of some pioneers in Germany, Russia, the UK and the USA, the field of neuropsychological rehabilitation was born.

WHAT IS COGNITIVE REHABILITATION? AND WHAT IS IT NOT?

Cognitive rehabilitation involves addressing cognitive impairments that result from brain injury. Cognitive impairments include memory, attention, executive function, behaviour, speed of processing and language. Most commonly, cognitive rehabilitation involves cognitive retraining or compensation as stated above. Cognitive rehabilitation usually involves the therapy of patients with non-progressive brain injuries. However, cognitive stimulation has also been found to be helpful in patients with dementia, which involves a progressive loss of cognitive abilities. Most of the processes described in this chapter are for patients with non-progressive conditions. The aim of cognitive rehabilitation is to facilitate independent living and improve quality of life. Table 11.1 displays what cognitive rehabilitation can do and what it may not do.

Table 11.1   What cognitive rehabilitation can do and may not do

Cognitive rehabilitation can	Cognitive rehabilitation may not
• Improve awareness about one's strengths and weaknesses • Facilitate better functioning for someone with cognitive impairment • Improve quality of life for a brain injury survivor and their family • Facilitate optimising one's capacity	• Offer complete recovery to pre-morbid levels • Offer treatment • Always generalise to improving problems in everyday life

Having established what the aims of cognitive rehabilitation are, it is then important to work out what will allow clinicians to help their clients achieve these goals. An international survey conducted by Nowell et al. (2020) looking at current practices of cognitive rehabilitation in patients post-TBI illustrated a thematic map of factors that do and *do not* facilitate cognitive rehabilitation (Figure 11.1). They outlined three main factors that influence cognitive rehabilitation: those relating to the patient or client, those relating to the rehabilitation setting and finally the factors relating to the clinician. Factors relating to the client play an important role in mediating cognitive rehabilitation and these include their knowledge about the impact of *their* brain injury, the social support they have around them in their everyday lives and finally their motivation to engage in therapy. With regards to the clinician, their skill and their rapport with the patient seem significant in contributing to the success of the cognitive rehabilitation. Finally, a good rehabilitation team that is involved in helping physical, cognitive, emotional and vocational needs by integrating engagement in daily life are recognised contributing factors to the rehabilitation setting.

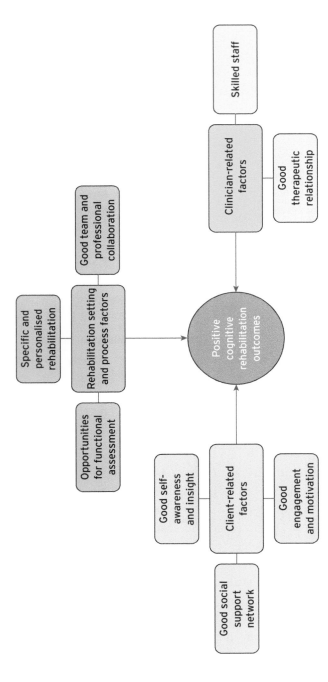

Figure 11.1 Thematic map of factors that facilitate cognitive rehabilitation (Nowell et al., 2020. Reprinted with permission from Taylor & Francis Ltd)

The vital importance of contextualising *cognitive* rehabilitation for the needs of the patient with their *psychosocial background* has been emphasised by a number of pioneers in the field. This is because focusing singularly on a cognitive function may lead to improvement or even mastery on *that* isolated task or even result in improved scores on cognitive tests; however it does not necessarily show improved functional outcome. For instance, training someone with a memory problem on a list of words may help improve their ability to remember that specific list, but it may not improve their memory to recall a shopping list from their everyday chores. Wilson et al. (2009) emphasise that the purpose of rehabilitation is not to improve cognitive test scores as the relationship between test performance and real-life skills is only moderate. Rehabilitation helps patients reach their highest level of functioning possible in the community given their disabilities.

Brain injury rehabilitation can be complex and, if done appropriately rather than with a 'one-size-fits all' method, is unique to each individual as deficits arise not just from lesions in one area of the brain, but shared networks connecting to other parts of the brain too. Other factors including behaviour and emotions following brain injury can also interfere with cognitive function. Just as you or I would find it difficult to do something (for example, writing an essay for your course) if we were not feeling well physically or emotionally, it is important to take these factors into consideration when working in neuropsychological rehabilitation, since sleep, pain, fatigue and mood influence cognitive performance. This is particularly important since these factors are also most commonly affected in a brain injury. Hence, as a therapist it is important to identify and manage these factors. Setting a patient's sleep cycle right or managing their fatigue better can have a direct impact on cognitive abilities such as the individual's speed of processing, attention and memory.

THE REHABILITATION PROCESS

Figure 11.2 shows the biopsychosocial model of the consequences of a brain injury showing the complex interactions between the psychosocial factors and the brain injury in planning functional goals. Mapping the patient's strengths and weaknesses, support systems and their goals also bring clarity to the patient about the process of rehabilitation. If the therapist only focuses on a particular cognitive deficit experienced by their patient, they may start working on strategies for improving that cognitive skill, but this may have no value in the person's everyday life or their main outcome goal. This is the reason that the cognitive deficit cannot be viewed in isolation but a more holistic approach is necessary. This holistic approach to the rehabilitation process begins with a comprehensive assessment. Who the person was before the brain injury changed their life, a detailed interview of the injury itself and how it came about, the patient's pre-morbid personality and their background are all crucial for the goal-setting process. The comprehensive assessment would entail a clinical interview (which would include the difficulties the patient is presenting with and any relevant medical conditions they may be suffering), a cognitive assessment (of major domains such as memory, language and visuo-spatial abilities) and an evaluation of mood and behaviour. By following this holistic process, the rehabilitation programme that emerges is unique for each patient as it has been tailored to the individual's particular circumstances, their needs and the goals set by them and their families.

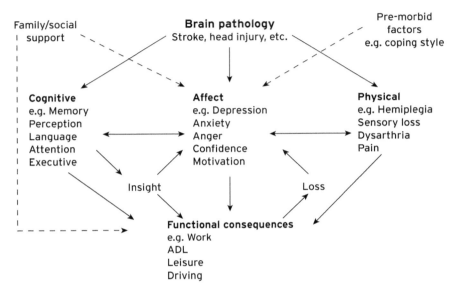

Figure 11.2 A biopsychosocial model of the consequences of brain injury (Wilson et al., 2009. Reprinted with permission from Cambridge University Press)

There are two main approaches to rehabilitation, namely restoration and compensation. The more intuitive approach to overcome an impairment is to improve it or retrain the function. Often complete restoration of lost function may not be possible, therefore compensatory strategies are encouraged in helping the patient to engage in everyday life. Restoration requires retraining of a cognitive skill by repetitive practice of a specific cognitive task, starting with simple exercises, gradually increasing the difficulty over the rehabilitation programme until the patient has achieved mastery. For example, for a patient who has suffered a problem in speaking fluently, speech training for articulation would be appropriate. Depending on the severity of the impairment, the therapist may start by training the patient on articulating simple sounds, then moving on to words and sentences as the patient improves. On the other hand, rather than trying to improve the specific ability, compensation involves using an aid to *overcome* the problem, for example where retraining may have not been completely successful it may be possible to use text-to-voice technology to articulate speech. As will be seen in the following section, depending on the cognitive domain that has been affected, there are different restorative and compensatory strategies that have been developed and evaluated.

REHABILITATION OF DIFFERENT COGNITIVE DOMAINS

Attention

As seen in Chapter 4, attention is one of the most essential and basic abilities that forms the foundation for other cognitive functions. If you do not pay attention in class, you are going to have difficulty remembering what is taught. Similarly, if you are not paying attention in everyday life, you can make errors on more complex tasks like driving a car. Therefore, Fish (2017) has suggested that assessing and including the understanding of a patient's attentional abilities can be central to understanding the patient's impairment and planning their rehabilitation programme.

Several studies have looked at restorative or repetitive exercises to improve attention. Sohlberg & Mateer (2001) developed the Attention Process Training (APT) methodology which is a structured programme in training attention that targets the five types of attention that guide our functioning: focused, selective, sustained, divided and alternating attention. It involves repetitive exercises, based on training of these five areas in a hierarchical and graded manner. Following the exercises in a clinic setting, the clinician makes plans for generalisation of these five areas of attention. The ability to focus attention is less commonly impaired. Focused attention is the most basic ability to mediate other attentional processes. If a patient is unable to focus attention it would be difficult to train them on other aspects of attention. Therefore, if this is impaired, much of the rehabilitation would be spent training the patient to focus on a target either through auditory or visual training. Once this basic skill is improved, other types of attention can be trained.

Let's take cooking as an example of an activity to train the other four types of attention, since generally one needs to continually monitor one's behaviour and react to what is happening, adding ingredients or changing the heat, etc. If a patient gets easily distracted and is unable to cook a meal on their own, the basic cooking activity to improve a patient's ability to sustain attention may be making a sandwich or a cup of coffee; then this could be scaled up in complexity all the way to preparing a five-course meal. Using the cooking activity in the context of alternating attention could include cooking while monitoring the washer/dryer cycles. In a selective attention training task, the cooking activity can take place in a setting with children playing in the background, therefore requiring the individual to focus *selectively* on the cooking task. Finally, for divided attention, the individual is expected to focus on the cooking task while listening to the lottery numbers on the television (Sohlberg & Mateer, 2001). Any activity may be used for retraining, however Sohlberg & Mateer (2001) emphasised that the training must be carried out in an organised manner starting with basic skills increasing in difficulty; they also stressed the importance of repetition and practice of these skills and the need to keep records of how the patient performs. The success of the training programme is when there is improvement in everyday life.

Fish & Manly (2017) propose other strategies to help improve attentional abilities, and describing them all would be beyond the scope of this chapter but one strategy that you may relate to while studying for exams is reducing distractions. While patients with brain injury struggle with processing information quickly or processing too much information at the same time, reducing distractions can help them focus on a task better. Reducing external distractions such as noise by using noise-cancellation headphones, reducing or avoiding clutter, switching off mobile phones and completing complex work in a quiet space can be helpful. Further, managing internal distractions including mood, pain and thoughts by means of mindfulness can be useful to improve attention.

Working Memory

Working memory in this section is referring to the ability to temporarily hold information and use it effectively; as such it is different to the specific Working Memory Model described in Chapter 8. Impairment in working memory is a common cognitive deficit and an important function to address in rehabilitation. However, the evidence on restorative techniques for working memory is somewhat limited. Studies have looked into evaluating simple exercises including basic math problems and word games. Some studies have also evaluated the benefits of retraining working memory using the traditional n-back test that was described in Chapter 8. Here the task may require you to name a series of colours that may be shown to you, however the *n-back* factor would require you to name the colour just before the colour displayed at present. The second level may require you to name the colour *2-back*, two turns ago. The third level may require you to name the number and the circle of the previous stimuli. Figure 11.3 demonstrates this exercise. You could try this with your friend by adding more stimuli. As working memory is an ability to *hold information* temporarily, other compensatory strategies have been suggested including changing communication style to short and precise sentences to aid comprehension and using a notepad to write down important information; technology has also been found to be helpful.

Level 1		Level 2		Level 3	
Stimuli	Correct response	Stimuli	Correct response	Stimuli	Correct response
●	-	●	-	5	-
●	Red	●	-	4	5 red
●	Blue	●	Red	2	4 blue
●	Green	●	Blue	8	2 green

Figure 11.3   An example of the n-back training exercise

Other Executive Functions

As seen in Chapter 9, executive functions encompass a variety of abilities and there-fore many strategies related to the deficits have been proposed. Two commonly used techniques to improve deficits of executive function are metacognitive strategies and goal management training. Metacognitive strategy training is also an integral part of attention training. It helps improve a patient's awareness about their deficits and assist in regulating their behaviour when required. Ownsworth et al. (2006) illustrate an example of one of their patients JM, a 32-year-old male who sustained a severe open head injury in a car accident. His brain injury led to significant cognitive and physical deficits, however he showed some improvement over the course of two years. JM continued to have significant deficits in executive function and self-awareness. He was unaware of his own difficulties, he only complained of reduced strength in his left side, while his family reported extensive physical, cognitive and behavioural changes. One of JM's goals in therapy was to cook independently; this was facilitated by giving JM education about his deficits and using effective feedback and prompts to reduce any errors (metacognitive strategies) while cooking. There were three factors that would classify an error: 1) a risk to his own or others' safety; 2) the outcome of the meal; and 3) time efficiency. When JM was being trained on the cooking task he was given feedback at three levels to improve his awareness: 1) he was given time to *self-correct*; when unable to self-correct; 2) *non-specific prompts* were given such as 'Can I get you to stop and tell me what you are up to right now?'; if JM was unable to correct the error with an unspecific prompt; 3) a more *specific prompt* was presented, e.g. 'Can you check the recipe and see what goes in the mixing bowl first?' Figure 11.4

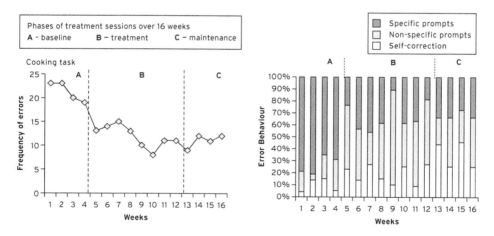

Figure 11.4   Results from Ownsworth et al. (2006) indicating reduction in error frequency on the cooking task over 16 weeks of therapy (graph on the left). The graph on the right indicates changes in the proportions of self-correction and prompts over the 16 weeks of therapy (Reprinted with permission from Cambridge University Press)

shows the 44% reduction in his error frequency (left graph) from the *baseline* or time before therapy (A), to the *treatment* phase (B), to the *maintenance* or after therapy phase (C). On the graph on the right, it's also important to take note of the reduction in the specific prompts required from before the treatment to after the treatment and the increase in self-corrections. Therapists may use different ways to aid in building awareness, including using technology to alert and set reminders, using videos of behaviour to give feedback or sometimes just verbal feedback from the therapist, family or friends.

Goal management is a useful tool for patients with deficits in executive function. It can help patients in planning, problem solving and goal setting. Goal management training (GMT) was proposed by Levine et al. (2000), and various versions of the framework are now used. GMT encourages patients to monitor and evaluate their own performance in everyday life. Levine et al. (2000) presented the effectiveness of GMT using a randomised controlled trial (considered as a gold standard research methodology for treatment studies). In their study of 30 mild to severe traumatic brain injury patients, they randomly allocated 15 patients to GMT and 15 patients to motor skills training (MST) groups. The GMT involved about four to eight hours of training on brain injury education and a five-stage process of goal management: 1) STOP – orienting and alerting to task; 2) Define main task – goal setting; 3) List steps – partitioning goals into subgoals; 4) Learn steps – encoding and retention of subgoals; 5) Check – monitor goals. The MST involved training processes unrelated to goal management including the reading and tracing mirror-reversed test. Following their training period the two groups were assigned tasks to test the use of the strategies they learnt. Three paper-pencil tasks were presented to them: 1) *proofreading*: participants were given a paragraph of text that required proofreading (e.g. circle all numbers); 2) *grouping*: participants were given a sheet with two columns, each listing 23 individuals' age and sex, participants were given instructions to group them in different ways (e.g. grouping individuals below the age of 30 as the first group and those above the age of 30 as the second group); 3) *room layout*: a 5×5 grid represented columns and rows of a seating scheme for a meeting. The rows and columns were numbered from 1 to 5. In each of the 25 cells, a letter ('A' to 'E') indicated an employee from one of five companies (company A to company E). Participants had to answer a series of questions based on the grid. All participants were evaluated based on accuracy and speed of working on the task. Figure 11.5 shows the decrease in pre- to post-training errors on all three tasks. It also shows an increase in time spent on the task for patients who underwent GMT which is indicative of the greater care and attention taken to complete the task, which the authors relate to the GMT effects. A recent review of all related studies in GMT and brain injury rehabilitation stresses the increased effectiveness of GMT when coupled with other strategies like using external alerting systems (reminders on a phone) and other patient-specific goal setting (Krasny-Pacini et al., 2014).

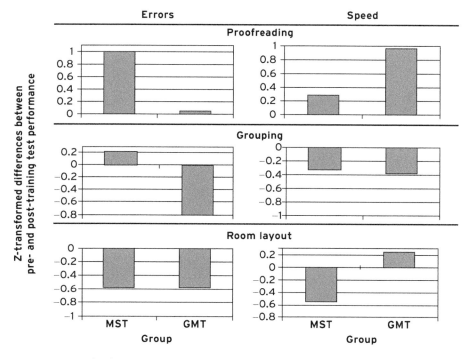

Figure 11.5 Results from Levine et al. (2000) indicate pre- to post-training changes in errors and speed for three tasks. For the purposes of presentation, post-training data were subtracted from pre-test data and the difference was transformed to a standard (z) score. For errors, negative scores indicate a reduction in errors from pre- to post-training. For speed, positive scores indicate increased time (and presumably increased care and attention) from pre- to post-training

Memory

Memory impairment can be variable in patients depending on the injury and severity of symptoms. There are two common approaches to memory rehabilitation, namely compensatory strategies and specific instructional techniques.

Compensatory Strategies

Compensatory strategies are based on internal and external strategies. Internal strategies are techniques used to process, learn, and retain information, usually in patients with mild memory impairment. They include different strategies to encode and recall information. Refer to Table 11.2 to see how some of the common strategies could be used to remember a shopping list such as *bread, butter, coffee, sugar.*

Table 11.2   Common strategies to encode and recall information

Association	If your mother has this for breakfast every day, you can associate this list with your mother's breakfast to strengthen recall
Imagery	You could make a mental image of your mother enjoying her bread and butter while stirring the sugar in her coffee
Rehearsal	This will involve repetitive learning and recalling of the list to ensure storage of information
Chunking	You could group the bread and butter together and the coffee and sugar as one to remember fewer items
Mnemonics	Making an acronym such as **bbc-s** may help you recall what the letters stood for

There are many external strategies which include routines, by means of a time-table, checklists, technology assisted devices, and planners, used for people with moderate-to-severe memory impairment. External strategies along with using an electronic aid have proven to be more successful in patients with acquired brain injury. Various electronic aids including digital calendars, voice organisers and paging systems have proven to be useful, particularly when combined with internal strategies (for example, mnemonics and visual imagery; see Table 11.2) and incorporated into structured training programmes.

Instructional Techniques

Instructional techniques are the guiding principles of learning and memory. The most common and widely studied techniques are errorless learning and spaced retrieval which have been found to be useful in learning functionally relevant information, including names of people, locations and educational facts (Clare & Jones, 2008, Evans et al., 2000; Landis et al., 2006; Wilson et al., 1994). Remember the famous phrase 'You learn from your mistakes'? Well, for a patient with brain injury, they tend to learn *the* mistake and later, when they try to recall the information, they have both the correct information and this mistake now as possibilities for recall; not being able to distinguish between the original correct information and the mistaken information that they have now also learnt makes the likelihood of more errors high. The errorless learning technique aims to reduce or eliminate error while learning new information. This can be done by providing patients with the right answer when asked a question with cues that would lead them to generate the right answer. Wilson et al. (1994) studied 16 young, 16 elderly control and 16 densely amnesic patients on learning new material. They compared performance on standard techniques that allow errors to be generated (known as errorful learning) and a technique that resulted in errorless learning. Wilson et al. (1994) found that each of the amnesic people learned better if prevented from making mistakes during learning.

The spaced retrieval technique aims to improve memory by repeated retrieval and practice of the information learnt over spaced time intervals (Brush & Camp, 1998; Camp &

Schaller, 1989). If you want to learn an important piece of information for your exam it might be helpful to retrieve the learnt material over a few days. For example, retrieving the information 30 minutes after you learn it, then maybe two hours later, again at the end of the day and then maybe after a week will help in the learning process, rather than just repetitive reading. The temporal spacing of retrieval practice results in enhanced learning relative to large amounts of learning in one go (Donovan & Radosevich, 1999).

Visuospatial

Since visuospatial difficulties can impair a person's interaction with the world, it is important to address these to avoid the patient hurting themselves. As seen in Chapter 4, following some types of strokes, some patients may neglect part of the visual world and therefore rehabilitation for visual inattention primarily focuses on 'scanning' to encourage patients to consciously pay attention to objects that are presented to them on the affected side. This can be done in a controlled environment through exercises where the patient scans a given set of items, and it can also be incorporated as a practice in their everyday life. This could include a digit detection task, copying tasks, or reading and writing tasks. The main goal is to work towards paying attention to each part of the person's visual field. Other visual scanning and attention-based tasks that can be implemented are cancellation tasks, word searches and mazes.

Figure 11.6a shows a picture of a patient with visual neglect undergoing visual scanning training where he is made to sit in front of a screen with four arrays of lights. Dundon et al. (2015) in their visual training task required patients to identify patterns of red light (e.g. a square of four lights), requiring them to scan the whole board. Participants filled out a questionnaire about activities of daily living both before (pre-) and after (post-) these training activities. As a visual neglect usually leads to patients missing objects on the left side of their field, it can affect their daily life as they may bump into things on the left or have difficulty finding things in the left side. The results showed significantly reduced problems in everyday life including in activities like reading, crossing the street, etc. (see Figure 11.6b).

Language

As seen in Chapter 10, the domain of language is extremely complex and it can be affected by brain damage in a number of ways, and the resulting impairment can be very disabling. As a social species where individual members are constantly communicating with one another, when an individual is unable to express themselves, they can tend to feel isolated and experience low mood.

There seems to be substantial evidence about the benefits of speech therapy following brain injury (Cicerone et al., 2000). Even evidence from meta-analyses of

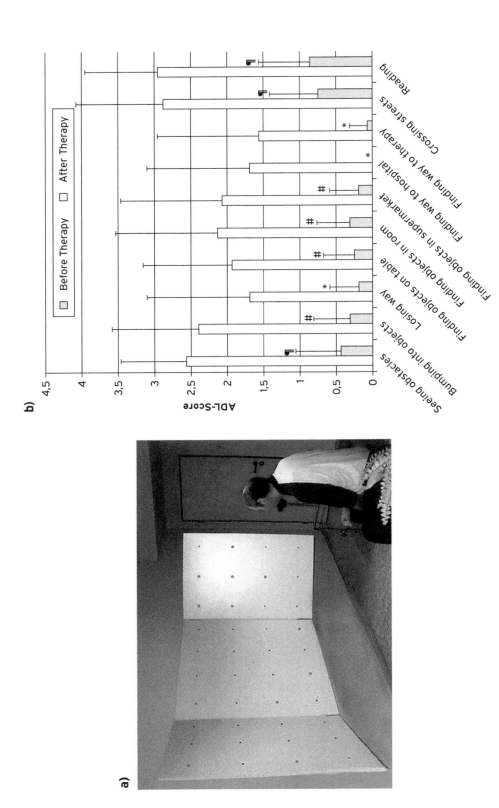

Figure 11.6 a) A patient undergoing visual scanning training; b) Reduced difficulty on activities of daily living post-training (right) in Nelles et al. (2001) (Reproduced with permission from Elsevier)

speech rehabilitation studies following brain injury indicate patients with treatment have better outcomes than those untreated (Greener et al., 1999; Robey, 1998; Whurr et al., 1992). Studies have found therapies of longer duration (more than six months) and intensive programmes (greater number of sessions) to be more effective than shorter duration and low-intensity programmes (Basso & Caporalli, 2001; Marshall et al., 1982).

There are three main approaches that have influenced the field of rehabilitation for aphasia. Encouraging social participation is an important aspect of therapy. Therefore, therapy aims to transition from language training (impairment focused therapy), to encouraging the use of compensatory strategies (compensatory therapies), building confidence, and to finally use language skills learnt in therapy in the community (conversational therapies).

Impairment-Focused Therapy

Impairment-focused therapy is a specific intervention to restore particular language skills including auditory comprehension, word retrieval, sentence production, reading and writing. The therapy may involve language-based exercises to develop and practise the deficient skill. Auditory comprehension training may include repetitive practice with auditory verbal tasks. Impairment therapy has been shown to improve scores on specific language tests including naming (Rayme & Gonzalez Rothi, 2001) and sentence production (Marshall, 2002). Some studies have also indicated generalisation of these skills to conversations (Best et al., 2013). Similar to other cognitive-based exercises it may be appreciated that exercises of a particular skill (e.g. naming) are different from naming ability in daily life. Hence generalisations of these exercises may not always take place. An example of this is that practising the word 'banana' with repetitive pairing of the picture and qualities of a banana may not offer an automatic generalisation of producing the response 'banana' to a question in everyday life such as 'What did you have for breakfast?'

Compensatory Therapies

Compensatory therapies include employing other means of communication, such as using gestures, drawing, pointing to symbols, or communication books. Figure 11.7a shows an example of what a communication book could include. Patients having difficulty naming objects or expressing their needs could point to pictures in the books to communicate their needs. Figure 11.7b displays a communication board that can be used by patients who have difficulty articulating speech. They can be taught to spell out sentences by pointing to the letters on the communication board. Modifying environmental factors to improve communication by means of training a communication partner (e.g. spouse) or context-based modifications (for example, creating simplified versions of books for a book club) can also be helpful (Raymer & Turkstra, 2017).

Figure 11.7 a) A page from a communication book; b) A communication board to help patients spell out what they might be trying to communicate

Conversational Therapies

The conversational therapies approach focuses on improving direct conversations in everyday life. This approach is tailored to the needs of the individual and their context. For instance, Lustig & Tompkins (2002) saw that their patient LG had better expressive writing than speech. Therefore, they taught LG to use written communication in everyday conversations. Conversational therapy may also include therapy sessions with the significant other (such as a partner or family member) who the patient will be communicating with regularly. The therapist could include conversational analysis (CA) to understand the pattern of conversations between the patient and the carer. The therapist may use this information to mediate improving conversational skills for the patient and the significant other. Therapy with the significant other would also include education on the language disorder and the psychosocial aspects of the condition. Once the significant other understands the strengths and weaknesses of the patient, they are also empowered to communicate more effectively with the patient.

Praxis

As seen in Chapter 5, apraxia is a complex condition which impairs the ability to perform previously learned movements used in everyday life. Patients with apraxia can have difficulty carrying out tasks of daily living independently. The condition can be very disabling depending on the severity and kind of apraxia – ideational or ideomotor (see Chapter 5). The presence of apraxia predicts inability to return to work after stroke (Saeki et al., 1995), greater deficits in simulated activities of daily living (Sunderland et al., 1999; Wetter et al., 2005; Goldenberg et al., 2001), eating (Foundas et al., 1995) and caregiver ratings of functioning (Hanna-Pladdy et al., 2003). Unfortunately, despite the presence of apraxia being a strong predictor of being able to return to work after a brain injury, there has been little research in the rehabilitation of apraxias. Restorative-based exercises including gestural training have been found to improve apraxia and also improve activities of daily living (Smania et al., 2000). Studies have also shown positive results for strategy training on specific tasks along with improvement in trained and untrained tasks (Donkervoort et al., 2001). Studies have found observing an action repeatedly can also aid in improving coordinated movements (Pazzaglia & Galli, 2019). Figure 11.8 gives an example of grasping a cup of coffee. Although patients with apraxia identify the cup, they may have difficulty recalling the series of movements associated with the cup. In this study the patient observes correct movement and also receives feedback about his/her movement that tends to aid in the correct usage of the cup. Vanbellingen & Bohlhalter (2011) proposed that ideomotor apraxia required gestural training therapy and patients with ideational apraxia benefited from strategy training.

ASSISTIVE TECHNOLOGY

Given the technological age that we live in, assistive technology has become an increasingly important part of the rehabilitation clinician's arsenal. As much of cognitive rehabilitation relies on compensatory strategies, it can play a critical role in helping a patient lead a more independent life. A systematic review bringing together all the existing literature in the field by Gillespie et al. (2012) on assistive technology for cognition indicated effectiveness in cognition relating to calculation, attention, emotion, experience of self, planning, time management and memory. Below is an overview of the various technologies available.

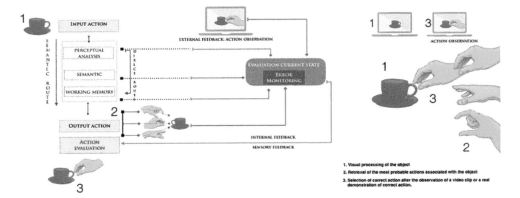

Figure 11.8 A demonstration of the steps displayed to a patient with apraxia to learn the skill of picking up a cup (Pazzaglia & Galli, 2019. Reproduced with permission from Frontiers in Neurology)

Attention and Alerting Systems

As seen in Chapter 4, patients with unilateral neglect can fail to pay attention to one side of space, usually the left. The focus in therapy is to bring the patient's attention to the neglected side, and for this, Robertson & Frasca (1992) developed the Limb Activation Device. It's a device worn by the patient on the *neglected limb*; if the patient has not moved their neglected limb for a long period of time, the device will set off an alarm that will be turned off only when the patient attends to the neglected space. In a later study Robertson et al. (2002) reported improved motor function two years after the intervention, demonstrating a long-term impact of the device.

Another alerting system, found to be helpful to remind a patient about the task and goals she was to focus on, was reported by Evans et al. (1998). Their patient, RP, who sustained bilateral frontal lobe damage, seemed to be unable to carry out goals she intended to despite the fact that her memory was unaffected. Evans et al. (1998) found that introducing an automated alerting system reminding RP of her daily activities (such as taking her medication, going to the voluntary work that she was doing, etc.) was effective in meeting her everyday goals. Fish et al. (2007) found similar effects while training patients on an alerting system to think about their goals. In this study patients were asked to make telephone calls to a voicemail service at four set times each day for ten days. In addition, a simple text saying 'stop' was sent to patients on eight random occasions to cue them to think about their goals. Striking improvements on remembering to carry out the task (making telephone calls) was found on days that patients were cued, indicating that a simple cue can help the brain's monitoring system and in turn help patients achieve their daily goals.

One of the largest studies in assistive technology and cognition is the NeuroPage randomised controlled trial (Wilson et al., 2001). The study involved a paging system that delivered reminders for the performance of everyday tasks in people with cognitive impairment. The paging system was found to successfully assist patients in carrying out everyday activities (for example, taking medication, self-care, keeping appointments), reducing everyday failures of memory and planning. Wilson et al. (2001) noted an increase in the percentage of successful task completion from 37% during baseline to 85% during treatment, and then to 75% at the post-treatment phase. Since the seminal work in NeuroPage many studies have investigated other technologies for reminders and time management, including receiving voice calls, mobile phone text messages and reminders on a smartphone (Pijnenborg et al., 2007; Svoboda & Richards, 2009; van Den Broeck et al., 2000).

Virtual Reality and Technology

Virtual reality (VR) offers a virtual environment (VE) created by computer graphics that the patient can interact with. It also offers various levels of immersive sensations and gamification of the interaction to make the experience more fun (Maggio et al., 2018). VR can offer an ecological and real-world experience of practising cognitive strategies (e.g. carrying out actions, shopping, etc.) VR has been used to rehabilitate motor and cognitive deficits following brain injury with good outcome (Bohil et al., 2011). The field of VR has been fast growing with improving and more affordable technology. A review by Schiza et al. (2019) described the successful use of different types of VR technology across various neurological conditions including dementia, multiple sclerosis, strokes and Parkinson's disease. The VE offers a 'real-life–like' experience that gives the individual with a brain injury a chance to practise or train on skills in a safe environment. Figure 11.9 shows a game where the patients with hemiplegic strokes are required to use a limb as part of the game. This study stressed the importance of administering tasks that are balanced in enjoyment and difficulty levels to engage patients in therapy. As physical therapy post-stroke can be difficult and sometimes painful, the gamification of VR-based tasks can help make the rehabilitation more enjoyable.

There are many VR games developed for the healthy population. These can be used by patients with brain injury too, however some of the games may be too complex for patients to process, particularly for patients who find it difficult to multitask and focus attention. There are apps and games developed specifically targeting skills that require training, such as walking for patients with Parkinson's disease and multiple sclerosis. Walking-related exercises on a treadmill using VR have been tried in a virtual city scene with a tree-lined walking path (Peruzzi et al., 2017). Gamito et al. (2017) developed a VR system to train post-stroke cognitive deficits including attention and memory embedded in everyday tasks. The games offered tasks including buying several items (working

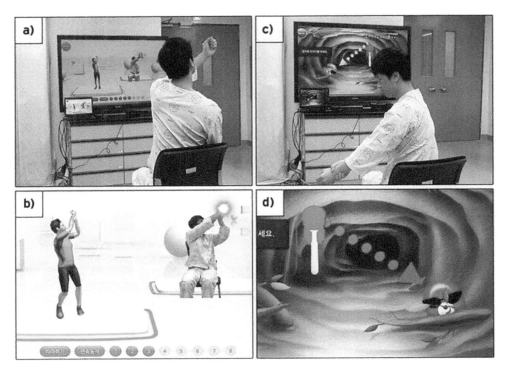

Figure 11.9   VR-based rehabilitation software for patients with hemiplegic stroke: a) and b) show a participant performing the workout mode of training and the VR content reflected back to the participant; c) and d) show a participant performing the game mode of training and the VR content including a hammer (participant's hand movement) and a mole target (Lee et al., 2016. Reprinted with permission from Oxford University Press)

memory), finding a virtual character dressed in yellow (selective attention), recognising advertisements (recognition memory and finding their way in the supermarket (visuo-spatial ability). However, this area is fast evolving and needs further efficacy studies to determine its use in clinical practice.

Another exciting and promising addition to the VR system is the ability to tailor the cognitive training to the level required for the patient using machine learning and artificial intelligence. As cognitive retraining usually takes place in a graded manner with increasing complexity to optimise the training of a skill, being able to identify the level of the patient and assigning exercises specifically for their needs could eventually be very important as we move into an era of personalised medi-cine which moves away from a 'one-size-fits-all' approach and instead caters for the individual. The enormous leaps being made in the technological world generally will greatly help this pursuit in capitalising on the use of virtual reality for rehabilitation in the future.

Chapter Summary

Cognitive rehabilitation is an integral part of neuropsychological rehabilitation. However, the rehabilitation needs to be planned around each individual patient by means of prioritising their goals. The field of cognitive rehabilitation is fast evolving, particularly in the realm of cutting-edge technology. It is important to integrate technology where possible as it could facilitate independence earlier and compensate for deficits that may not be recoverable.

Important Researcher

Barbara Wilson

Barbara Wilson is a British clinical neuropsychologist who has spent her career working to help patients with brain damage transition back to their lives. She has championed a holistic approach to rehabilitation and fought for the UK's National Health Service to fund a centre using this approach. She was successful and founded the Oliver Zangwill Centre for Neuropsychological Rehabilitation in Ely, Cambridgeshire. Her work has always put the patient at the centre of rehabilitation and is more interested in functional outcomes than scores on clinical assessments that are divorced from everyday behaviour; indeed, many of her papers include her patients as co-authors because of their centrality to the work. Barbara Wilson has published more than 200 peer-reviewed manuscripts and 26 books; in addition she has developed eight neuropsychological tests. Her passion for the field resulted in her organising the first ever Symposium on Neuropsychological Rehabilitation that took place at Uluru in Australia in 2004. The meeting was so successful that it has become an annual conference bringing together clinicians from around the world. Barbara has won numerous awards both from the academic community and society (including an Order of the British Empire from Her Majesty Queen Elizabeth II). She is an avid traveller constantly chalking up more new countries that she has visited and has helped neuropsychology in so many countries that there is even a rehabilitation centre named after her in Brazil.

Questions for Reflection

- What are the different approaches to cognitive rehabilitation?
- Why does retraining of one cognitive ability not fix a cognitive problem?
- What are the various factors that affect cognitive recovery?
- What role can technology play in reducing the impact of cognitive impairment?

Go Further

- There is a fast-developing field of technology and virtual reality in cognitive rehabilitation which will be of interest to explore.

- In this chapter, it has been possible to only give a sample of the many rehabilitation strategies. Look at the Further Reading for suggestions of where to find out about other strategies for rehabilitation of memory, language, visuospatial ability, executive function and social cognition.

Further Reading

- Wilson, B. A., Gracey, F., Evans, J. J., & Bateman, A. (2009). *Neuropsychological Rehabilitation: Theory, Models, Therapy and Outcome*. Cambridge University Press.
- Wilson, B. A., Winegardner, J., & Ashworth, F. (2013). *Life after Brain Injury: Survivors' Stories*. Psychology Press.
- Wilson, B. A., Winegardner, J., van Heugten, C. M., & Ownsworth, T. (Eds.) (2017). *Neuropsychological Rehabilitation: The International Handbook*. Psychology Press.

12
SYNAESTHESIA & SENSORY PROCESSING

MARY JANE SPILLER

Chapter Overview

While the rest of this book has dealt with conditions which have resulted in the *loss* of an ability, this chapter will explore a fascinating condition where along with the typical perceptual experiences, some people have *additional* perceptual experiences. For most of us, listening to music is a sound-based experience, whereas for some people with this condition, it can be both a visual and sound-based experience. For other people, reading or hearing words can induce additional colours in their mind's eye, and months or days of the week can have precise spatial locations around their body. This condition is known as synaesthesia and can be something that has been experienced since early childhood, or something acquired after brain damage or sometimes even regular use of certain drugs. This chapter will outline the key research and findings relating to synaesthesia, in terms of how it is measured, how closely it relates to typical perception, and thinking about likely causes. Important questions about why some of us do and some of us do not experience synaesthesia will be explored, keeping in mind the wider individual differences that can be associated with how we make sense of our multi-sensory world. Synaesthesia has been referred to as a window into our perceptual systems which may show some of the ways that the brain interprets and integrates sensory information.

Chapter Outline

- Introduction
- Why Study Synaesthesia?
- Exploring Synaesthesia
- Why Do Some People Have Synaesthesia?
- What Do We Know about Acquired Synaesthesia?
- Is Synaesthesia Associated with Anything Else?
- Chapter Summary

INTRODUCTION

Our perception of the world around us is built upon information we take in through our senses. For example, if we hear the sound of a dog barking, it is because of the particular pattern of sound waves generated from the vibrations of the dog's vocal chords that hit our ear drums. However, the brain plays a crucial role in this as well; our perceptual experience is greatly shaped by the way our brain processes and organises the incoming information. In order for us to have the perception of the dog's bark, the brain needs to process that incoming auditory information. This is why we talk about the role of both 'bottom-up' processing (sensory input from the world around us) and 'top-down' processing (the role of the brain). The dog's bark may trigger other thoughts or feelings, such as fear, or remembering to buy Rover his doggie biscuits, but for the majority of the population, the initial pattern of sound waves will not elicit any other *sensory* perceptions. The human sensory system works in such a way that a sensory stimulus presented in one modality will 'typically' generate the conscious perception of that stimulus within the same sensory modality. However, for some individuals it is more complex than this; the sound of the dog's bark may also generate the additional perception of colours, or additional tactile sensations. For others it could be that hearing music induces the visual perception of colour, or particular tastes might induce tactile sensations on different parts of the body.

The term 'synaesthesia' has been used to describe this perceptual phenomenon, wherein the attributes of certain sensory stimuli (referred to as inducers) elicit additional sensory experiences. These additional sensory perceptions (referred to as concurrents) seemingly happen without any additional effort, and people with synaesthesia, known as 'synaesthetes', describe the concurrents as having percept-like qualities. The colours triggered by music for example, look as real as the colours in a rainbow seen in the sky. These additional sensory experiences are not merely metaphorical associations, like when we say a cheese has a sharp taste or someone is wearing loud colours. Importantly, they are not memories or images generated at will either, like we might imagine the delicious taste of a chocolate cake when we see one in a shop window. The concurrents are also generally consistent over time, so when a synaesthete says they see the colour red whenever they hear the note E flat, they will always see the exact same shade of red with E flat.

Some synaesthetes report that they have experienced synaesthesia for as long as they can remember, and this type is referred to as 'developmental synaesthesia'. In contrast, for other synaesthetes the additional concurrents have only been experienced after some form of change in their sensory processing. This change may have been caused by damage to the brain, or in some cases from hallucinogenic drugs. This form is known as 'acquired synaesthesia'. The chapter will introduce the more common forms of both developmental and acquired synaesthesia, discussing different ways the experience has been studied and measured. It will explore how similar the synaesthetic experience is to typical (non-synaesthetic) perception, and also consider the possible causal mechanisms. As with the other conditions acquired following brain damage covered in the rest of the book, one aim is to understand how typical healthy cognitive functions work relating to synaesthesia. Generally, the developmental form has received greater interest from researchers so far. Important questions that remain about acquired synaesthesia, and how we can use what we know about developmental synaesthesia and neural plasticity to help further our understanding of neural processes, will be considered.

WHY STUDY SYNAESTHESIA?

The key question to consider at the start of this chapter is 'why study synaesthesia?' Other than being an inherently fascinating phenomenon, why should we be interested in synaesthesia as neuropsychologists? What can studying synaesthesia tell us about typical cognition and perception?

Synaesthesia can be seen as a perceptual phenomenon that illustrates how the brain actively forms our individual perceptions of the world, emphasising the role of top-down processes. We have a great deal of sensory information coming into our awareness at all times, and this refers to the work our brain does in order for us to make sense of this. We can experience many different auditory, visual, tactile, and olfactory sensations at the same time, which are processed by each sensory system in the associated areas of the brain in order for us to make sense of our worlds. However, our sensory systems do not work in isolation from each other. For example, what we taste is clearly influenced by what we smell, but interestingly it can also be influenced by what we see or hear. Consequently, we need to understand how information is shared both across and within the senses. By studying synaesthesia, a condition in which there are anomalous cross-modal interactions, we can explore the processes involved.

Studying acquired synaesthesia may help us to understand how our perceptual experiences change as a result of sensory deafferentation (which is when you lose a sense, such as vision, as a result of damage to the neural pathways involved). In the examples of acquired auditory-visual synaesthesia, individuals with partial or complete loss of visual processing acquire the conscious experience of visual concurrents associated with auditory input. Importantly, initial neuroimaging evidence suggests that the brain areas usually associated with processing the impaired modality have become associated with the other modality. For example, Rao et al. (2007) found in a case of auditory-visual synaesthesia that activity in the occipital cortex which would *typically* be correlated with visual processing was found to be associated with activity in the auditory cortex. This suggests that there has been some cortical reorganisation, as areas of the brain are not showing typical patterns of activity. It is widely recognised that the adult human brain has a high level of plasticity, meaning that following damage the brain can make changes to its neuronal circuits in order to cope with the loss of the damaged/affected areas (see Chapter 3). Studying acquired synaesthesia will therefore allow the further exploration of the impact of sensory impairment on cross-modal plasticity.

Developmental synaesthesia provides an opportunity to explore the neuronal mechanisms associated with different subjective 'normal' or 'typical' perceptual experiences. For example, as we learn more about developmental synaesthesia, which is thought to have a genetic basis, we will be able to better understand the effect our genes can have on our perception of the world.

In addition to the experience of synaesthesia, it is also possible to look at other aspects of perception and cognition that might differ between synaesthetes and non-synaesthetes. Living with additional sensory experiences either throughout your life or when acquired later in life could be associated with differences in memory, mental imagery, creativity, attention and mental health. Alternatively, the neuronal activity or structures that elicit the experience of synaesthesia could be related to other differences in our brain and behaviour beyond just the synaesthetic experience. Researchers are therefore trying to unpick this 'synaesthetic constitution'.

EXPLORING SYNAESTHESIA

What are the different forms of developmental synaesthesia?

There are many different types of developmental synaesthesia, with reports listing more than 50 (Day, 2013). Table 12.1 provides a list of example types. This section provides an overview of the more common different types and looks at different types of inducers and concurrents.

With developmental synaesthesia, inducer-concurrent pairings can be both between different sense modalities (*inter-modal*) and within the same modality (*intra-modal*). Examples of the inter-modal types include sound-colour synaesthesia, where sounds such as music induce colours, and lexical-gustatory synaesthesia, in which certain words induce particular tastes. Intra-modal synaesthesia usually involves the visual modality, such as grapheme-colour synaesthesia, where letters and numbers induce colours. With developmental synaesthesia the inducers can be both sensory stimuli (e.g. sounds and tastes) and cognitive stimuli (e.g. letters, numbers, days of the week, months of the year, etc.).

Table 12.1   Examples of reported inducer-concurrent pairings found in developmental synaesthesia

Inducers	Concurrents
Graphemes, Time units, Musical sounds, General sounds, Phonemes, Musical notes, Smells, Tastes, Pain, Touch, Temperatures, Orgasm, Personalities	Colour
Sound, Vision, Touch, Musical notes, Phonemes, Pain	Taste
Sound, Vision, Smell, Tastes	Touch
Sound, Vision, Personalities, Touch	Smells
Vision, Smells, Touch	Sound
Sound, Vision, Smells, Taste, Touch	Temperature

Coloured Words and Coloured Sounds

Many synaesthetes report experiencing colours from words or sounds (see Figure 12.1). For some it is the grapheme (the written symbol used to represent speech) that induces the colour, and for others it is the phoneme (the actual speech sound). For example, a grapheme-colour synaesthete may experience the same green colour when reading or hearing the word 'cheese' as they do for the word 'cake', as it has the same initial grapheme. However, a phoneme-colour synaesthete may experience two very different colours due to the different phoneme sounds. Synaesthetes also report that for some it is the initial grapheme or phoneme that colours a word, and for others it may be the dominant or more stressed one (Simner et al., 2006). Grapheme-colour synaesthesia is the most commonly studied form of this condition.

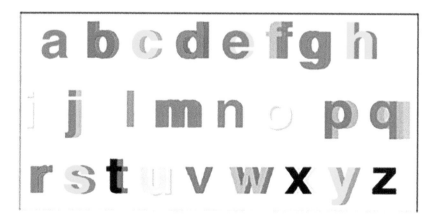

Figure 12.1   A representation of the 'prototypical' coloured alphabet of 70 grapheme-colour synaesthetes. Letters in two or more colours represent those with more than one significant shared colour preference (k was omitted because it had no significant colour preference) (Reprinted from Simner, Julia, Ward, Jamie et al., "Non-random associations of graphemes to colours insynaesthetic and non-synaesthetic populations" in *Cognitive Neuropsychology, 22*(8), Copyright (2005) with permission of the publisher, Taylor & Francis Ltd)

It is also worth making a clear distinction between sound-colour and music-colour synaesthesia. With sound-colour synaesthesia an individual experiences colours elicited from a range of environmental sounds, such as the ticking of a clock, or the sound of a cat meowing. Music-colour synaesthesia refers to the experience of perceiving colours upon hearing music. This can be broken down still further, as some synaesthetes report that it is the different tones which induce the distinct colours, while others report it being the key, or the timbre, or the emotion evoked by the music (Zamm et al., 2013).

Rather than this simply being a list of various types of synaesthesia, it is important to make distinctions between the different types of inducers. This is because in order to understand why someone has synaesthesia, we may want to look at the brain activity associated with the synaesthetic experience. A good starting point is to focus on the neural areas typically involved in processing both the inducer and the concurrent. As discussed throughout this book, certain areas of the brain have been found to be more associated with specific types of sensory or cognitive processing than others. For example, areas found to be important for processing the spoken word /cat/ are different to those associated with processing the written word CAT, or a musical sound such as a G flat. As will be discussed later, neuroimaging studies have found support for activation in the inducer-related areas being associated with subsequent activity in the concurrent areas of the brain (Rouw et al., 2011).

Synaesthesia with Smell, Taste and Touch

Synaesthesia with taste or touch as either inducers or concurrents has also been reported. One documented case of taste-shape synaesthesia involves the experiences of MW, who was described as 'The man who tasted shapes' (Cytowic, 1993).

Another example is the case of JIW who has word-taste synaesthesia (Ward & Simner, 2003). For certain speech sounds (phonemes) JW experiences very specific tastes in his mouth, but this is not the case for other more general environmental sounds. For JIW the word 'safety' tastes of lightly buttered toast, and the word 'jail' tastes of hard cold bacon.

There is also the case of ES who has musical interval-taste synaesthesia (Beeli et al., 2005). She is a professional musician, and upon hearing different musical intervals she experiences specific tastes. For example, she reports that the musical interval known as a 'minor second' tastes sour, while a 'major third' tastes sweet, and a 'major sixth' tastes of low-fat cream (see Table 12.2).

Touch has been documented as the concurrent in what is known as mirror-touch synaesthesia. Individuals with this form of synaesthesia feel the sensation of touch when they see another person being touched. For example, Blakemore et al. (2005) report the case of C, a 41-year-old woman, who reports that when she sees someone else being

Table 12.2 Tastes triggered by tone intervals for synaesthete ES (Beeli et al., 2005)

Tone interval	Taste experienced
Minor second	Sour
Major second	Bitter
Minor third	Salty
Major third	Sweet
Fourth	(Mown grass)
Tritone	(Disgust)
Fifth	Pure water
Minor sixth	Cream
Major sixth	Low-fat cream
Minor seventh	Bitter
Major seventh	Sour
Octave	No taste

touched on the face, she has the conscious perception of being touched on her own face. The tactile perceptions are a direct mirror of the person she is observing. It is thought that there are two distinct sub-types of mirror-touch synaesthesia (Banissy & Ward, 2007). The first, like C, report the synaesthetic touch to be a mirrored version of the observed touch, referred to as a 'specular sub-type'. The second group report a direct mapping, so that if they observe someone being touched on their left cheek, the synaesthetic touch is also felt on their own left cheek.

Sequence Space Synaesthesia

The inducers in this form of synaesthesia, such as numbers, days of the week, months of the year, time of day, have a sequential format (see Figure 12.2). The concurrent is a spatial location, such that when thinking about the days of the week, for example, someone with sequence-space synaesthesia will have a spatial location in mind for where that concept is located (Sagiv et al., 2006). Someone who has sequence-space synaesthesia for months of the year may have an idea of the year located around the middle part of their body, and they know exactly where each month of the year would be located in the physical space around their body (see Figure 12.2). The patterns can be simple or complex, and some have additional colours related to the sequences. There are examples of individuals reporting that their sequence-space synaesthesia has a functional format, with some reporting prodigious talent based on these spatial layouts.

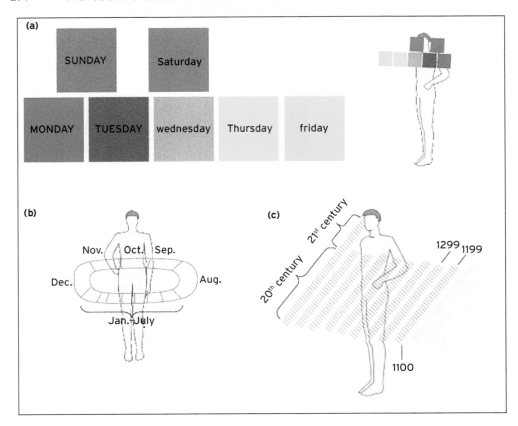

Figure 12.2 The visuospatial forms of synaesthete IB. (a) Days are seen as white or black text against coloured blocks and are projected into peripersonal space onto a vertical plane approximately 50 cm from the face. (b) Months are colourless and run anti-clockwise at hip level on a horizontal plane, which IB views from any positional perspective. (c) Years group into centuries and form columns on an inclined plane. Each turn of the century starts at arm's length and moves up towards the body. The exception is for the year 2000 onwards, which (as IB noticed in 2001) did not return to arm's length as expected, but continued over his right shoulder. All forms are involuntarily evoked when IB hears, says or thinks about time units. All arrangements (for example, the slight off-centring of Sunday above Monday and the permutations of upper- and lower-case text on day names) are precise, automatically generated and have existed (without conscious construction) for as long as IB can remember' (Reprinted from *Trends in Cognitive Sciences, 11*(1), Simner, Julia, "Beyond perception: synaesthesia as a psycholinguistic phenomenon", pp. 23–29, Copyright (2007) with permission from Elsevier)

How Do We Study Synaesthesia?

When someone says they see pink and purple swirls when listening to music, or that they taste chocolate when they think of the word 'Thursday', a question that comes to mind is how 'real' are these experiences? Are they experienced in the same way as actually seeing those visual patterns or experiencing that taste? For someone who does not experience synaesthesia, it might be difficult to imagine having these additional sensory experiences. Indeed, synaesthetes report that often their synaesthetic experiences have been dismissed as being merely metaphorical, or just aspects of an overactive imagination. How have researchers studied the 'realness' of these experiences and whether they are consistent and automatic? In exploring questions such as these, not only can we better understand synaesthesia, but more generally we can learn about how our perceptual systems work.

One approach has been the use of subjective reports, such as found in *The Man Who Tasted Shapes* (Cytowic, 1993), where Cytowic describes his encounter with his friend, MW. When cooking a chicken for a dinner party, MW commented 'there aren't enough points on the chicken' (p. 3). For MW flavours have shape, and this is something he says he has experienced all his life. When tasting something with a strong flavour he described the resulting sensations as 'the feeling sweeps down my arm into my fingertips. I feel it – its weight, its texture, whether it's warm or cold, everything' (p. 4). For MW these shapes feel so real it is as if they are actually in his hands.

The subjective reports are useful to illustrate differences in perceptual experiences, both between synaesthetes and non-synaesthetes, and also between individual synaesthetes. However, subjective reports cannot be objectively verified. Further, they are limited in scope when exploring more detailed questions about synaesthesia. For this purpose, researchers use other methods to further document and unpick the phenomenon.

Consistency measures are one of the key methods used to assess synaesthesia, both for developmental and acquired synaesthesia. With this method synaesthetes are asked to report their synaesthetic experiences for a range of stimuli at two different time points. The consistency between the two different time points is then used as a 'test of genuineness', with synaesthetes generally having more consistent responses than non-synaesthetes (for example, Baron-Cohen et al., 1987). This consistency measure was used by Baron-Cohen and colleagues (1996) in one of the first attempts to work out the prevalence of synaesthesia. An advertisement was placed in a newspaper in a UK city that described synaesthesia and asked people to respond if they thought they had synaesthesia. The prevalence rate found by this early study was 1 in 2000, however more recent studies report much higher prevalence rates of 2 in 100 (Simner et al., 2006).

Variations of this consistency measure have since been used throughout synaesthesia research, with increased colour-picking options (Simner et al., 2006), and cut-off scores that indicate whether someone falls into the typical synaesthesia scoring range (Rothen et al., 2013). Consistency measures are used in all forms of synaesthesia research, for example, with word-taste synaesthesia showing much higher levels of consistency with the synaesthete JW compared to controls (see Figure 12.3). An online measure for many different types of synaesthesia has also been developed (Eagleman et al., 2007). More recently, research has used it for assessing synaesthesia-like responses in the general population (Spiller et al., 2019), as shown in Figure 12.4.

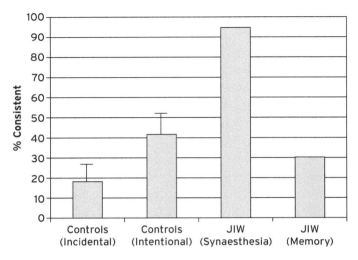

Figure 12.3 A graph showing the consistency levels (%) for word-taste associations. Non-synaesthetes learnt the associations either incidentally (controls incidental) or intentionally (controls intentional) and the synaesthete JIW tested both his synaesthetic associations (JIW synaesthesia) and another set of learnt associations (JIW memory). This shows the clear difference in consistency levels, with the synaesthesia being almost 100% consistent; this is common with synaesthetes (Reprinted from *Cognition*, 89(3), Ward, Jamie and Simner, Julia, "Lexical-gustatory synaesthesia: linguistic and conceptual factors", pp. 237–261, Copyright (2003), with permission from Elsevier)

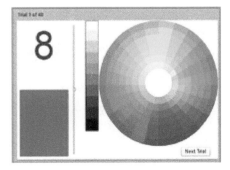

Figure 12.4 Example screenshot during colour-picking consistency task (Spiller et al., 2019. Reprinted with permission from Elsevier)

Behavioural measures are useful for looking at questions about the perceptual nature of synaesthesia. For example, synaesthetes report that the concurrent is elicited from the inducer effortlessly and that it is an involuntary experience. Researchers have therefore designed studies to test whether synaesthesia is automatic. One way this has been done is with a variation of the Stroop paradigm (see Chapter 9). In the synaesthetic-Stroop paradigm, grapheme-colour synaesthetes are visually presented with coloured graphemes and asked to name the visual colour of each grapheme. When the grapheme colour does not match the colour of the concurrent experienced with that particular grapheme, synaesthetes are inhibited in their colour naming response time. For example, if some-one has a blue concurrent for the letter S, and are shown a green S they will be slower to name the visually presented colour (green) than when the S is presented in blue (the colour that matched the synaesthetic colour). This has been interpreted as showing the interference caused to the synaesthetes' ability to name the visual colour of a grapheme when it is presented in a colour that is incongruent with the synaesthetic colour elicited by that grapheme (in comparison to when the colour is congruent, or in baseline non-graphemic conditions). As expected, non-synaesthetes show no such difference in colour naming times, as they do not have to contend with any interference from any extra synaesthetic colour.

Researchers have also explored the perceptual qualities of the synaesthetic colour induced by graphemes. For example, 'real' colour is known to make the task of picking out an object from the background much easier (figure-ground segregation) than if the picture is shown in greyscale. A grey (or 'achromatic') object would be difficult to distinguish from a grey background, whereas a red object from a blue background would be comparatively easy. Researchers have therefore run experiments to find out if synaesthetic colours would work in the same way. In a single case study, Smilek et al. (2001) showed a synaesthete a series of coloured screens which contained achromatic target and distractor graphemes. The screens were coloured to either match or not match the synaesthetic colour of the target. The synaesthete's task was to locate one of two possible target graphemes. The results showed that when the background was congruent with the concurrent colour of the target, the synaesthete was significantly slower to detect it than when the background was incongruently coloured (and there was no difference for the controls). The authors proposed that this 'congruency effect' was due to a difficulty in segregating the digit from the background when the 'real' colour of the background matched the synaesthetic concurrent elicited by the digit, as the colour of the concurrent produced a 'camouflage effect'. This illustrates a potential interaction between the synaesthetic colour induced by the grapheme and the 'real' colour of the background, in the same way as a coloured digit would be difficult to locate if it matched the colour of the search background.

Neuroimaging methods have been used to understand what is happening in many different aspects of synaesthesia. One question addressed is whether synaesthetic colour uses the same areas of the brain as 'real' colour. We know from previous research that certain early visual areas are activated when presented with coloured stimuli or during colour-related cognitive tasks (the posterior fusiform gyrus or V4) and during tasks that require colour knowledge (medial ventral occipital regions) (Zeki, 1998). With regards to synaesthesia, researchers were therefore interested in finding out whether there would be increased activation of these early colour-selective regions when synaesthetes are presented with graphemes; in other words, was the concurrent report of 'seeing' a colour just an abstract idea or was there a neural reality to it? Although the findings have been mixed, a number of studies have shown activation of these colour areas (Hubbard et al., 2005; Nunn et al., 2002; Sperling et al., 2006; see Figure 12.5). As well as differences in the methods used across these studies, the mixed findings may also highlight a subjective difference in the experience of the concurrent.

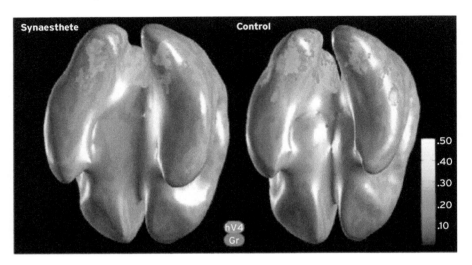

Figure 12.5 fMRI ventral surface activation in synaesthetes and non-synaesthetes to graphemic versus non-graphemic stimuli. It shows an inflated cortex of a representative synaesthete and non-synaesthete (labelled 'Control' on the image). The colour-selective area hV4 is purple and the grapheme region of interest is blue. See Hubbard et al. (2005) for full image details. Importantly, the image illustrates that while both the synaesthete and non-synaesthete show activation in the grapheme region, only the synaesthete shows activation of hV4 (Reprinted from Hubbard, E., Arman, A., Ramachandran, V. and Boynton, G., Copyright (2005). "Individual Differences among Grapheme-Color Synesthetes: Brain-Behavior Correlations". *Neuron, 45*(6), pp. 975–985, with permission from Elsevier)

Researchers have also asked whether other areas of the brain involved in more general perceptual processing might play a role in the generation of a synaesthetic concurrent. Parts of the parietal lobes have been shown to play an important role in 'normal' shape-colour binding (see Robertson, 2003 for a review). Binding is argued to be an essential stage in our perceptual processes, as this is what allows us to experience all features of an object as 'belonging' to that object; so the shape, colour and sound of your pet cat Jasmine need to be bound together so that they all form part of your perceptual experience of her. Synaesthesia can be viewed as an anomalous binding phenomenon, with the binding of an *additional* internally generated feature to an externally perceived object (the binding of colour to a grapheme). If this is the case, then activity would be predicted in the parts of the parietal lobes known to be involved with feature binding in grapheme-colour synaesthesia. Accordingly, synaesthetic concurrents were found to be associated with enhanced activity in the left intraparietal sulcus (IPS) (Weiss et al., 2005).

Furthermore, a study using a neuroimaging technique called diffusion tensor imaging that measures the strength of structural connections between different parts of the brain, found that, compared to controls, synaesthetes had increased connectivity not only in the word processing region of the brain, but also in the left IPS and frontal lobes (Rouw & Scholte, 2007). This greater level of structural connectivity within the regions of the brain involved in colour-form binding can be used as support for the argument that this region is critical for synaesthetic binding. Furthermore, the functional role of these key areas has been shown with studies using transcranial magnetic stimulation (TMS) (Esterman et al., 2006; Muggleton et al., 2007). While the majority of neuroimaging studies of synaesthesia have, so far, focused on grapheme-colour synaesthesia, more recently there have been some studies of the neural correlates of other types of synaesthetes (for example, see Zamm et al., 2013).

WHY DO SOME PEOPLE HAVE SYNAESTHESIA?

So far, we have looked at different forms of developmental synaesthesia, and considered some of the methods used to study the experience. It is estimated that approximately 2–4% of the population experience synaesthesia (Simner et al., 2006). A key question that arises is why do some people have the developmental form of synaesthesia?

Some of the earliest studies of developmental synaesthesia noted the tendency for the condition to run in families. For example, at the end of the nineteenth century, Sir Frances Galton observed that it was a heritable condition (Galton, 1883). Although synaesthesia is heritable, it does not follow that family members will all experience the same forms of synaesthesia (Barnett et al., 2008). Furthermore, even if particular forms of synaesthesia are the same within a family, the inducer-concurrent pairings will not be identical (siblings report having very different grapheme-colour alphabets).

It is now generally accepted that developmental synaesthesia has a genetic basis, and studies are underway to try to identify the genes that play a role (Asher et al., 2009; Nelson et al., 2009). Preliminary findings indicate that the genetic basis is likely to be more complex than involving a single gene, being referred to as a 'polygenic' condition (Tilot et al., 2018). Identifying the genetic substrates underlying synaesthesia will be an important step forward, illustrating how our genes can influence the way we perceive the world. For example, a possible genetic mechanism proposed is a gene that helps to produce more neuronal axons (Tilot et al., 2019) and as we will see below, this links well with the theories proposed about the neural mechanisms of synaesthesia.

While the genetic component in synaesthesia seems very likely, some findings show that the environment can also play a key role. This is particularly important when culturally specific inducers such as graphemes or units of time are involved. For example, one study has even shown the role of refrigerator magnets / coloured toy letter sets in the colour of alphabets for some grapheme-colour synaesthetes (see Figure 12.6;

Figure 12.6　Picture from Witthoft et al. (2015) of the Fisher-Price letter set owned by a child who is now an adult synaesthete with colours influenced by the toy (Reused with the permission of PLoS One)

Witthoft et al., 2015). Therefore, although there may be a genetic causal mechanism for developmental synaesthesia, the environment, particularly during childhood, will play a big role in the way synaesthesia develops, along with memory, learning and languages processes.

The neonatal synaesthesia hypothesis is one of the key theories about why some of us experience developmental synaesthesia (Maurer & Maurer, 1988; Maurer & Mondloch, 2006). This theory is based on the idea that synaesthesia results from additional neural connections in synaesthete brains, providing the connections between the necessary neural areas. With the example of grapheme-colour synaesthesia, this would be from the grapheme-processing area and the colour processing area, which are near each other. The neonatal hypothesis builds on the idea that we are all born with additional neural connections, many of which are not needed, and so a natural pruning process occurs for those unnecessary connections (Falchier et al., 2002). However, in synaesthetes, this pruning is more selective, and so additional connections remain which consequently permit the development of synaesthesia. However, the idea that we are all born as synaesthetes and then most of us lose this ability does not explain *why* only some retain it.

A greater proportion of research so far has focused on what the actual neural mechanisms for synaesthesia are (rather than why some of us may have them). From the familial studies that have been conducted, we know that synaesthesia is likely to have a genetic basis, and we know that there is evidence of activation of the areas of the brain associated with the perception of the concurrent (i.e. colour or touch). There is also evidence with grapheme-colour synaesthesia that areas of the parietal lobes play a functional role, potentially in binding the perception of the grapheme-form with the perception of the concurrent. What is still unclear, however, is how these additional sensory experiences arise. In Chapter 1 a computer analogy was used to describe how we can think about the brain, and this is also useful for understanding the possible neural mechanisms involved in synaesthesia. The analogy described the idea that input to the brain is processed by the software to give certain outputs. With the example of grapheme-colour synaesthesia, we can think of printed letters on the page as the input. The brain of a synaesthete would produce the same 'reading' output as the brain of a non-synaesthete, but *in addition* to this there would be the extra 'colour' output. What we need to try to understand is whether this additional output is due to differences in the hardware of the synaesthete brain, or differences in their software.

The analogy of synaesthetes having different hardware would support the idea of additional neuronal connections, as suggested by the already mentioned neonatal synaesthesia hypothesis, and also the 'cross-activation' theory (Ramachandran & Hubbard, 2001). The cross-activation theory proposes that synaesthesia is caused by additional neural pathways between the relevant parts of the brain, such as between the grapheme processing area and the colour processing area for grapheme-colour synaesthesia. Support for this theory has been taken from studies that show additional connections in these areas in the brain of synaesthetes compared to non-synaesthetes (e.g. Rouw et al., 2011).

An alternative idea is that rather than additional hardware, synaesthesia may be caused by differences in the software, i.e. the way the existing hardware is used. Some researchers have suggested that synaesthesia may make use of existing connections that are not unique to the synaesthete brain (e.g. Grossenbacher & Lovelace, 2001). Instead, feedback along pathways that is typically inhibited is disinhibited in the synaesthete brain, resulting in the synaesthetic experience. There is less evidence to support this idea for developmental synaesthesia. However, it may be the neural mechanism behind drug-induced acquired synaesthesia, when there is not the time required for additional neuronal connections.

Section Summary

When considering why some people have developmental synaesthesia, as with most complex human behaviours, the role of genetics and the environment are clear causal mechanisms. In terms of the neural mechanisms that then give rise to the synaesthetic experience, there are important differences between the brains of synaesthetes and non-synaesthetes, which indicate additional neuronal connections are likely to play a key role. However, as will be discussed in the final section of this chapter, it may be that these differences do not only give rise to synaesthesia, but a wider profile of individual differences, due to the diffuse area these additional connections are located within the brain (Ward, 2019).

WHAT DO WE KNOW ABOUT ACQUIRED SYNAESTHESIA?

Some people experience synaesthesia for the first time later in life, after an accident or illness. It can also occur with the use of certain psychedelic drugs. This is known as acquired synaesthesia. Acquired synaesthesia is often triggered by a *loss* of input into one sensory modality (i.e. through stroke or a brain tumour). For example, an individual who has become visually impaired experiences visual flashes when hearing a clock ticking, or from the tactile sensation of tapping their finger. Seemingly, a change in the visual, auditory or somatosensory perceptual processing systems has generated new sensory pairings.

Acquired synaesthesia is interesting to neuropsychologists, because we want to understand why the initial change in the sensory system can sometimes lead to the condition emerging. In the same way as we learn about language processing by studying the consequence of damage to areas of the brain involved with language, cases of acquired synaesthesia help us understand how the brain integrates and binds information across the senses to form a coherent view of the world around us. We need to understand that integration process, and by studying *anomalous* forms of cross-sensory processing we can learn about the *typical* processes involved.

As with a number of conditions considered elsewhere in this book (for example, apraxia, dyslexia and prosopagnosia) in which acquired forms are rarer and also heterogeneous, the same is the case with synaesthesia. It is a developing situation, but from the cases reviewed to date we can start to understand the different ways our brains sometimes make sense of the world around us following changes to our sensory systems.

Auditory-Visual Acquired Synaesthesia

Auditory-visual synaesthesia is one of the more documented types of acquired synaesthesia. It usually occurs following loss of visual input due to sensory deafferentation. The result is that everyday sounds trigger visual experiences such as flashes of white or coloured lights in the blind area. A study of nine patients with loss of visual input following damage to the anterior parts of the visual pathway (the optic nerve or optic chasm) found that their auditory visual synaesthesia was mostly reported to start within one to three days after initial visual loss, and was consistent over time (Jacobs et al., 1981). Further cases of these 'sound-induced phosphenes' (visual flashes) in other patients with sensory deafferentation report similar patterns of simple flashes induced by sudden or unexpected sounds, mostly starting within a few days or weeks of initial visual problems (Kim, 2006; Lessell & Cohen, 1979; Page et al., 1982).

As found with the developmental forms, neuroimaging evidence illustrates the correlation between activity in the visual and auditory areas of the brain with this form of acquired synaesthesia. An individual, referred to as PS, lost his sight in a car accident that destroyed both optic nerves (but with no lasting cognitive deficits, and no diffuse or localised structural damage to the brain). His synaesthesia developed about one year after the accident, and for him sudden loud noises induced illusory flashes of light (Rao et al., 2007). Using EEG which records the small electrical currents generated by neural activity on the scalp, PS was studied while being presented with a series of different sounds. The electrical activity showed that the occipital lobe visual activity was positively correlated with the temporal auditory activity. The authors concluded that auditory stimulation for the sounds that induced the synaesthesia resulted in atypical occipital visual activity, and that this activity seemingly originated in the auditory cortex. They proposed that the fact that this has been shown in a late-blind individual is important, as it suggests extensive cortical *reorganisation* is possible following late-blindness. It is known that the brain is 'plastic' to some extent and reorganisation is possible, but generally these ideas are linked to younger brains that are developing; therefore, this work on changes happening in adult brains is interesting at a number of levels.

Auditory Tactile Acquired Synaesthesia

With auditory-tactile synaesthesia the perception of sounds induces tactile sensations. Ro et al. (2007) studied patient SR, a female 40-year-old university lecturer who, following a stroke, was left with a small discrete lesion to the right ventrolateral nucleus of the thalamus (VL). The VL is thought to be involved with motor function due to its connections to the cerebellum and motor cortex. Usually lesions to this area are large and diffuse, and so typically affecting more than one of the nuclei. Therefore, studying the impact of SR's small lesion to only the right VL provided a unique opportunity to explore the potential consequences of VL thalamic brain damage.

After the stroke, SR experienced various changes to her sensory perception of touch, including experiencing tactile sensations in response to auditory stimulation. Certain sounds, such as someone's voice, produced intense tingling sensations on the left side of her body. SR described the tactile sensations as tingles or pressures, and at times the sensations could be uncomfortable for her. Consistency testing three and six years after the stroke showed support for these subjective reports, and neuroimaging showed some reorganisation of connections from the right thalamus to the cerebral cortex (Beauchamp & Ro, 2008). This longitudinal study of the impact of a small lesion to the right VL at both a behavioural and neurological level illustrates the effect of both the neural and functional reorganisation on sensory processing.

The fact that SR wasn't a 'one-off' has been seen with the case of ER, who about nine months after a stroke (involving the left lateral posterior nucleus of the thalamus) started to experience auditory-tactile synaesthesia, as well as auditory-colour and grapheme-taste synaesthesia (Fornazzari et al., 2012).

Tactile Visual Acquired Synaesthesia

The tactile modality has been reported as the inducer in a single case of tactile-visual synaesthesia in which tactile sensations of the body induce visual experiences. Armel & Ramachandran (1999) describe the case of PH, who experienced a gradual loss of sight from age five (due to retinitis pigmentosa) and was completely blind by the age of 40. However, two years after losing his sight, PH started to experience visual sensations when reading Braille; he reported experiencing coloured dots that would visually shift. Systematic testing of various thresholds of tactile stimulation and the associated subjective descriptions showed that his experiences were consistent.

Drug-Induced Acquired Synaesthesia

Synaesthesia-like experiences have been reported to be induced with the use of some recreational drugs (see Luke & Terhune, 2013 for a review). Usually, however, these experiences are transient and therefore do not meet the usual 'consistency over time' measures used by synaesthesia researchers more generally. Like other forms of acquired synaesthesia, this is a growing area of research. It is important to understand why these experiences may occur with certain drugs as it could help to unpick the chemical processes involved in other forms of synaesthesia.

Interestingly, one study has documented drug-induced acquired synaesthesia which has been shown to be consistent over time (Yanakieva et al., 2019). LW has regularly used large doses of 2C-B, a psychedelic recreational drug, and consequently experienced several different forms of synaesthesia, including face-colour synaesthesia whereby he saw specific colours when he saw individual faces. With this form, an experiment showed that when primed with a face, he was significantly slower at subsequently naming a colour that was incongruent to the one induced by the face than a congruent colour (whereas there was no such difference with non-synaesthete matched control participants). This supports the idea that the synaesthetic colours are induced without effort as they are shown to hinder task performance. As this is similar to the findings from other studies of developmental synaesthesia, this supports the idea that drug-induced synaesthesia has potentially similar attributes to the developmental forms. Yanakieva et al. (2019) suggest that the automaticity and consistency of drug-induced acquired synaesthesia, and potentially even developmental synaesthesia, may be a consequence of the over-learning of associations, rather than an inherent aspect of synaesthesia. Importantly, a recent neuroimaging study has shown important differences between the visual cortex excitability of drug-induced acquired synaesthesia and developmental synaesthesia, suggesting that they do not share the same neural mechanisms (Lungu et al., 2020).

So What Have We Learned about Acquired Synaesthesia?

From the handful of studies of acquired synaesthesia described above it is possible to make some key observations about the condition. While the exact trigger for acquired synaesthesia varies, most involve some type of sensory deafferentation either to the visual or somatosensory modality. The actual degree of sensory loss varies across the cases, as sometimes it is partial and sometimes it is complete. Similarly, the onset of the experience of synaesthesia after the deafferentation varies. Afra (2009) makes the distinction of onsets being 'acute' (one to three days), 'sub-acute' (one to four weeks) and 'chronic' (in months). For example, most of the cases of auditory-visual synaesthesia reported by Jacobs et al. (1981) developed within days of the initial visual loss which is in sharp contrast to the reported case of tactile-visual (Armel & Ramachandran, 1999) and auditory-tactile (Ro et al., 2007) synaesthesia developed two years after the initial sight loss / stroke.

In terms of the concurrent and the inducer, for all cases of acquired synaesthesia these are only both sensory in nature; this contrasts with developmental synaesthesia in which the inducers can be cognitive stimuli such as words or numbers. Often the concurrents have a simple form such that the visual or tactile perceptions are not complex. For example, the cases of auditory-visual synaesthesia report visual flashes (for example, Jacobs et al., 1981) and the case with auditory-tactile synaesthesia reports tingling and pressure (Ro et al., 2007). As with developmental synaesthesia, the objective nature is demonstrated in some initial neuroimaging evidence that shows that the brain areas associated with the concurrent are activated (Beauchamp & Ro, 2008; Rao et al., 2007; Ro et al., 2007), providing further support for the synaesthetes' subjective reports. These studies have highlighted the cortical reorganisation that seems to have occurred following the initial sensory loss.

What Remains Unknown about Acquired Synaesthesia?

It is important to keep in mind that acquired synaesthesia has not been as thoroughly documented as developmental synaesthesia. For example, there have not been any attempts yet to estimate the prevalence of this condition, and it is acknowledged in the literature that it is probably often under-reported. For example, Jacobs et al. (1981) report that auditory-visual synaesthesia was experienced by at least seven of the 20 patients they assessed with optic nerve lesions, and two of the nine patients with optic chiasm lesions. However, they noted that patients needed to be specifically questioned about this as they often did not spontaneously report the experiences. The reports have also generally been single case studies, with the exception of Jacobs et al., and so this method has the associated limitations as discussed in Chapter 3.

Important questions remain concerning the documented differences in initial onset timing and the nature of the onset trigger (Afra, 2009; Ward, 2007). We need to be able to understand why, for some, the acquired synaesthesia occurs almost immediately after the change in sensory perception, while for others it occurs months or even years later. It is also important to understand why the acquired synaesthesia can develop after partial, complete or even no sensory deafferentation. Finally, we need to be able to explain why not all cases of sensory deafferentation result in acquired synaesthesia; whether some people have a pre-disposition to it, or there are factors relating to their condition which have an impact on any neural reorganisation of neural pathways, and whether this relates to a conscious experience of cross-sensory perception.

An essential question relates to the neuronal mechanisms that result in this cross-modal plasticity. The 'reorganisation hypothesis' argues that this plasticity is due to the development or growth of new neural pathways. In contrast, the 'unmasking hypothesis' argues that it occurs as a result of changes to already existing networks. With the example of auditory-visual synaesthesia, the reorganisation hypothesis would propose that the auditory-related activity in the visual cortex occurred as a result of new pathways being formed between the two areas. In contrast, the unmasking hypothesis would argue that it was due to changes in already existing pathways.

One way that this question has been explored is by looking at the timing of the onset of the synaesthesia after the initial trigger or start of sensory deafferentation, as using pre-existing pathways in a different way (unmasking) could be an almost immediate development, whereas the formation of new pathways (reorganisation) would be a much slower process (Ward, 2007). SR's case of auditory-touch synaesthesia (Ro et al., 2007) provides support for the 'reorganisation hypothesis' as the synaesthesia developed 18 months after the initial sensory impairment. It is therefore unlikely to be due to the unmasking of pre-existing pathways, as that would have happened much more quickly. In contrast, unmasking may be important in other cases where synaesthesia is faster to appear – within a few days of the sensory loss (for example, Jacobs et al., 1981).

IS SYNAESTHESIA ASSOCIATED WITH ANYTHING ELSE?

Previous sections have looked at synaesthesia (developmental or acquired), in terms of what it is, how we measure it and how similar it is to typical perception. The possible causal mechanisms have also been considered. Importantly, for both forms, a key question concerns the reasons why some of us experience synaesthesia and most of us do not.

With the developmental form a genetic cause is likely. Research to date suggests it involves more than one gene, and environment clearly plays a key role too given the cultural specificity of some inducers. Further, given the polygenic basis and widespread neuronal differences, it is likely that there may be *other* differences between synaesthetes' and non-synaesthetes' perceptual and cognitive profiles other than simply having synaesthetic experiences.

With the acquired form, the trigger is usually some form of sensory loss. What remains unclear is why acquired synaesthesia is triggered in the rare cases so far documented, as many other people who experience the same sensory loss do *not* go on to report acquiring synaesthesia. Potentially there could be some pre-existing factors (either genetic or environmental or both) that make some individuals more likely to develop acquired synaesthesia following sensory loss than others.

There are only a handful of studies exploring acquired synaesthesia, and the question of what other individual differences may accompany the development of acquired synaesthesia has not yet been addressed in any depth. However, with developmental synaesthesia there is a growing body of research that has noted a possible wider profile of individual differences beyond just the synaesthetic experience. Are these differences a result of having experienced synaesthesia (for example, harnessing synaesthetic associations as a tool to aid memory or inspire creativity), or could they actually be part of a broader 'synaesthetic constitution'?

Synaesthesia and Creativity

One of the first individual differences to be considered in relation to synaesthesia is creativity. Many artists (for example, Kandinsky and David Hockney) and musicians (for example, Lady Gaga and Thom Yorke) have discussed how they have used their synaesthesia to inspire their art. This has been supported by studies that find synaesthetes are more likely to report having careers relating to the arts and have more creative hobbies (e.g. Rich et al., 2005). Furthermore, although there are mixed findings, most likely due to different creativity measurements used, it does seem that synaesthesia is related to enhanced creativity (e.g. Lunke & Meier, 2019). The question that remains though is whether this creativity is a consequence of synaesthesia, as potentially having these 'unusual' sensory combinations has allowed the synaesthetes to think about things in a different way throughout their creative development. Alternatively, it may be that there is something about the synaesthete brain that allows greater levels of creative thinking, such as the additional neuronal connections.

Synaesthesia and Mental Imagery

Mental imagery refers to the ability to internally form an image of something in our mind, without external stimulation (Pearson et al., 2015). This could be a visual image such as imagining a friend's face or the layout of furniture in your bedroom. Imagery can also be formed in any other sensory modality such as an auditory image of the sound of a trumpet, or a smell image of a favourite perfume. It may seem that mental images are similar to the synaesthetic experiences discussed so far, but there are important differences. A key difference is that mental images are usually created with intention and require effort, whereas synaesthetic concurrents happen without conscious effort and are difficult to suppress. So for example, it takes a conscious effort to think of a taste you imagine upon hearing the brand name of your favourite chocolate, whereas for a word-taste synaesthete the synaesthetic taste associated with the word would happen automatically. However, the similarities, such as experiencing a perception in the absence of a sensation, suggest that there could be a relationship between the two. Studies have found that synaesthetes report more vivid imagery than non-synaesthetes (Barnett & Newell, 2008). Across all sensory modalities synaesthetes report more vivid imagery than controls (Spiller et al., 2015). Further, they report even more vivid imagery in the modalities relating to their synaesthesia, so that for example, someone with word-taste synaesthesia reported more vivid taste imagery than other synaesthetes without taste as a concurrent. Of course, there are important limitations to research based on self-report. To date the support for enhanced mental imagery with behavioural measures is less clear (for example, see Spiller et al., 2019). However, overall evidence has supported the idea that synaesthesia is associated with more vivid mental imagery. As with creativity, the question remains about whether this is a *by-product* or 'epiphenomenon of experiencing synaesthesia, or whether the differences between the synaesthete and non-synaesthete brain (such as the differences in neural connectivity) make this more vivid imagery more likely.

Synaesthesia and Memory

The potential link between enhanced memory and synaesthesia has been studied a lot over the years. Like creativity, it is easy to see how the two could be linked. There are many reports of individuals using their synaesthesia as a mnemonic device to aid their memory; the classic example is a case reported by the great Luria (1968), S, who famously could remember vast lists of words and recall them decades later. Some of the early group studies showed that synaesthetes had a memory advantage, but the findings in subsequent studies have been more mixed (e.g. Rothen et al., 2012; Yaro & Ward, 2007). A key issue for clarification was whether the memory advantage held by synaesthetes related to their use of synaesthesia as a memory tool, or whether there was something more general about the synaesthete brain that caused the memory enhancement. Importantly, a recent meta-analysis bringing together the findings from many studies objectively has found that the memory advantage does not appear to be restricted to memory forms relating to the synaesthesia form (Ward et al., 2019). Indeed, synaesthesia was found to be associated with a memory advantage across all aspects of memory including working memory and long-term memory. This would suggest that it is not caused by living with synaesthesia, but rather something about the way the synaesthete brain is different to the non-synaesthete.

Synaesthesia and Autism Spectrum Conditions

Neuroimaging studies of synaesthesia suggest that increased neuronal connections may be the neural causal mechanism (Rouw et al., 2011), and similarly, studies of autism spectrum conditions (ASC) show that increased local connections may play a causal role (Belmonte et al., 2004). This, along with subjective reports, has led researchers to explore the co-occurrence of synaesthesia and ASC. Overall, it is now recognised that rates of synaesthesia are higher among those with ASC (Baron-Cohen et al., 2013), and also reciprocally people with synaesthesia have higher rates of autistic traits (Ward et al., 2018). There is also some initial support for the link between synaesthesia and ASC from genetic studies (Asher et al., 2009). It is thought that the similarities may be more with the perceptual profile (van Leeuwen et al., 2020), as for example, both synaesthetes and people with ASC report greater sensory sensitivity, and have a tendency to focus more on local level processing than global level (Ward et al., 2017). Interestingly, the co-occurrence of synaesthesia and ASC has also been linked with increased likelihood to display prodigious talent (Hughes et al., 2017; Spiller & Jansari, 2012). The link between synaesthesia and ASC is an exciting ongoing area of research and could help us to understand the broader implications of individual differences associated with synaesthesia.

Section Summary

Overall, there appear to be consistent individual differences, beyond the synaesthetic experience, between synaesthetes and non-synaesthetes. This is still a developing area, but with memory for example, research suggests this advantage goes beyond the types of synaesthesia and synaesthetes may have a general memory advantage across all types of information and irrespective of type of synaesthesia. The research with creativity and imagery is not so advanced, but there are signs that suggest it could be a similar situation. Finally, the growing interest in synaesthesia and autism brings us back to the genetic causal mechanism. Potentially, the co-occurrence of synaesthesia and autism, that may be based on a shared genetic background, shows how our perceptual systems are shaped by our genes as well as our environments. In relation to acquired synaesthesia, it will be interesting to see if there are any consistent individual differences that co-occur with the emergence of acquired synaesthesia following sensory loss, and whether any of these are similar to those with the developmental form.

Chapter Summary

- Synaesthesia is an excellent example of the different ways people can perceive the world, and the role that our brains play in making sense of the environment around us.

- There is a developmental *and* an acquired form of synaesthesia, with the developmental form being the more studied and understood form. For both forms, as our knowledge of them expands we learn more about the complexity of this perceptual experience and the possible neuronal mechanisms giving rise to it. One of the aims of neuropsychological research is to study atypical cognition in order to inform our knowledge and understanding of typical perception.
- We have considered the different forms of synaesthesia, how it can be studied, and how closely it resembles typical perception. The likely casual mechanisms for developmental synaesthesia and likely associated individual differences in cognition and perception have been discussed.
- In relation to acquired synaesthesia we have highlighted key questions that are yet to be tackled concerning differences in when and how the synaesthesia develops, and if there are associated individual differences that might preclude this.
- Overall, studying both developmental and acquired synaesthesia helps us to further understand the organisation of multisensory perceptual processing.

Questions for Reflection

- Does synaesthesia involve *any* combination of senses or is there a 'logic' behind which senses end up being 'paired'?
- Can we learn anything about 'normal' cognitive processing from studying synaesthesia or is it just an interesting phenomenon?
- Whilst synaesthesia can occur both from brain damage and more commonly as a developmental condition, are there any major differences between the two forms?

Go Further

- There is a literature looking at how synaesthesia might be harnessed which would be interesting to explore.
- While synaesthesia comes across as a fascinating condition, is it the case that for some individuals it can *negatively* affect their lives?

Go Further

Dr Jansari's YouTube Videos
When hearing 'two plus four' looks like gold! What is synaesthesia?

When I ask you 'What is two plus four?' you are likely to think of the number six; however, 2% of people would think of the number six but also think of a colour such as blue! This video gives an overview of the emerging understanding of synaesthesia, and what can be learned about standard brain functions by looking at this intriguing phenomenon.

Further Reading

- Ward, J. (2009). *The Frog Who Croaked Blue: Synesthesia and the Mixing of the Senses*. Routledge.
- Cytowic, R. E., & Eagleman, D. M. (2011). *Wednesday Is Indigo Blue: Discovering the Brain of Synesthesia*. MIT Press.
- Cytowic, R. E. (2003). *The Man Who Tasted Shapes*. Imprint Academic.

GLOSSARY

Abstract words: concepts that are more difficult to visually imagine (e.g. love or harmony)

Accelerated long-term forgetting: (also known as long-term amnesia), a disruption in the consolidation process that results in delayed amnesia weeks or months after an event; currently this is difficult to diagnose with standard memory tests

Achromatopsia: an impairment in extracting colour from other aspects of information in a visual scene

Acquired brain injury (ABI): any injury to the brain that is *not* inherited, degenerative or caused by trauma during the process of birth

Acquired disorder: atypical cognitive or neural abilities due to physical brain damage

Acquired dyslexia: a reading disorder that develops due to a traumatic brain injury, stroke or dementia

Acquired synaesthesia: multisensory perception that has only been experienced after some form of change in sensory processing, which may have been caused by damage to the brain, or in some cases from hallucinogenic drugs

Aetiology: underlying cause of a disorder, disease or condition (also known as etiology)

Agnosia: loss or diminution of the ability to recognise objects, sounds, smells, tastes or other sensory stimuli

Allesthesia: reporting a physical sensation such as being touched on the contralesional side as having happened on the ipsilesional side; so a patient experiencing allesthesia would say that they were tapped on their right shoulder when someone touches them on the left shoulder

Allocentric neglect: (also known as 'object-centred' neglect); the difficulty with the left-hand side of each particular object irrespective of where it is in the visual scene

Altitudinal neglect: a form of neglect which occurs along the vertical axis (up or down) rather than the more common form which is along the horizontal axis (left and right)

Amnesia: severe difficulty in creating new long-term memories

Anterograde amnesia: an impairment in learning or retaining new information in the post-morbid period (after sustaining brain injury)

Alzheimer's disease: a degenerative disorder that slowly destroys memory and thinking skills and, eventually, the ability to carry out the simplest tasks

Amnesic episode: the point at which the individual sustained brain damage

Aneurysm: a swelling in the wall of a weak blood vessel that looks like a blister protruding from the vessel; if this bursts (ruptures) then it can cause a lot of brain damage

Angular gyrus: an area at the front of the parietal lobes that is involved in transferring information from the visual areas to Wernicke's area; this area is thought to be involved in allowing us to 'translate' the squiggles that you see on a page or screen into a sound that you 'hear' and understand in your mind

Anomia: a loss or impairment in the ability to *find* certain words but with no impairment in comprehension or the capacity to repeat the words

Anosognosia: lack of awareness of cognitive deficits

Anoxia: (also known as hypoxia) an interruption in the steady flow of oxygen to the brain

Aphasia: an impairment in producing spoken language

Apperceptive agnosia: inability to group the information together to create a coherent visual image of what one is seeing

Apperceptive prosopagnosia: stage of prosopagnosia in which different facial information can be seen and understood *individually* but cannot be *integrated*

Apraxia: refers to the inability to carry out movements in the absence of primary motor, sensory or comprehension deficits

Arcuate fasciculus: fibre tract that connects Broca's and Wernicke's areas in the brain

Association of symptoms: symptoms that co-occur (but may not actually be related to each other)

Associations: cognitive problems that tend to occur together

Associative agnosia: describes individuals who have intact intellect and visual acuity, who can copy line drawings and who *pass* perceptual tests, but who nonetheless are unable to recognise objects; they experience 'a normal percept, stripped of its meaning' (Farah, 2000)

Associative prosopagnosia: difficulty in accessing stored visual representations of known faces

Asymptote: poorer recall for items in the middle of a list of to-be-remembered words

Attention: the cognitive system that filters out what is important from all of the perceptual input in one's environment

Autism spectrum conditions (ASC): overarching term used to describe autism, Asperger's syndrome, pathological demand avoidance (PDA) and pervasive developmental disorder (PDD)

Autobiographical memory: one of the most important aspects of episodic memory; autobiographical memory is memory for events that occurred in one's life such as holidays, birthdays and other personal events

Axon: the major fibre that transmits information from the cell body of a neuron to the dendrites of other neurons

Baseline: a fixed point of reference that is used for comparison purposes; in experimental work, this usually refers to performance of either a control group or of a control condition so that it is possible to see the impact of either a manipulation or of brain damage

Behavioural neurology: subspecialty of neurology that studies the impact of neurological damage and disease upon behaviour, memory and cognition, and the treatment thereof

Broca's aphasia: disorder in being able to speak fluently (also known as motor aphasia)

Brodmann areas: originally defined and numbered by German anatomist Korbinian Brodmann, refers to a system that divides the cerebral cortex into approximately 52 areas according to cytoarchitectural organisation of neurons

Capgras syndrome: the irrational belief that a familiar person or place has been replaced with an exact duplicate that can be observed in some patients with dementia or specific forms of traumatic brain injury

Cell body: region of a neuron that contains the nucleus and connects the dendrites to the axon (also known as the soma)

Chronic traumatic encephalopathy (CTE): multiple small lesions caused by repeated small head injuries that can lead to memory problems, which are effectively a form of dementia; often seen following a long period of playing contact sports

Cognition: the 'software' that processes information in the brain

Cognitive neuroscience: subfield of neuroscience that studies the biological processes that underlie human cognition

Compensation: reorganising of function to minimise a disability

Computerised axial tomography (CAT/CT): a structural imaging technique that utilises X-ray to see the brain at a certain point in time

Concurrent: in **synaesthesia** research, this refers to the synaesthetic experience, i.e. the colour experienced when hearing music by someone with **music-colour synaesthesia**

Concreteness: refers to the difference between **concrete words**, which are those that refer to physical things that can be visualised or imagined (e.g. a cat or a chair), and **abstract words**, which refer to concepts that are more difficult to imagine (e.g. love or harmony) (also known as **imageability**)

Concrete words: those that refer to physical things that can be visualised or imagined (e.g. a cat or a chair)

Conduction aphasia: a language disorder in which one has the ability to comprehend and create language but not to repeat what is said to them

Configural processing: 'seeing the whole' as one entity (also known as: holistic processing and gestalt processing)

Connectionist modelling: a research methodology which describes mental processes (such as how you translate the visual input CAT into the sound /*cat*/) by very simple units in an interconnected programmed network

Consistency measures: one of the key methods used to assess synaesthesia; synaesthetes report their synaesthetic experiences for a range of stimuli at two different time points, and the consistency between the two different time points is then used as a 'test of genuineness'

Consolidation: the process where our brains convert short-term memories into long-term ones

Contention scheduling: a cognitive mechanism that is thought to be active in routine situations where decision making and other executive functions are not required

Contralesional: side of space opposite to the hemisphere that has suffered brain damage

Declarative memory: fact-based knowledge

Deep dyslexia: type of reading error whereby an individual provides a word that is *semantically* related to the target word, for example, reading ORANGE as /*lemon*/

Dendrites: smaller fibres connected to the soma that allow the nerve cell to communicate with other nerve cells at a junction known as a synapse

Developmental coordination difficulty (DCD): developmental variant of apraxia which individuals have from childhood

Developmental disorder: atypical cognitive or neural abilities with no known brain injury (therefore not acquired)

Developmental synaesthesia: synaesthetes who report that they have experienced synaesthesia for as long as they can remember

Diencephalon: a structure that is located deep within the brain and divided into four parts: the epithalamus, thalamus, subthalamus, and hypothalamus; it acts as a primary relay and processing centre for sensory information and autonomic control

Digit span: number of digits one can remember in their correct order

Direct retraining: involves repeated practice or training of a lost ability, like physiotherapy may do for a weak limb

Dissociation: separation of cognitive functions

Dorsolateral: area relating to or involving both the back and the sides of the brain or a specific brain area (usually used for the frontal lobes)

Dorsomedial: area located toward the back and near the midline (usually used for the frontal lobes)

Dorsomedial prefrontal cortex: area of the frontal lobes, more specifically an area in the prefrontal cortex, that is mostly associated with executive functions including working memory and selective attention

Double dissociation: when two related mental processes are shown to function independently of each other (for example, short-term and long-term memory)

Dual Route Model: currently accepted theoretical model in explaining how single words are understood, processed and produced; central to this model is the fact that there are two independent routes, one which involves the 'sounding out' of the constituent parts of a word (just as we did when we were young children learning to read), and the other a kind of 'matching' against a dictionary called the lexicon of all the words that you are already familiar with

Dual-task paradigms: a procedure in experimental psychology where the individual must perform two tasks simultaneously in order to compare performance with single-task conditions

Dysgraphia: a neurological disorder that impairs (hand)writing ability and fine motor skills in someone of normal or above-average intelligence

Ecological validity: refers to tests being more realistic and examining whether the results of a study are representative of real-world behaviour

Egocentric neglect: the difficulty in perceiving information that is on the left side of someone's perceptual world

Encephalitis: inflammation within brain tissue

Epilepsy: a disorder in which damaged cells produce 'unprogrammed' electrical activity that causes a sort of avalanche effect spreading to connected brain regions, resulting in a seizure

Epileptic focus: area of the brain creating the excess of electrical stimulation in epilepsy

Episodic memory: refers to the ability to remember specific events such as the last time that you rode a bicycle

Errorless learning: aims to reduce or eliminate error while learning new information

Etiology: underlying cause of a disorder, disease or condition (also known as aetiology)

Everyday outcome: an important measure that is used by clinicians regarding the transition back towards the life that the individual had prior to their brain injury

Explicit memory: any test that requires the subject to recall a specific learning episode (and therefore the information that was learnt) consciously

Extinction: neglecting the information on the contralesional side when information is presented on both sides simultaneously

Extra-personal: anything beyond the physical reach of a person

Face-blindness: particularly for use with individuals who suffer a developmental form of prosopagnosia, or the inability to recognise faces

Featural processing: adding up the individual elements of a visual scene

Fissure: a deep sulcus (or groove) in the cerebral cortex

Focal retrograde amnesia (FRA): very dense retrograde amnesia; being virtually incapable of remembering any events from one's life before sustaining brain injury but with memory since that period being relatively intact

Fornix: white matter between the hippocampus and the hypothalamus; when damaged, can lead to amnesia

Frontal lobe: the front of the brain responsible for higher cognitive functions such as planning, problem solving, impulse control, social interactions, etc.

Functional imaging: techniques that allow us to go beyond structure and examine certain functional properties of the brain (or seeing the brain 'in action')

Functional MRI (fMRI): measures brain activity by detecting changes associated with blood flow

Functional specialisation: the idea that our mental abilities are separable into modules (such as memory and language) and that these modules may be localised in specific parts of the human brain

Generalisation: training the foundational levels of cognition first, which can later be built upon by more advanced skills in practical settings

Gestalt processing: 'seeing the whole' as one entity (also known as: configural processing and holistic processing)

Goal management training: a useful tool for patients with deficits in executive function by helping with planning, problem solving and goal setting

Grapheme: the written symbol used to represent speech

Grapheme-colour synaesthesia: a form of synaesthesia in which letters and numbers induce colours

Grapheme-to-phoneme conversion (GPC): using pronunciation rules that you've learnt through your life to 'sound out' words

Grey matter: unmyelinated neurons and other cells of the central nervous system

Gyrus: (plural: gyri) a ridge or fold between two clefts on the surface of the brain

Haemorrhagic stroke: (or haemorrhage) bursting of a blood vessel that causes downstream brain damage due to oxygen deprivation

Hemianopia: the inability to see information in one of the two visual fields; tends to involve a *total* lack of response to information in that particular hemispace

Hemispatial neglect: the lack of attention paid to information in the contralesional side of space

Heschl's gyrus: an area within the auditory cortex that is involved in the transfer of sounds to Wernicke's area where meaning can be extracted to allow us to comprehend what we are hearing

Hippocampus: brain structure deep in the temporal lobe that is involved in learning and memory

Holistic processing: 'seeing the whole' as one entity (also known as: configural processing and gestalt processing)

Hypoxia: (also known as anoxia) an interruption in the steady flow of oxygen to the brain

Ideational apraxia: a form of apraxia in which the individual actions themselves are intact but there is inappropriate use of objects and a failure in discriminating between gestures

Ideomotor apraxia: a form of apraxia in which the sensorimotor programmes that allow an individual to start and control any motor activity are impaired resulting in impaired timing, sequencing and spatial organisation of movements

Imageability: refers to the difference between concrete words which are those that refer to physical things that can be visualised or imagined (e.g. a cat or a chair) and abstract words which refer to concepts that are more difficult to imagine (e.g. love or harmony) (also known as concreteness)

Implicit memory: learning that is assessed by any test which does not require any specific reference to the previous learning episode, and is testing your recall indirectly

Inducers: in people with synaestheisa inducers elicit additional sensory experiences (known as concurrents)

Inferior parietal lobe: area most implicated in neglect, containing the right supramarginal gyrus and the angular gyrus

Information processing approach: the view that human mental abilities can be seen as a sequence of processing stages

Input modality: the modality receiving sensory information (visual, tactile, gustatory, olfactory or auditory)

In silico neuropsychology: studying brain-damaged deep neural networks

Integrative agnosia: a form of visual agnosia in which individuals are able to perceive the elements of an object but find it difficult to combine them into a perceptual whole; typically, symptoms of both apperceptive and associative agnosia are present

Introspection: involves the observation of one's own thoughts, feelings and mental states to try to derive theories of general human behaviour

Ipsilesional: the space on the same side as the hemisphere that has suffered brain damage

Irregular words: words for which standard grapheme-to-phoneme conversion rules cannot work, and can only be read using the lexical route

Ischemia: interruption of blood flow to the brain

Ischemic stroke: occurs when there is a clot in a blood vessel which blocks the flow of the oxygen to downstream brain areas

Kuhnian paradigm shift: this is when a fundamental shift in thinking and methodology is required

Lateral fissure: prominent sulcus that separates the frontal (and parietal) lobes from the temporal lobe (also known as: Sylvian fissure)

Lesion: a region in an organ or tissue which has suffered damage through injury or disease

Lesion overlap analysis: method that made it possible to look at patients who have the same cognitive disorder and to locate the common area of damage; this then allows for the potential localisation of specific functions

Lexical-gustatory synaesthesia: certain words induce particular tastes

Lexicon: mental dictionary of all the words that you are already familiar with

Localisationalists: those who believed that certain functions were firmly localised in particular areas of the brain, e.g. speech production in Broca's area and comprehension in Wernicke's area

Long-term amnesia: (also known as accelerated long-term forgetting), a disruption in the consolidation process that results in delayed amnesia weeks or months after an event; currently this is difficult to diagnose with standard memory tests

Long-term store (LTS): long-term storage of information beyond short-term memory, so for more than a minute or so; duration of time that information can be held in this store is said to be unlimited

Magic number (7 plus or minus 2): capacity of short-term storage; most people can hold between 5 and 9 items at a time

Mammillary Bodies: a pair of structures on either side of the midline of the brain that consist of groups of nuclei and are best known for their role in recollective memory; part of the diencephalon

Meningitis: inflammation in the lining of cells (known as the meninges) around the brain and the spinal cord

Metacognitive strategies: an integral part of attention training, which helps improve a patient's awareness about their deficits and assist in regulating their behaviour when required

Magnetic resonance imaging (MRI): type of scan that uses strong magnetic fields and radio waves to produce detailed images of the inside of the body

McGurk Effect: illusion that demonstrates that when we 'hear' someone speaking, we are actually also lip reading, and what we *see* will influence what we think we *hear*

Middle cerebral artery: most common artery that bursts in a stroke that causes neglect

Mild cognitive impairment (MCI): the stage between the expected cognitive decline of normal aging and the more serious decline of dementia

Mirror neurons: neurons that are hypothesised to hold motor representations of actions that we are already familiar with; it is thought that these get played back when we observe others performing the same actions

Mirror-touch synaesthesia: individuals with this form of synaesthesia feel the sensation of touch when they see another person being touched

Modal Model: an influential model of memory in which information is processed in a serial manner, meaning that information needs to go through one stage before it goes onto the next

Modality-specific: a means of processing information through a certain module, such as a specific sense (gustatory, auditory, visual, etc.)

Modules: a hypothetical centre of information in a process which is assumed to be relatively independent and highly specialised in the role it fulfils

Motor aphasia: disorder in being able to speak fluently (also known as Broca's aphasia)

Motor neglect: the underutilisation of the contralesional limbs to perform actions or to interact with objects

Motor neuron disease (MND): a rare neurodegenerative disorder which affects the functioning of the nerve cells that are specialised for controlling the muscles around the body

Motor strip: area of the brain that controls our motor movement

Music-colour synaesthesia: perceptual phenomenon whereby music induces colours

Musical interval – taste synaesthesia: a form of synaesthesia whereby musical intervals induce taste experiences

Negative temporal gradient: memory for events just before the onset of Wernicke-Korsakoff syndrome (WKS) is extremely poor and then gets progressively better as one delves further back into the patient's life

Non-traumatic brain injury (NTBI): brain damage caused internally, such as by lack of oxygen, pressure from a tumour, infections, etc.

Non-word: made-up word

Norms: the score of the control group of healthy participants that raw scores can be compared to, in order to assess brain damage or cognitive disabilities

Nuclei: clusters of neurons in the central nervous system (the brain and spinal cord)

Nucleus: an individual cluster of neurons with similar functions in the central nervous system

Occipital lobe: lobe at the back of the brain responsible for visual processing

Optic ataxia: in this disorder, individuals can give perceptual information about objects, but have difficulty knowing the correct action to perform for them (e.g. not being able to reach out to objects placed in front of them)

Output modality: outgoing information, such as verbal responses, after receiving sensory input (input modality)

Papez circuit: a very old circuit of brain structures including the hippocampus, thalamus and mammillary bodies are all linked and involved in a number of different functions such as memory and emotion

Parallel: when a number of processes can occur at the same time

Paresis: a condition in which muscle movement in an area of the body has become weakened or impaired.

Parietal lobe: lobe at the top and back of the brain responsible for reception and integration of sensory information

Parkinson's disease: a degenerative disease of the nervous system marked by tremors, muscular rigidity and slow, imprecise movement

Percentile: involves drawing a line in the (usually normal) distribution where the patient's score falls and computing the proportion of people who have *lower* scores – this number then tells the researcher what proportion of population the patient scores *better* than

Percept: a mental concept that is developed as a consequence of the process of perception following intake of sensory information

Perception: process or result of becoming aware of objects, relationships and events by means of the senses

Peri-personal: space that is within physical reach of a person

Perseveration: the difficulty to shift from one concept to another or to change or cease a behaviour once it has been initiated

Personal neglect: an aspect of hemispatial neglect where a patient might, for example, even only shave or put make-up on one side of the face

Personalised medicine: treatment that moves away from a 'one-size-fits-all' approach and instead caters to the individual

Phrenology: a pseudoscience which was the study of bumps on the skull based on the belief that they are indicative of mental faculties and character

Post-acute: usually refers to rehabilitation services that support the patients' continued recovery from a brain injury or chronic illness

Procedural memory: skill-based knowledge

Prosopagnosia: neurological disorder characterised by the inability to recognise familiar faces, including one's own face

Phoneme: the sounds that constitute a spoken language

Plasticity: the ability of the brain to repair itself both at the neuronal and even cognitive level

Polygenic: the genetic basis of a disorder is likely to be more complex than involving a single gene

Pre-morbid IQ: one's intellectual capacities before brain damage

Primacy: good recall for the earliest items in the list

Raw score: the unaltered data before statistical analysis (e.g. the number of correct words remembered in a memory test)

Recency: good recall for the most recent items in the list

Recognition: experience of 'knowing'

Regularisation error: pronouncing an irregular word according to GPC rules, which is incorrect (e.g. 'colonel' as /kollonel/)

Rehearsal: processing information by repeating it over and over again, that can move the information to long-term storage

Repetition blindness: a symptom of neglect which results in only showing extinction of information on the contralesional side when two identical items are presented in the two visual fields

Repetition priming: the change in response to an item (word, object, etc.) as a result of having previously encountered it

Replication crisis: concern within psychology and cognitive neuroscience in particular that many past studies are not replicable, even though statistically, if a result is significant, someone repeating the same study *should* get similar results

Representational neglect: neglect does not occur simply because of a deficit with external input but can happen on internally generated information, neglecting the contralesional side of their mental image

Restoration: overcoming an impairment by improving it or retraining the function

Retrograde amnesia: difficulty in remembering events that occurred in the pre-morbid period (the period before sustaining brain damage)

Retrosplenial cortex: an area of the brain that is important in the formation of memories, and therefore damage to this area can also cause amnesia

Right supramarginal gyrus: part of the somatosensory association cortex, which interprets tactile sensory data and is involved in perception of space and limb location

Rostral: area situated toward the front end of the body, in this case, toward the front of the brain

Schemas: a cognitive framework or pattern of thought that helps organise categories of information and interpret the relationship among them

Seizure: an event in the brain that results when there is 'unprogrammed' electrical activity from damaged nerve cells, that causes a sort of avalanche effect spreading to connected brain regions

Semantic dementia: usually associated with ageing, individuals slowly lose their understanding of once common objects

Semantic memory: knowing facts, such as understanding the concept of a bicycle

Semantic system: how meaning is stored in the mind

Semanticisation: the trend in recall such that when a new event is experienced, recall for it tends to be more episodic but with constant repetition, later events of the same type tend to be largely semantic in nature

Sensory aphasia: inability to comprehend spoken language (also known as: Wernicke's aphasia)

Sensory deafferentation: elimination or interruption of sensory nerve impulses by destroying or injuring the sensory nerve fibres

Serial position curve: the graph of how many people remember the first word in the list, the second word, etc., as a function of its original position in the list

Short-term store (STS): short-term memory storage with limited capacity that holds only a finite number of items

Soma: region of a neuron that contains the nucleus and connects the dendrites to the axon (also known as the cell body)

Somatoparaphrenia: a delusional belief in which one thinks that the limb contralateral to a brain pathology, usually the left upper one, does not belong to them

Somatosensory neglect: patient will ignore tactile, thermal or painful stimuli that are applied to the contralesional side of the body

Somatic marker hypothesis: influential theory put forward by Antonio Damasio suggesting that logic is not the only important thing for decision-making, as our emotions (that come from our body or 'soma') are central; losing this results in purely logical decisions that can result in major errors

Sound-colour synaesthesia: perceptual phenomenon whereby a range of environmental sounds such as the ticking of a clock or the sound of a cat meowing can induce colours

Spaced retrieval: a rehabilitation technique that is used to improve memory by repeated retrieval and practice of the information learnt over spaced time intervals

Spoken modality: ability to communicate verbally

Standard deviation: a measure of how 'spread out' or varied the distribution is across all the scores in a dataset

Standardised tests: cognitive tests that are used to evaluate performance on different abilities in a clear and objective manner

Stored visual representations: stored memories of others' faces that are not accessible to individuals with prosopagnosia

Stroke: a serious life-threatening medical condition that happens when the blood supply to part of the brain is cut off

Structural brain imaging: techniques that take static 'pictures' or 'snapshots' of the brain at a given point in time

Structural description system: holds a visual representation of all objects in the mind

Substitution: a technique in rehabilitation which involves learning a new way of doing something due to the damage to the brain

Subtractivity: one of the major assumptions behind the use of damaged cognitive systems to infer normal intact processing which states that the brain-damaged system is the same as the unimpaired system except with some pieces missing

Sulci: (singular: sulcus) shallow grooves in the brain

Supervisory attentional system (SAS): an executive monitoring system that oversees and controls scheduling by influencing schema activation probabilities and allowing for general strategies to be applied to novel problems or situations during automatic attentional processes

Surface dyslexia: errors in reading irregularly spelt words, those in which the word cannot be made up simply by 'adding up' the constituent elements of the written word

Synapse: junction between two neurons where neurotransmitters are released, which then bind to the dendrites of the receiving neuron

Synaesthesia: a perceptual phenomenon whereby the attributes of certain sensory stimuli (referred to as inducers) elicit additional sensory experiences (known as concurrents)

Synaesthetes: people with synaesthesia

Syndrome: a cluster of cognitive problems that consistently co-occur

Sylvian fissure: prominent sulcus that separates the frontal (and parietal) lobes from the temporal lobe

Task demands: the difficulty of the assessment in testing cognitive deficits can impact how impaired a patient can seem

Taste-shape synaesthesia: a form of synaesthesia whereby tastes induce shape experiences, which can be tactile and/or visual in nature

Temporal lobes: lobes on each side of the brain (lying beneath the temples) responsible for auditory processing, language comprehension and memory encoding

Temporal pole: the front end of each of the temporal lobes

Theory-driven research: a biased research method in which researchers only study patients who fit into their particular theoretical framework

Top-down processes: the cognitive processes that occur later in the processing pathways and feedback to influence our perception of the world

Tracts: clusters of axons in the central nervous system

Traumatic brain injury (TBI): damage caused by a sudden external impact on the brain which can either penetrate the skull or leave it intact

Transparency: a principle coined by Alfonso Caramazza (1986), that the rest of the brain is assumed to function in exactly the same way as that of a healthy brain-intact individual, despite specific damaged areas (also known as: universality)

Transcortical motor aphasia: a form of language impairment which results in an inability to produce spontaneous speech; occurs when there is damage between the area of the brain that contains word concepts and Broca's area

Transcortical sensory aphasia: a form of language impairment caused by a disconnection between the word concept area and the 'sensory images' in Wernicke's area that results in the inability to comprehend or repeat spoken language

Transient epileptic amnesia: long-term amnesia that occurs due to epileptic interruptions in the consolidation processes

Tumour: an abnormal growth of a particular type of tissue, whether benign or malignant

Universality: a principle coined by Alfonso Caramazza (1986), that the rest of the brain is assumed to function in exactly the same way as that of a healthy brain-intact individual, despite specific damaged areas (also known as **transparency**)

Ventromedial: area extending towards the middle of the ventral (or lower) side

Veridicality: a concept that refers to how much performance on the test matches everyday functioning

Verisimilitude: a concept that refers to how much the cognitive demands of a test resemble what is required in a real everyday environment

Visual dyslexia: a form of reading disorder which involves reading errors whereby one verbalises a word based on how it visually appears written down

Visual neglect: a form of neglect which usually involves patients missing objects on the left side of their field

Visuokinesthetic engrams: part of a theoretical model in which action programmes are stored and processed within the parietal lobes, particularly in the left hemisphere, allowing one to perform familiar movements very rapidly and efficiently

Vocational rehabilitation: a structured programme to help a patient retain a job or find a new one that they are able to carry out given their disabilities

Wernicke's aphasia: inability to comprehend spoken language (also known as: **sensory aphasia**)

Wernicke-Korsakoff syndrome: constellation of deficits that can occur following very chronic alcohol abuse (although there are other causes as well), including the inability to lay down new memories, difficulties retrieving past memories and disrupted walking gait

White matter: areas of the brain made up of cells that transmit brain signals, primarily axons that are covered in white myelin sheaths

Word frequency: a measure of how often a particular word is used in a language

Word taste synaesthesia: a form of synaesthesia whereby words induce taste experiences

REFERENCES

Adolphs, R., Tranel, D., Damasio, H., & Damasio, A. R. (1994). Fear and the human amygdala. *The Journal of Neuroscience*, *15*(9), 5879–5891. https://doi.org/10.1523/JNEUROSCI.15-09-05879.1995

Afra, P. (2009). Acquired auditory-visual synesthesia: A window to early cross-modal sensory interactions. *Psychology Research and Behavior Management*, *2*, 31–37. https://doi.org/10.2147/PRBM.S4481

Aggleton, J. P., McMackin, D., Carpenter, K., Hornak, J., Kapur, N., Halpin, S., Wiles, C. M., Kamel, H., Brennan, P., Carton, S., & Gaffan, D. (2000). Differential cognitive effects of colloid cysts in the third ventricle that spare or compromise the fornix. *Brain*, *123*(4), 800–815. https://doi.org/10.1093/brain/123.4.800

Albert, M. S., Butters, N., & Levin, J. (1979). Temporal gradients in the retrograde amnesia of patients with alcoholic Korsakoff's disease. *Archives of Neurology*, *36*(4), 211–216. https://doi.org/10.1001/archneur.1979.00500400065010

Alexander, M. P., Stuss, D. T., & Benson, D. F. (1979). Capgras syndrome: A reduplicative phenomenon. *Neurology*, *29*(3), 334–339. https://doi.org/10.1212/WNL.29.3.334

Ali, S. S., Lifshitz, M., & Raz, A. (2014). Empirical neuroenchantment: from reading minds to thinking critically. *Frontiers in Human Neuroscience*, *8*, 357.

Armel, K. C., & Ramachandran, V. S. (1999). Acquired synesthesia in retinitis pigmentosa. *Neurocase*, *5*(4), 293–296. https://doi.org/10.1080/13554799908411982

Asher, J. E., Lamb, J. A., Brocklebank, D., Cazier, J.-B., Maestrini, E., Addis, L., Sen, M., Baron-Cohen, S., & Monaco, A. P. (2009). A whole-genome scan and fine-mapping linkage study of auditory-visual synesthesia reveals evidence of linkage to chromosomes 2q24, 5q33, 6p12, and 12p12. *The American Journal of Human Genetics*, *84*(2), 279–285. https://doi.org/10.1016/j.ajhg.2009.01.012

Atkinson, R. C., & Shiffrin, R. M. (1968). Human memory: A proposed system and its control processes. In K. W. Spence & J. T. Spence (Eds.), *Psychology of Learning and Motivation* (Vol. 2, pp. 89–195). Academic Press. https://doi.org/10.1016/S0079-7421(08)60422-3. Retrieved January 30, 2022, from www.rca.ucsd.edu/speeches/ScientistsMakingADifference_Human-Memory-A-Proposed-System-and-its-Control-Processes.pdf

Baddeley, A. D. (1966). The influence of acoustic and semantic similarity on long-term memory for word sequences. *Quarterly Journal of Experimental Psychology*, *18*(4), 302–309. https://doi.org/10.1080/14640746608400047

Baddeley, A. D., & Hitch, G. (1977). Commentary on "working memory". In *Human Memory* (pp. 191–197). Academic Press.

Baddeley, A. D., & Warrington, E. K. (1970). Amnesia and the distinction between long- and short-term memory. *Journal of Verbal Learning and Verbal Behavior*, *9*(2), 176–189. https://doi.org/10.1016/S0022-5371(70)80048-2

Baddeley, A.D., Della Sala, S., Papagno, C., & Spinnler, H. (1997). Dual-task performance in dysexecutive and nondysexecutive patients with a frontal lesion. *Neuropsychology*, *11*(2), 187.

Baddeley, A. D., Thomson, N., & Buchanan, M. (1975). Word length and the structure of short-term memory. *Journal of Verbal Learning and Verbal Behavior*, *14*(6), 575–589. https://doi.org/10.1016/S0022-5371(75)80045-4

Bálint, R. (1909). Seelenlähmung des 'Schauens', optische Ataxie, räumliche Störung der Aufmerksamkeit. *European Neurology*, *25*(1), 51–66. https://doi.org/10.1159/000210464

Banich, M. T. (2004). *Cognitive neuroscience and neuropsychology.* Houghton Mifflin College Division.

Banissy, M. J., & Ward, J. (2007). Mirror-touch synesthesia is linked with empathy. *Nature Neuroscience, 10*(7), 815–816. https://doi.org/10.1038/nn1926

Barnett, K. J., & Newell, F. N. (2008). Synaesthesia is associated with enhanced, self-rated visual imagery. *Consciousness and Cognition, 17*(3), 1032–1039. https://doi.org/10.1016/j.concog.2007.05.011

Barnett, K. J., Finucane, C., Asher, J. E., Bargary, G., Corvin, A. P., Newell, F. N., & Mitchell, K. J. (2008). Familial patterns and the origins of individual differences in synaesthesia. *Cognition, 106*(2), 871–893. https://doi.org/10.1016/j.cognition.2007.05.003

Baron-Cohen, S., Burt, L., Smith-Laittan, F., Harrison, J., & Bolton, P. (1996). Synaesthesia: prevalence and familiality. *Perception, 25*(9), 1073-1079. https://doi.org/10.1068/p251073

Baron-Cohen, S., Johnson, D., Asher, J., Wheelwright, S., Fisher, S. E., Gregersen, P. K., & Allison, C. (2013). Is synaesthesia more common in autism? *Molecular Autism, 4*(1), 40. https://doi.org/10.1186/2040-2392-4-40

Baron-Cohen, S., Wyke, M. A., & Binnie, C. (1987). Hearing words and seeing colours: An experimental investigation of a case of synaesthesia. *Perception, 16*(6), 761–767. https://doi.org/10.1068/p160761

Bartlett, J. C., & Searcy, J. (1993). Inversion and configuration of faces. *Cognitive Psychology, 25*(3), 281–316.

Bartley, A. J., Jones, D. W., & Weinberger, D. R. (1997). Genetic variability of human brain size and cortical gyral patterns. *Brain, 120*(2), 257–269. https://doi.org/10.1093/brain/120.2.257

Bartolomeo, P., Bachoud-Lévi, A. C., Azouvi, P., & Chokron, S. (2005). Time to imagine space: a chronometric exploration of representational neglect. *Neuropsychologia, 43*(9), 1249–1257.

Bartolomeo, P., Bachoud-Lévi, A.-C., & Denes, G. (1997). Preserved imagery for colours in a patient with cerebral achromatopsia. *Cortex, 33*(2), 369–378. https://doi.org/10.1016/S0010-9452(08)70012-1

Basso. A., Caporali A., (2001). Aphasia Therapy or the importance of being earnest. *Aphasiology,* 15, 307–332.

Bates, E., & Roe, K. (2001). Language development in children with unilateral brain injury. In C.A. Nelson & M. Luciana (Eds.), *Handbook of Developmental Cognitive Neuroscience* (pp. 447–476). MIT Press.

Bauer, R. M. (1984). Autonomic recognition of names and faces in prosopagnosia: A neuropsychological application of the guilty knowledge test. *Neuropsychologia, 22*(4), 457–469.

Baylis, G. C., Driver, J., & Rafal, R. D. (1993). Visual extinction and stimulus repetition. *Journal of Cognitive Neuroscience, 5*(4), 453–466.

Beauchamp, M. S., & Ro, T. (2008). Neural substrates of sound-touch synesthesia after a thalamic lesion. *Journal of Neuroscience, 28*(50), 13696–13702. https://doi.org/10.1523/JNEUROSCI.3872-08.2008

Beeli, G., Esslen, M., & Jäncke, L. (2005). When coloured sounds taste sweet. *Nature, 434*(7029), 38. https://doi.org/10.1038/434038a

Behrmann, M., Moscovitch, M., & Winocur, G. (1994). Intact visual imagery and impaired visual perception in a patient with visual agnosia. *Journal of Experimental Psychology: Human Perception and Performance, 20*(5), 1068–1087. https://doi.org/10.1037/0096-1523.20.5.1068

Belmonte, M. K., Allen, G., Beckel-Mitchener, A., Boulanger, L. M., Carper, R. A., & Webb, S. J. (2004). Autism and abnormal development of brain connectivity. *Journal of Neuroscience, 24*(42), 9228–9231. https://doi.org/10.1523/JNEUROSCI.3340-04.2004

Bennett, C. M., Miller, M. B., & Wolford, G. L. (2009). Neural correlates of interspecies perspective taking in the post-mortem Atlantic Salmon: an argument for multiple comparisons correction. *Neuroimage, 47*(Suppl 1), S125.

Benson, D. F., & Greenberg, J. P. (1969). Visual form agnosia: A specific defect in visual discrimination. *Archives of Neurology, 20*(1), 82–89.

Benton, A. L., & Van Allen, M. W. (1968). Impairment in facial recognition in patients with cerebral disease. *Cortex, 4*(4), 344–358. https://doi.org/10.1016/S0010-9452(68)80018-8

Best, W., Greenwood, A., Grassly, J., Herbert, R., Hickin, J., & Howard, D. (2013). Aphasia rehabilitation: Does generalisation from anomia therapy occur and is it predictable? A case series study. *Cortex, 49*(9), 2345–2357. ISSN 0010-9452, https://doi.org/10.1016/j.cortex.2013.01.005

Bisiach, E., & Luzzatti, C. (1978). Unilateral neglect of representational space. *Cortex, 14*(1), 129–133.

Bisiach, E., Luzzatti, C, &. Perani, D. (1979). Unilateral neglect, representational schema and consciousness. *Brain, 102,* 609–618.

Boake, C. (1991). History of cognitive rehabilitation following head injury. In J. S. Kreutzer & P. H. Wehman (Eds.), Cognitive rehabilitation for persons with traumatic brain injury (pp. 1–12). Baltimore: Brookes.

Bodamer, J. (1947). Die prosop-agnosie. *Archiv für Psychiatrie und Nervenkrankheiten, 179*(1), 6–53.

Bohil, C. J., Alicea, B., & Biocca, F. A. (2011). Virtual reality in neuroscience research and therapy. *Nature Reviews Neuroscience, 12*(12), 752–762. doi: 10.1038/nrn3122. PMID: 22048061

Bonato, M. (2012). Neglect and extinction depend greatly on task demands: A review. *Frontiers in Human Neuroscience, 6.* www.frontiersin.org/article/10.3389/fnhum.2012.00195

Boore, J., Cook, N., & Shepherd, A. (2016). *Essentials of anatomy and physiology for nursing practice.* Sage.

Bornstein, B., Sroka, H., & Munitz, H. (1969). Prosopagnosia with animal face agnosia. *Cortex, 5*(2), 164–169.

Bowles, D. C., McKone, E., Dawel, A., Duchaine, B., Palermo, R., Schmalzl, L., Rivolta, D., Wilson, C. E., & Yovel, G. (2009). Diagnosing prosopagnosia: Effects of ageing, sex, and participant–stimulus ethnic match on the Cambridge Face Memory Test and Cambridge Face Perception Test. *Cognitive Neuropsychology, 26*(5), 423–455. https://doi.org/10.1080/02643290903343149

Breen, N., Caine, D., & Coltheart, M. (2000). Models of face recognition and delusional misidentification: A critical review. *Cognitive Neuropsychology, 17*(1–3), 55–71.

Bruce, V., & Young, A. (1986). Understanding face recognition. *British Journal of Psychology, 77*(3), 305–327.

Brunsdon, R. K., Hannan, T. J., Nickels, L., & Coltheart, M. (2002). Successful treatment of sublexical reading deficits in a child with dyslexia of the mixed type. *Neuropsychological Rehabilitation, 12*(3), 199–229. https://doi.org/10.1080/09602010244000048

Brush, J. A., & Camp, C. J. (1998). Spaced retrieval during dysphagia therapy: A case study. *Clinical Gerontologist: The Journal of Aging and Mental Health, 19*(2), 96–99.

Bruyer, R., Laterre, C., Seron, X., Feyereisen, P., Strypstein, E., Pierrard, E., & Rectem, D. (1983). A case of prosopagnosia with some preserved covert remembrance of familiar faces. *Brain and Cognition, 2*(3), 257–284.

Burgess, P. W., Alderman, N., Forbes, C., Costello, A., Laure, M. C., Dawson, D. R., … & Channon, S. (2006). The case for the development and use of "ecologically valid" measures of executive function in experimental and clinical neuropsychology. *Journal of the International Neuropsychological Society, 12*(2), 194–209.

Burton, A. M., Bruce, V., & Johnston, R. A. (1990). Understanding face recognition with an interactive activation model. *British Journal of Psychology, 81*(3), 361–380.

Butler, C. R., Graham, K. S., Hodges, J. R., Kapur, N., Wardlaw, J. M., & Zeman, A. Z. J. (2007). The syndrome of transient epileptic amnesia. *Annals of Neurology*, *61*(6), 587–598. https://doi.org/10.1002/ana.21111

Buttaro, M. (2018). Gollin figures. In J. S. Kreutzer, J. DeLuca, & B. Caplan (Eds.), *Encyclopedia of Clinical Neuropsychology* (pp. 1601–1603). Springer International Publishing. https://doi.org/10.1007/978-3-319-57111-9_1369

Butter, C. M., & Trobe, J. D. (1994). Integrative agnosia following progressive multifocal leukoencephalopathy. *Cortex*, *30*(1), 145–158.

Butters, N., & Brandt, J. (1985). The continuity hypothesis: The relationship of long-term alcoholism to the Wernicke-Korsakoff Syndrome. *Recent Developments in Alcoholism*, 207–226.

Buxbaum, L. J. (2001). Ideomotor apraxia: A call to action. *Neurocase*, *7*(6), 445–458. https://doi.org/10.1093/neucas/7.6.445

Buxbaum, L. J. (2006). On the right (and left) track: Twenty years of progress in studying hemispatial neglect. *Cognitive Neuropsychology*, *23*(1), 184–201.

Buxbaum, L. J., & Kalénine, S. (2010). Action knowledge, visuomotor activation, and embodiment in the two action systems. *Annals of the New York Academy of Sciences*, *1191*(1), 201–218.

Buxbaum, L. J., Veramontil, T., & Schwartz, M. F. (2000). Function and manipulation tool knowledge in apraxia: Knowing 'what for' but not 'how'. *Neurocase*, *6*(2), 83–97. https://doi.org/10.1080/13554790008402763

Calder, A. J. (1996). Facial emotion recognition after bilateral amygdala damage: Differentially severe impairment of fear. *Cognitive Neuropsychology*, *13*(5), 699–745. https://doi.org/10.1080/026432996381890

Camp, C. J., & Schaller, J. R. (1989). Epilogue: Spaced-retrieval memory training in an adult day-care center. *Educational Gerontology*, *15*(6), 641–648. https://doi.org/10.1080/0380127890150608

Campbell, R., Landis, T., & Regard, M. (1986). Face recognition and lipreading: A neurological dissociation. *Brain*, *109*(3), 509–521.

Capgras, J., & Reboul-Lachaux, J. (1923). L'illusion dessosies' dans un dlire systmatise chronique. *Bulletin de la Socite Clinique de Medecine Mentale*, *2*, 616.

Capitani, E., Della Sala, S., Logie, R. H., & Spinnler, H. (1992). Recency, primacy, and memory: Reappraising and standardising the serial position curve. *Cortex*, *28*(3), 315–342. https://doi.org/10.1016/S0010-9452(13)80143-8

Caramazza, A. (1986). On drawing inferences about the structure of normal cognitive systems from the analysis of patterns of impaired performance: The case for single-patient studies. *Brain and Cognition*, *5*(1), 41–66.

Castle, A., Bates, T., & Coltheart, M. (2006). John Marshall and the developmental dyslexias. *Aphasiology*, *20*(9), 871–892. https://doi.org/10.1080/02687030600738952

Cermak, L. S. (1984). The episodic-semantic distinction in amnesia. *Neuropsychology of Memory*, 55–62.

Chao, L. L., & Martin, A. (2000). Representation of manipulable man-made objects in the dorsal stream. *NeuroImage*, *12*(4), 478–484. https://doi.org/10.1006/nimg.2000.0635

Charcot, J. M. (1883). *Lectures on the Localisation of Cerebral and Spinal Diseases*. New Sydenham Society.

Chatterjee, A., Mennemeier, M., & Heilman, K. M. (1992). A stimulus-response relationship in unilateral neglect: The power function. *Neuropsychologia*, *30*(12), 1101–1108.

Chaytor, N., & Schmitter-Edgecombe, M. (2003). The ecological validity of neuropsychological tests: A review of the literature on everyday cognitive skills. *Neuropsychology Review*, *13*(4), 181–197.

Chestnut, C., & Haaland, K. Y. (2008). Functional significance of ipsilesional motor deficits after unilateral stroke. *Archives of Physical Medicine and Rehabilitation, 89*(1), 62–68. https://doi.org/10.1016/j.apmr.2007.08.125

Chevignard, M. P., Catroppa, C., Galvin, J., & Anderson, V. (2010). Development and evaluation of an ecological task to assess executive functioning post childhood TBI: The children's cooking task. *Brain Impairment, 11*(2), 125–143. https://doi.org/10.1375/brim.11.2.125

Chia, L. G., & Kinsbourne, M. (1987). Mirror-writing and reversed repetition of digits in a right-handed patient with left basal ganglia haematoma. *Journal of Neurology, Neurosurgery and Psychiatry, 50*(6), 786–788. https://doi.org/10.1136/jnnp.50.6.786

Cicerone, K. D., Dahlberg, C., Kalmar, K., Langenbahn, D. M., Malec, J. F., Bergquist, T. F., Felicetti, T., Giacino, J. T., Harley, J. P., Harrington, D. E., Herzog, J., Kneipp, S., Laatsch, L., Morse, P. A. (2000). Evidence-based cognitive rehabilitation: recommendations for clinical practice. *Archives of Physical Medicine and Rehabilitation, 81*(12), 1596–1615. Doi: 10.1053/apmr.2000.19240

Clarapede, E. (1911). Récognition et moiité. *Archives de Psychologie, 11*, 79–90.

Clare, L., & Jones, R. S. P. (2008). Errorless learning in the rehabilitation of memory impairment: A critical review. *Neuropsychology Review, 18*(1), 1–23.

Cocchini, G., Beschin, N., & Jehkonen, M. (2001). The fluff test: A simple task to assess body representation neglect. *Neuropsychological Rehabilitation, 11*(1), 17–31.

Cohen, N. J. (1984). Preserved learning capacity in amnesia. In L. R. Squire & N. Butters (Eds.), *Neuropsychology of Memory.* The Guilford Press.

Cohen, N. J., & Squire, L. R. (1981). Retrograde amnesia and remote memory impairment. *Neuropsychologia, 19*(3), 337–356. https://doi.org/10.1016/0028-3932(81)90064-6

Coltheart, M., Patterson, K., & Marshall, J. C. (1987). *Deep Dyslexia Since 1980.* Routledge.

Conrad, R. (1964). Acoustic confusions in immediate memory. *British Journal of Psychology, 55*(1), 75–84. https://doi.org/10.1111/j.2044-8295.1964.tb00899.x

Corbetta, M., & Shulman, G. L. (2002). Control of goal-directed and stimulus-driven attention in the brain. *Nature Reviews Neuroscience, 3*(3), 201–215.

Corkin, S. (2002). What's new with the amnesic patient HM? *Nature Reviews Neuroscience, 3*(2), 153–160. https://doi.org/10.1038/nrn726

Corti, E. J., Gasson, N., & Loftus, A. M. (2021). Cognitive profile and mild cognitive impairment in people with chronic lower back pain. *Brain and Cognition, 151*, 105737. https://doi.org/10.1016/j.bandc.2021.105737

Craik, F. I. M., & Lockhart, R. S. (1972). Levels of processing: A framework for memory research. *Journal of Verbal Learning and Verbal Behavior, 11*(6), 671–684. https://doi.org/10.1016/S0022-5371(72)80001-X

Craik, K. J. W. (1943). Physiology of colour vision. *Nature, 151*(3843), 727–728. https://doi.org/10.1038/151727a0

Crawford, J. R., & Garthwaite, P. H. (2002). Investigation of the single case in neuropsychology: Confidence limits on the abnormality of test scores and test score differences. *Neuropsychologia, 40*(8), 1196–1208. https://doi.org/10.1016/S0028-3932(01)00224-X

Crovitz, H. F., Harvey, M. T., & McClanahan, S. (1981). Hidden memory: A rapid method for the study of amnesia using perceptual learning. *Cortex, 17*(2), 273–278. https://doi.org/10.1016/S0010-9452(81)80047-0

Cytowic, R. E. (1993). *The Man Who Tasted Shapes: A Bizarre Medical Mystery Offers Revolutionary Insights into Emotions, Reasoning and Consciousness.* Putnam.

Damasio, A. R. (1985). Prosopagnosia. *Trends in Neurosciences, 8*, 132–135.

Damasio, A. R. (2006). *Descartes' Error: Emotion, Reason and the Human Brain*. Vintage Books.

Damasio, H., & Damasio, A. R. (1990). *Lesion Analysis in Neuropsychology*. Oxford University Press.

Damasio, H., Grabowski, T., Frank, R., Galaburda, A. M., & Damasio, A. R. (1994). The return of Phineas Gage: Clues about the brain from the skull of a famous patient. *Science, 264*(5162), 1102–1105. https://doi.org/10.1126/science.8178168

David, A. S. (1992). Frontal lobology: Psychiatry's new pseudoscience. *The British Journal of Psychiatry, 161*(2), 244–248.

Davis, J. P., Forrest, C., Treml, F., & Jansari, A. (2018). Identification from CCTV: Assessing police super-recogniser ability to spot faces in a crowd and susceptibility to change blindness. *Applied Cognitive Psychology, 32*(3), 337–353. https://doi.org/10.1002/acp.3405

Day, S. (2013). Synesthesia: A first-person perspective. In J. Simner & E. Hubbard (Eds.), *The Oxford Handbook of Synesthesia* (pp. 903–923). Oxford University Press.

De Haan, E. H. F., Young, A. W., & Newcombe, F. (1987). Faces interfere with name classification in a prosopagnosic patient. *Cortex, 23*(2), 309–316. https://doi.org/10.1016/S0010-9452(87)80041-2

De Haan, E. H. F., Young, A. W., & Newcombe, F. (1991). Covert and overt recognition in prosopagnosia. *Brain, 114*(6), 2575–2591. https://doi.org/10.1093/brain/114.6.2575s

De Renzi, E., Faglioni, P., & Spinnler, H. (1968). The performance of patients with unilateral brain damage on face recognition tasks. *Cortex, 4*(1), 17–34. https://doi.org/10.1016/S0010-9452(68)80010-3

Del Gaizo, J., Fridriksson, J., Yourganov, G., Hillis, A. E., Hickok, G., Misic, B., Rorden, C., & Bonilha, L. (2017). Mapping language networks using the structural and dynamic brain connectomes. *ENeuro, 4*(5). https://doi.org/10.1523/ENEURO.0204-17.2017

Denmark, T., Fish, J., Jansari, A., Tailor, J., Ashkan, K., & Morris, R. (2019). Using Virtual Reality to investigate multitasking ability in individuals with frontal lobe lesions. *Neuropsychological Rehabilitation, 29*(5), 767–788.

Descartes, R. (1989). The passions of the soul (1649). *The Philosophical Writings of Descartes, 1*, 11.

Donkervoort, M., Dekker, J., Stehmann-Saris, F. C., & Deelman, B. G. (2001). Efficacy of strategy training in left hemisphere stroke patients with apraxia: A randomised clinical trial. *Neuropsychological Rehabilitation, 11*(5), 549–566.

Donovan, J. J., & Radosevich, D. J. (1999). A meta-analytic review of the distribution of practice effect: Now you see it, now you don't. *Journal of Applied Psychology, , 84*(5), 795–805.

Driver, J., & Halligan, P. W. (1991). Can visual neglect operate in object-centred co-ordinates? An affirmative single-case study. *Cognitive Neuropsychology, 8*(6), 475–496.

Driver, J., Baylis, G. C., & Rafal, R. D. (1992). Preserved figure-ground segregation and symmetry perception in visual neglect. *Nature, 360*(6399), 73–75.

Dronkers, N. F., Plaisant, O., Iba-Zizen, M. T., & Cabanis, E. A. (2007). Paul Broca's historic cases: High resolution MR imaging of the brains of Leborgne and Lelong. *Brain, 130*(5), 1432–1441. https://doi.org/10.1093/brain/awm042

Dronkers, N. F., Redfern, B., & Knight, R. (2000). The neural architecture of language disorders. *The New Cognitive Neurosciences, 2*, 949–960.

Dundon, N. M., Bertini, C., Làdavas, E., Sabel, B. A., & Gall, C. (2015). Visual rehabilitation: visual scanning, multisensory stimulation and vision restoration trainings. *Frontiers in Behavioral Neuroscience, 9*, 192. doi: 10.3389/fnbeh.2015.00192. PMID: 26283935; PMCID: PMC4515568

Eagleman, D. M., Kagan, A. D., Nelson, S. S., Sagaram, D., & Sarma, A. K. (2007). A standardized test battery for the study of synesthesia. *Journal of Neuroscience Methods, 159*(1), 139–145. https://doi.org/10.1016/j.jneumeth.2006.07.012

Eglin, M., Robertson, L. C., & Knight, R. T. (1989). Visual search performance in the neglect syndrome. *Journal of Cognitive Neuroscience*, *1*(4), 372–385.

Eglin, M., Robertson, L. C., Knight, R. T., & Brugger, P. (1994). Search deficits in neglect patients are dependent on size of the visual scene. *Neuropsychology*, *8*(3), 451.

Eklund, A., Nichols, T. E., & Knutsson, H. (2016). Cluster failure: Why fMRI inferences for spatial extent have inflated false-positive rates. *Proceedings of the National Academy of Sciences*, *113*(28), 7900–7905. https://doi.org/10.1073/pnas.1602413113

Ellis, A. W., & Young, A. W. (1988/2013). *Human Cognitive Neuropsychology: A Textbook with Readings*. Psychology Press.

Ellis, A. W., Young, A. W., & Anderson, C. (1988). Modes of word recognition in the left and right cerebral hemispheres. *Brain and Language*, *35*(2), 254–273. https://doi.org/10.1016/0093-934X(88)90111-3

Ellis, H. D., & Lewis, M. B. (2001). Capgras delusion: a window on face recognition. *Trends in cognitive sciences*, *5*(4), 149–156.

Eslinger, P. J., & Damasio, A. R. (1985). Severe disturbance of higher cognition after bilateral frontal lobe ablation: Patient EVR. *Neurology*, *35*(12), 1731. https://doi.org/10.1212/WNL.35.12.1731

Esterman, M., Verstynen, T., Ivry, R. B., & Robertson, L. C. (2006). Coming unbound: Disrupting automatic integration of synesthetic color and graphemes by transcranial magnetic stimulation of the right parietal lobe. *Journal of Cognitive Neuroscience*, *18*(9), 1570–1576. https://doi.org/10.1162/jocn.2006.18.9.1570

Evans, J. J., Emslie, H., & Wilson, B. A. (1998). External cueing systems in the rehabilitation of executive impairments of action. *Journal of the International Neuropsychological Society*, *4*(4), 399–408.

Evans, J. J., Wilson, B. A., Schuri, U., Andrade, J., Baddeley, A., Bruna, O., Canavan, T., Sala, S. D., Green, R., Laaksonen, R., Lorenzi, L., & Taussik, I. (2000). A comparison of "errorless" and "trial-and-error" learning methods for teaching individuals with acquired memory deficits. *Neuropsychological Rehabilitation*, *10*(1), 67–101..

Falchier, A., Clavagnier, S., Barone, P., & Kennedy, H. (2002). Anatomical evidence of multimodal integration in primate striate cortex. *The Journal of Neuroscience*, *22*(13), 5749–5759. https://doi.org/10.1523/JNEUROSCI.22-13-05749.2002

Farah, M. J. (2000a). Agnosias. In A. E. Kazdin. (Ed.), *Encyclopedia of Psychology, Vol. 1* (pp. 106–108). American Psychological Association.

Farah, M. J. (2000b). *The Cognitive Neuroscience of Vision*. Blackwell Publishing.

Farah, M. J. (2004). *Visual Agnosia*. The MIT Press.

Farah, M. J., & Feinberg, T. E. (2000). Visual object agnosia. In M. J. Farah & T. E. Feinberg (Eds.), *Patient-Based Approaches to Cognitive Neuroscience* (pp. 79–95). The MIT Press.

Farah, M. J., & McClelland, J. L. (1991). Neural network models and cognitive neuropsychology. *Psychiatric Annals*, *22*(3), 148–153. https://doi.org/10.3928/0048-5713-19920301-12

Ferro, J. M., & Santos, M. E. (1984). Associative visual agnosia: A case study. *Cortex*, *20*(1), 121–134.

Fish, J. (2017). Rehabilitation of attention disorders: a) adults. In B. A. Wilson, J. Winegardner, C. M. van Heugten, & T. Ownsworth (Eds.), *Neuropsychological Rehabilitation: The International Handbook*. Routledge.

Fish, J., & Manly, T. (2017). Rehabilitation of working memory disorders. In B. A. Wilson, J. Winegardner, C. M. van Heugten & T. Ownsworth (Eds.), *Neuropsychological Rehabilitation: The International Handbook*. Routledge.

Fish, J., Evans, J. J., Nimmo, M., Martin, E., Kersel, D., Bateman, A., ... & Manly, T. (2007). Rehabilitation of executive dysfunction following brain injury:"Content-free" cueing improves everyday prospective memory performance. *Neuropsychologia*, *45*(6), 1318–1330.

Fornazzari, L., Fischer, C. E., Ringer, L., & Schweizer, T. A. (2012). 'Blue is music to my ears': Multimodal synesthesias after a thalamic stroke. *Neurocase, 18*(4), 318–322. https://doi.org/10.108 0/13554794.2011.608362

Foundas, A. L., Macauley, B. L., Raymer, A. M., Maher, L. M., Heilman, K. M., & Rothi, L. J. G. (1995). Ecological implications of limb apraxia: evidence from mealtime behavior. *Journal of the International Neuropsychological Society, 1*(1), 62–66.

Frank, R. J., Damasio, H., & Grabowski, T. J. (1997). Brainvox: An interactive, multimodal visualization and analysis system for neuroanatomical imaging. *NeuroImage, 5*(1), 13–30. https://doi.org/10.1006/nimg.1996.0250

Freud, S. (1891). *Zur auffassung der aphasien: eine kritische studie.* F. Deuticke.

Funnell, E. (1983). Phonological processes in reading: New evidence from acquired dyslexia. *British Journal of Psychology, 74*(2), 159–180. https://doi.org/10.1111/j.2044-8295.1983.tb01851.x

Funnell, E., & Sheridan, J. (1992). Categories of knowledge? Unfamiliar aspects of living and nonliving things. *Cognitive Neuropsychology, 9*(2), 135–153.

Fuster, J. M. (2002). Frontal lobe and cognitive development. *Journal of Neurocytology, 31*(3), 373–385.

Gabrieli, J. D., Cohen, N. J., & Corkin, S. (1988). The impaired learning of semantic knowledge following bilateral medial temporal-lobe resection. *Brain and Cognition, 7*(2), 157–177.

Gaffan, D., & Heywood, C. A. (1993). A spurious category-specific visual agnosia for living things in normal human and nonhuman primates. *Journal of Cognitive Neuroscience, 5*(1), 118–128. https://doi.org/10.1162/jocn.1993.5.1.118

Gajardo-Vidal, A., Lorca-Puls, D. L., PLORAS team, Warner, H., Pshdary, B., Crinion, J. T., Leff, A. P., Hope, T. M. H., Geva, S., Seghier, M. L., Green, D. W., Bowman, H., & Price, C. J. (2021). Damage to Broca's area does not contribute to long-term speech production outcome after stroke. *Brain, 144*(3), 817–832. https://doi.org/10.1093/brain/awaa460

Galton, F. (1883). *Inquiries into Human Faculty and its Development.* Macmillan.

Gamito, P., Oliveira, J., Coelho, C., Morais, D., Lopes, P., Pacheco, J., Brito, R., Soares, F., Santos, N., & Barata, A. F. (2017). Cognitive training on stroke patients via virtual reality-based serious games. *Disability Rehabilitation, 39*(4), 385–388. doi: 10.3109/09638288.2014.934925. Epub 2015 Mar 5. PMID: 25739412

Garrett, B., & Hough, G. (2017). *Brain & behavior: An introduction to behavioral neuroscience.* Sage Publications.

Gascoigne, M. B., Smith, M. L., Barton, B., Webster, R., Gill, D., & Lah, S. (2019). Accelerated long-term forgetting and behavioural difficulties in children with epilepsy. *Cortex, 110*, 92–100. https://doi.org/10.1016/j.cortex.2018.03.021

Gauthier, I., & Tarr, M. J. (1997). Becoming a 'greeble' expert: Exploring mechanisms for face recognition. *Vision Research, 37*(12), 1673–1682. https://doi.org/10.1016/S0042-6989(96)00286-6

Ghent, L. (1956). Perception of overlapping and embedded figures by children of different ages. *The American Journal of Psychology, 69*(4), 575–587. https://doi.org/10.2307/1419081

Gilboa, Y., Jansari, A., Kerrouche, B., Uçak, E., Tiberghien, A., Benkhaled, O., … & Chevignard, M. (2019). Assessment of executive functions in children and adolescents with acquired brain injury (ABI) using a novel complex multi-tasking computerised task: The Jansari assessment of Executive Functions for Children (JEF-C©). *Neuropsychological Rehabilitation, 29*(9), 1359–1382.

Gillespie, A., Best, C., & O'Neill, B. (2012). Cognitive function and assistive technology for cognition: A systematic review. *Journal of the International Neuropsychological Society, 18*(1), 1–19. doi: 10.1017/S1355617711001548. Epub 2011 Dec 12. PMID: 22152338

Gogtay, N. J., Jakhere, S. G., Waingankar, S. P., Dalvi, S. S., & Kshirsagar, N. A. (2004). Therapeutic drug monitoring as a tool to identify medication errors. *Drug Safety*, *27*(2), 143–144. https://doi.org/10.2165/00002018-200427020-00005

Goldenberg, G., Daumüller, M., & Hagmann, S. (2001). Assessment and therapy of complex activities of daily living in apraxia. *Neuropsychological Rehabilitation*, *11*(2), 147–169.

Gollin, E. S. (1960). Developmental studies of visual recognition of incomplete objects. *Perceptual and Motor Skills*, *11*(3), 289–298.

Gonzalez Rothi, L. J., Ochipa, C., & Heilman, K. M. (1991). A cognitive neuropsychological model of limb praxis. *Cognitive Neuropsychology*, *8*(6), 443–458. https://doi.org/10.1080/02643299108253382

Goodale, M. A., Milner, A. D., Jakobson, L. S., & Carey, D. P. (1991). A neurological dissociation between perceiving objects and grasping them. *Nature*, *349*(6305), 154–156. https://doi.org/10.1038/349154a0

Goodglass, H., Kaplan, E., & Weintraub, S. (2001). *BDAE: The Boston Diagnostic Aphasia Examination*. Lippincott Williams & Wilkins.

Graf, P., Squire, L. R., & Mandler, G. (1984). The information that amnesic patients do not forget. *Journal of Experimental Psychology: Learning, Memory and Cognition*, *10*(1), 164–178. https://doi.org/10.1037/0278-7393.10.1.164

Graves, R. E. (1997). The legacy of the Wernicke-Lichtheim model. *Journal of the History of the Neurosciences*, *6*(1), 3–20.

Greener, J., Enderby, P., & Whurr, R. (1999). Speech and language therapy for aphasia following stroke. *Cochrane Database of Systematic Reviews*, Issue 4. Art. No.: CD000425. DOI: 10.1002/14651858.CD000425

Grossenbacher, P. G., & Lovelace, C. T. (2001). Mechanisms of synesthesia: Cognitive and physiological constraints. *Trends in Cognitive Sciences*, *5*(1), 36–41. https://doi.org/10.1016/S1364-6613(00)01571-0

Haaland, K. Y., Harrington, D. L., & Knight, R. T. (2000). Neural representations of skilled movement. *Brain*, *123*(11), 2306–2313. https://doi.org/10.1093/brain/123.11.2306

Hanna-Pladdy, B., Heilman, K. M., & Foundas, A. L. Ecological implications of ideomotor apraxia: Evidence from physical activities of daily living. *Neurology*, *60*(3), 489–490. doi: 10.1212/wnl.60.3.487. PMID: 12578932

Harlow, J. M. (1868). Recovery after severe injury to the head. *Publication of the Massachusetts Medical Society*, *2*(327), 990–992.

Hassabis, D., Kumaran, D., Vann, S. D., & Maguire, E. A. (2007). Patients with hippocampal amnesia cannot imagine new experiences. *PNAS*, *104*(5), 1726–1731. https://doi.org/10.1073/pnas.0610561104

Haxby, J. V., Hoffman, E. A., & Gobbini, M. I. (2000). The distributed human neural system for face perception. *Trends in Cognitive Sciences*, *4*(6), 223–233. https://doi.org/10.1016/S1364-6613(00)01482-0

Hécaen, H., Goldblum, M. C., Masure, M. C., & Ramier, A. M. (1974). Une nouvelle observation d'agnosie d'objet. Deficit de l'association ou de la categorisation, specifique de la modalite visuelle?. *Neuropsychologia*, *12*(4), 447–464.

Heilman, K. M., & Van Den Abell, T. (1980). Right hemisphere dominance for attention: the mechanism underlying hemispheric asymmetries of inattention (neglect). *Neurology*, *30*(3), 327–330.

Heilman, K. M., Rothi, L. J., & Valenstein, E. (1982). Two forms of ideomotor apraxia. *Neurology*, *32*(4), 342. https://doi.org/10.1212/WNL.32.4.342

Higgins, I., Chang, L., Langston, V., Hassabis, D., Summerfield, C., Tsao, D., & Botvinick, M. (2021). Unsupervised deep learning identifies semantic disentanglement in single inferotemporal face patch neurons. *Nature Communications*, *12*(1), 1–14.

Hillis, A. E., & Caramazza, A. (1991). Category-specific naming and comprehension impairment: A double dissociation. *Brain*, *114*(5), 2081–2094. https://doi.org/10.1093/brain/114.5.2081

Hitch, G. J., & Baddeley, A. D. (1976). Verbal reasoning and working memory. *The Quarterly Journal of Experimental Psychology*, *28*(4), 603–621.

Holdnack, H. A. (2001). *Wechsler test of adult reading: WTAR*. The Psychological Corporation.

Hørlyck, L. D., Obenhausen, K., Jansari, A., Ullum, H., & Miskowiak, K. W. (2021). Virtual reality assessment of daily life executive functions in mood disorders: associations with neuropsychological and functional measures. *Journal of Affective Disorders*, *280*, 478–487.

Horster, I., Nickel, K., Holovics, L., Schmidt, S., Endres, D., Tebartz van Elst, L., Zeeck, A., Maier, S., & Joos, A. (2020). A neglected topic in neuroscience: Replicability of fMRI results with specific reference to anorexia nervosa. *Frontiers in Psychiatry*, *11*. www.frontiersin.org/article/10.3389/fpsyt.2020.00777

Huang, T. L., Liu, C. Y., & Yang, Y. Y. (1999). Capgras syndrome: Analysis of nine cases. *Psychiatry and Clinical Neurosciences*, *53*(4), 455–460.

Hubbard, E. M., Arman, A. C., Ramachandran, V. S., & Boynton, G. M. (2005). Individual differences among grapheme-color synesthetes: Brain-behavior correlations. *Neuron*, *45*(6), 975–985. https://doi.org/10.1016/j.neuron.2005.02.008

Huberle, E., Rupek, P., Lappe, M., & Karnath, H. O. (2012). Perception of biological motion in visual agnosia. *Frontiers in Behavioral Neuroscience*, *6*, 56.

Hughes, J. E. A., Simner, J., Baron-Cohen, S., Treffert, D. A., & Ward, J. (2017). Is synaesthesia more prevalent in autism spectrum conditions? Only where there is prodigious talent. *Multisensory Research*, *30*(3–5), 391–408. https://doi.org/10.1163/22134808-00002558

Humphreys, G. W., & Riddoch, M. J. (1984). Routes to object constancy: Implications from neurological impairments of object constancy. *The Quarterly Journal of Experimental Psychology*, *36*(3), 385–415.

Humphreys, G. W., & Riddoch, M. J. (2013). *To See but Not to See: A Case Study of Visual Agnosia*. Psychology Press.

Humphreys, G. W., Donnelly, N., & Riddoch, M. J. (1993). Expression is computed separately from facial identity, and it is computed separately for moving and static faces: Neuropsychological evidence. *Neuropsychologia*, *31*(2), 173–181.

Hunkin, N. M., Parkin, A. J., Bradley, V. A., Burrows, E. H., Aldrich, F. K., Jansari, A., & Burdon-Cooper, C. (1995). Focal retrograde amnesia following closed head injury: A case study and theoretical account. *Neuropsychologia*, *33*(4), 509–523.

Husain, M. (2008). Hemispatial neglect. *Handbook of Clinical Neurology*, *88*, 359–372.

Husain, M., Mannan, S., Hodgson, T., Wojciulik, E., Driver, J., & Kennard, C. (2001). Impaired spatial working memory across saccades contributes to abnormal search in parietal neglect. *Brain*, *124*(5), 941–952.

Jacobs, L., Karpik, A., Bozian, D., & Gothgen, S. (1981). Auditory-visual synesthesia sound-induced photisms. *Archives of Neurology*, *38*(4), 211–216. https://doi.org/10.1001/archneur.1981.00510040037005

Jansari, A. S., & McGibbon, T. (2022). Towards an earlier diagnosis of memory deterioration in dementia: VALMT (The Verbal Associative Learning & Memory Test). *The Cognitive Psychology Bulletin*, *7*, 36–42.

Jansari, A., Cole, S., & McCarthy, R. (2004). Selective short-term memory impairment following closed head injury: Possible role of the Central Executive. *Journal of the International Neuropsychological Society, 10*(2), 47.

Jansari, A. S., Davis, K., McGibbon, T., Firminger, S., & Kapur, N. (2010). When 'long-term memory' no longer means 'forever': Analysis of accelerated long-term forgetting in a patient with temporal lobe epilepsy. *Neuropsychologia, 48*, 1707–1715.

Jansari, A. S., Devlin, A., Agnew, R., Akesson, K., Murphy, L., & Leadbetter, T. (2014). Ecological assessment of executive functions: A new virtual reality paradigm. *Brain Impairment, 15*(2), 71–87. https://doi.org/10.1017/BrImp.2014.14

Jansari, A., Edmonds, E., Gordon, R., Nwosu, U., & Leadbetter, T. (2012). Towards a novel ecologically-valid assessment of executive functions in children and adolescents: Could virtual reality be the answer? *Brain Impairment, 13*, 146.

Jansari, A. S., Froggatt, D., Edginton, T., & Dawkins, L. (2013). Investigating the impact of nicotine on executive functions using a novel virtual reality assessment: Effects of nicotine on executive functions. *Addiction, 108*(5), 977–984. https://doi.org/10.1111/add.12082

Jansari, A. S., Miller, S., Pearce, L., Cobb, S., Sagiv, N., Williams, A. L., Tree, J. J., & Hanley, J. R. (2015). The man who mistook his neuropsychologist for a popstar: When configural processing fails in acquired prosopagnosia. *Frontiers in Human Neuroscience, 9*, 390. https://doi.org/10.3389/fnhum.2015.00390

Jansari, A. S., Spiller, M. J., & Redfern, S. (2006). Number synaesthesia: When hearing 'four plus five' looks like gold. *Cortex, 42*(2), 253–258. https://doi.org/10.1016/S0010-9452(08)70350-2

Jeannerod, M., & Rossetti, Y. (1993). Visuomotor coordination as a dissociable visual function: Experimental and clinical evidence. *Baillieres Clinical Neurology, 2*(2), 439–460.

Jurado, M. B., & Rosselli, M. (2007). The elusive nature of executive functions: A review of our current understanding. *Neuropsychology Review, 17*(3), 213–233. https://doi.org/10.1007/s11065-007-9040-z

Kapur, N., Millar, J., Colbourn, C., Abbott, P., Kennedy, P., & Docherty, T. (1997). Very long-term amnesia in association with temporal lobe epilepsy: Evidence for multiple-stage consolidation processes. *Brain and Cognition, 35*(1), 58–70. https://doi.org/10.1006/brcg.1997.0927

Karnath, H. O., Fruhmann Berger, M., Küker, W., & Rorden, C. (2004). The anatomy of spatial neglect based on voxelwise statistical analysis: a study of 140 patients. *Cerebral Cortex, 14*(10), 1164–1172.

Kartsounis, L. D., & Warrington, E. K. (1991). Failure of object recognition due to a breakdown of figure-ground discrimination in a patient with normal acuity. *Neuropsychologia, 29*(10), 969–980. https://doi.org/10.1016/0028-3932(91)90061-C

Kay, J., Lesser, R., & Coltheart, M. (1996). Psycholinguistic assessments of language processing in aphasia (PALPA): An introduction. *Aphasiology, 10*(2), 159–180. https://doi.org/10.1080/02687039608248403

Kim, I. K. (2006). Melanocytoma of the optic nerve associated with sound-induced phosphenes. *Archives of Ophthalmology, 124*(2), 273. https://doi.org/10.1001/archopht.124.2.273

Kinsbourne, M. (1987). Mechanisms of unilateral neglect. *Advances in Psychology, 45*, 69–86.

Kopelman, M. (1989). Human organic memory disorders. *Journal of Neurology, Neurosurgery and Psychiatry, 52*(11), 1327–1328. https://doi.org/10.1136/jnnp.52.11.1327-b

Krasny-Pacini, A., Chevignard, M., & Evans, J. (2014) Goal Management Training for rehabilitation of executive functions: a systematic review of effectiveness in patients with acquired brain injury. *Disability Rehabilitation, 36*(2), 105–16. doi: 10.3109/09638288.2013.777807. Epub 2013 Apr 18. PMID: 23597002.

Landis, J., Hanten, G., Levin, H. S., Li, X., EwingCobbs, L., Duron, J., & High Jr., W. M. (2006). Evaluation of the errorless learning technique in children with traumatic brain injury. *Archives of Physical Medicine and Rehabilitation*, 87, 799–805.

Lashley, K. S. (1929). *Brain Mechanisms and Intelligence: A Quantitative Study of Injuries to the Brain* (pp. xi, 186). University of Chicago Press. https://doi.org/10.1037/10017-000

Law, S.-P., & Or, B. (2001). A case study of acquired dyslexia and dysgraphia in Cantonese: Evidence for nonsemantic pathways for reading and writing Chinese. *Cognitive Neuropsychology*, *18*(8), 729–748. https://doi.org/10.1080/02643290143000024

Lee, M., Pyun, S. B., Chung, J., Kim, J., Eun, S. D., & Yoon, B. (2016). A further step to develop patient-friendly implementation strategies for virtual reality-based rehabilitation in patients with acute stroke. *Physical Therapy*, *96*(10), 1554–1564. doi: 10.2522/ptj.20150271. Epub 2016 May 5. PMID: 27149961

Leibniz, G. W. (1916). *New Essays Concerning Human Understanding with an Appealing...: Translated from the Original Latin, French and German Writeen*. Open Court Publishing Company.

Lessell, S., & Cohen, M. M. (1979). Phosphenes induced by sound. *Neurology*, *29*(11), 1524. https://doi.org/10.1212/WNL.29.11.1524

Levine, B., Robertson, I. H., Clare, L., Carter, G., Hong, J., Wilson, B. A., Duncan, J., & Stuss, D. T. (2000). Rehabilitation of executive functioning: An experimental–clinical validation of goal management training. *Journal of the International Neuropsychological Society*, *6*(3), 299–312. https://doi.org/10.1017/S1355617700633052

Lichtheim, L. (1885). On aphasia. *Brain*, 7, 433–484

Linton, M. (1982). Transformations of memory in everyday life. In U. Neisser (Ed.), *Memory Observed: Remembering in Natural Contexts*. Freeman.

Lissauer, H. (1890). Ein Fall von Seelenblindheit nebst einem Beitrage zur Theorie derselben. *Archiv für Psychiatrie und Nervenkrankheiten*, *21*(2), 222–270.

Losier, B. J., & Klein, R. M. (2001). A review of the evidence for a disengage deficit following parietal lobe damage. *Neuroscience & Biobehavioral Reviews*, *25*(1), 1–13.

Luke, D. P., & Terhune, D. B. (2013). The induction of synaesthesia with chemical agents: A systematic review. *Frontiers in Psychology*, *4*. https://doi.org/10.3389/fpsyg.2013.00753

Lungu, L., Stewart, R., Luke, D. P., & Terhune, D. B. (2020). Primary visual cortex excitability is not atypical in acquired synaesthesia. *Brain Stimulation*, *13*(2), 341–342. https://doi.org/10.1016/j.brs.2019.10.021

Lunke, K., & Meier, B. (2019). Creativity and involvement in art in different types of synaesthesia. *British Journal of Psychology*, *110*(4), 727–744. https://doi.org/10.1111/bjop.12363

Luria, A. R. (1968). *The Mind of a Mnemonist: A Little Book about a Vast Memory*. Trans. L. Solotaroff. Basic Books.

Luria, A. R. (1979). *The Making of Mind: A Personal Account of Soviet Psychology*. Harvard University Press.

Lustig, A., & Tompkins, C. (2002). A written communication strategy for a speaker with aphasia and apraxia of speech: Treatment outcomes and social validity. *Aphasiology*, *16*, 507–521. 10.1080/02687030244000211

Maggio, M. G., De Cola, M. C., Latella, D., Maresca, G., Finocchiaro, C., La Rosa, G., Cimino, V., Sorbera, C., Bramanti, P., De Luca, R., Calabrò, R. S. (2018). What about the role of virtual reality in Parkinson Disease's cognitive rehabilitation? Preliminary findings from a randomized clinical trial. *Journal of Geriatric Psychiatry and Neurology*, *31*(6), 312–318. doi: 10.1177/0891988718807973

Manes, F., Serrano, C., Calcagno, M. L., Cardozo, J., & Hodges, J. (2008). Accelerated forgetting in subjects with memory complaints. *Journal of Neurology, 255*(7), 1067–1070.

Marr, D. (1976). Early processing of visual information. *Philosophical Transactions of the Royal Society of London. B, Biological Sciences, 275*(942), 483–519.

Marr, D., & Nishihara, H. K. (1978). Representation and recognition of the spatial organization of three-dimensional shapes. *Proceedings of the Royal Society of London. Series B. Biological Sciences, 200*(1140), 269–294.

Marshall, J. (2002). Assessment and treatment of sentence processing disorders: A review of the literature. In A. E. Hillis (Ed.), *The Handbook of Adult Language Disorders: Integrating Cognitive Neuropsychology, Neurology, and Rehabilitation* (pp. 351–372). Psychology Press.

Marshall, J. C., & Halligan, P. W. (1988). Blindsight and insight in visuo-spatial neglect. *Nature, 336*(6201), 766–767.

Marshall, J. C., & Newcombe, F. (1966). Syntactic and semantic errors in paralexia. *Neuropsychologia, 4*(2), 169–176. https://doi.org/10.1016/0028-3932(66)90045-5

Marshall, J. C., & Newcombe, F. (1973). Patterns of paralexia: A psycholinguistic approach. *Journal of Psycholinguistic Research, 2*(3), 175–199. https://doi.org/10.1007/BF01067101

Marshall, R. C., Tompkins, C. A. and Phillips, D. S. 1982. Improvement in treated aphasia: Examination of selected prognostic factors. *Folia Phoniatrica, 34*: 305–315.

Maurer, D., & Maurer, C. (1988). *The World of the Newborn.* Basic Books.

Maurer, D., & Mondloch, C. J. (2006). The infant as synesthete. *Attention and Performance, 21,* 449–471.

McCabe, D. P., & Castel, A. D. (2008). Seeing is believing: The effect of brain images on judgments of scientific reasoning. *Cognition, 107*(1), 343–352.

McCarthy, R. A., & Warrington, E. K. (1986). Phonological reading: Phenomena and paradoxes. *Cortex, 22*(3), 359–380. https://doi.org/10.1016/S0010-9452(86)80002-8

McCarthy, R. A., & Warrington, E. K. (1988). Evidence for modality-specific meaning systems in the brain. *Nature, 334*(6181), 428–430.

McCarthy, R. A., & Warrington, E. K. (1990). *Cognitive Neuropsychology: A Clinical Introduction.* Academic Press.

McGibbon, T., & Jansari, A. S. (2013). Detecting the onset of accelerated long-term forgetting: Evidence from temporal lobe epilepsy. *Neuropsychologia, 51*(1), 114–122. https://doi.org/10.1016/j.neuropsychologia.2012.11.004

McGibbon, T., Jansari, A., Demirjian, J., Nemes, A., & Opre, A. (in press). Accelerated forgetting in healthy older samples: implications for methodology, future ageing studies and early identification of risk of dementia. *Quarterly Journal of Experimental Psychology.*

McGlinchey-Berroth, R., Milberg, W. P., Verfaellie, M., Grande, L., D'Esposito, M., & Alexander, M. (1996). Semantic processing and orthographic specificity in hemispatial neglect. *Journal of Cognitive Neuroscience, 8*(3), 291–304. https://doi.org/10.1162/jocn.1996.8.3.291

McGurk, H., & MacDonald, J. (1976). Hearing lips and seeing voices. *Nature, 264*(5588), 746–748.

McNeil, J. E., & Warrington, E. K. (1993). Prosopagnosia: A face-specific disorder. *The Quarterly Journal of Experimental Psychology, 46*(1), 1–10.

Medina, J., & Fischer-Baum, S. (2017). Single-case cognitive neuropsychology in the age of big data. *Cognitive Neuropsychology, 34*(7–8), 440–448. https://doi.org/10.1080/02643294.2017.1321537

Miller, G. A. (1956). The magical number seven, plus or minus two: Some limits on our capacity for processing information. *Psychological Review, 63*(2), 81–97. https://doi.org/10.1037/h0043158

Milner, A. D., Perrett, D. I., Johnston, R. S., Benson, P. J., Jordan, T. R., Heeley, D. W., … & Davidson, D. L. W. (1991). Perception and action in 'visual form agnosia'. *Brain, 114*(1), 405–428.

Milner, B. (2003). Visual recognition and recall after right temporal-lobe excision in man. *Epilepsy & Behavior, 4*(6), 799–812. https://doi.org/10.1016/j.yebeh.2003.08.027

Montgomery, C., Ashmore, K. V., & Jansari, A. (2011). The effects of a modest dose of alcohol on executive functioning and prospective memory. *Human Psychopharmacology, 26*(3), 208–215. https://doi.org/10.1002/hup.1194

Montgomery, C., Fisk, J. E., Murphy, P. N., Ryland, I., & Hilton, J. (2012). The effects of heavy social drinking on executive function: A systematic review and meta-analytic study of existing literature and new empirical findings. *Human Psychopharmacology, 27*(2), 187–199. https://doi.org/10.1002/hup.1268

Montgomery, C., Hatton, N. P., Fisk, J. E., Ogden, R. S., & Jansari, A. (2010). Assessing the functional significance of ecstasy-related memory deficits using a virtual paradigm. *Human Psychopharmacology, 25*(4), 318–325. https://doi.org/10.1002/hup.1119

Moravec, H. (1988). *Mind Children: The Future of Robot and Human Intelligence.* Harvard University Press.

Morris, R. G. M., Garrud, P., Rawlins, J. N. P., & O'Keefe, J. (1982). Place navigation impaired in rats with hippocampal lesions. *Nature, 297*(5868), 681–683. https://doi.org/10.1038/297681a0

Moscovitch, M., & Winocur, G. (1992). The neuropsychology of memory and aging. In F. I. M. Craik & T. A. Salthouse (Eds.), *The Handbook of Aging and Cognition* (pp. 315–372). Lawrence Erlbaum Associates, Inc.

Moscovitch, M., Winocur, G., & Behrmann, M. (1997). What is special about face recognition? Nineteen experiments on a person with visual object agnosia and dyslexia but normal face recognition. *Journal of Cognitive Neuroscience, 9*(5), 555–604. https://doi.org/10.1162/jocn.1997.9.5.555

Muggleton, N., Tsakanikos, E., Walsh, V., & Ward, J. (2007). Disruption of synaesthesia following TMS of the right posterior parietal cortex. *Neuropsychologia, 45*(7), 1582–1585. https://doi.org/10.1016/j.neuropsychologia.2006.11.021

Murdock Jr., B. B. (1962). The serial position effect of free recall. *Journal of Experimental Psychology, 64*(5), 482–488. https://doi.org/10.1037/h0045106

National Aphasia Association (2022). *Types of Aphasia.* National Aphasia Association. https://www.aphasia.org/aphasia-definitions/

Nelles, G., Esser, J., Eckstein, A., Tiede, A., Gerhard, H., Diener, H. C. (2001). Compensatory visual field training for patients with hemianopia after stroke. *Neuroscience Letters, 306*(3), 189–192. doi: 10.1016/ s0304-3940(01)01907-3.

Nelson, H. E., & Williams, J. R. (1991). *The National Adult Reading Test (NART)* (pp. 1–26). Windsor: NFER-Nelson.

Nelson, S., Avidan, N., Sarma, A., Tushe, R., Milewicz, D., Lee, K., Bray, M., Leal, S., & Eagleman, D. (2009). The genetics of colored sequence synesthesia: Evidence of linkage to chromosome 16q and genetic heterogeneity for the condition. *Nature Precedings.* https://doi.org/10.1038/npre.2009.3987.1

Newcombe, F. (1969). *Missile Wounds of the Brain: A Study of Psychological Deficits* (pp. vi, 145). Oxford University Press.

Newcombe, F., & Ratcliff, G. (1974). Agnosia: a disorder of object recognition. In F. Michel & B. Schott (Eds.), *Les Syndromes de Disconnexion Calleuse Chez l'Homme. Actes du Colloque International* (pp. 317–340). Lyon.

Norman, D. A., & Shallice, T. (1986). Attention to Action. In R. J. Davidson, G. E. Schwartz, D. Shapiro, (Eds.), *Consciousness and Self-Regulation.* Springer. https://doi.org/10.1007/978-1-4757-0629-1_1

Nowell, C., Downing, M., Bragge, P., & Ponsford, J. (2020). Current practice of cognitive rehabilitation following traumatic brain injury: An international survey. *Neuropsychological Rehabilitation, 30*(10), 1976–1995. Doi: 10.1080/09602011.2019.1623823

Nunn, J. A., Gregory, L. J., Brammer, M., Williams, S. C. R., Parslow, D. M., Morgan, M. J., Morris, R. G., Bullmore, E. T., Baron-Cohen, S., & Gray, J. A. (2002). Functional magnetic resonance imaging of synesthesia: Activation of V4/V8 by spoken words. *Nature Neuroscience, 5*(4), 371–375. https://doi.org/10.1038/nn818

Ochipa, C., & Gonzalez Rothi, L. J. (1989). Recovery and evolution of a subtype of crossed aphasia. *Aphasiology, 3*(5), 465–472. https://doi.org/10.1080/02687038908249007

Orkin Simon, N., Jansari, A., & Gilboa, Y. (2020). Hebrew version of the Jansari assessment of Executive Functions for Children (JEF-C©): Translation, adaptation and validation. *Neuropsychological Rehabilitation.* https://doi.org/10.1080/09602011.2020.1821718

Ownsworth, T., Desbois, J., Grant, E., Fleming, J., & Strong, J. (2006). The associations among self-awareness, emotional well-being, and employment outcome following acquired brain injury: A 12-month longitudinal study. *Rehabilitation Psychology, 51*(1), 50–59. https://doi.org/10.1037/0090-5550.51.1.50

Page, N., Bolger, J., & Sanders, M. (1982). Auditory evoked phosphenes in optic nerve disease. *Journal of Neurology, Neurosurgery & Psychiatry, 45*(1), 7–12. https://doi.org/10.1136/jnnp.45.1.7

Patterson, K., Marshall, J. C., & Coltheart, M. (2017). *Surface Dyslexia: Neuropsychological and Cognitive Studies of Phonological Reading.* Routledge.

Pazzaglia, M., & Galli, G. (2019). Action observation for neurorehabilitation in apraxia. *Frontiers in Neurology, 10.* www.frontiersin.org/article/10.3389/fneur.2019.00309

Pazzaglia, M., Smania, N., Corato, E., & Aglioti, S. M. (2008). Neural underpinnings of gesture discrimination in patients with limb apraxia. *Journal of Neuroscience, 28*(12), 3030–3041. https://doi.org/10.1523/JNEUROSCI.5748-07.2008

Pearson, J., Naselaris, T., Holmes, E. A., & Kosslyn, S. M. (2015). Mental imagery: Functional mechanisms and clinical applications. *Trends in Cognitive Sciences, 19*(10), 590–602. https://doi.org/10.1016/j.tics.2015.08.003

Peruzzi, A., Zarbo, I. R., Cereatti, A., Della Croce, U., & Mirelman, A. (2017). An innovative training program based on virtual reality and treadmill: effects on gait of persons with multiple sclerosis. *Disability and Rehabilitation, 39*(15), 1557–1563, DOI: 10.1080/09638288.2016.1224935

Pijnenborg, G. H. M., Evans, J. J., Withaar, F. K., van den Bosch, R. J., & Brouwer, W. H. (2007). SMS text messages as a prosthetic aid in the cognitive rehabilitation of schizophrenia. *Rehabilitation Psychology, 52*(2), 236–240.

Pisella, L., & Mattingley, J. B. (2004). The contribution of spatial remapping impairments to unilateral visual neglect. *Neuroscience & Biobehavioral Reviews, 28*(2), 181–200.

Posner, M. I., Cohen, Y., & Rafal, R. D. (1982). Neural systems control of spatial orienting. *Philosophical Transactions of the Royal Society of London. B, Biological Sciences, 298*(1089), 187–198.

Prigatano, G. P. (1999). *Principles of Neuropsychological Rehabilitation.* Oxford University Press.

Ramachandran, V. S., & Hubbard, E. M. (2001). Synaesthesia – A window into perception, thought and language. *Journal of Consciousness Studies, 8,* 3–34.

Rao, A., Nobre, A. C., Alexander, I., & Cowey, A. (2007). Auditory evoked visual awareness following sudden ocular blindness: An EEG and TMS investigation. *Experimental Brain Research, 176*(2), 288–298. https://doi.org/10.1007/s00221-006-0616-2

Raymer, A. M., & Rothi, L. J. G. (2001). Cognitive neuropsychological approaches to assessment and treatment: Impairments of lexical comprehension and production. In R. Chapey (Ed.), *Language Intervention Strategies in Adult Aphasia,* 4th edn (pp. 524–550). Lippincott, Williams, & Wilkins.

Raymer, A., & Turkstra, L. (2017). Rehabilitation of language disorders in adults and children. In B. A. Wilson, J. Winegardner, C. M. van Heugten, & T. Ownsworth (Eds.), *Neuropsychological Rehabilitation: The International Handbook* (pp. 220–233). Routledge/Taylor & Francis Group.

Rich, A. N., Bradshaw, J. L., & Mattingley, J. B. (2005). A systematic, large-scale study of synaesthesia: Implications for the role of early experience in lexical-colour associations. *Cognition, 98*(1), 53–84. https://doi.org/10.1016/j.cognition.2004.11.003

Riddoch, M. J., & Humphreys, G. W. (1990). *The Smiling Giraffe: An Illustration of a Visual Memory Disorder.*

Riddoch, M. J., & Humphreys, G. W. (1993). *Birmingham Object Recognition Battery.* Lawrence Erlbaum Associates.

Ringman, J. M., Saver, J. L., Woolson, R. F., Clarke, W. R., & Adams, H. P. (2004). Frequency, risk factors, anatomy, and course of unilateral neglect in an acute stroke cohort. *Neurology, 63*(3), 468–474.

Rizzolatti, G., Fadiga, L., Gallese, V., & Fogassi, L. (1996). Premotor cortex and the recognition of motor actions. *Cognitive Brain Research, 3*(2), 131–141. https://doi.org/10.1016/0926-6410(95)00038-0

Ro, T., Farnè, A., Johnson, R. M., Wedeen, V., Chu, Z., Wang, Z. J., Hunter, J. V., & Beauchamp, M. S. (2007). Feeling sounds after a thalamic lesion. *Annals of Neurology, 62*(5), 433–441. https://doi.org/10.1002/ana.21219

Ro, T., Rorden, C., Driver, J., & Rafal, R. (2001). Ipsilesional biases in saccades but not perception after lesions of the human inferior parietal lobule. *Journal of Cognitive Neuroscience, 13*(7), 920–929. https://doi.org/10.1162/089892901753165836

Robertson, I. H. & Frasca, R. (1992). Attentional load and visual neglect. *International Journal of Neuroscience, 62*: 45–56.

Robertson, I. H., McMillan, T. M., MacLeod, E., Edgeworth, J., & Brock, D. (2002). Rehabilitation by limb activation training reduces left-sided motor impairment in unilateral neglect patients: A single-blind randomised control trial. *Neuropsychological Rehabilitation, 12*(5), 439–454.

Robertson, L. C. (2003). Binding, spatial attention and perceptual awareness. *Nature Reviews Neuroscience, 4*(2), 93–102. https://doi.org/10.1038/nrn1030

Robey, R. R. (1998) A meta-analysis of clinical outcomes in the treatment of aphasia. *Journal of Speech, Language, and Hearing Research, 41*(1), 172–87. doi: 10.1044/jslhr.4101.172. PMID: 9493743

Roby-Brami, A., Hermsdörfer, J., Roy, A. C., & Jacobs, S. (2012). A neuropsychological perspective on the link between language and praxis in modern humans. *Philosophical Transactions of the Royal Society B: Biological Sciences, 367*(1585), 144–160. https://doi.org/10.1098/rstb.2011.0122

Rode, G., Pagliari, C., Huchon, L., Rossetti, Y., & Pisella, L. (2017). Semiology of neglect: an update. *Annals of Physical and Rehabilitation Medicine, 60*(3), 177–185.

Rose, F. D., & Johnson, D. A. (1996). Brains, Injuries and Outcome (Ch. 1, p. 14) - In F. D. Rose & D. A. Johnson (Eds.), *Brain Injury and After. Towards Improved Outcome.* John Wiley & Sons.

Rothen, N., Meier, B., & Ward, J. (2012). Enhanced memory ability: Insights from synaesthesia. *Neuroscience & Biobehavioral Reviews, 36*(8), 1952–1963. https://doi.org/10.1016/j.neubiorev.2012.05.004

Rothen, N., Seth, A. K., Witzel, C., & Ward, J. (2013). Diagnosing synaesthesia with online colour pickers: Maximising sensitivity and specificity. *Journal of Neuroscience Methods, 215*(1), 156–160. https://doi.org/10.1016/j.jneumeth.2013.02.009

Rouw, R., & Scholte, H. S. (2007). Increased structural connectivity in grapheme-color synesthesia. *Nature Neuroscience, 10*(6), 792–797. https://doi.org/10.1038/nn1906

Rouw, R., Scholte, H. S., & Colizoli, O. (2011). Brain areas involved in synaesthesia: A review. *Journal of Neuropsychology*, *5*(2), 214–242. https://doi.org/10.1111/j.1748-6653.2011.02006.x

Roy, E. A., Square, P. A. (1985). Common considerations in the study of limb, verbal and oral apraxia. In E. A. Roy (Ed.), Advances in Psychology: *Neuropsychological Studies of Apraxia and Related Disorders*. Vol. 23 (pp. 1–61). North Holland.

Russell, R., Duchaine, B., & Nakayama, K. (2009). Super-recognizers: People with extraordinary face recognition ability. *Psychonomic Bulletin & Review*, *16*(2), 252–257. https://doi.org/10.3758/PBR.16.2.252

Ryle, G. (1949). Meaning and Necessity1. *Philosophy*, *24*(88), 69–76.

Sacchett, C., & Humphreys, G. W. (1992). Calling a squirrel a squirrel but a canoe a wigwam: A category-specific deficit for artefactual objects and body parts. *Cognitive Neuropsychology*, *9*(1), 73–86. https://doi.org/10.1080/02643299208252053

Sacks, O. (1985). *The Man Who Mistook His Wife for a Hat*. Summit Books.

Sacks, O., & Wasserman, R. L. (1987). The Painter Who Became Colour Blind. *New York Review of Books*, 34(18), 25–33.

Saeki, S., Ogata, H., Okubo, T., Takahashi, K., & Hoshuyama, T. (1995). Return to work after stroke. *Stroke*, *26*(3), 399–401. https://doi.org/10.1161/01.STR.26.3.399

Sagiv, N., Simner, J., Collins, J., Butterworth, B., & Ward, J. (2006). What is the relationship between synaesthesia and visuo-spatial number forms? *Cognition*, *101*(1), 114–128. https://doi.org/10.1016/j.cognition.2005.09.004

Sartori, G., & Job, R. (1988). The oyster with four legs: A neuropsychological study on the interaction of visual and semantic information. *Cognitive Neuropsychology*, *5*(1), 105–132. https://doi.org/10.1080/02643298808252928

Schacter, D. L. (1987). Implicit memory: History and current status. *Journal of Experimental Psychology: Learning, Memory, and Cognition*, *13*(3), 501.

Schiza, E., Matsangidou, M., Neokleous, K., & Pattichis, C. S. (2019). Virtual Reality Applications for Neurological Disease: A Review. *Frontiers in Robotics and AI*, vol. 6. doi:=10.3389/frobt.2019.00100

Schneider, G. E. (1967). Contrasting visuomotor functions of tectum and cortex in the golden hamster. *Psychological Research*, *31*(1), 52–62. https://doi.org/10.1007/BF00422386

Scoville, W. B., & Milner, B. (1957). Loss of recent memory after bilateral hippocampal lesions. *Journal of Neurology, Neurosurgery and Psychiatry*, *20*(1), 11–21. https://doi.org/10.1136/jnnp.20.1.11

Shallice, T. (1986). Single and multiple component central dyslexic syndromes. *Deep Dyslexia*, 119–145.

Shallice, T. (1988). *From Neuropsychology to Mental Structure*. Cambridge University Press.

Shallice, T., & Burgess, P. W. (1991). Deficits in strategy application following frontal lobe damage in man. *Brain*, *114*(2), 727–741. https://doi.org/10.1093/brain/114.2.727

Shallice, T., & Jackson, M. (1988). Lissauer on agnosia. *Cognitive Neuropsychology*, *5*(2), 153–156.

Shallice, T., & Warrington, E. (1970). Independent functioning of verbal memory stores: A neuropsychological study. *The Quarterly Journal of Experimental Psychology*, *22*, 261–273. https://doi.org/10.1080/00335557043000203

Simner, J. (2007). Beyond perception: synaesthesia as a psycholinguistic phenomenon. *Trends in Cognitive Sciences*, *11*(1), 23–29. https://doi.org/10.1016/j.tics.2006.10.010

Simner, J., Mulvenna, C., Sagiv, N., Tsakanikos, E., Witherby, S. A., Fraser, C., Scott, K., & Ward, J. (2006). Synaesthesia: The prevalence of atypical cross-modal experiences. *Perception*, *35*(8), 1024–1033. https://doi.org/10.1068/p5469

Sirigu, A., Duhamel, J.-R., & Poncet, M. (1991). The role of sensorimotor experience in object recognition: A case of multimodal agnosia. *Brain, 114*(6), 2555–2573. https://doi.org/10.1093/brain/114.6.2555

Smaers, J. B., Gómez-Robles, A., Parks, A. N., & Sherwood, C. C. (2017). Exceptional evolutionary expansion of prefrontal cortex in great apes and humans. *Current Biology, 27*(5), 714–720. https://doi.org/10.1016/j.cub.2017.01.020

Smania, N., Girardi, F., Domenicali, C., Lora, E., & Aglioti, S. (2000). The rehabilitation of limb apraxia: a study in left-brain-damaged patients. *Archives of Physical Medicine and Rehabilitation, 81*(4), 379–388. https://doi.org/10.1053/mr.2000.6921

Smilek, D., Dixon, M. J., Cudahy, C., & Merikle, P. M. (2001). Synaesthetic photisms influence visual perception. *Journal of Cognitive Neuroscience, 13*(7), 930–936. https://doi.org/10.1162/089892901753165845

Soar, K., Chapman, E., Lavan, N., Jansari, A. S., & Turner, J. (2016). Investigating the effects of caffeine on executive functions using traditional Stroop and a new ecologically-valid virtual reality task, the Jansari assessment of Executive Functions (JEF©). *Appetite, 105*, 156–163. https://doi.org/10.1016/j.appet.2016.05.021

Sohlberg, M. M., & Mateer, C. A. (2001). *Cognitive Rehabilitation: An Integrative Neuropsychological Approach*. The Guilford Press.

Søraas, A., Bø, R., Kalleberg, K. T., Støer, N. C., Ellingjord-Dale, M., & Landrø, N. I. (2021). Self-reported memory problems 8 months after COVID-19 infection. *JAMA Network Open, 4*(7), e2118717. https://doi.org/10.1001/jamanetworkopen.2021.18717

Sperling, J., Prvulovic, D., Linden, D., Singer, W., & Stirn, A. (2006). Neuronal correlates of colour-graphemic synaesthesia: Afmri study. *Cortex, 42*(2), 295–303. https://doi.org/10.1016/S0010-9452(08)70355-1

Spiller, M. J., & Jansari, A. (2012). Synesthesia and savantism. In J. Simner & E. M. Hubbard (Eds.), *The Oxford Handbook of Synesthesia* (pp. 707–727). Oxford University Press.

Spiller, M. J., Harkry, L., McCullagh, F., Thoma, V., & Jonas, C. (2019). Exploring the relationship between grapheme colour-picking consistency and mental imagery. *Philosophical Transactions of the Royal Society B: Biological Sciences, 374*(1787), 20190023. https://doi.org/10.1098/rstb.2019.0023

Spiller, M. J., Jonas, C. N., Simner, J., & Jansari, A. (2015). Beyond visual imagery: How modality-specific is enhanced by mental imagery in synesthesia? *Consciousness and Cognition, 31*, 73–85. https://doi.org/10.1016/j.concog.2014.10.010

Squire, L. R., & Moore, R. Y. (1979). Dorsal thalamic lesion in a noted case of human memory dysfunction. *Annals of Neurology, 6*(6), 503–506. https://doi.org/10.1002/ana.410060607

Starowicz-Filip, A., Chrobak, A. A., Moskała, M., Krzyzewski, R. M., Kwinta, B., Kwiatkowski, S., Milczarek, O., Rajtar-Zembaty, A., & Przewoźnik, D. (2017). The role of the cerebellum in the regulation of language functions. *Psychiatria Polska, 51*(4), 661–671. https://doi.org/10.12740/pp/68547

Stewart, F., Parkin, A. J., & Hunkin, N. M. (1992). Naming impairments following recovery from herpes simplex encephalitis: Category-specific? *The Quarterly Journal of Experimental Psychology, 44*(2), 261–284.

Stuss, D. T. (2011). Functions of the frontal lobes: relation to executive functions. *Journal of the International Neuropsychological Society, 17*(5), 759–765.

Stuss, D. T., Alexander, M. P., Shallice, T., Picton, T. W., Binns, M. A., Macdonald, R., ... & Katz, D. I. (2005). Multiple frontal systems controlling response speed. *Neuropsychologia, 43*(3), 396–417.

Stuss, D. T., & Benson, D. F. (1986). *The Frontal Lobes*. Raven Press.

Sunderland, A., Bowers, M. P., Sluman, S. M., Wilcock, D. J., & Ardron, M. E. (1999). Impaired dexterity of the ipsilateral hand after stroke and the relationship to cognitive deficit. *Stroke, 30*(5), 949–955. https://doi.org/10.1161/01.str.30.5.949

Sutherland, N. S. (1989). *Dictionary of Psychology*. MacMillan.

Svoboda, E., & Richards, B. (2009). Compensating for anterograde amnesia: A new training method that capitalizes on emerging smartphone technologies. *Journal of the International Neuropsychological Society*, *15*(4), 629–638.

Taira, M., Mine, S., Georgopoulos, A. P., Murata, A., & Sakata, H. (1990). Parietal cortex neurons of the monkey related to the visual guidance of hand movement. *Experimental Brain Research*, *83*(1), 29–36. https://doi.org/10.1007/BF00232190

Taylor, A., & Warrington, E. K. (1971). Visual agnosia: A single case report. *Cortex*, *7*(2), 152–161. https://doi.org/10.1016/S0010-9452(71)80011-4

Teuber, H. L. (1955). Physiological psychology. *Annual Review of Psychology*, *6*(1), 267–296. https://doi.org/10.1146/annurev.ps.06.020155.001411

Thompson, P. (1980). Margaret Thatcher: A new illusion. *Perception*, *9*(4), 483–484. https://doi.org/10.1068/p090483

Tilot, A. K., Kucera, K. S., Vino, A., Asher, J. E., Baron-Cohen, S., & Fisher, S. E. (2018). Rare variants in axonogenesis genes connect three families with sound–color synesthesia. *Proceedings of the National Academy of Sciences*, *115*(12), 3168–3173. https://doi.org/10.1073/pnas.1715492115

Tilot, A. K., Vino, A., Kucera, K. S., Carmichael, D. A., van den Heuvel, L., den Hoed, J., Sidoroff-Dorso, A. V., Campbell, A., Porteous, D. J., St Pourcain, B., van Leeuwen, T. M., Ward, J., Rouw, R., Simner, J., & Fisher, S. E. (2019). Investigating genetic links between grapheme–colour synaesthesia and neuropsychiatric traits. *Philosophical Transactions of the Royal Society B: Biological Sciences*, *374*(1787), 20190026. https://doi.org/10.1098/rstb.2019.0026

Tranel, D., & Damasio, A. R. (1985). Knowledge without awareness: An autonomic index of facial recognition by prosopagnosics. *Science*, *228*(4706), 1453–1454. https://doi.org/10.1126/science.4012303

Tranel, D., Damasio, H., & Damasio, A. R. (1997). A neural basis for the retrieval of conceptual knowledge. *Neuropsychologia*, *35*(10), 1319–1327. https://doi.org/10.1016/S0028-3932(97)00085-7

Tranel, D., Kemmerer, D., Adolphs, R., Damasio, H., & Damasio, A. R. (2003). Neural correlates of conceptual knowledge for actions. *Cognitive Neuropsychology*, *20*(3–6), 409–432. https://doi.org/10.1080/02643290244000248

Tulving, E. (1972). Episodic and semantic memory. In E. Tulving & W. Donaldson (Eds.). *Organization of Memory* (pp. 381–403). Academic Press. https://doi.org/10.1016/j.cortex.2012.10.014

Ungerleider, L. G., & Mishkin, M. (1982). Two cortical visual systems. In D. J. Ingle, M. A. Goodale, & R. J. W. Mansfield (Eds), *Analysis of Visual Behavior* (pp. 549–586). The MIT Press.

Vallar, G., & Perani, D. (1986). The anatomy of unilateral neglect after right-hemisphere stroke lesions. A clinical/CT-scan correlation study in man. *Neuropsychologia*, *24*(5), 609–622.

Van den Broek, M. D., Downes, J., Johnson, Z., Dayus, B., & Hilton, N. (2000). Evaluation of an electronic memory aid in the neuropsychological rehabilitation of prospective memory deficits. *Brain Injury*, *14*(5), 455–462.

van Heugten, C. M., Dekker, J., Deelman, B. G., van Dijk, A. J., & Stehmann-Saris, J. C. (1998). Outcome of strategy training in stroke patients with apraxia: A phase II study. *Clinical Rehabilitation*, *12*(4), 294–303. https://doi.org/10.1191/026921598674468328

van Leeuwen, T. M., Neufeld, J., Hughes, J., & Ward, J. (2020). Synaesthesia and autism: Different developmental outcomes from overlapping mechanisms? *Cognitive Neuropsychology*, *37*(7–8), 433–449. https://doi.org/10.1080/02643294.2020.1808455

Vanbellingen, T., & Bohlhalter, S. (2011). Apraxia in neurorehabilitation: Classification, assessment and treatment. *NeuroRehabilitation*. *28*(2), 91–98. doi: 10.3233/NRE-2011-0637. PMID: 21447909.

Vargha-Khadem, F., Gadian, D. G., Watkins, K. E., Connelly, A., Van Paesschen, W., & Mishkin, M. (1997). Differential effects of early hippocampal pathology on episodic and semantic memory. *Science, 277*(5324), 376–380. https://doi.org/10.1126/science.277.5324.376

Verfaellie, M., Bauer, R. M., & Bowers, D. (1991). Autonomic and behavioral evidence of 'implicit' memory in amnesia. *Brain and Cognition, 15*(1), 10–25. https://doi.org/10.1016/0278-2626(91)90012-W

von Arx, S. W., Müri, R. M., Heinemann, D., Hess, C. W., & Nyffeler, T. (2010). Anosognosia for cerebral achromatopsia: A longitudinal case study. *Neuropsychologia, 48*(4), 970–977. https://doi.org/10.1016/j.neuropsychologia.2009.11.018

Ward, J. (2007). Acquired auditory-tactile synesthesia. *Annals of Neurology, 62*(5), 429–430. https://doi.org/10.1002/ana.21281

Ward, J. (2019). Synaesthesia: A distinct entity that is an emergent feature of adaptive neurocognitive differences. *Philosophical Transactions of the Royal Society B: Biological Sciences, 374*(1787), 20180351. https://doi.org/10.1098/rstb.2018.0351

Ward, J., & Simner, J. (2003). Lexical-gustatory synaesthesia: Linguistic and conceptual factors. *Cognition, 89*(3), 237–261. https://doi.org/10.1016/S0010-0277(03)00122-7

Ward, J., Brown, P., Sherwood, J., & Simner, J. (2018). An autistic-like profile of attention and perception in synaesthesia. *Cortex, 107*, 121–130. https://doi.org/10.1016/j.cortex.2017.10.008

Ward, J., Field, A. P., & Chin, T. (2019). A meta-analysis of memory ability in synaesthesia. *Memory, 27*(9), 1299–1312. https://doi.org/10.1080/09658211.2019.1646771

Ward, J., Hoadley, C., Hughes, J. E. A., Smith, P., Allison, C., Baron-Cohen, S., & Simner, J. (2017). Atypical sensory sensitivity as a shared feature between synaesthesia and autism. *Scientific Reports, 7*(1), 41155. https://doi.org/10.1038/srep41155

Warrington, E. K. (1982). Neuropsychological studies of object recognition. *Philosophical Transactions of the Royal Society of London. B, Biological Sciences, 298*(1089), 15–33.

Warrington, E. K. (1986). Visual deficits associated with occipital lobe lesions in man. *Experimental Brain Research Supplementum, 11*, 247–261.

Warrington, E. K., & James, M. (1988). Visual apperceptive agnosia: a clinico-anatomical study of three cases. *Cortex, 24*(1), 13–32.

Warrington, E. K., & McCarthy, R. A. (1994). Multiple meaning systems in the brain: A case for visual semantics. *Neuropsychologia, 32*, 1465–1473.

Warrington, E. K., & Shallice, T. (1969). The selective impairment of auditory verbal short-term memory. *Brain, 92*(4), 885–896.

Warrington, E. K., & Shallice, T. (1984). Category specific semantic impairments. *Brain, 107*(3), 829–853. https://doi.org/10.1093/brain/107.3.829

Warrington, E. K., & Taylor, A. M. (1973). The contribution of the right parietal lobe to object recognition. *Cortex, 9*(2), 152–164.

Weiss, P. H., Zilles, K., & Fink, G. R. (2005). When visual perception causes feeling: Enhanced cross-modal processing in grapheme-color synesthesia. *NeuroImage, 28*(4), 859–868. https://doi.org/10.1016/j.neuroimage.2005.06.052

Wetter, S., Poole, J. L. & Haaland, K. Y. (2005). Functional implications of ipsilesional motor deficits after unilateral stroke. *Archives of Physical Medicine and Rehabilitation, 86*, 776–781.

Whurr, R., Lorch, M. P., & Nye, C. (1992). A meta-analysis of studies carried out between 1946 and 1988 concerned with the efficacy of speech and language therapy treatment for aphasic patients. *International Journal of Language & Communication Disorders, 27*(1), 1–17.

Wilbrand, H. (1892). Ein fall von seelenblindheit und hemianopsie mit sectionsbefund. *Deutsche Zeitschrift für Nervenheilkunde, 2*(5), 361–387.

Wilson, B. A. (2009). *Memory Rehabilitation: Integrating Theory and Practice*. The Guildford Press.

Wilson, B. A., & Wearing, D. (1995). Prisoner of consciousness: A state of just awakening following herpes simplex encephalitis. In *Broken Memories: Case Studies in Memory Impairment* (pp. 14–30). Blackwell Publishing.

Wilson, B. A., Baddeley, A. D., Evans, J., & Shiel, A. (1994). Errorless learning in the rehabilitation of memory impaired people. *Neuropsychological Rehabilitation*, *4*(3), 307–326. https://doi.org/10.1080/09602019408401463

Wilson, B. A., Baddeley, A. D., & Young, A. W. (1999). LE, a person who lost her 'mind's eye'. *Neurocase*, *5*(2), 119–127. https://doi.org/10.1080/13554799908415476

Wilson, B. A., Emslie, H. C., Quirk, K., & Evans, J. J. (2001). Reducing everyday memory and planning problems by means of a paging system: a randomised control crossover study. *Journal of Neurology, Neurosurgery & Psychiatry*, *70*(4), 477–482.

Wilson, B. A., Gracey, F., Evans, J. J., & Bateman, A. (2009). *Neuropsychological Rehabilitation: Theory, Models, Therapy and Outcome*. Cambridge University Press.

Wilson, B. A., Winegardner, J., van Heugten, C. M., & Ownsworth, T. (2017). *Neuropsychological rehabilitation: The international handbook*. Routledge.

Witthoft, N., Winawer, J., & Eagleman, D. M. (2015). Prevalence of learned grapheme-color pairings in a large online sample of synesthetes. *PloS One*, *10*(3), e0118996. https://doi.org/10.1371/journal.pone.0118996

Yanakieva, S., Luke, D. P., Jansari, A., & Terhune, D. B. (2019). Acquired synaesthesia following 2C-B use. *Psychopharmacology*, *236*(7), 2287–2289. https://doi.org/10.1007/s00213-019-05242-y

Yaro, C., & Ward, J. (2007). Searching for Shereshevskii: What is superior about the memory of synaesthetes? *Quarterly Journal of Experimental Psychology*, *60*(5), 681–695. https://doi.org/10.1080/17470210600785208

Yin, R. K. (1969). Looking at upside-down faces. *Journal of Experimental Psychology*, *81*(1), 141.

Young, A. W., de Haan, E. H., Newcombe, F., & Hay, D. C. (1990). Facial neglect. *Neuropsychologia*, *28*(5), 391–415.

Young, A. W., Hellawell, D., & Hay, D. C. (1987). Configurational information in face perception. *Perception*, *42*(11), 1166–1178. https://doi.org/10.1068/p160747n

Young, A. W., Newcombe, F., De Haan, E. H. F., Small, M., & Hay, D. C. (1993). Face perception after brain injury: Selective impairments affecting identity and expression. *Brain*, *116*(4), 941–959. https://doi.org/10.1093/brain/116.4.941

Yuan, S. H., & Wang, S. G. (2018). Alzheimer's dementia due to suspected CTE from subconcussive head impact. *Case Reports in Neurological Medicine*, *2018*, e7890269. https://doi.org/10.1155/2018/7890269

Zamm, A., Schlaug, G., Eagleman, D. M., & Loui, P. (2013). Pathways to seeing music: Enhanced structural connectivity in colored-music synesthesia. *NeuroImage*, *74*, 359–366. https://doi.org/10.1016/j.neuroimage.2013.02.024

Zeki, S. (1998). Three cortical stages of colour processing in the human brain. *Brain*, *121*(9), 1669–1685. https://doi.org/10.1093/brain/121.9.1669

Zhou, B., Sun, Y., Bau, D., & Torralba, A. (2018). Revisiting the importance of individual units in cnns via ablation. *arXiv preprint arXiv*:1806.02891

Zola-Morgan, S., Squire, L. R., & Amaral, D. G. (1986). Human amnesia and the medial temporal region: Enduring memory impairment following a bilateral lesion limited to field CA1 of the hippocampus. *Journal of Neuroscience*, *6*(10), 2950–2967. www.jneurosci.org/content/6/10/2950.short.

INDEX

Page numbers in *italics* refer to figures; page numbers in **bold** refer to tables.